Designs on Democracy

OXFORD HISTORICAL MONOGRAPHS

The *Oxford Historical Monographs* series publishes some of the best
Oxford University doctoral theses on historical topics, especially
those likely to engage the interest of a broad academic readership.

Editors

P. BETTS, F. DEVJI, P. GAUCI,
J. MCDOUGALL, D. PARROTT, R. REID,
H. SKODA, J. SMITH, W. WHYTE

Designs on Democracy

Architecture and the Public in Interwar London

NEAL SHASORE

OXFORD
UNIVERSITY PRESS

Great Clarendon Street, Oxford, OX2 6DP,
United Kingdom

Oxford University Press is a department of the University of Oxford.
It furthers the University's objective of excellence in research, scholarship,
and education by publishing worldwide. Oxford is a registered trade mark of
Oxford University Press in the UK and in certain other countries

© Neal Shasore 2022

The moral rights of the author have been asserted

First Edition published in 2022

All rights reserved. No part of this publication may be reproduced, stored in
a retrieval system, or transmitted, in any form or by any means, without the
prior permission in writing of Oxford University Press, or as expressly permitted
by law, by licence or under terms agreed with the appropriate reprographics
rights organization. Enquiries concerning reproduction outside the scope of the
above should be sent to the Rights Department, Oxford University Press, at the
address above

You must not circulate this work in any other form
and you must impose this same condition on any acquirer

Published in the United States of America by Oxford University Press
198 Madison Avenue, New York, NY 10016, United States of America

British Library Cataloguing in Publication Data
Data available

Library of Congress Control Number: 2022933688

ISBN 978-0-19-284972-4

DOI: 10.1093/oso/9780192849724.001.0001

Printed and bound in the UK by
TJ Books Limited

Links to third party websites are provided by Oxford in good faith and
for information only. Oxford disclaims any responsibility for the materials
contained in any third party website referenced in this work.

To Meena, Abbey, and Zara Leah Shasore

Acknowledgements

The book that follows has changed much from the D.Phil. thesis on which it was based. That seems par for the course, but the themes and ideas that underpin it have—in the decade of its development—gained an unexpected currency, reframing its core arguments. This is not a book in which material has been selected on the basis of taste; quite the contrary. These are not buildings or personalities with which it has been easy to empathize, and I hope that this book is not read as a defence or an apology. It is intended as a dispassionate analysis of the rhetorics of modern architectural professionalism.

The strange and recondite architectural culture of interwar Britain (hardly a fashionable subject when I set out) has nonetheless a real relevance to the ethical conundrums that the modern profession has faced in recent years: the legacy of the tragedy at Grenfell Tower, for instance; the ever-accelerating challenges born of climate emergency (to which construction practices are a major contributing factor); the manifestation of racial inequality and social injustice in debates about heritage and the built environment. These have all thrown into question what obligations the architectural profession has to its publics. I have found the material that I grappled with in the research for *Designs on Democracy* surprisingly resonant when contextualizing contemporary practice and professionalism, and though this may seem oblique, if not opaque, to the reader, it has informed my own teaching practice within architecture schools profoundly.

These ideas have taken a long time to germinate, and I have been immensely fortunate to have been surrounded by friends, students, colleagues, and mentors who have nurtured and trained the resulting shoots. I am truly grateful to William Whyte, who supervised the thesis and then endured as Advising Editor for the preparation of the book; his gregariousness and good-humour have leavened darker moments, and his subtle methods of tuition—encouraging immersion in the material, using intuition as much as method—have taught me a great deal. Unending thanks are owed to Jane Garnett who for fifteen years has provided such encouragement, support, love, and friendship. I could not have finished this

viii ACKNOWLEDGEMENTS

book without her, and the thinking and writing have been enriched by her rigour and care.

Since I completed my D.Phil., this book has followed me to three different institutions, and then unexpectedly back to Oxford: special thanks are owed to the whole History of Art community there but particularly Gervase Rosser, from whom I have learnt so much, and who has been a constant friend and role model. I must also thank Alastair Wright, my departmental supervisor, and Clare Hills-Nova, librarian of the Sackler Library. My gratitude too to St John's College and the AHRC, which jointly funded my doctoral studies.

Elizabeth Darling, who was my external examiner, and Elizabeth McKellar, who reviewed the text, have offered support and friendship. They have both subsequently read earlier versions of this text, as did Alan Powers, whose inexhaustible knowledge of this period and the life that animated it has been invaluable. Some of the framing and wider context for this research was enlivened by conversations and connections made at the SAHGB Annual Symposium which I convened in 2018, 'Reconstruction: Architecture, the Built Environment and the Aftermath of the First World War'. Indeed, many thanks are owed to colleagues and friends in and around the Society of Architectural Historians of Great Britain (SAHGB) including Ann-Marie Akehurst, Murray Fraser, Ewan Harrison, Neil Jackson, Jessica Kelly, David Lewis, Otto Saumarez-Smith, Mark Swenarton, and Susie West, who have all been immensely encouraging. The SAHGB also provided me with a Publications Grant which contributed significantly to the illustrations. Chater Paul Jordan patiently and ably assisted in the organisation of my images. JWH Pockson RIBA—always too generous with this time—designed the beautiful book cover using an image by Raymond Myerscough-Walker.

Staff at countless libraries and archives enabled the research that informed this project: they include the National Archives at Kew, the London Metropolitan Archives, the Architectural Association Archives and the Bodleian Library among others. Colleagues and friends at the RIBA Library and Archives and Drawings Collections have been especially patient: particular thanks are owed to Lil Adams, Valeria Carullo, Brian Glover, Kurt Helfrich, Charles Hind, Jonathan Makepeace, Fiona Orsini, Liliana Perrone, Richard Reed, and Karen Wilman.

I also owe a huge debt of gratitude to former colleagues in the RIBA Practice Department, in particular Lucy Carmichael, Alex Tait, Bobbie Williams and Ann Dye, as well as Flora Samuel. My experience working there helped to reframe my doctoral research in a way that connects more explicitly to architectural practice and professionalism.

The residents of Pyrland Road past and present had to live first with the D.Phil. and then with the book, for which I can only apologize. Of them, Angus Hodder—*primus inter pares*—has demonstrated more investment in the completion of this book than he ever should have, and was confident it would be finished long before I believed it could be. Love and thanks are owed to so many wonderful, intelligent, and interested friends who have offered advice and encouragement, and to my extended family, the Patels and Shasores alike.

Contents

List of Illustrations	xiii
List of Abbreviations	xxv
Introduction: Reconstructing the Profession for a Democratic Age	1
1. Propaganda: Publicity and the Arts of Display at the British Empire Exhibition, Wembley	49
2. Slump: Public Relations and the Building World	97
3. Machine-Craft: Forging Public Institutions	127
4. Vigilance: Preservationism and a Proprietary Public	207
5. Manners: Public Propriety and Civic Design	263
6. The Architectural Mind: Topographical Projections on the Public Realm	327
Bibliography	407
Index	425

List of Illustrations

0.1. Invitation to an exhibition of modern architecture by Erich Mendelsohn (1930), AA/02/05/02/03/08, Architectural Association Archives — 2

0.2. Plan of the ground floor of 36 Bedford Square as remodelled by Easton and Robertson (1928), AA/01/04/01/03, Architectural Association Archives — 3

0.3. Caricature of sixteen well-known architects of the 1930s attending a function in the RIBA's Florence Hall by Fred May (1939), RIBA21580, RIBA Collections — 15

0.4. 'Drawing Illustrating the Union of the Art of Architecture and Allied Societies and Arts', by John Murray (1918), RIBA, SCM 8, Future of Architecture Committee (17 June 1918), RIBA Collections — 30

1.1. Portrait of Sir Lawrence Weaver by Walter Stoneman (1920), NPG x28057, © National Portrait Gallery, London — 50

1.2. Buildings for the National Institute of Agricultural Botany, commissioned by Lawrence Weaver, by Percy Morley Horder (1921), photographer and date unknown, NIAB — 55

1.3. 'A General Plan of the British Empire Exhibition', AR (June 1924), p.209, RIBA Collections, courtesy of the Architectural Review — 57

1.4. The east quadrant of the garden just inside the north entrance to the exhibition site, photograph by Katherine Jane Macfee (1924), MCF01/02/0815, Source: Historic England Archive — 58

1.5. Aerial view of the exhibition site showing the main boulevard, Kingsway, from Wembley Park to the twin towers of the Stadium, photography by Aerofilms Ltd (1925), EPW012752, © Historic England — 59

1.6. Crowds in front of the Palace of Industry at the British Empire Exhibition in Wembley Park, with a 'Railodock' electric bus in the foreground, photograph by Katherine Jane Macfee (1924), MCF01/02/0806, Source: Historic England Archive — 59

1.7. Palace of Industry, British Empire Exhibition, photograph by Campbell Gray, published by Fleetway Press (1924), 0985, Courtesy Brent Museum and Archives — 60

xiv LIST OF ILLUSTRATIONS

1.8. The 'Gate of Harmony', entrance to the Palace of Industry, by
John Simpson and Maxwell Ayrton, photograph by Walter Benington
(1924), *AR* (June 1924) 55.331, p.207, RIBA Collections, courtesy
of *Architectural Review*   60

1.9. '"Enterprise Made Visible and Vocal": The Advertising Convention
Declared Open', *ILN* (19 July 1924), pp.134–5, photograph by
Campbell Gray, published by Fleetwood Press, 13419361/ILN,
© Illustrated London News Ltd/Mary Evans   62

1.10. 'Truth In Advertising', lithograph poster designed for use in connection
with the Advertising Convention, designed by Frederick Charles Herrick
(c.1923–4), E.144-1976, © Frederick Charles Herrick/Victoria and
Albert Museum, London   63

1.11. Design for Yardley & Company's Stand, British Empire Exhibition,
Wembley, London, plans and perspective, by Clough Williams-Ellis
(1923), RIBA126425, RIBA Collections   67

1.12. 'Plan of the Palace of Industry, Wembley 1924, Showing Arrangement
of Sections', reproduced in Lawrence Weaver, *Exhibitions and the Arts
of Display* (London, 1925), p.9, Wellcome Collection   71

1.13. 'South Walk, Palace of Industry, Wembley, 1924', reproduced in
Lawrence Weaver, *Exhibitions and the Arts of Display* (1925), plate ix,
Wellcome Collection   72

1.14. The interior of the Palace of Industry building at the British Empire
Exhibition in Wembley Park, showing people standing near the Cauldon
China stand, MCF01/02/0824, Source: Historic England Archive   73

1.15. 'Porticos to Cotton and Wool Sections, North Walk, Palace of Industry,
Wembley, 1924', reproduced in Lawrence Weaver, *Exhibitions and the
Arts of Display* (1925), plate xxxiii, Wellcome Collection   74

1.16. People on the tea balcony at the British Empire Exhibition in Wembley
Park, photography by Katherine Jane Macfee (1924), MCF01/02/0811,
Source: Historic England Archive   74

1.17. The 'Wembley Lion', lithograph poster, designed by Frederick Charles
Herrick for the Baynard Press (c.1923–4), Twentieth Century Posters Ltd 75

1.18. (a) Steel, glass, and concrete construction in the Palace of Industry
'hangar' (November 1923) and (b) East Walk, Palace of Industry, looking
east, reproduced in Lawrence Weaver, *Exhibitions and the Arts of Display*
(1925), plate v, Wellcome Collection   76

1.19. The Lion Kiosk, Palace of Industry, designed by Joseph Emberton,
sculpted by Percy Metcalfe (1924), reproduced in Lawrence Weaver,
Exhibitions and the Arts of Display (1925), plate LXV, Wellcome Collection 77

LIST OF ILLUSTRATIONS   XV

1.20. 'Ulster Pavilion, Palace of Industry, Wembley, 1924', reproduced in
Lawrence Weaver, *Exhibitions and the Arts of Display* (1925), plate XXI,
Wellcome Collection   78

1.21. Design for the Pottery section (for Wedgwood) of the British Empire
Exhibition, Wembley, London, by Oliver Hill (1924), RIBA20238, RIBA
Collections   79

1.22. Porticos, showrooms, and galleries for the Pottery section designed
by Oliver Hill, reproduced in Lawrence Weaver, *Exhibitions and the Arts
of Display* (1925), plate LXXXVIII, Wellcome Collection   80

1.23. Pavilions for the Electricity Development Association, by Imrie and
Angell, reproduced in Lawrence Weaver, *Exhibitions and the Arts
of Display* (1925), plate XXVIII, Wellcome Collection   82

1.24. Six of the seven tableaux of 'The Seven Ages of Women': gas exhibit,
reproduced in Lawrence Weaver, *Exhibitions and the Arts of Display*
(1925), plate XXIII, Wellcome Collection   84

1.25. The seventh tableau and other images of the gas exhibit, reproduced in
Lawrence Weaver, *Exhibitions and the Arts of Display* (1925),
plate XXIV, Wellcome Collection   85

1.26. A gallery in the Advertising Art Exhibition, Palace of Arts, reproduced
in Lawrence Weaver, *Exhibitions and the Arts of Display* (1925),
plate LXX, Wellcome Collection   88

1.27. Poster Street, designed by Westood and Emberton, reproduced in
Lawrence Weaver, *Exhibitions and the Arts of Display* (1925),
plate LXX, Wellcome Collection   89

3.1. *AR* (December 1934), plate ii, image courtesy of the Museum of
Domestic Design & Architecture, Middlesex University,
http://www.moda.mdx.ac.uk   129

3.2. *AR* (December 1934), plate v, image courtesy of the Museum of
Domestic Design & Architecture, Middlesex University,
http://www.moda.mdx.ac.uk   131

3.3. *AR* (December 1934), plate vii, images courtesy of the Museum
of Domestic Design & Architecture, Middlesex University,
http://www.moda.mdx.ac.uk   132

3.4. *AR* (December 1934), plate viii, image courtesy of the Museum
of Domestic Design & Architecture, Middlesex University,
http://www.moda.mdx.ac.uk   133

3.5. *AR* (December 1934), plate xi, image courtesy of the Museum
of Domestic Design & Architecture, Middlesex University,
http://www.moda.mdx.ac.uk   134

xvi LIST OF ILLUSTRATIONS

3.6. *AR* (December 1934), plate xiv, image courtesy of the Museum
of Domestic Design & Architecture, Middlesex University,
http://www.moda.mdx.ac.uk   135

3.7. *AR* (December 1934), plate xvi, image courtesy of the Museum
of Domestic Design & Architecture, Middlesex University,
http://www.moda.mdx.ac.uk   136

3.8. *AR* (December 1934), plate xvii, image courtesy of the Museum of
Domestic Design & Architecture, Middlesex University,
http://www.moda.mdx.ac.uk   137

3.9. *AR* (December 1934), plate xix, image courtesy of the Museum of
Domestic Design & Architecture, Middlesex University,
http://www.moda.mdx.ac.uk   138

3.10. *AR* (December 1934), plate xxi, image courtesy of the Museum
of Domestic Design & Architecture, Middlesex University,
http://www.moda.mdx.ac.uk   139

3.11. *AR* (December 1934), plate xxv, image courtesy of the Museum of
Domestic Design & Architecture, Middlesex University,
http://www.moda.mdx.ac.uk   140

3.12. John Gloag, photographer and date unknown, PP.8.17.1,
Pritchard Papers, University of East Anglia   142

3.13. George Grey Wornum, photograph by Bassano Ltd (1934),
NPG x151237, © National Portrait Gallery, London   148

3.14. Miriam Wornum painting the fixed shutters in the Members' Room of
66 Portland Place, photographer unknown (c.1934), Wornum Family
Private Collection   149

3.15. Cover of a prospectus for the Building Centre (1932), F203A,
Architectural Association Archive   154

3.16. 'Plans of the Building Centre', *AAJ* (September 1932), p.81, Architectural
Association Archive   157

3.17. View of the main entrance hall of the Building Centre with the enquiries
desk to the left, photographer unknown (c.1932), © Building Centre   158

3.18. Enquiries counter at the Building Centre, photographer unknown
(c.1932), © Building Centre   159

3.19. View of paint section on the first floor of the Building Centre,
photographer unknown (c.1932), © Building Centre   160

3.20. Ceiling lights in the vestibule of the Building Centre, photographer
unknown (c.1932), © Building Centre   162

3.21. Venesta Ltd, Vintry House, London: the secretary's office panelled
in birch plywood, designed by Lois de Soissons and Grey Wornum,

photograph by Dell & Wainwright (1930), RIBA72582, Architectural
Press Archive/RIBA Collections   163

3.22. Bellometti's Restaurant, Soho Square, London: detail of the wall
decoration, photograph by Sydney Newberry, RIBA72003,
RIBA Collections   164

3.23. Empire Timbers Exhibit on the first floor of the Building Centre,
photographer unknown (c.1932), © Building Centre   165

3.24. Empire Timbers Exhibit, showing the parquet flooring laid by
Hollis Brothers & Co. and EF Ebner, photographer unknown (c.1932),
© Building Centre   166

3.25. 9 Conduit Street, 1920s. Drawing by Walter Monckton Keesey,
RIBA114066, RIBA Collections   169

3.26. 9 Conduit Street, Meeting Room, photograph by Herbert Felton
(c.1934), RIBA113992, RIBA Collections   170

3.27. 9 Conduit Street, general office towards counter, photograph by
Herbert Felton (c.1934), RIBA114064, RIBA Collections   171

3.28. *AR* (December 1934), p. 199, image courtesy of the Museum of
Domestic Design & Architecture, Middlesex University,
http://www.moda.mdx.ac.uk   176

3.29. Royal Institute of British Architects, 66 Portland Place, London:
incised sculpture by Bainbridge Copnall in the Henry Florence
Memorial Hall depicting Maurice Webb, Grey Wornum, and Ragnar
Ostberg, photograph by Dell & Wainwright (1934), RIBA15119,
Architectural Press Archive/RIBA Collections   179

3.30. Royal Institute of British Architects, 66 Portland Place, London:
the Aston Webb committee room, photograph by Dell & Wainwright
(1934), RIBA15112, Architectural Press Archive/RIBA Collections   180

3.31. Royal Institute of British Architects, 66 Portland Place, London: the
Members' Room on the second floor, photograph by Dell & Wainwright
(1934), RIBA15091, Architectural Press Archive/RIBA Collections   181

3.32. Miriam Wornum painting at 66 Portland Place, photographer
unknown (c.1934), Wornum Family Private Collection   182

3.33. 'Working Details: Disappearing Partition', *AJ* (22 November 1934),
p.783, RIBA Collections   184

3.34. Bainbridge Copnall (seated) and his assistant Nicholas Harris
(standing) at work on the Henry Jervis Memorial Hall screen,
photographer unknown (c.1934), Leeds Museums & Galleries (Henry
Moore Institute Archive), part purchased and part presented by
Jill Copnall Neff   185

xviii LIST OF ILLUSTRATIONS

3.35. Royal Institute of British Architects, 66 Portland Place, London: the
Henry Florence Memorial Hall, photograph by Dell & Wainwright
(1934), RIBA15087, Architectural Press Archive/RIBA Collections 186

3.36. Entrance foyer to Ivar Tengbom's Konserthuset, photograph by
August Malmström (1926), SSM D2367, Stadsmuseum, Stockholm 190

3.37. Royal Institute of British Architects, 66 Portland Place, London:
the Henry Florence Memorial Hall, photograph by Dell &
Wainwright (1934), RIBA15101, Architectural Press
Archive/RIBA Collections 191

3.38. Royal Institute of British Architects, 66 Portland Place, London: the
main elevation by night, photograph by Dell & Wainwright (1934),
RIBA15097, Architectural Press Archive/RIBA Collections 192

3.39. Royal Institute of British Architects, 66 Portland Place, London:
clay model made by Bainbridge Copnall (c.1933), photographer
unknown, RIBA113984, RIBA Collections 193

3.40. Royal Institute of British Architects, 66 Portland Place, London: the
Library, photograph by Dell & Wainwright (1934), RIBA15090,
Architectural Press Archive/RIBA Collections 196

3.41. Programme for RIBA Centenary Celebration Reception, cover
designed by Raymond McGrath (1934), AA/02/05/03/13,
Architectural Association Archive 199

3.42. 'Progress and Period Charts of English Design' designed by Raymond
McGrath, AR (July 1933), plate ii, image courtesy of the Museum
of Domestic Design & Architecture, Middlesex University,
http://www.moda.mdx.ac.uk 200

3.43. British Art in Industry, Royal Academy, Burlington House, Piccadilly,
London: the Plastics Gallery, photograph by Sydney W Newbery (1935),
RIBA73645, RIBA Collections 201

3.44. Dressing table equipment exhibited at the 'Everyday Things' exhibition,
66 Portland Place, photograph by Herbert Felton (1936), RIBA60662,
RIBA Collections 202

4.1. Design for Regent Street Quadrant, London W1: part-elevation, Richard
Norman Shaw (c.1905), 11/4302, © Royal Academy of Arts, London;
photographer: Prudence Cuming Associates Limited 216

4.2. 32–4 Regent Street, London, photograph by Bedford Lemere & Co.
(1910), RIBA7796, RIBA Collections 218

4.3. 67–71 Regent Street, Westminster LB: redevelopment, photographer
unknown (1925), 136641, image © London Metropolitan Archives
(City of London) 222

LIST OF ILLUSTRATIONS   xix

4.4. Rex House, Lower Regent Street, London, Rex Cromie, photograph
by Charles Borup (1939), RIBA23481, RIBA Collections   227

4.5. 'Obituaries of Buildings: Nos 120 and 122 Maida Vale', *ABN*
(3 January 1936), RIBA139645, RIBA Collections   231

4.6. The Mutilated House, 'Shutters up in Portland Place', *AR* (June 1938),
p.292, image courtesy of the Museum of Domestic Design &
Architecture, Middlesex University, http://www.moda.mdx.ac.uk 232

4.7. Local residents of Portland Town, photograph by Margaret
Monck (c.1938), IN15002, Museum of London, © The Estate of
Margaret Monck   233

4.8. Joseph Bunyan outside his fruit shop in Portland Town,
photograph by Margaret Monck (c.1938), IN14985, Museum of
London, © The Estate of Margaret Monck   234

4.9. Rear of terraced housing in Portland Town, photograph by
Margaret Monck (c.1938), IN14977, Museum of London,
© The Estate of Margaret Monck   234

4.10. Construction of Townshend Court, Portland Town, photograph by
Margaret Monck (c.1938), IN14971, Museum of London,
© The Estate of Margaret Monck   235

4.11. Oslo Court, Prince Albert Road, Regent's Park, London: the entrance
façade on Charlbert Street seen from the north, Robert Atkinson,
photograph by Dell & Wainwright (1938), RIBA8253, Architectural
Press Archive/RIBA Collections   236

4.12. Bentick Close, Prince Albert Road, Regent's Park, London: corner of
the main elevation, Robert James Hugh Minty, photograph by Alfred
Cracknell (1938), RIBA64754, Architectural Press Archive/RIBA
Collections   237

4.13. 'Shutters up in Portland Town', *AR* (June 1938), pp.286–7, image
courtesy of the Museum of Domestic Design & Architecture, Middlesex
University, http://www.moda.mdx.ac.uk   243

4.14. 'Shutters up in Portland Town', *AR* (June 1938), pp.290–1, image
courtesy of the Museum of Domestic Design & Architecture, Middlesex
University, http://www.moda.mdx.ac.uk   244

4.15. 'Shutters up in Portland Town', *AR* (June 1938), p.289, image courtesy
of the Museum of Domestic Design & Architecture, Middlesex
University, http://www.moda.mdx.ac.uk   245

5.1. 'What the Building Said—I. Overheard in Regent Street', *AR* (June 1926),
pp.294–5, image courtesy of the Museum of Domestic Design &
Architecture, Middlesex University, http://www.moda.mdx.ac.uk 265

xx LIST OF ILLUSTRATIONS

5.2. At Piccadilly Circus', showing the new Swan and Edgar's rising behind the old, 'What the Building Said—I. Overheard in Regent Street', *AR* (June 1926), pp.294–5, image courtesy of the Museum of Domestic Design & Architecture, Middlesex University, http://www.moda.mdx.ac.uk 266

5.3. The new Quadrant, Vigo House, Ingersoll and Carrington's, Regent Street, 'What the Building Said—I. Overheard in Regent Street', *AR* (June 1926), pp.294–5, image courtesy of the Museum of Domestic Design & Architecture, Middlesex University, http://www.moda.mdx.ac.uk 266

5.4. 'The Domed Shop. Liberty's, facing Regent Street' and 'Dickins and Jones. Liberty's in Great Marlborough Street', 'What the Building Said—II. Overheard in Regent Street', *AR* (July 1926), pp.34–5, image courtesy of the Museum of Domestic Design & Architecture Middlesex University, http://www.moda.mdx.ac.uk 268

5.5. Studio portrait of Arthur Trystan Edwards, Owen, Merthyr, photographer unknown (c.1918), DXQN/25/14, Cardiff, Glamorgan Archives 271

5.6. AT Edwards, *Good and Bad Manners in Architecture* (London: Philip Allan & Co., 1924), 1st edn., pp.138–9 282

5.7. 'Hours of Sunlight in Broad and in Narrow Streets', reproduced in Arthur Trystan Edwards, 'Sunlight in Streets', *TPR*, 8.2 (April 1920), pp.93–8 (Liverpool University Press) 286

5.8. Back cover of the original promotional pamphlet, showing one of Edwards's type plans, AT Edwards, *A Hundred New Towns for Britain: An Appeal to the electorate by Ex-Serviceman J47485* (London: Simpkin Marshall, 1934) 294

5.9. A map of mainland Britain showing the disposition of the new towns, AT Edwards, *A Hundred New Towns for Britain: An Appeal to the electorate by Ex-Serviceman J47485* (London: Simpkin Marshall, 1934), p.36 295

5.10. The 'archetype' town plan, elsewhere referred to as 'A "Model" Town Designed for Traffic', reproduced in the *TPR* 14.1 (May 1939), p.35, this version reproduced in AT Edwards, *A Hundred New Towns for Britain: An Appeal to the electorate by Ex-Serviceman J47485* (London: Simpkin Marshall, 1934), p.40 299

5.11. 'A Town in a Valley', AT Edwards, *A Hundred New Towns for Britain: An Appeal to the electorate by Ex-Serviceman J47485* (London: Simpkin Marshall, 1934), p.44 300

LIST OF ILLUSTRATIONS xxi

5.12. 'A Town on Special Site', AT Edwards, *A Hundred New Towns for Britain: An Appeal to the electorate by Ex-Serviceman J47485* (London: Simpkin Marshall, 1934), p.45   301

5.13. Perspective view of terraced housing in quadrangular formation, AT Edwards, *A Hundred New Towns for Britain: An Appeal to the electorate by Ex-Serviceman J47485* (London: Simpkin Marshall, 1934), p.48   302

5.14. AT Edwards, *A Hundred New Towns for Britain: An Appeal to the electorate by Ex-Serviceman J47485* (London: Simpkin Marshall, 1934), p.50   303

5.15. 'Houses at 40 to the Acre with blocks of Flats at Corners', AT Edwards, *Modern Terrace Houses: Researches on High Density Development* (London: John Tiranti Ltd, 1946), p.xiv   307

5.16. Plans and a section showing 'Street houses at 40 to the acre with Blocks of Flats at junction of Roads', AT Edwards, *Modern Terrace Houses: Researches on High Density Development* (London: John Tiranti Ltd, 1946), p.xv   308

6.1. Waterloo Bridge: sightseers inspecting cracks in the parapet, photographer unknown (1924), 236070, image © London Metropolitan Archives (City of London)   333

6.2. 'The Waterloo Bridge Subsidence: Causes of the Controversy', *ILN* (12 April 1924), p.11, © Illustrated London News Ltd/Mary Evans   334

6.3. 'The End of Waterloo Bridge', *ILN* (30 June 1934), p.1047, © Illustrated London News Ltd/Mary Evans   336

6.4. A view of men working on the demolition of the old Waterloo Bridge with buildings on the north side of the river in the background, photograph by Charles William Prickett (1936), CXP01/01/102, Source: Historic England Archive   337

6.5. A view across the River Thames showing the demolition of the old Waterloo Bridge, photograph by Charles William Prickett (1936), CXP01/01/097, Source: Historic England Archive   338

6.6. A view of the old Waterloo Bridge during its demolition with people working on a boat beneath the bridge, Charles William Prickett (1936), CXP01/01/100, Source: Historic England Archive   339

6.7. A view across the River Thames showing the demolition of the old Waterloo Bridge, with the shot tower at the Lambeth Lead Works on the right of the background, photograph by Charles William Prickett (1936), CXP01/01/099, Source: Historic England Archive   340

xxii LIST OF ILLUSTRATIONS

6.8. Waterloo Bridge: demolition work in progress, photographer unknown
(1935), 236187, image © London Metropolitan Archives (City
of London) — 341

6.9. Unexecuted designs for Waterloo Bridge, London, for the London
County Council: part plan and elevation, Giles Gilbert Scott (1932),
RIBA97454, RIBA Collections — 348

6.10. Unexecuted designs for Waterloo Bridge, London, for the London
County Council: perspective, Giles Gilbert Scott (1932), RIBA97455,
RIBA Collections — 349

6.11. Design as built for Waterloo Bridge, London, for the London County
Council: 1/4" details of the arches, Giles Gilbert Scott (1937, with
revisions dated 1938–40), RIBA97456, RIBA Collections — 350

6.12. Waterloo Bridge, London: the steps leading down to the Embankment
with Somerset House, Strand, in the background on the right,
Giles Gilbert Scott (1945), photograph by Dell & Wainwright (1946),
RIBA25307, RIBA Collections — 351

6.13. Waterloo Bridge under construction, River Thames, London,
Giles Gilbert Scott, photograph by Dell & Wainwright (1945),
RIBA25308, RIBA Collections — 353

6.14. Waterloo Bridge, London: structural detail of an arch span,
Giles Gilbert Scott, photograph by Sam Lambert (1968), RIBA25215,
Architectural Press Archive/RIBA Collections — 354

6.15. Designs for Waterloo Bridge, London, for the London County Council:
details of south abutment (with amendments), Giles Gilbert Scott (1935,
amended between 1937 and 1938), RIBA97457, RIBA Collections — 355

6.16. Waterloo: detail of parapets and arches of Waterloo Bridge from
South Bank Exhibition Site, photographer unknown (1948), 236093,
image © London Metropolitan Archives (City of London) — 356

6.17. The south-west side of the newly built Waterloo Bridge viewed from
the south bank of the River Thames, with a hut occupied by Peter Lind
and Co., the company responsible for the bridge's construction, under
one of the arches, photograph by JJ Samuels Ltd (1942–7),
SAM01/03/0564, Source: Historic England Archive — 357

6.18. Hungerford Bridge by Herbert George Hampton (c.1920), 32367,
image © London Metropolitan Archives (City of London) — 359

6.19. 'London's Cross-River Traffic: The Commission's Great Scheme', *ILN*
(18 December 1926), p.14, © Illustrated London News Ltd/Mary Evans — 363

6.20. 'Charing Cross Bridge: the Scheme of the Royal Commission' (1926),
Arthur Keen, *Charing Cross Bridge* (1930), p.54 — 364

LIST OF ILLUSTRATIONS   xxiii

6.21. 'Plan of the Scheme Proposed by the Committee of Engineers as an Alternative to that of the Royal Commission on Cross-River Traffic London' (1928), Arthur Keen, *Charing Cross Bridge* (1930), p.56   365

6.22. One of several sheets of rough sketches for a bridge head at Charing Cross by Edwin Lutyens (c.1929–30), PA1624/3/12, RIBA Collections   366

6.23. 'Charing Cross Bridge: Copy of Sketch Proposals by Sir Edwin Lutyens': sent with a letter from Mott, Hay & Anderson (4 June 1929), PA1624/3(2), RIBA Collections   366

6.24. 'Scheme for Charing Cross Bridge and its approaches. With or without an elevated roadway across the new Charing Cross Square and a sub-way under York Road: John Murray, FSA, FRIBA, September, 1929', Arthur Keen, *Charing Cross Bridge* (1930), p.49   371

6.25. Reginald Blomfield's proposal for a suspension bridge, LCC/MIN/12506, Plan 2, London Metropolitan Archives (City of London)   372

6.26. A proposal for a low-level station on the Lion Brewery site by Sir Murdoch Macdonald, William Muirhead, David Barclay Niven, WD Caröe, Edwin Maxwell (Max) Fry and Thomas Adams, LCC/MIN/1250 Fig. 6. Plan 4, London Metropolitan Archives (City of London)   373

6.27. Giles Gilbert Scott's proposal for a high-level station west of the bridge head, LCC/MIN/12506, Plan 5, London Metropolitan Archives (City of London)   374

6.28. Variation on the Parliamentary Scheme by the LCC Engineers (recommended by the Majority Report), LCC/MIN/12506, Plan 7, London Metropolitan Archives (City of London)   375

6.29. 'Charing Cross Bridge Scheme' prepared by Sir Murdoch Macdonald, William Muirhead, David Barclay Niven, WD Caröe, E Maxwell (Max) Fry and Thomas Adams, drawing by Max Fry (c.1930), LCC/MIN/12506. Plan 23, London Metropolitan Archives (City of London)   376

6.30. The 'Wipers' scheme, 'Scheme for Charing Cross Bridge: W.D. Caröe, 1917', Arthur Keen, *Charing Cross Bridge* (1930), p.41   377

6.31. 'A Sketch for a Suspension Bridge, Near Charing Cross, 800 feet span', by Reginald Blomfield (1930), LCC/MIN/12506, Plan 18, London Metropolitan Archives (City of London)   378

6.32. 'A section of the sunk ring road round inner London, showing the banks of the cutting turfed and planted with trees, ramps connecting with a three-level roundabout', drawing by AC Webb, Royal Academy Planning Committee, *Road, Rail and River in London* (1944), p.5, image courtesy of Penn State University Libraries   397

xxiv LIST OF ILLUSTRATIONS

6.33. 'Model of a roundabout at a junction with the ring road', maker and photographer unknown, Royal Academy Planning Committee, *Road, Rail and River in London* (1944), p.15, image courtesy of Penn State University Libraries · 398

6.34. 'Plan for the south bank of the Thames from Lambeth to Blackfriars', Royal Academy Planning Committee, *Road, Rail and River in London* (1944), p.8, image courtesy of Penn State University Libraries · 399

6.35. 'Isometric view of the south bank of the Thames between Lambeth and London Bridge', drawing AC Webb, Royal Academy Planning Committee, *Road, Rail and River in London* (1944), p.10, image courtesy of Penn State University Libraries · 400

6.36. 'Waterloo Bridge, looking south, with Charing Cross Road Bridge on the right', drawing by AC Webb, Royal Academy Planning Committee, *Road, Rail and River in London* (1944), p.11, image courtesy of Penn State University Libraries · 401

List of Abbreviations

Institutions

AA	Architectural Association
AASTA	Association of Assistant Surveyors, Technologists and Architects
ARCUK	Architects Registration Council of the United Kingdom
AUC	Architectural Union Company
BBC	British Broadcasting Corporation
BEE	British Empire Exhibition
BICR	Building Industry Council of Review
BIIA	British Institute of Industrial Art
BINC	Building Industries National Council
BRS	Building Research Station
CEB	Central Electricity Board
CIAM	Congrès Internationaux d'Architecture Moderne
CPRE	Council for the Preservation of Rural England
DIA	Design and Industries Association
ERC	Economic Reform Club
EDA	Electricity Development Association
ELMA	Electrical Lamp Manufacturers' Association
EMB	Empire Marketing Board
FAS	Faculty of Architects and Surveyors
GLCC	Gas Light and Coke Company
GPO	General Post Office
HNTA	Hundred New Towns Association
IAAS	Incorporated Association of Architects and Surveyors
ICF	Industrial Christian Fellowship
JCT	Joint Contracts Tribunal
LCC	London County Council
LPC	London Power Company
LPE	London Press Exchange
LSB	Lighting Service Bureau
MARS	Modern Architectural Research Group
MO	Mass Observation

xxvi LIST OF ABBREVIATIONS

PIC	Population Investigation Committee
RA	Royal Academy
RFAC	Royal Fine Arts Commission
RIBA	Royal Institute of British Architects
Scapa	Society for Checking the Abuses of Public Advertising
SoA	Society of Architects
SPAB	Society for the Protection of Ancient Buildings
TDA	Timber Development Association
TPI	Town Planning Institute

Publications

AAJ	*Architectural Association Journal*
ABJ	*Architect and Builder's Journal*
ABN	*Architect and Building News*
AH	*Architectural History*
AJ	*Architects' Journal*
AR	*Architectural Review*
JRIBA	*Journal of the Royal Institute of British Architects*
JSAH	*Journal of the Society of Architectural Historians*
ODNB	*Oxford Dictionary of National Biography*
TPR	*Town Planning Review*
TRIBA	*Transactions of the Royal Institute of British Architects*

Archives

AA Archives	Architectural Association Archives
AA, BMB	AA, Buildings Materials Bureau
CLAC	Crown Lands Advisory Committee
Glasgow U, ASC	University of Glasgow, Archives & Special Collections
LMA	London Metropolitan Archives
LSA	London Society Archive
NLA	National Library of Australia
RIBA, CCMP	RIBA, Centenary Committee Minutes and Papers
RIBA, ECM	RIBA, Executive Committee Minutes
RIBA, NPCM	RIBA, New Premises Committee Minutes
RIBA, PCM	RIBA, Publication Committee Minutes
RIBA, PRCM	RIBA, Public Relations Committee Minutes
RIBA, RCM	RIBA, Registration Committee Minutes
RIBA, SCM	RIBA, Special Committee Minutes

RIBA, URCM	RIBA, Unification and Registration Committee Minutes
SPAB Archives, GGGC	Society for the Protection of Ancient Buildings Archives, Georgian Group General Correspondence, May 1938–1947
TNA	The National Archives
WFPC	Wornum Family Private Collection

Introduction

Reconstructing the Profession for a Democratic Age

In May 1930, Erich Mendelsohn, perhaps the best-known Modernist architect of his day, arrived in London. Although he was to move to Britain just three years later, fleeing Nazi Germany, this was his first visit to a very foreign environment. Indeed, at least in architectural terms, it might have been a hostile environment—one that was either unaware of Mendelsohn's ethos and approach, or even contemptuous of it. In fact, Mendelsohn's visit was much feted. Coordinated by the Architectural Association (AA), it coincided with a month-long exhibition of drawings, photographs, and sketches of his works at their premises on Bedford Square (Fig. 0.1); Howard Robertson, the principal of the AA, delivered a radio broadcast recording Mendelsohn's impressions of London;[1] and a dinner was held in his honour at JC Squire's Architecture Club, of which many leading figures in architectural practice, criticism, and policy were members. The centrepiece of Mendelsohn's trip was a lecture delivered to the AA on the 'Laws of Architecture', probably in the dining room of the ground floor recently refurbished by Easton and Robertson (Fig. 0.2). Entitled 'Architecture of Our Own Time', the proceedings were recorded in the *Architectural Association Journal* of the following month.[2] Mendelsohn spoke as a 'representative of a movement which is certainly not at war with the past, which recognises the beauty of the past, created by the past; but which realises that this beauty belongs irrevocably to the past, and has turned to find a separate path of its own towards a modern beauty'.[3] Probably a version of a lecture given in Pittsburgh in 1924,[4] it was informed by the vestiges of Mendelsohn's engagement with Expressionism in

---

[1] Howard Robertson, 'Modern Architecture of Europe', *Listener* 72.3 (28 May 1930), p.930.

[2] 'AA General Meeting: Architecture of Our Own Times', *AAJ* 46 (June 1930), pp.4–22.

[3] Ibid., p.4.

[4] Arnold Whittick, *Eric Mendelsohn* (1940), p.112; Kathleen James, 'Expressionism, Relativity and the Einstein Tower', *JSAH* 53.4 (December 1994), pp.392–413, p.412. Place of publication for books is London unless otherwise stated.

Designs on Democracy: Architecture and the Public in Interwar London. Neal Shasore, Oxford University Press.
© Neal Shasore 2022. DOI: 10.1093/oso/9780192849724.003.0001

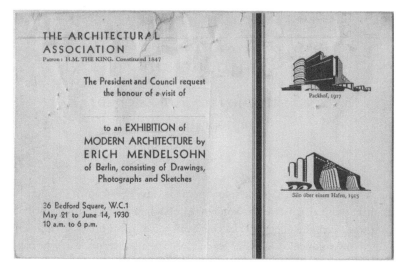

Fig. 0.1 Invitation to an exhibition of modern architecture by Erich Mendelsohn (1930), AA/02/05/02/03/08, Architectural Association Archives

the 1910s and early 1920s, in particular the Einstein Tower in Potsdam (built between 1919 and 1921). This work owed much to the expressionist sketches he had produced in the 1910s of industrial and monumental architecture, displayed in Berlin to some acclaim in 1919.

Echoing contemporary concerns in Germanophone art history, Mendelsohn expounded a set of contrasting classifications to describe the difference between surface and space. These included 'mere front' versus wall, line against contour, inert mass set against living mass—a version of Swiss art historian Heinrich Wölflinn's formulae of classification for Classical and Baroque art and architecture. In Mendelsohn's conception, the façade to the Palazzo Strozzi was a wall which, though it 'clearly lacks all sensuous appeal', nonetheless expressed *and* represented three-dimensional space. The façade of the Palazzo Balbarano, Venice, was still structural but its decoration—'attractive, facile, suggestive'—exemplified a transition from wall to front. The Admiralspalast Theatre in Berlin, in its fussiness and stylistic eclecticism, had become 'mere front'. In his defence of dynamic functionalism, Mendelsohn talked of the need for 'organic unity', and 'energy' alongside 'form':

> Functional architecture is collective architecture, real purposeful architecture; but such slogans which are still living their shadow life in all the

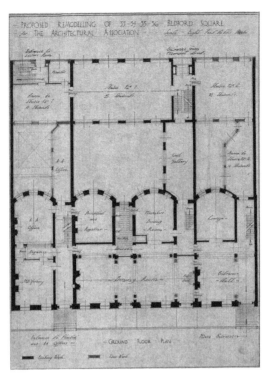

Fig. 0.2 Plan of the ground floor of 36 Bedford Square as remodelled by Easton and Robertson (1928), AA/01/04/01/03, Architectural Association Archives

> European art magazines may be quickly reduced to their insignificance by stripping them of their covering of sounding words. Instead of function put reality, conscience, reason, figures: instead of dynamics put unreality, unconscience, feeling, imagination. It is perfectly obvious that real creative power is the result of the interplay of dynamics and function. Both components, intellect and temperament, are essential in the creative process. It is the union between them which leads to mastery over space.[5]

Mendelsohn's distinction between wall and 'mere front' tapped into an international debate about the expression of structure in modern architecture. Mendelsohn's own interventions were expressionist—the 'dynamic functionalism' of the Einstein Tower (incidentally, brick built with a concrete

---

[5] 'AA General Meeting: Architecture of Our Own Times', p.16.

4 DESIGNS ON DEMOCRACY

skin), the Hermann Hat Factory and the Schocken Department Stores in Chemnitz and Stuttgart were in contrast with the increasing move 'toward austerity as a metaphor for rationalism' among other Modernists of the International Style. Mendelsohn proclaimed, however, that 'to speak in London on modern architecture requires both daring and confidence'; England 'is still very much in love with its old fashions, and has striven long to adapt Queen Anne and Queen Elizabeth not to speak of Queen Victoria, with all that they imply, to modern times'.[6] This characterization of the backwardness of English architecture, and in particular London street architecture, was difficult for some to refute. Robertson had confessed in his broadcast 'that in England the full force of the modern movement is not yet felt'.[7] But he did count as exceptions a number of recent buildings in London: Burnet and Tait's Adelaide House at London Bridge, Joseph Emberton's New Olympia, Leo Sylvester Sullivan's new offices for Courtauld's on St Martin's-le-Grand, Ideal House for the National Radiator Company on Argyll Street by the American architect Raymond Hood, Percy Morley Horder and Verner Rees's School of Hygiene and Tropical Medicine on Gower Street, and the headquarters of the London Underground at 55 Broadway by Charles Holden, as well as the various tube stations he was designing at the same time.[8] Incidentally, these were largely steel-frame, commercial buildings.[9] In Britain, and in London in particular, the cladding of the steel frame in often classical or stripped classical dress, denying constructional honesty and limiting the expressive capacity of a building's architectonic, was seen as characteristic of the conservatism of English architecture in the early twentieth century, akin to the sins of the Admiralspalast Theatre in Berlin— all 'mere front'. Robertson's list, by contrast, comprised buildings that deliberately exposed or represented their constructional method, in particular through the vertical emphases of their façades, such as at Adelaide House and Courtauld's. Others, like 55 Broadway, New Empire Hall at Olympia, and the School of Hygiene and Tropical Medicine, used the possibilities of the steel frame for bold massing and stepped profiles, or punctured voids in façades. Many of these buildings, however, still deployed

---

[6] Ibid., p.4.   [7] Robertson, 'Modern Architecture of Europe', p.930.

[8] Andrew Saint, 'Americans in London: Raymond Hood and the National Radiator Building; Architects: Stanley Gordon Jeeves, in association with Raymond Hood', *AA Files* 7 (September 1984), pp.30–43; Eitan Karol, *Charles Holden, Architect* (Donington, 2007).

[9] Jonathan Clarke, *Early Structural Steel in London Buildings: A Discreet Revolution* (Swindon, 2014).

INTRODUCTION 5

conventional planning tropes and 'historicist' ornamental motifs: symmetrical façades, stone facings, classical porticos, Egyptianizing cornices.

Mendelsohn's lecture implied, in other words, a criticism commonly held that England lagged behind in architectural terms. He had come, prophetically, to his hosts at the AA to impart the new 'laws' of architecture. Prominent members of the largely metropolitan architectural elite were present, and the response was laudatory, if cautious. Grey Wornum, an architect of a neo-Georgian sensibility and with a particular interest in craft and interior decoration, thanked the speaker for his 'several words of warning', despite the fact that Mendelsohn had offered 'us no ready means of designing successfully in this modern style'.[10] Austen Hall, who had produced a number of notable Edwardian Baroque town halls in partnership with Septimus Warwick, was interested in the 'many definitions he gave' and the idea of 'modern architecture as being an expression of intellect and emotion'.[11] Howard Robertson, who had proposed the first vote of thanks, Austen Hall, and Wornum were central figures at the AA at this time, along with the recently stepped-down director of education, Robert Atkinson. They were among a number of middle-aged architects who, according to Alan Powers, at the end of the 1920s 'began to show a greater interest in Modernism in their work and pronouncements', and who, though largely forgotten by history, 'occupied many crucial positions in teaching and journalism'.[12]

Arthur Trystan Edwards, an eccentric architect-planner and critic, was also at the AA that evening. Irritated by the lecture, he argued with another journalist, Frederick Towndrow, who by contrast had felt that Mendelsohn was 'saying all the things which some of us have been saying for years'.[13] So vociferous was their disagreement that 'no one else had much chance to talk'.[14] The editor of the journal *Building* light-heartedly recounted that, indeed, 'we would not have got to bed before dawn had I not suggested, amid acclamation from the rest of the party, that their eloquence was being largely wasted, and others ought to "listen in"'.[15] The resulting debate, entitled 'The New Religion', carried out through an exchange of letters between Edwards and Towndrow, ran for a further six months in the pages

---

[10] 'AA General Meeting: Architecture of Our Own Times', p.20. [11] Ibid., p.21.
[12] Alan Powers, *Britain: Modern Architectures in History* (2007), p.33.
[13] '"The New Religion": A Discussion on Traditionalism and Modernism between A. Trystan Edwards, MA, ARIBA, and Frederic Towndrow, ARIBA', *Building* (July 1930), p.296.
[14] Ibid. [15] Ibid.

6 DESIGNS ON DEMOCRACY

of *Building*, during which 'Modernism', defended by Towndrow, was pitted against 'Traditionalism', represented by Edwards.[16] Edwards—a mathematician and classicist before his conversion to architecture—could not tolerate Mendelsohn's pseudo-mathematical and pseudo-scientific language. Instead he advocated for 'reason' and his own universal principles of form and composition derived from classical Georgian and Regency architecture. Towndrow defended the 'scientific' approach to modern architecture which lay at the core of Mendelsohn's paper but was disappointed by his interpretation of dynamic functionalism. Mendelsohn's method, upon further probing, was to study the functional aspect of the problem first, 'but only apparently for a little while; for then he has one of those dreadful things—an "inspiration"; an artist's preconception of what he is going to do, which shapes all the good and necessary factors into those which we see illustrated'.[17]

This vignette of Mendelsohn's lecture and its reception has all the elements of a prevailing view of interwar architecture—all the clichés—of Britain's uneasy relationship with architectural Modernism. Here the 'white hats' of Modernism were lined up against the 'black hats' of traditionalism, as Powers has described it (though perversely, as John Summerson later reflected, 'black hats' were typically donned by Modernists in the 1930s).[18] But it also includes those whom Powers describes as the 'middle of the field', sitting on the 'boundary line' where white 'can sometimes fade to grey'.[19] Mendelsohn represents the archetypal 'white hat', supported by figures like Towndrow, unremitting in their commitment to and advocacy of the new architecture even where they themselves parted company. It also conforms to a view that Modernism in Britain was an 'import' of émigré architects in the 1930s. The 'black hat' is Trystan Edwards's, deeply sceptical of Mendelsohn's 'new' architecture, blindly defending conservative and traditional values. And between them, the grey (indeed, grey-haired) muddled middle of Atkinson, Austen Hall, Wornum, and Robertson, practising, or having practised, one thing, and now starting, perhaps, to preach another, almost unthinkingly ignorant of the gulf between them. From this we might expect a familiar narrative of the interwar years in Britain to follow: the white hats in

---

[16] Ibid., pp.296–7; *Building* (August 1930), pp.352–3; *Building* (September 1930), pp.404–5; *Building* (October 1930), pp.446–7; *Building* (November 1930), pp.486–7; *Building* (December 1930), pp.534–9.

[17] '"The New Religion"', *Building* (July 1930), p.297.

[18] 'It showed they were intellectuals, persons apart, detached.' See 'History and Criticism: The Sense of the Modern', *AJ* (16 December 1987), p.28.

[19] Powers, *Britain*, p.7.

INTRODUCTION 7

the end overcoming the black, the turncoat grey hats hedging their bets, pursuing weak stylistic compromises, only to be rewarded with obscurity.

But is such a monochromatic view plausible or useful? Should we settle for shades of grey to add depth and texture to a period and architectural culture that were in fact much more colourfully dynamic and contradictory? Instead of defining stylistic camps—diametric opposites and 'middle-lines'—we might more profitably explore the simple fact that all the agents in this opening vignette were engaging and interacting with each other. The reciprocity of the debate and the breadth of the discourse are what is important. There were fiercely contested terms and concepts, but there were also often shared fundamental concerns and points of consensus. This scene at the AA presents a remarkably cohesive cross-section of architectural culture and its media in London: an engaged audience, open-minded to international trends in design, drawn from influential elite institutions like the Architecture Club and Architectural Association; and the media and techniques used to disseminate ideas and debate, namely an exhibition, the print press, and radio broadcasting.

We should recall the injunction of the editor of *Building*—to 'listen in'. This was a metaphor drawn from the relatively new medium of radio broadcast. There was, in other words, something performative about this pitting of 'Modernist' and 'Traditionalist' against each other—participants took on certain roles, and stuck to certain positions, in a polarized head-to-head that was designed to entertain. This was a trope which reached its apogee on the BBC in 1934 in a famous debate between the Edwardian grandee Sir Reginald Blomfield and the young gun Amyas Connell of the avant-garde practice Connell, Lucas and Ward—'For and Against Modern Architecture'—which prompted a series of further debates, one of which included Towndrow himself.[20] This has been taken as a seminal moment in which normally unequal opponents were 'levelled': 'In airing competing viewpoints, radio did for architecture what the professional press could not do and the lay press did not do.'[21] These cultural moments certainly mattered, but for significantly different reasons. The *Journal of the Royal Institute of British Architects* commented at the time on 'the wireless debate between the staunch champions of two schools of architectural thought':

---

[20] Reginald Blomfield and Amyas Connell, 'For and Against Modern Architecture', *Listener* (28 November 1934), pp.885–8.

[21] Shundana Yusaf, *Broadcasting Buildings: Architecture on the Wireless, 1927–1945* (Cambridge, Mass, 2014), p.68.

8 DESIGNS ON DEMOCRACY

In a careless moment we almost wrote 'architecture old and new,' but realised in time that the supporters of both traditionalism and modernism claim that theirs is the only true traditional form of building and the only architecture of the future. The other is dead, so says one side, or sterile says the other. In fact the only thing in common is the opinion that the other man's architecture is not architecture at all. The debate must have interested innumerable listeners, but surely it is a pity, even as recreation for an evening, to stimulate again a battle of the styles.[22]

This was at a moment when the Institute was trying to show 'that the essential purpose of good building is wide enough to allow scope for the united efforts of the whole profession without the disconcerting note of polemical debate'.[23]

The tableau at the AA—Mendelsohn pontificating, Wornum bemused, Edwards agitated, Towndrow intransigent—is perhaps also an unhelpfully limited and static image. This was, after all, one group of architects, in one institution, attending a particular lecture in 1930 about an individual's idiosyncratic interpretation of the formal aspects of modern architecture. The reality of debates about architecture and the built environment was much more diverse and complex—neither so easily abstracted into laws, nor so easily divided into oppositional camps, nor fixed in time. Contemporaries recognized this. While Edwards and Towndrow understood that there was something profoundly different about the way they conceived of architecture, even Edwards could concede that the 'common distinction between "Modernist" and "Traditionalist" is a somewhat artificial one, inasmuch as those of us who revere the element of reason in the architecture of the past are anxious to discover and uphold a new reason such as may give to twentieth-century architecture a characteristic quality of its own'.[24] Edwards, though anti-Modernist, was not a great supporter of the 'conservative' element, having spilt 'a lot of ink in attempting to expose the inconsequence of much of the traditionalist work'. For his part Towndrow, at this time the architectural critic of the *Observer*, had in the 1920s worked first for the architects' branch office at the British Empire Exhibition at Wembley and then as an assistant architect in the Office of Works, including a stint under Sir James West, designing details on public buildings such as the Law Courts in Northern Ireland, additions to the National Gallery and National Portrait

---

[22] 'Report of the Centenary Conference', *JRIBA* (8 December 1934), p.151.   [23] Ibid.
[24] '"The New Religion"', *Building* (July 1930), p.296.

INTRODUCTION 9

Gallery, and minor alterations to Buckingham Palace.[25] These were no doubt among 'the spineless imitations of ancient architecture' he railed against in his exchange with Edwards: 'the half-columns stuck on to the face of Sir Thingumytight's building, the swags of fruit and flowers as employed by Sir Youknowhow, the handsome rustications four-and-a-half inches thick, the cornices which are an arrant waste of money, the mouldings which collect flies and dust, and the foolish sentimental arches which do not support anything, and are themselves—poor things—supported by steel'.[26]

Unlike many histories of twentieth-century British architecture, in particular those dealing with the decades before the Second World War, this book stresses the interconnectedness and common bases of architectural culture. The rhetorics of avowed difference and the adversarial framework—the 'battle of the styles'—through which contemporaries often sought to present the profession, and which architects at times deployed for effect, are resituated as part of a project to put architecture at the heart of civic consciousness. The strong formalist inflection of architectural discussion, encapsulated by Mendelsohn's paper and the response to it, often suggests a more limited debate than was in fact the case and obscures points of fundamental consensus as well as complexity as the profession of architecture continued to modernize. This is not to elide meaningful differences of opinion or to pretend that Modernism was totally indistinct from a wider modernizing architectural culture. On the contrary, examining intersections, interactions, and contiguities may allow for a clearer articulation of what was in fact distinct about avant-garde design and practice.

It was, after all, through Wornum, Robertson, and Austen Hall's energies and receptivity to 'modern' ideas about architecture that Mendelsohn had come to present his ideas to the AA. Despite their tentativeness, their intentions were genuine. Mendelsohn and his wife went on to enjoy a long friendship with the Wornums, for example. Later, Mendelsohn's emigration to Britain was secured through representations to the Home Office by the president, Giles Gilbert Scott, and secretary, Ian MacAlister, of the Royal Institute of British Architects (RIBA). Even the gruff and contrived exchange between Towndrow and Edwards makes a different sense in the context of their professional relationship. Both had served on a short-lived Publicity Committee for the RIBA under the chairmanship of Clough Williams-Ellis

---

[25] NLA, Oral History and Folklore Collection, ORAL TRC 1/56, 'An Interview with FE Towndrow' (1964). I am grateful for Steve Parnell for this reference.
[26] '"The New Religion"', *Building* (September 1930), p.405.

10   DESIGNS ON DEMOCRACY

in 1926, a body convened to examine how to garner wider public interest in the profession. It is significant too that Towndrow commissioned Edwards regularly in the early issues of *Architectural Design and Construction*, of which Towndrow was editor from 1933. Both men admired Reginald Blomfield; Edwards had served articles with him for three years from 1908, and Towndrow as late as 1932 (although before the publication of his anti-Modernist tract, *Modernismus* in 1934) wrote an enthusiastic review of Blomfield's memoirs, praising his books on the French and English Renaissance for establishing 'the principles on which—as distinct from the details—some of our best modern work is based'.[27] His part in 'setting the foundations of architectural education' and his 'almost revolutionary proposals for the reformation of the Royal Academy' were equally admired, along with his campaigning work for preserving significant London monuments.[28] In his book *Architecture in the Balance*—in which he quoted Edwards—Towndrow himself reflected that no one should:

> suppose that there is, somewhere, an isolated modern doctrine, cut off in some perverse way from the major part of architectural thought: an imaginary school which has its own canons, its own convictions and its own stock-in-trade of design. To assume that would be to assume that there is a curious cult with a number of duly-initiated practitioners who had sworn to clothe their buildings in one new style rather than in any of the old ones. There may be such people. I hope not. All that I know is that there are all shades of thought between the academically-minded copyist and the out-and-out pure and simple constructivist.[29]

The polemic and performativity—Towndrow *versus* Edwards, Connell *versus* Blomfield—were necessitated by a perceived crisis of criticism, itself the consequence of a commonly shared concern in the interwar years that architecture and (of greater concern to professionals) *architects* did not matter to the public and were peripheral to public debate. *The Pleasures of Architecture* (first published in 1924), by Clough and Amabel Williams-Ellis, took on this theme at length, their purpose being to forge 'a *rapprochement* between practitioners of this long-neglected art [architecture] and the

---

[27] 'The Architect Militant', *Observer* (13 November 1932), p.8.   [28] Ibid.
[29] Frederick Towndrow, *Architecture in the Balance: An Approach to the Art of Scientific Humanism* (1933), p.3.

public'.[30] Public indifference directly impacted the quality of design and the capacity of designers: 'any set of artists whose products are not exposed to plenty of criticism, degenerate. They become either affected, lethargic, over-wild or over-fastidious, or else they lose heart and make money.'[31] This apathy, the Williams-Ellises complained, was reinforced by the dearth of architectural writing in the general press, and in the technical press 'the treatment is, as a rule, descriptive rather than critical.'[32] This was a result of the enduring convention of nineteenth-century criticism, that living archi-tects could not criticize one another's work: these public bouts of Modernist *versus* Traditionalist were intended to get round this convention and recap-ture an imagined ideal of architectural knockabout in the nineteenth cen-tury. Architecture required 'besides the technical appraisers, a second type of interpretative or go-between critic to write for the general cultivated public...Certain it is that without this public interest we shall not see another great age of this enduring, expensive, satisfactory, cumbersome art.'[33] Williams-Ellis's concluding words made it clear what was at stake:

> Our cities might be growing into proud places, we have got plenty of capable designers. Instead, for every beautiful new building that goes up we shall still have a dozen or more which are absurd, ignorant and ugly, and give pleasure to nobody, but carry on the bad old Victorian tradition of building without hope or enjoyment. The future of English poetry lies with the poets, the future of English architecture with the public. We have reached the moment when they may, if they think it worth while [*sic*], enjoy the pleasures of architecture.[34]

Clough and Amabel Williams-Ellis were not the only writers and architects to reflect on this perceived crisis in the early 1920s. WG Newton, then editor of the *Architectural Review*, used his editorials to take on the 'Bases of Criticism' later published as a *Prelude to Architecture* (1925), in which he discussed the relationship between Citizen and Artist, and discussed how architecture should express plan and structure, as well as challenging the primacy of style.[35] The purposes of these editorials were to prompt the

---

[30] Clough and Amabel Williams-Ellis, *The Pleasures of Architecture* (1930), p.17.
[31] Ibid., p.235. [32] Ibid., p.238. [33] Ibid., p.240. [34] Ibid., p.242.
[35] William Godfrey Newton, *Prelude to Architecture* (1925). The editorials comprising the volume were published as 'The Bases of Criticism' in *AR* (1924).

12 DESIGNS ON DEMOCRACY

public press to stake a claim in questions surrounding the built environment. Countless other examples in a similar tone and on similar themes abound.

These concerns about an enervated critical discourse, public apathy, and their impact on design and the profession persisted, ironically, given how frequently the issue was discussed in the columns of the architectural press. By November 1938, however, celebrating the opening of Norwich City Hall, designed in partnership by Charles Holloway James and Stephen Rowland Pierce, the *AR* was able to reflect that 'perhaps once in a couple of years, architecture becomes news, and an architectural event...becomes a public event. Architects for once receive acknowledgement of the public significance that they themselves know attaches to their profession.'[36] Recent such buildings, all covered extensively by the *AR* in the preceding fifteen years, included 'Liberty's in Great Marlborough Street, off Regent Street, the Shakespeare Memorial Theatre at Stratford-upon-Avon, Cambridge University Library, the RIBA building in Portland Place and the De La Warr Pavilion at Bexhill'.[37] Proposed additions to the University of London and St George's Hospital would do the same. In civic architecture, new municipal buildings at Worthing, Southampton, Swansea, Leeds, Hornsey, and Slough had all been 'the direct expression of an age which is increasingly organized as a bureaucracy', and all had fostered growing public interest in the practice of architecture.[38]

The current common conception of interwar architecture would struggle to make much either of the *Review*'s statement or of the range of buildings it listed as somehow coherently representative of 'an age'. Instead, the modern reader might focus on the stylistic variety covered by those examples: Modernist, or International Style at Bexhill (1935, Eric Mendelsohn and Serge Chermayeff) and Hornsey (1935, Reginald Uren); *moderne* at Stratford (1932, Elisabeth Scott) and Swansea (1934, Percy Thomas); neo-Georgian at Norwich, Slough (1937, both by James and Pierce), and, arguably, at Cambridge (1934, Giles Gilbert Scott); Queen Anne at Worthing (1933, Cowles-Voysey); Classical and Beaux-Arts Classical at Leeds (1933, Vincent Harris) and Southampton (1932–9, Ernest Berry Webber); Swedish Grec at the RIBA (1934, Grey Wornum); Tudoresque at Liberty (1924, Edwin Thomas Hall and Edwin Stanley Hall, father and son). Yet, the writer of the *AR*'s editorial seems to have been largely unbothered by this. Indeed, despite their stylistic, typological, political, and chronological range, he seems to have observed some

---

[36] 'Foreword', *AR* (November 1938), p.201.   [37] Ibid.   [38] Ibid.

more fundamental connection—they all, in late 1938, seemed adequately and collectively to represent 'architecture', they were all part of a common architectural culture and they all shared the capacity to generate and in turn receive attention from the public.

Today we are inclined to view that list as representative of something rather eclectic, non-committal, historicist in English architecture of the interwar period. We have grown accustomed to a narrative of stylistic chaos and insularity with a few, highly fetishized, truly 'Modernist' buildings, like the pavilion at Bexhill, as somehow redemptive of a period of national embarrassment in which the mainstream of architectural design and practice was staunchly traditional and non-, if not anti-Modernist. Even those who have offered more nuanced views have tended to find only occasional instances of vitality in monographic studies of particular architects, practices, and typologies. Much more energy has been given to uncovering early and pre-histories of British Modernism in the 1920s and 1930s, in which a small avant-garde and their private, corporate, and institutional patrons established new design practices, discourses, and architectural 'consumers' almost as an act of subterfuge. Internationalist by definition—especially because of the presence of émigrés in the early 1930s—this small coterie and the supposedly transnational language of the 'International Style' in which they were engaged, were allegedly drowned out by the parochial concerns of the establishment voices predominant in England. The more nuanced account of Mendelsohn's visit to the AA shows what a (persistent) caricature the received view is. In fact, the situation was much more complex. Despite the rhetoric even of contemporaries themselves, there was broad coalition and consensus in architectural culture in the early twentieth century, in particular about the need to forge a meaningful relationship with the public.

The 1920s and 1930s have been too often neglected by historians of architecture and the built environment, in particular those of the long nineteenth century for whom the interwar years represent a weak coda to the more substantial Victorian era, and those of the twentieth century whose politics and tastes more easily align with the optimism of the postwar years. The 'interwar' period is left defined as merely 'between' subjects of much greater interest and ambition. When the 1920s and 1930s have been considered they have normally been discussed in regard to the stylistic eclecticism and historicism which typified design culture in the period: the anachronistically identified 'Art Deco', the neo-Georgian, the Tudoresque, and so on, so pithily lampooned even by contemporaries like Osbert Lancaster

14   DESIGNS ON DEMOCRACY

in *From Pillar to Post* (1938).[39] The intense focus on style in existing scholarship, its oppositionality—often itself caught up in later iterations of 'style wars'—and eclecticism have obscured much of the historical interest and dynamism of the interwar years.

Definitions: Architects, Their Publics, and Interwar Britain

The title of the present book has a double meaning. On one level, it alludes to the ways in which architects had to map their work literally and figuratively onto a maturing mass democracy, heralded by universal franchise and other social changes such as the reduction of the working week. This was reflected superficially in terms of typology—in entirely new types of building like community centres, or in developing ones such as civic centres, which incorporated municipal building complexes evolving from Victorian and Edwardian precedents. On another level, however, to have designs on democracy implies a desire to co-opt and shape it. The title thus drives at the fundamental tension in architectural culture's obsession with democratization—between cultivating and engaging an architecturally minded public, and the concern that such a public might not in fact have need for or pay much heed to architectural expertise, and might therefore need guidance. The insistent emphases on publics thus served as a set of rhetorical procedures and tools to bolster the position of the professional architect, whilst at the same time shaping architectural forms and the meanings ascribed to them.

This book recovers a highly energetic and connected, if sometimes fragile, 'public sphere' of architectural culture in the first decades of the twentieth century. It is striking the extent to which perceived or constructed needs and wants of the 'public' underpin controversies, campaigns, innovations, reform, and development throughout the period in question. It is also striking that this was felt to be a new (or perhaps revived) phenomenon which made the early twentieth century distinct from the laissez-faire individualism of the Victorian era. In certain instances, it also expressed progressive ideals of social liberalism. Through foregrounding deeper questions about democratization and 'cultures of democracy', and properly historicizing attitudes to style at this time, we can get at the history of the formation, or more accurately consolidation, of the modern architectural profession. This book,

---

[39] Osbert Lancaster, *From Pillar to Post: The Pocket Lamp of Architecture* (1938).

therefore, looks at a broad coalition of architects, their allies, and patrons, who were neither necessarily Modernist nor explicitly excluded from its ranks, who were indeed part of the architectural establishment, and who fashioned a liberal consensus about the nature of architecture which prevailed in the interwar years (Fig. 0.3). Even those normally considered to represent 'extremes'—such as Edwards to the right, Towndrow to the left—were in fact part of this broader consensus.

This liberal consensus was characterized by an acceptance that for the architectural profession to exist, and to continue to enjoy its particular privileges, it would need to address and meet the socio-political demands of a mass democracy. This was not, in other words, a communitarian radicalism, for the most part, but it was often politically progressive despite its mischaracterization as crudely or unthinkingly conservative. The book explores this interaction between architecture and the public by examining new conceptions of consumption and ownership, shifting attitudes towards

Fig. 0.3 Caricature of sixteen well-known architects of the 1930s attending a function in the RIBA's Florence Hall by Fred May (1939), RIBA21580, RIBA Collections

16   DESIGNS ON DEMOCRACY

practice and professionalism, developing themes in architectural discourse and criticism, the formation of new institutions and associations, and attention paid to programme and design. All of these were frequently and self-consciously cast in terms of their relationship to 'the public', a shorthand for these demands of mass democracy, frequently invoked as the ultimate client body politic.

This is not to claim that architects and their institutions acted altruistically in relation to the needs and wants of the public; architecture remained an elite profession, and architects were driven often by thinly concealed self-interest. Rather, the aim here is to examine to what ends professional architects and their collaborators mobilized various constructs of 'the public' and its means of expression. In so doing, individual chapters look at various 'vehicles' of public expression and engagement: publicity and public relations, public opinion and public interest, public proprietorship, public propriety, public amenity, and the public realm. These are explored through 'landmark' projects and events in architectural culture in the 1910s, 1920s, and 1930s. Using a number of canonical, though in some cases still relatively unknown, projects and major controversies of the period, this book looks at architectural culture as a whole. 'Non-Modernist' design, practice, and discourse are foregrounded because of their political and cultural significance, not as a matter of personal or current taste. The book also looks beyond the world of built monuments, their designers, and patrons, taking in an expanded cultural field of politicians, commentators, administrators, and advocates. It takes as read that all of architectural culture operated 'under the rule of modernity', to paraphrase the art historian David Peters Corbett; there was a range of architectural practice, all of which engaged with the experience of modernity in different ways and not necessarily under the rubrics of 'Modernism'.[40]

In doing so, the book seeks to provide an explanatory framework for architectural design, discourse, practice, and professionalism in the interwar years that captures prevalent anxieties, dynamic attempts at problem-solving, and new modes of criticism and practice, especially civic design and the emergence of the interwar 'architect-planner'. A conception of buildings as ensembles, constituting an environment, was repeatedly articulated as a distinguishing feature from the individualistic nineteenth century. The book addresses 'the public' as an idea and a construct—it does not a provide a

---

[40] David Peters Corbett, *The Modernity of English Art, 1914–1930* (Manchester, 1997), p.11.

sociological analysis of the general public's physical interactions with the built environment, nor does it quantitatively measure public engagement or public use of buildings. This may well constitute an underdeveloped methodology in the social history of architecture, but it is not the present concern. Nor does it investigate architecture in relation to the crowd, a powerful motif in the polarized politics of interwar Europe—indeed, British political rhetoric often eschewed the 'masses', those who might constitute the crowd in a visual and spatial imaginary, in favour of the 'public'.[41] The distinction was purposeful, and spoke to a liberal conception of the political subject. 'The public' is therefore used here as an expression of broadly conceived cultures of democracy and civil society. The book examines how evolving cultures of democracy interacted with the built environment. Processes of democratization also helped to shape ideals of professionalism and the collective or corporate identity of architects, including their interaction with the client body politic, 'the public'. Constructing and configuring 'the public' in architectural culture was as much part of modernity and modernization as technological and constructional innovation.

Such a reconsideration of the constructed and multifaceted nature of 'the public' and democratization is timely; recent debates within and outside the architectural profession and construction industry have stressed the need for recalibrating the relationship with the public and public interest. In doing so they have also reflected on the still relatively underplayed history of architectural practice and professionalism which this book tackles. Flora Samuel, former RIBA Vice President for Research, for instance, in *Why Architects Matter* (2016) has lamented our 'very poor understanding of how architects have operated as professionals over time and in relationship with others'.[42] Simon Foxell, active in the influential industry think-tank 'The Edge', has in a similar vein questioned how 'institutions currently understand their public service remit and in what way it influences their activities'. They have no 'clearly articulated narrative explaining their public interest obligations either to themselves, the public or even to the Privy Council'.[43]

---

[41] For an account of the politics and spectacle of the crowd in 1930s Britain, discussed in spatial terms, see Murray Fraser, 'Germania-on-Thames' in Graham Cairns (ed.), *Architecture, Media and Populism* (Abingdon and New York, forthcoming, 2022).

[42] Flora Samuel, *Why Architects Matter: Evidencing and Communicating the Value of Architects* (2018), p.6.

[43] Simon Foxell, *Professionalism in the Built Environment* (2018), p.235. For 'The Edge' see https://edgedebate.com [accessed 6 June 2020].

18 DESIGNS ON DEMOCRACY

In fact, the public interest case—however flawed or disingenuous—is intrinsic to the ideal of modern professionalism. As Foxell observes, 'the principal opposing poles attracting the professions have been public service on one side and self-interest on the other and high levels of institutional energy have been devoted to maintaining a degree of balance between them.'[44] 'It is this position: "between market and state"…that the professions have forgotten to properly maintain or interest themselves in.'[45]

Architects have begun to interrogate the 'dark matter' of practice and professionalism: institutional infrastructure, regulatory frameworks, procurement, management, governance. This encompasses the praxis of architecture. Writers and practitioners like Indy Johar—founder of 'Dark Matter Labs', a think-tank connected to the interdisciplinary collaborative design studio, Zero Zero, have argued that to create better architecture—architecture that is ethical, sustainable, beneficial to the community and to the public—these 'dark matter' processes and frameworks should be subject to more sophisticated scrutiny by the design professions, receiving as much intensity of focus as is given to systems of design education and practice. They are constructs and artefacts as much as buildings and environments. Johar calls frequently for a 'boring revolution'; an overhaul, reimagining, and refining of democratic governance, in particular in the built environment.[46] This overhaul is framed not in the self-interest of the profession, but in terms of architects' professional obligations to the public and civic life.

This has profound implications for how we understand the role of history, and history and theory, in architectural education and practice. The fundamentally technocratic premise that better bureaucracy, better policy, better regulation, better governance open up possibilities for a better built environment needs interrogation; history and historical method offer us rich opportunities to engage critically with that questioning. We need not just chronologies of typological evolution and design, but to use the tools of historical analysis and critical thinking to nuance this 'boring revolution', to test and reimagine institutions and techniques of governance on an institutional, architectural, and urban scale. We need to understand the history

---

[44] Foxell, *Professionalism*, p.xviii.   [45] Ibid., p.xix.

[46] See https://darkmatterlabs.org [accessed 6 June 2020]; Dark Matter Laboratories, 'Practice' in *AA Files* 76 (2019), pp.134–8. Johar also participated in the RIBA's recent Ethics and Sustainable Development Commission. See 'Findings of the RIBA Ethics and Sustainable Development Commission', (2018), https://www.architecture.com/knowledge-and-resources/resources-landing-page/ribas-ethics-and-sustainable-development-commission-final-report [accessed 6 June 2020].

INTRODUCTION   19

of architectural institutions, to understand in historically located ways why architects do the things they do and think the way they think. The praxis of architecture has historical dimensions which must be properly understood to help find creative, sustainable, sound solutions not only to architecture, but to the whole world of construction and the built environment. This challenge is far from boring.

There is a growing corpus of work in this area, and construction history in particular has contributed significantly.[47] The 1920s and 1930s, however, are particularly ripe for such an exploration because they were also witness, arguably, to an earlier 'boring revolution', in which important but barely noticeable or barely noted changes took place, like the formation of the Joint Contracts Tribunal (JCT) which produced the first standard form of contract agreed between the architectural profession and the construction industry. Or the establishment of the Building Industries National Council (BINC) to coordinate construction industry activity. Or the Building Research Station (BRS) and the definition of space standards of social housing.[48] Or the expansion of the Office of Works to deliver the social infrastructure of the pre-welfare state. These are stories which might not be well known but which played an important role in the formalizing and cementing of the modern architectural profession. They enshrined a vision of architectural practice and professionalism which arguably still endures. At the heart of this book are questions about how the new practice of public relations impacted architectural professionalism and the construction industry in the interwar years; what regulatory instruments were pondered to control elevations in rural and urban settings; how new and better-evidenced space standards might be designed for housing; about the means and ends of preservation; the place of associational culture; and about public scrutiny of major urban improvement schemes.

In the study of twentieth-century architectural history as a whole, far greater emphasis has been placed on the post-war period and the implication

---

[47] Katie Lloyd Thomas, Tilo Amhoff, and Nick Beech (eds), *Industries of Architecture* (2015); Andrew Saint, *The Image of the Architect* (New Haven, 1983); Linda Clarke, *Building Capitalism: Historical Change and the Labour Process in the Production of the Built Environment* (1992); Mark Swenarton, *Building the New Jerusalem: Architecture, Housing and Politics 1900–1930* (Watford, 2008); Bill Addis, 'The Contribution made by the Journal *Construction History* towards Establishing the History of Construction as an Academic Discipline' in *Proceedings of the First Construction History Society Conference* (Cambridge, 2014), pp.iii–x.

[48] Mark Swenarton, 'Breeze Blocks and Bolshevism: Housing Policy and the Origins of the Building Research Station 1917–1921', *Construction History* 21 (2005–6), pp.69–80. FM Lea, *Science and Building: A History of the Building Research Station* (1971).

20 DESIGNS ON DEMOCRACY

of architecture and planning in the formation of the Welfare State. As Mark Swenarton and others have suggested, the planning of the built environment 'was one of the key areas in which the welfare state sought to achieve its ambitions of economic redistribution and social welfare'.[49] The lionizing of architects' and architecture's 'heroic' place in the Welfare State has begun to be questioned,[50] but there is still an overemphasis on its intersection with post-war Modernism and the shift in practice towards 'official architecture'. This is partly because the histories of post-war architecture have been largely written by those who lived through it or in it, leading, perhaps, to an implicit optimism that its founding tenets might be revived. Elain Harwood's encyclopaedic *Space, Hope and Brutalism* opens with the assertion that 'The values of the Welfare State formed me and I grew up believing that they would last forever'.[51]

Contained in that statement is, of course, the implication that these values have *not* lasted forever, certainly not in unadulterated form. After the recent decimation of architecture and planning in local authorities in the context of neo-liberalism's ambivalence towards welfarism, an examination of architects in private practice negotiating with the public interest and public or semi-public institutions holds particular value. This book reflects on architecture's relationship with the state and its institutions before the post-war Welfare State, in which associational culture played an important role, and in which the limits of private interest were being tested against the needs of the community. An underlying argument of the book is that aspects of this scenario resemble our own *realpolitik*—however dismal that reality may be—in particular after the assault on public institutions by recent Conservative-led administrations under the banner of austerity. In the febrile atmosphere of today's politics, comparisons with the 1930s have become clichés. But there is a case to be made, in particular for built environment professionals, to understand better the socio-political context in which a consensus view about architectural practice and professionalism was forged, and the strategies—rightly or wrongly—used by the profession and its institutions to articulate a meaningful relationship with the state and its obligations to 'the public'. It is telling that when the Conservative government's 'Review of the Architects (Registration) Acts 1931–1969'

---

[49] Mark Swenarton, Tom Avermaete, and Dirk van den Heuvel (eds.), *Architecture and the Welfare State* (2015), pp.1–2.

[50] Ewan Harrison, ' "Money Spinners": R Seifert & Partners, Sir Frank Price and Public-Sector Speculative Development in the 1970s', *AH* (2018), pp.259–80.

[51] Elain Harwood, *Space, Hope and Brutalism* (New Haven, 2015), p.vi.

(known as the Warne Report) was published in 1993—recommending the end of statutory protection of title—it noted in Thatcherite language that the first Architects Registration Act (1931) was passed 'at a time when governments were not greatly concerned with competition or consumer protection policies'.[52] That problematic emphasis on 'competition' and 'consumer protection'—with very real implications for policy—evidenced an ahistorical ignorance of the importance of corporatism and the ethical check of public interest in the framing of that legislation in the interwar years.

In order to investigate this conception of architecture, I use the phrase 'architectural culture' as an expression to capture the diversity of architectural opinion and practice in the period: it is the intersection of design (methods, forms, styles), practice (including pedagogy, but also the 'industries of architecture'), professionalism (the individual and corporate identities and rituals of architects, their ethical proposition, their *habitus*), discourse (through a proliferating number of media, from the printed to exhibitions, radio, films, lectures, etc.), and institutions or associations (both formal and informal networks and corporate bodies, from the social to the regulatory). Architectural history privileges formal exegesis, and—in the case of British interwar architectural history—a narrative still overly concerned with stylistic delineation and evolution. What this book shows is that it is possible to write a history of this period without recourse to style, but while still attending to the historical specificity of stylistic debate and meaning, and indeed to form. I also show how these various aspects of architectural culture have operated on each other, at times de-centring style altogether. Some of my case studies were executed monuments, some were 'unbuilt'; some institutions endured and thrived, others were ephemeral. Taken together, they give a rounded picture of the architectural world at this time, and one situated in a wider cultural field. It is for this reason that a range of methods are deployed, from urban history to design history, and a range of sources embraced, from buildings and their conventional representations, to literary representation and film.

I have chosen London as my focus because architectural culture was particularly concentrated in the capital city. Provincial architectural culture was at this time vibrant and diverse—regional associations and societies were not yet subsumed into a formal national network, and although they were represented in the governance of the profession, they had lively

---

[52] EJD Warne, *Review of the Architects (Registration) Acts 1931–1969* (1993), p.2.

22 DESIGNS ON DEMOCRACY

traditions and cultures of their own. These extended not only to the provinces and regions of Great Britain but to colonies and dominions throughout the Empire. Although urban historians have long been interested in these more regionally based studies,[53] architectural history of this period tends to look at the regional through the monographic—studies of particular practices, like Bradshaw, Gass and Hope in Bolton, the Worthington dynasty in Manchester, or George Oatley in Bristol, rather than looking critically and holistically at provincial architectural cultures and their relationships with one another.[54] Liverpool is perhaps the exception, where there have been a number of studies of the local architectural culture and its links to the Liverpool School of Architecture, dominated by the charismatic figure of Charles Herbert Reilly.[55] London had a distinct architectural culture of its own, but one which was also defined by its interconnectivity with, and jurisdiction over, other places. It is where the preeminent institutions of the period had physical presence: the RIBA, the Architects' Registration Council of the United Kingdom (ARCUK), the Building Centre, and the BINC were all located, and indeed had been founded, in London. Important centres of architectural education were in London—from the AA to the Regent Street Polytechnic to the Brixton School of Building. The leading titles of the architectural press were primarily London-based, certainly the titles with the highest circulation and greatest reach: the *Architectural Review*, the *Architects' Journal*, *Architecture*, *The Builder*, *Building*, *Country Life* were all published in London. There were other conduits back to regional centres—the *Manchester Guardian*'s London editor, James Bone, wrote frequently on architectural subjects; Charles Herbert Reilly, a Londoner by birth, operated a significant metropolitan network, and his deputies at the Liverpool School, first Stanley Adshead and later Patrick Abercrombie, graduated from professorships in Civic Design at Liverpool to Town Planning at the University of London. The ancillary institutions of architecture—the BBC chief among them, but others too, like the Architecture Club, the Design and Industries Association (DIA), the Georgian Group, the London Society, the Town Planning Institute

[53] Charlotte Wildman, *Urban Development and Modernity in Liverpool and Manchester, 1918–1939* (2016).

[54] Jane Lingard and Timothy Lingard, *Bradshaw Gass & Hope: The Story of an Architectural Practice—The First One Hundred Years 1862–1962* (2007); Sarah Whittingham, *Sir George Oatley: Architect of Bristol* (Bristol, 2011).

[55] Joseph Marples, Alan Powers, and Michael Shippabottom, *Charles Reilly and the Liverpool School of Architecture, 1904–1933* (Liverpool, 1996).

INTRODUCTION 23

(TPI), the Council for the Preservation of Rural England (CPRE)—all had headquarters in London, with a national purview.

The RIBA—central to our story—had specifically metropolitan origins, having begun life as a London-based club in 1834, and had been housed in 9 Conduit Street from 1859 in a property owned by the Architectural Union Company (AUC). Independent but architect-owned, the AUC had been formed to promote an annual 'Architectural Exhibition' and other joint professional initiatives, run by a board of directors drawn mainly from RIBA member shareholders.[56] Its aspirations were, as *The Builder* put it, to create 'the home of the architectural bodies of the metropolis,—the centre, it may be hoped, of architectural progress in England.'[57] Many of the other bodies housed at 9 Conduit Street were eventually absorbed by the RIBA, which from the 1880s began to exert a stronger grip over the 'Allied' and 'Provincial' societies.

The Builder's characterization of the relationship of the metropolitan to the national shows how architectural culture in London from the nineteenth century operated at different scales. To the civic or municipal and the national we might also add the imperial. There was a centripetal tendency towards the financial hub of the Empire; wealthy clients were concentrated in London, and—in particular for our theme—public institutions and public debate were more often than not located in London. When I have referred to Britain it is not to deny the specificity of architectural culture in Scotland, Wales or Northern Ireland or anywhere else, but instead to emphasize London as a significant centre of the British imperial polity. Chapters deal with all three of these scales—the 'Little Londons' evoked in preservationist battles, the creation or reform of national institutions, and the presence of Empire in London, as well as the casting of architectural debate in terms of the imperial capital. Therefore, while I do not discuss here architectural culture in other imperial locations, I have conceived of London as an imperial city. Alex Bremner has recently called for not merely 'a history of architecture in the British Empire', but an 'architectural history of British imperialism'—a history, we can extrapolate, engaged in the material and spatial turns in history, that uses urbanism and the built environment as means of exploring wider historical questions, and that analyses architecture as constitutive of Empire and imperialism as much as

---

[56] Angela Mace, *The Royal Institute of British Architects: A Guide to Its Archive and History* (1986), p.310.
[57] 'The Architectural Galleries, Conduit-Street', *Builder* (12 March 1859), p.188.

24 DESIGNS ON DEMOCRACY

politics and ideas.[58] This architectural history of imperialism should address architectural manifestations of Empire in London: 'The metropolis was...a centre in more ways than one, both *of* and *within* the wider imperial system.'[59]

Architectural culture was inflected by imperialism. Architects and the institutions with which and for whom they worked were profoundly implicated in the later imperial project. Empire was inscribed into buildings and the urban environment, sometimes literally, through sculpture and ornament, in others respects more subtly, through patronage or building materials. This aspect of architectural culture has been rarely acknowledged in or written into histories of the period, certainly by comparison with analysis of the long nineteenth century culminating in the overt imperial pomp of the Edwardian Baroque. This is partly because the interwar years have been so strongly associated with the beginning of British imperial decline. More significantly, few architectural historians have engaged with the complexity of an architectural history of British imperialism in the 1920s and 1930s. Architectural histories of this period seem to have been untouched by the New Imperial History, where design and art histories have been more seriously engaged, save for accounts of the particular relationship of Modernism to imperialism.[60] More recently, it is striking that the Rhodes Must Fall campaigns in Cape Town and Oxford have not yet prompted much reflection in the UK discipline, despite the fact that the controversy has concerned history, architecture, urbanism, and heritage so directly, and despite the large corpus of material on the contemporaneous American Confederate monuments controversy which led directly to the Charlottesville attack in 2017.[61] At the time of writing, the Black Lives Matter campaign has secured the removal of the statue to Robert E Lee on Virginia's Monument Avenue, and in Britain that of a statue of the seventeenth-century slave trader Edward Colston, erected in Bristol in 1895. Significantly, these campaigns directly relate not only to the late nineteenth

---

[58] GA Bremner, 'Introduction' in GA Bremner (ed.), *Architecture and Urbanism in the British Empire* (Oxford, 2016), p.15.

[59] Bremner, 'The Metropolis: Imperial Buildings and Landscapes in Britain', ibid., p.125.

[60] Mark Crinson, *Modern Architecture and the End of Empire* (Aldershot, 2006); Crinson, 'Imperial Story-lands: Architecture and Display at the Imperial and Commonwealth Institutes', *Art History* 22.1 (1999), pp.99–123; Crinson, 'The Powers that Be: Architectural Potency and Spatialized Power', *Architecture Beyond Europe* 4 (2013), http://journals.openedition.org/abe/3389 [accessed 6 June 2020].

[61] These themes are beginning to be explored. See N Coetzer, 'An Imperial axis, counter-memorials, and the double bind: the rise and fall of Rhodes at the University oc Cape Town', *arq* 24.1 (May 2020), pp.67-82; and Eva Branscome, 'Colston's Travels, or Should We Talk About Statues?', *Arena Journal of Architectural Research* 6.1 (2021), p.1.

century but also the early twentieth and in particular the 1920s and 1930s. The Rhodes Building on Oxford's High Street was built by Oriel College in 1911. The Upper Campus of the University of Cape Town—where the original Rhodes Must Fall campaign began, initially directed at the statue of Rhodes on axis with the Memorial (now Sarah Baartman) Hall—was put up to designs by JM Solomon in the late 1920s; Solomon had served articles with Herbert Baker, whose patron was Rhodes, and who designed Rhodes House in Oxford for the Rhodes Trust, as well as, better known, the Union Building in Pretoria.

The neglect of Empire in architectural histories of the mainstream in the 1920s and 1930s may reflect the colonization of interwar classicism and 'traditionalism' by the right in the 1970s, manifested in David Watkin's defence of figures like Geoffrey Scott and Trystan Edwards. Furthermore, the perception of parochialism and obsolescence in the architecture of the 1920s and 1930s has failed to attract postcolonial perspectives. On both counts I have tried to open up a different angle on this period. The book is neither an apology for architectural traditionalism nor an anti-Modernist polemic. I have aimed to recover the complex politics of architectural culture, in some instances showing how 'traditionalist' and 'conservative' agents were in fact more often than not part of the liberal consensus I have identified. I have placed London's architectural culture in its imperial context. As a second-generation immigrant of West African and East African Indian parentage, I have been able at least to *see* it and name it: in suburban Wembley where the British Empire Exhibition (BEE) was organized in 1924; in the imperial iconography and materiality of the RIBA's headquarters at 66 Portland Place; in the 'civilizing' language of architectural good manners; in the peculiar hold of 'relics' of the imperial metropolis at Waterloo Bridge and Regent Street; and in the making of a 'New London', a 'worthy' capital of Empire in the central urban improvements proposed around Charing Cross and the South Bank.

The architectural world I address was strongly gendered; the profession was unquestionably male-dominated, despite the fact that the early twentieth century saw the admission of women into architectural schools, at the AA from 1917.[62] Their representation in the RIBA was recognized (although in separatist terms) through the establishment of the Women Architects Committee in 1932, with Gertrude Leverkus serving as chair. Women were more likely to be trained in architecture schools rather than the increasingly

---

[62] Elizabeth Darling and Lynne Walker (eds.), *AA Women in Architecture 1917–2017* (London: Architectural Association Publications, 2017).

26 DESIGNS ON DEMOCRACY

old-fashioned, indeed gentlemanly, system which prevailed, and notable women practitioners in this period designed in a Modernist idiom or were associated with progressive and avant-garde projects. This is not to downplay the other significant contributions made by women in the making and use of the built environment, as clients and patrons, as active philanthropists and members of civil society, as astute commentators and critics—as members of an architectural public. There was, however, an undeniably chauvinistic attitude prevalent in the homosociality of professional politics, and indeed in the approach to designing and making space by many of the architects under discussion. The conspicuous absence of female presence in the myriad public and professional proposals for and commentary about new bridges at Waterloo and Charing Cross shows the ongoing barriers to full and representative participation in mainstream architectural culture.

Where possible, I have drawn attention to the wider historiography that addresses gender more explicitly, and have highlighted the specific contributions of women to the projects I discuss, such as Miriam Wornum whose professional partnership with Grey Wornum was significant in the interiors of the RIBA's building and in defining his practice more widely. Conceptions of different 'publics', moreover, often contained assumptions and distinctions about gender. At the BEE and the Building Centre, for instance, women's roles as consumers, and not solely in the domestic sphere, were reflected in the displays and exhibits. Women also played highly significant roles in preservationist campaigns of the 1920s and 1930s, from Dorothy Warren Trotter and her Londoners' League, to Katherine Ada Esdaile's active participation in the Georgian Group. There remains, nevertheless, more work to be done on the role gender played in defining architectural culture of the period, not just in design but in professionalization and discourse, and indeed in the enduring sexism of the architectural profession.

Reconstruction

Architecture as a civic art, one directed at the needs of the community, and as a subject of judgement in the public eye has, of course, a long history. Discussions in the interwar years were almost always informed by pre-war debates; there was no neat caesura between 1914 and 1918. The ripples of reconstruction and democratization created by the disturbance of the war had significant ongoing impacts on architectural culture, as they did on society as a whole.

INTRODUCTION   27

In 1917, the energies of the state, industry, and institutions were turning towards reconstruction—economic, social, and physical. At a national level, various commissions and committees set up ad hoc were brought under the aegis of a new Ministry of Reconstruction, established by the Lloyd George administration. But reconstruction extended beyond the arena of high government policy.[63] Many contemporaries understood that the war had fundamentally changed the nature of society; returning servicemen expected and would demand fairer opportunities and a greater stake in the running of the country.[64] Institutions of all complexions would need to accommodate this shift to stymie the perceived ever-present risk of violent revolution. Industries too, including the construction industry, would require reorganization.

The professions and their corporate bodies were also prompted to reflect. Architects anxiously seized the opportunity to engage with bold and radical ideas to strengthen, or even remake, their own profession and definitively resolve tensions which had dogged them for decades. The RIBA convened a number of 'Informal Conferences' over 1917 and 1918, which dealt in detail with professional challenges and opportunities. The tone of optimism, the clarity of thought, and prescience are striking in the papers and the subsequent exchanges, especially compared to the inaction and infighting which characterized the 1920s. FM Simpson, professor of architecture at London University (earlier Charles Herbert Reilly's predecessor at the Liverpool School), spoke, for example, on the need for unity in the profession, emphasizing the need for a register of architects, sanctioned by Parliament and maintained by the RIBA.[65] From the floor, HH Wigglesworth imagined a federation of architectural societies dealing with different aspects of professional life: a registering body, for example, would be distinct from an Institute reformulated to represent the 'art' of architecture; an alternative body might deal explicitly with the 'business interests' of the profession. He proposed new professional services, such as a 'Parliamentary Watch Committee', a 'Legal Defence Committee', and a Bureau for technical information.[66]

---

[63] Jessica Kelly and Neal Shasore, *Reconstruction: Architecture, Society and the Aftermath of the First World War* (2022).

[64] Paul Barton Johnson, *London Fit for Heroes: The Planning of British Reconstruction, 1916–1919* (Chicago, 1968).

[65] FM Simpson, 'Unity of the Profession: The Tenth Informal Conference held at the Royal Institute of British Architects, 5th December 1917', *JRIBA* (January 1918), pp.49–51.

[66] Ibid., p.52.

28 DESIGNS ON DEMOCRACY

Other papers came from outside the profession. Sidney Webb, who had written a series on the architectural profession for *The Architect* in 1916, rehearsed his arguments in a paper on 'The Function of an Architectural Society'. This was a Fabian vision of the 'brain-working' professions, as the Webbs defined them; professional associations whose role it would be to criticize public policy actively, but foremost 'to bring to the public notice, and to agitate for, the supply of a sufficiency of its service to the community as a whole'.[67] It was a theme that ran through many of the discussions. WR Lethaby, chairing Simpson's conference, gave an especially lucid concluding observation that 'It is only by getting the public's consent and interest that we can exist'.[68]

The active and excitable group that gathered for these conferences later formalized their discussions by constituting a 'Future of Architecture Committee' chaired by the president of the Institute, Henry T Hare.[69] This body included Lethaby, alongside figures such as HV Lanchester, Guy Dawber, Aston Webb, and Reginald Blomfield. Over the summer of 1918 they discussed a number of areas of enquiry that would galvanize new policy on, among other areas, inter- and intra-professional collaboration, practice, remuneration, policy, and propaganda. These discussions were used to formulate a questionnaire circulated to eminent practitioners, including Edwin Lutyens, Edward Prior, and FC Eden, many of whom provided written replies and some of whom were interviewed. Record of only one set of responses survives, those of John Murray (1864–1940). Murray, who was Crown Architect and Surveyor to the Commissioners of Crown Lands, had a particularly valuable perspective as both an 'official architect' and a private practitioner.

Murray's responses echoed Sidney Webb's argument: the issue of the reform of the profession was 'one that primarily concerns the public; it is of national importance, and should be considered primarily from that point of view'.[70] He identified a number of failures in professional practice and governance, many of which sound startlingly contemporary: the architect, he suggested, failed to deliver an integrated service across all

---

[67] Sidney Webb, 'The Function of an Architectural Society: the Ninth Informal Conference held at the Royal Institute of British Architects, 22nd November', *JRIBA* (December 1917), p.33.

[68] Simpson, 'Unity of the Profession', pp.49–58, p.57.

[69] RIBA, SCM (8) (14 June 1915–21 February 1919), Future of Architecture Committee and Sub-Committee, fos.304, 310, 312, 335, 340, 344, 352.

[70] RIBA, SCM (8) (14 June 1915–21 February 1919), Minutes of the Future of Architecture Committee (17 June 1918), fo.310 (appended report, 'The Future of Architecture and the Architectural Profession', p.1).

stages of design and construction; architects were poorly remunerated; the professional associations were unable to keep practitioners abreast of technological innovation; younger architects were disengaged from the task of professional governance; and the profession failed to have a say on major policy issues and participate fully in political institutions.

To remedy these ills, Murray proposed a reorganization of the RIBA, amalgamation with its main rival body, the Society of Architects (SoA), and meaningful collaboration with other societies largely governed by architects, such as the London Society, the TPI, the Concrete Institute, the Quantity Surveyors' Association, the Royal Sanitary Institute and even the Arts and Crafts Society and Society of British Sculptors. As an appendix to his report, Murray volunteered a diagram to illustrate 'the Union of the Art of Architecture and Allied Sciences and Arts' (Fig. 0.4). Murray depicted a circular plan, perhaps intended to evoke a tholos, with a distyle portico leading to a long entrance hall. A vista on axis terminated in a grand central staircase. At the centre of the plan, the RIBA was placed within a peristyle, with the words 'The Art of Architecture BC 600' engraved round its periphery. The rest of the plan was segmented for the different institutions Murray named in his report, with provision for Exhibition Galleries, Examination Halls, a Library, administrative offices, committee rooms, and a lecture theatre. The diagram was intended as a proposal for a 'new "Home of Architecture"'.[71]

Though rudimentary and schematic—only four apartments have entrances indicated—Murray's diagram represents an attempt to think through the reform of the governance and administration of the profession in spatial terms. It evoked not only a temple form, but also a parliament, although the seeming lack of means of entrance and exit for all of the constituents except the RIBA and TPI unintentionally also suggests a panopticon. Murray showed how a rejuvenated profession could bring together the technical, regulatory, infrastructural, learned, and artistic elements of design and construction that all fed into the self-image of the profession at this time, in a way in which histories of pre- and post-war architecture have perhaps not yet fully grasped. It also, arguably, represents a wider societal shift towards a more corporate conception of the profession through the rationalization and federalization of a number of ad hoc societies and associations across the construction industry. But most fundamentally, it links Murray's proposals explicitly to the idea of a new 'home' for architecture, and demonstrates an

[71] Ibid.

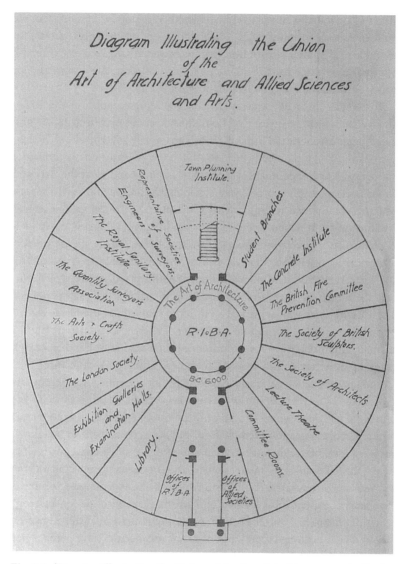

Fig. 0.4 'Drawing Illustrating the Union of the Art of Architecture and Allied Societies and Arts', by John Murray (1918), RIBA, SCM 8, Future of Architecture Committee (17 June 1918), RIBA Collections

INTRODUCTION 31

impulse for reform to be reified, to give architectural expression to a vision of bureaucracy and governance in the context of reconstruction. And in Murray's volunteering of this document, we can infer, there was an understanding that conceiving of the problem in this way opened up the potential for a more effectively communicated solution.

The Campaign for Statutory Registration

The dominating concern of the architectural profession in the post-war years was the question of professionalization and the campaign for statutory registration. This was a central ambition of the reconstruction of the profession for the democratic age, and although fuelled in large part by commercial and status imperatives, it was strongly promoted in terms of public interest. It also intersected with architects as a corporate body negotiating their relationship with the state, both central government and more local institutions. Indeed, it was an important aspect of professionalization that all these considerations interrelated—as well as being seen to do so.

Led by the RIBA—the preeminent professional association of architects in our period—these debates reached their climax in the Architects Registration Acts of 1931 and 1938. This campaign has been discussed most often in relation to the reform of architectural education in the late nineteenth and early twentieth centuries.[72] Without doubt, the reform of architectural education, or rather the codification of what constituted architectural qualification, was central to this effort. But equally, the campaign for statutory registration had immediate implications for architects already in professional practice. Registration, therefore, also touched on the question of the status of official architects and had implications for the procurement of architectural services, especially for state or state-subsidized projects. Moreover, though the campaign for statutory registration by the RIBA has been criticized for securing limited protection of title by an independent registering body, there was in fact an active campaign in the

---

[72] Mark Crinson and Jules Lubbock, *Architecture: Art or Professions? Three Hundred Years of Architectural Education in Britain* (Manchester, 1994), pp.61–86; Barrington Kaye, *The Development of the Architectural Profession in Britain: A Sociological Study* (1960), pp.147–56; Harry Barnes, 'Registration (The RIBA and the Statutory Registration of Architects)' in John Alfred Gotch (ed.), *The Growth and Work of the Royal Institute of British Architects, 1834–1934* (1934), pp.69–84.

32   DESIGNS ON DEMOCRACY

mid-1930s and into the post-war period for the statutory protection of function (i.e. the mandatory use of qualified architects for certain projects).

There had been an ongoing debate within the architectural profession since the last quarter of the nineteenth century as to whether architectural education 'should be closer to the practical craft of building and the visual arts or to the managerial professions'.[73] This split had culminated in the publication of Norman Shaw and TG Jackson's *Architecture: Profession or an Art* (1892) which helped to codify the various positions of a group that came to be known as the Memorialists against professionalization.[74] The issue of professionalization had been a controversial one for the RIBA since then, and part of the Memorialist complaint was the way in which a curriculum devised and governed by the RIBA was potentially to infiltrate every architectural school in the country.

Policy in favour of registration had been advanced by the RIBA Council since 1905. The SoA, a splinter group founded in 1884 and made up largely of members of the RIBA, had been continuously lobbying for an Act that would reserve the title of 'Architect' for those who had particular qualifications. Indeed, there was an international call for such legislation—resolutions to this end had been passed at the International Congresses of Architecture in Paris (1900), London (1906), Vienna (1908), and Rome (1911).[75] On the eve of war, under Reginald Blomfield's presidency, concrete proposals had been brought forward to alter the Institute's charter in favour of amalgamation with the SoA as a precursor to registration. This issue was front and centre of debates about reconstruction from 1917.

Through 1918 and 1919 there was almost continual debate about unity in the profession and registration. Accordingly, in July 1920 the RIBA convened a Registration and Unification Committee.[76] Chaired by John Simpson as president, it included representatives of the RIBA, its Allied Societies in the UK and Dominions, the AA, its main rival body the SoA, the Architects and Surveyors Assistants Professional Union (later the Association of Architectural Surveyors and Technical Assistants), representatives of official architects, and unattached architects (those with no professional affiliation). This meeting led to the appointment of a

---

[73] Crinson and Lubbock, *Architecture: Art or Professions?*, p.2.

[74] William Whyte, 'Memorialists (*act.* 1891–1903)', *Oxford Dictionary of National Biography* (October 2007), https://doi.org/10.1093/ref:odnb/96544 [accessed 25 August 2015].

[75] Barnes, 'Registration', p.70.

[76] RIBA, URCM (20 July 1920), fo.1. Cf. 'Unification and Registration. Charter Committee's Interim Report: Resolutions of the General Body', *JRIBA* (10 April 1920), pp.254–8.

INTRODUCTION   33

sub-committee representative of these diverse views and interests to report on the advisability of the RIBA absorbing the SoA and any other willing bodies, or the creation of a new federation of architectural societies.[77]

Majority opinion swung quickly to the principle of absorption, but this consensus quickly split into warring factions: one side adhered to the idea of absorption followed by a sustained campaign for statutory registration, bringing together the greatest number of architects possible to present a united front in promoting a bill; the other side, mainly comprising associates of the Institute, argued vociferously for registration first, then absorption, as a means of maintaining the RIBA's high standards of entry. This latter grouping felt that pursuing legislation with the RIBA as registrar would strengthen the Institute's role as gatekeeper; many were anxious not to drop standards of entry to accommodate members of other bodies, particularly the SoA, where the membership qualification threshold was felt to be lower.

This resistance coalesced into the RIBA Defence League, which in June 1922 stormed the Council elections after engaging in public criticism of Institute policy in the trade press. This body—the 'registration first and unification second' camp—dissolved the Unification and Registration Committee, instigating instead a new Registration Committee to promote a premature bill explicitly antagonistic to the SoA.[78] The League was, however, thrown off Council the following year, and formally withdrew opposition to the mainstream policy of unification followed by registration in June 1924 after a post-card referendum on the registration issue, which passed by 1,712 votes to 267.[79]

By December 1924, with the unification process now back on track, arrangements for the absorption of the SoA were in hand. Awaiting ratification in the form of a new charter, the two bodies meanwhile convened a joint Registration Committee chaired by Harry Barnes, a housing architect who was also serving as a Liberal MP and London County Council (LCC) alderman, and was therefore experienced in parliamentary affairs.[80] A new supplemental charter of the RIBA was approved by the king in March 1925, and the SoA membership transferred to the RIBA (including an absorption

---

[77] RIBA, URCM (2 February 1921), fo.21. See '(Draft) Report of the Sub-Committee' appended.

[78] 'The RIBA Registration Bill', *JRIBA* (24 January 1923), p.175.

[79] 'Unification of the Architectural Profession', *JRIBA* (16 July 1924), p.107.

[80] RIBA, RCM (5), fos.1–10; 'Amalgamation: The Great Meeting at Caxton Hall', *JRIBA* (26 June 1924), pp.1045–6; Harry Barnes, 'A Great Profession and a Supreme Institute', *JRIBA* (21 May 1924), p.876.

34   DESIGNS ON DEMOCRACY

of some of its staff).[81] At the same time a Draft Registration Bill was circulated. It included provisions to make the RIBA Council responsible for a register of architects. A 'Registration Board', comprising members of fifteen or more years of practical experience, would submit annual reports and accounts to the Council of the Institute.[82] Various draft bills were produced by Barnes's Registration Committee between 1927 and 1929 with little advancement through the Commons—a particular sticking point was the attempt by the RIBA to control the register directly, thereby monopolizing professional status and establishing itself as the statutory education board.[83] By the time the Architects Registration Act was passed in July 1931, ARCUK was established as an independent body with a registrar at its head to administer it, and an independent Board of Education. ARCUK was, however, limited to monitoring the use of the title 'Registered Architect'.

The campaign for registration was not solely to do with educational reform; it related centrally to professional practice. First and foremost, it required the RIBA to understand the new rules of public affairs; to gain statutory registration required the articulation of a clear public interest case. It is noteworthy that after the principle of unification was finally agreed, at the first meeting of the new Registration Committee the question emerged as to whether the bill was to 'be promoted in the interests of the profession or in the interests of the public'.[84] This was a question repeatedly raised by Ian MacAlister, secretary of the Institute. In May 1928, he submitted a memo on the importance of promoting the bill in terms of the 'public interest': 'The case is really a very simple one. This country is in extreme need of good architecture...It is obvious that there are many bad architects at work all round us, and that many buildings have lacked the services of any architect at all—good or bad.'[85]

The registration campaign was described by some contemporary commentators as a failure—the concessions of 'registered architect' as the protected title and the independent ARCUK and Board of Architectural Education were seen as too great to have warranted real success. Privately, however, senior figures in the RIBA were sanguine. Ian MacAlister was clear that the best strategy was to get some version of registration on the statute book to

---

[81] RIBA, RCM (5), (2 March 1925), fos.14–24.   [82] Ibid.

[83] RIBA, RCM (5), (28 June 1926), fo.61.

[84] RIBA, RCM (5), (23 May 1928), Minutes of Meeting (15 December 1924), fo.2.

[85] RIBA, RCM (5), (23 May 1928), fos.237–45; RIBA, Secretary's Correspondence (MacAlister), 4.1.1 (Box 5), Memorandum marked 'Secret. Private and Confidential' (17 April 1942).

INTRODUCTION 35

enable incremental lobbying for amendments eventually resulting in the protections the Institute wanted.[86] From mid-1935, the Public Relations Committee and Registration Committee of the RIBA was already pressing for the beginnings of statutory protection of function in housing schemes where any public money or subsidy was provided. Crucially, it lobbied (unsuccessfully) for provisions in the Housing Bill of 1935 for qualified architects to be used, regardless of whether they were in private practice or salaried employment.[87]

The nature of opposition to the RIBA's bill exposes some of the fault-lines in professional practice in this period. In 1925, once it was known the RIBA planned to amalgamate with the SoA and actively promote a registration bill, two bodies were quickly set up to oppose it. First was the Incorporated Association of Architects and Surveyors (IAAS), which grew out of the National Society of Landed Property, itself set up to oppose registration bills promoted by the Auctioneer, Surveyors and Land Agents Association.[88] Both of these bodies were formed by Alfred Sockett, a former town clerk to the Middleborough Corporation, and his sons and relatives. Their motivations—aside from financial—appear to have been anti-monopolistic. There was an ideological objection to the corporatist tendencies of chartered bodies to arbitrate professional qualification. Furthermore, the Association seemed to fight for the interests of private practitioners, particularly those unattached to any particular body. It was in that regard anti-corporatist.

The IAAS and the Socketts' coup was to pull together high-profile dissenting members of the profession. It attracted Edwin Lutyens, who had resigned membership of the Institute over two controversies in which his own professional ethics were clearly questionable, and Robert Tasker, a Conservative MP and long-serving member of the LCC, who had held a grudge against the RIBA from the 1910s when it failed to support his claims against the growth of the Council's official architects' department and its 'monopolization' of school design.[89] With these formidable allies, they opposed the RIBA at every turn. In the mid-1930s it was this same group

---

[86] Ibid., fo.242.

[87] RIBA, PRCM (1), (4 May 1934), fo.81, including memorandum 'Draft Proposals regarding the Statutory Recognition of Architects'; RIBA, PRCM (2), (3 May 1935), fos.24–39; cf. *JRIBA* (25 May 1935), pp.818–21.

[88] RIBA, Secretary's Correspondence (MacAlister), 4.1.1 (Boxes 1 and 2).

[89] RIBA, Secretary's Correspondence (MacAlister), 4.1.1 (Box 2), Folder entitled 'IAAS v RIBA, May 1934'; RIBA, Council Minutes 24 (20 January 1914–12 October 1915), Minutes of Meeting (23 February 1914), fo.53: 'Obituary: Sir Robert Tasker', *Builder* (1 March 1959), p.46.

36 DESIGNS ON DEMOCRACY

that established the Institute of Registered Architects in order to undermine the ambiguity of the protected title 'registered architect', making membership sound as though it was 'the necessary outcome of the Register of Architects which they had joined'.[90]

The Faculty of Architects and Surveyors (FAS) was another opposition group, founded in spring 1926, which had in fact emerged from the opposition of some IAAS members to the management of the IAAS by the Socketts.[91] It was established by hostile takeover, according to evidence from a later libel case between the RIBA and the IAAS, through the staging of a raid on the Socketts' offices. Again, this body had particular objections to monopolist claims by chartered bodies which, they believed, over-asserted their representation of the whole profession, propagating the idea 'that their members possess some sort of special qualification'.[92] Their objection, therefore, was to setting up the RIBA as a pseudo-legislative bureaucracy because it absolved the state of offering meaningful statutory definition of protected characteristics, leaving a powerful executive in the RIBA in charge of an important national activity, rather than Parliament.

These bodies were, broadly speaking, politically to the right of the RIBA; on the left was the Association of Assistant Surveyors, Technologists and Architects (AASTA), which, in Summerson's words, 'flushed a deep political colour' after the polarizing effects of the economic slump in the late 1920s and early 1930s.[93] This body claimed to represent salaried architects, indeed repeatedly asserting that up to 60–70 per cent of the profession was in fact in some form of salaried employ either in public departments, or even as assistants to private practitioners, and architectural assistants to non-architects.[94] Though occasionally collaborating with the RIBA—gaining representation on Council and driving the work of the Institute's Salaried Members Committee, for instance—it was overall hostile to a body whose

---

[90] RIBA, Secretary's Correspondence (MacAlister), 4.1.1 (Box 2), Folder entitled 'IAAS v RIBA, May 1934'. This issue rumbled into in the 1930s, as unpublished MSS letters (Private Collection) between Giles Gilbert Scott and Edwin Lutyens make clear.

[91] The FAS published a journal, *Portico*, and the IAAS published *Parthenon* as vehicles for their respective positions.

[92] 'The Architects Registration Bill 1926: A Criticism of the Provisions of the Bill', *Estates Review* (February 1926), p.247.

[93] John Summerson, 'Bread & Butter Architecture', *Horizon* 6.34 (October 1942), p.236; 'The Caxton Hall Meeting', *The Keystone* 4.2 (April 1928), pp.19–22.

[94] See '*History of Architects': A Few Notes, addressed to Architects in salaried employment, and to students on English architectural politics of the period 1919–1935* (London: Association of Building Technicians, 1935), n.p.

INTRODUCTION   37

'economic roots [were] not unconnected with the pressing needs of private practitioners.'[95]

In his essay 'Bread and Butter Architecture' (1942), Summerson presented an exaggerated view of the development of the profession—of country house and ecclesiastical work replaced with commercial projects, 'smaller houses, small factories, suburban churches, and the continual rebuildings in London and the provinces.'[96] This image continues to hold sway, as does his restricted view of the RIBA as a 'learned Society' at first blind and then resistant to shifts in architectural practice.[97] Although the RIBA's policy was not necessarily progressive, its accommodation of the public interest case demonstrates something more imaginative than reactionary conservatism. The recurring fear that central government, the Office of Works in particular, was designing public buildings using internal salaried staff, denying architects in private practice the normal opportunity to compete for prestige projects, was grounded in professional ethics. Special alarm was caused when the marquess of Londonderry, a Conservative Commissioner of Works, gave an inflammatory speech to the Architecture Club in May 1929—in the midst not only of the registration campaign, but also the moment at which the Institute was preparing to promote a competition for its new premises.[98] Londonderry boasted of the nearly 400 buildings designed by his office in the preceding year, including the British Museum's newspaper repository at Hendon, the National Physical Library at Teddington, new museum buildings in South Kensington, an extension to the National Portrait Gallery, as well as fifty-six employment exchanges and 300 post offices and telephone exchanges.[99] Goading the RIBA, he claimed that the Institute itself was 'wavering in its loyalty to the doctrine of open competition, even in regard to its own new building', a reference to the Council's consideration of direct appointment or invited competition, a suggestion wisely and ultimately abandoned.[100]

Londonderry's speech—which prompted the RIBA to call for a public inquiry into the state's policy on procurement of public buildings—was itself the climax of a growing schism in the architectural profession between

---

[95] Ibid.   [96] Summerson, 'Bread & Butter Architecture', p.233.   [97] Ibid., p.235.
[98] The speech is reported in 'Design in Public Buildings', *Times* (2 May 1929), p.11. Cf. 'Official Architecture', *Times* (2 May 1929), p.17; 'State Architecture', *AJ* (8 May 1929), p.707. See also a letter from Maxwell Fry on this subject published in 'Correspondence', *AJ* (15 May 1929), p.771. Cf. 'Notes and Comments', *Architect and Building News* (10 May 1929), pp.603–4.
[99] 'Design in Public Buildings', p.11.
[100] Ibid.; RIBA, Council Minutes (10 June 1929–11 May 1931), fos.2–5.

38   DESIGNS ON DEMOCRACY

'official architects', those in salaried employ of the state or commercial undertakings, and brass-plate private practitioners. By the late 1930s the ongoing agitation of the AASTA and growing dissent of salaried and official architects were seen as a serious threat to the predominance of the RIBA.[101] The war and subsequent growth of the power and prestige of the architect within the apparatus of the Welfare State effectively quelled this dissent.

The Professionalization of Management

Registration was the goal of professionalization, and professionalization was increasingly discussed in terms of the civic responsibilities of architects and in relation to the public. Professionalization, however, as a broad sociological phenomenon impacted architectural practice and professionalism beyond the questions of qualification and protection of title.[102] It also encompassed the professionalization of management of the architectural profession. All the major institutions of architecture had a governance structure which required increasingly sophisticated techniques of management, sometimes by architects themselves, at other times by administrators and clerks. The terms on which these institutions were established and the ways in which they operated could have consequences for how architecture was practised which were as profound as regulatory or legislative frameworks. Yet this context has never been taken seriously in an architectural history still with a tendency to focus on individual architects. The emergence of a body of executive administrators co-running the RIBA, headed by the secretary, Ian MacAlister, along with the Council and committees of architect-members, was hugely significant. In 1900 there were only 9 members of staff,[103] in 1925, around 25 Institute employees;[104] in 1935, there was a staff of 44;[105] and by 1948 the executive wing of the RIBA numbered around 80.[106]

This growing body of people typifies the development of the Institute and the architectural profession in the interwar years. It functioned in a way loosely analogous with the Civil Service, in which staff pursued policies determined by a self-governing membership. In reality, of course, the lines

---

[101] The Official and Staff Architects Association was established in 1938.
[102] Harold Perkin, *The Rise of Professional Society: England Since 1880* (1989), pp.295–8.
[103] 'The Work of the RIBA Part II', *JRIBA* (October 1948), p.530.
[104] RIBA, ECM (1), (22 October 1925), fo.9.
[105] 'The RIBA New Building—X: The Offices and Services', *JRIBA* (6 November 1934), p.68.
[106] 'The Work of the RIBA Part II', *JRIBA* (October 1948), p.530.

INTRODUCTION   39

between elected members and paid officials were often blurred. The executive and its leadership played a central role in coordinating the campaign for statutory registration, the development of the Institute, architectural profession and construction industry, and a series of spatial and material transformations which culminated in the design and construction of new premises for the RIBA. These underpin the subjects of Chapters 2 and 3 in particular.

The RIBA had begun as a society of architects nominally self-governed by its members through its General Body brought together at general meetings. The size and prominence of the Meeting Room in its apartments at 9 Conduit Street reflected the supremacy of this body. Typically for organizations of this kind, general meetings elected a Council annually, which took responsibility for routine business. In the nineteenth century, Council had been restricted to Fellows. In 1925, all membership classes were given equal rights in general meetings which helped to democratize the annual election of Council. In the same year, once a new Charter had ratified changes to by-laws, the Council also included the lower membership classes, namely Licentiates and Associates, as well as members from Allied Societies. The reformed Council emerged more powerfully during this period as the supreme decision-making body of the Institute, and through an extraordinarily labyrinthine committee structure it presented a new breadth in response to concerns about the unrepresentativeness and metropolitan bias of the General Body.[107]

Initially a fairly small committee-sized body of thirteen, by the mid-1930s Council had seventy-eight members.[108] It was claimed in 1935 that there were nearly 2,000 architects involved in the management of the profession's affairs, and that the governing machine of the RIBA contained around 320 individual members.[109] This growth reflected the federation of the Allied Societies in the provinces and increasingly the dominions of the British Empire. The RIBA saw itself as an imperial institute. Not only had Council grown larger, its workload had also increased; the presence of greater numbers of non-London members also made the fortnightly meetings of

---

[107] RIBA, Constitutional Committee (28 February 1927), letter from EB Kirby to TR Milburn, Chairman of the Allied Societies' Conference, and presented to the Executive Committee, fos.1–2.

[108] John Alfred Gotch, 'The Royal Institute of British Architects' in John Alfred Gotch (ed.), *The Growth and Work of the Royal Institute of British Architects, 1834–1934* (1934), pp.41–2.

[109] 'AA General Meeting: Tuesday, April 30th, 1935: The History and Work of the RIBA, by Sir Ian MacAlister, MA', *AAJ* (May 1935), p.428; RIBA, Constitutional Committee (October 1935–February 1937).

40 DESIGNS ON DEMOCRACY

Council impractical for many. A leaner and more agile executive function, therefore, was needed and in 1925 the Executive Committee was established to comprise the president, the secretary, the chairs of the four Standing Committees, the chair of the Board of Education, the chair of the Finance and House Committee, the chair of the Allied Societies Conference, and, notably, the chair of the Registration Committee.[110] This initiative was particularly important for the corporatist and managerialist shift in the RIBA's administration. Proposed rather innocuously to take on the routine business which was absorbing valuable Council time, within a year the Executive Committee had assumed responsibility for watching 'matters of general policy'.[111]

In February 1928 plans were brought forward by the then honorary secretary, Percy Thomas, for the 'Development of the RIBA'.[112] It provided an assessment of the RIBA's membership and governance in particular. It noted that although the Institute now had 6,000 members, and was 'very rightly launching out from a Metropolitan to a British, and from a British to an Imperial policy', the net increase of membership was in fact stalling.[113] Thomas also suggested that Council was not as efficient as it might be; the development programme proposed strengthening the Council's powers, making it more representative of the Allied Societies, and removing the supreme power of the general meeting altogether. Ultimately, the development programme was to support the registration initiative: 'The success of this movement would be a convincing demonstration of the fact that the profession (the *bona fide* architects of the country) are solidly organized in the demand that they are making for an improved and guaranteed status.'[114] These changes were passed by Privy Council in September 1930.

Corporatism and Institutional History

One of the implicit issues addressed in this book is the place of Modernists in architectural histories of the period. Elizabeth Darling's institutional history of Modernism elucidates with precision the complex circumstances

---

[110] RIBA, ECM (1), (30 July 1925), fos.1–2.
[111] RIBA, ECM (1), (12 October 1926), fo.152.
[112] RIBA, ECM (1), (28 February 1928), fo.295.   [113] Ibid.
[114] 'The Development of the RIBA', *JRIBA* (22 December 1928), p.170.

INTRODUCTION 41

of the emergence of the Modern Architectural Research Group (MARS) in February 1933, out of a number of earlier efforts in the late 1920s which are often omitted in standard accounts.[115] The establishment of MARS, a network of leading British Modernists, conformed to a more general policy of the Congrès Internationaux d'Architecture Moderne (CIAM), an international congress dedicated to the dissemination of Modernist principles, to distinguish 'an avant-garde from the broader anti-traditional tendencies of the day', legitimizing this through 'institutionalisation'.[116] Darling has argued that, under the aegis of MARS, Modernists 'inveigled' themselves into establishment institutions like the RIBA, conspiring to effect a hostile 'takeover' by stealth of the Institute and its governance.[117] The logical corollary of this argument is that this active avant-garde infiltrated an architectural establishment who were at best blissfully ignorant of these attempts, and at worst, exemplified by Reginald Blomfield's *Modernismus*, reactionary in their response. MARS, effectively the British chapter of CIAM, controlled by the driving forces of Maxwell Fry and Wells Coates, was certainly the result of a search 'to find the right organisational technique for the beginnings of an assault on the profession', with the RIBA as a prime target.[118] As part of this mission, it deliberately excluded modernistic, but not Modernist, architects like Howard Robertson and Grey Wornum from its ranks.[119]

The aim of this book is not to dispute the existence of this strategy or its ends—the so-called post-war Modernist hegemony—but instead to bring out the other side of the story, to question how unwitting or even antagonistic the prevailing architectural culture was. Rhetorical oppositions between 'Modernists' and 'non-Modernists' have been taken too much at face value, obscuring the common concerns and objectives which formed part of longer trajectories in architectural discourse. These included not only a general agreement on the need for a formalized architectural education system of pupillage or college training, but also protection of title (and function) through registration, resulting in strong central control by a professional governing body, and public engagement with and understanding of the role of the architect, whether in salaried employ or private practice. From these aims, it was claimed, good design—the expression of the art of

[115] Elizabeth Darling, 'Institutionalising British Modernism 1924–1933: From the Vers Group to MARS', *AH* 55 (2012), pp.299–320.
[116] Ibid., p.300.
[117] Darling, *Re-forming Britain: Narratives of Modernity Before Reconstruction* (2007), fn.16, p.236.
[118] Darling, 'Institutionalising British Modernism', p.311.   [119] Ibid., p.315.

42   DESIGNS ON DEMOCRACY

architecture—would more liberally flow. These measures would help protect the public from the prevalence of bad building, as well as defending architects' integrity (and income).

In the educational context, the historiographical emphasis placed on student activism in a number of privileged architectural schools in the 1930s—in particular, the venerable schools at Liverpool and the AA in London—has occluded the diversity of activity in professional practice.[120] Educational reform catalysed and empowered younger generations of architects, with sometimes immediate and tangible effects in practice. The establishment of Tecton by Lubetkin with a number of AA students shows this very well. But architectural practice in the interwar years was diverse and changing, and not solely driven by the schools, despite their considerable power. Furthermore, where it mattered, professional issues of substance were not discussed in terms of style or with reference to particular schools of thought; an individual's professional identity was the result of a number of intersecting factors. Design preferences constituted one of these. But more fundamental to professional identity was the distinction between private practice and salaried employment. An architect working in salaried employ might be working for a local authority, but could also work for a cooperative or a large commercial undertaking. The nature of these working environments varied significantly. A salaried architect could also describe an architectural assistant in a small or medium-sized brass-plate practice. Architects might, however, feel more antipathy to those professional brethren who were arguing against a formalized education system and statutory registration, in particular if they were salaried and felt critically vulnerable. Moreover, the significant minority of architects working in provincial centres or in the countryside faced very different issues from the metropolitan majority. Architects with progressive politics found a home in the AASTA, but not all members of the AASTA were Modernists. There were non-Modernist architects who held progressive views. Many local authority architects joined the IAAS and the FAS, though the AASTA was more sympathetic to their professional concerns. And there were Associates of the RIBA in all of these bodies too. Many of these divisions in practice and their intersections emerged or took on a new urgency in the early twentieth

---

[120] Patrick Zamarian, 'The Origins of the Oxford Conference within the Networks of 1930s Student Activism', *Journal of Architecture* 24.4 (2019), pp.571–92; Elizabeth Darling, '*Focus*: A Little Magazine and Architectural Modernism in 1930s Britain', *Journal of Modern Periodical Studies* 3.1 (2012), pp.39–63.

INTRODUCTION   43

century. They caused significant anxiety, not only for individuals, many of whom were workers in a squeezed and skewed job market; there were persistent concerns about 'overcrowding' from the left of the profession during the period.

Despite the internecine world of professional politics—a common feature of professional life—a corporatist trend which privileged the professional ideal above all else militated against further institutional fragmentation, and arguably kept the smaller rival professional associations weaker.[121] The RIBA achieved consensus by giving voice and institutional form to a liberal professional ideal. It easily accommodated and actively welcomed a plurality of views in the 1920s and 1930s. Indeed, it was anxious to do so—it was anxious in general to find allies who could help secure its overarching policy of assuring its own supremacy and the consolidation of the profession through statutory registration. How was this liberal consensus achieved? The evidence shows that at a senior executive level, the RIBA, in particular its secretary, Ian MacAlister, was accommodating of new ideas. In an undated memo (likely to have been written in 1933), MacAlister wrote to the RIBA librarian and *Journal* editor, Bobby Carter, on the subject of 'International Architectural Organisations', and specifically the affiliation of MARS to the CIAM.[122] The majority of MARS members, as Carter argued in response, 'are keen Institute people and inasmuch as they represent a point of view which is growing fast I think that, as a matter of policy, they should have the Institute support'.[123] 'If we disregard them,' he continued, 'it will only mean that the kudos as patron will go to the AA or some other body'.[124] Of Tecton, he wrote that its members were 'all very keen on the Institute', making 'a great deal of the use of the library'.[125]

Modernist architects, in other words, far from infiltrating the RIBA, found themselves pushing at an open door. This was at least in part because Modernists of the MARS kind in this period came from or aspired to be in the same elites as the mainstream of architectural culture; they were trained in the same schools and practices, were members of the same clubs, and moved in the same social circles. John Summerson later described MARS as

---

[121] Perkin, *Rise of Professional Society*, pp.286–91.

[122] RIBA, Librarian's Papers, 6.4, Box 2, 'Memorandum from Ian McAlister to EJC' (undated).

[123] Ibid., 'Memorandum to Mr MacAlister from Mr Carter: International Architectural Organisations' (undated).

[124] Ibid.   [125] Ibid.

44 DESIGNS ON DEMOCRACY

a 'round-table of architectural highbrows', 'introvert and supine'.[126] Often the most extreme disagreements—evidenced by the Blomfield and Connell or Edwards and Towndrow debates described earlier—were as much generational as anything else, and deliberately and performatively polemical.

Structure

The book is organized thematically, within an overarching chronological span; the opening chapter begins in the early 1920s, and the final one ends in the 1940s. Each chapter is titled with a keyword, chosen by listening carefully to the tenor of the discourse and its most articulate voices. Just as I have used primarily contemporary images throughout, these words are also contemporaneous. Images and titles, in other words, are not just fundamental to the presentation of my argument but are constitutive parts of it, intended to immerse the reader in the architectural culture under discussion and to anchor the analysis in its wider cultural, social, and political context. The keywords are also intended to jolt the reader, particularly readers broadly familiar with the architecture of the period, out of some prevailing clichés and stereotypes, especially formal ones. I have therefore avoided words like 'streamline' or 'jazz', and invented or anachronistic stylistic categories, such as 'medieval Modernism', 'Baroque', and 'Art Deco'. Each keyword is paired with a different aspect of the public sphere: 'Propaganda' with 'Publicity', 'Manners' with 'Public Propriety' and 'Vigilance' with a 'Proprietary Public'. The final chapter, 'The Architectural Mind'—an expression and concept discussed in the 1930s—pulls together these various conceptions of the public sphere, and also discusses a number of interventions and proposed interventions into the physical public realm.

The first chapters of the book discuss architecture in relation to propaganda, from publicity to public relations. They also situate architectural debates in a wider context of the design reform movement and the 'Long Arts and Crafts'. Chapter 1 looks at the British Empire Exhibition at Wembley, and in particular at the contribution of the journalist, civil servant, and businessman, Lawrence Weaver who was a hugely important figure in the design reform movement and in architectural culture. This combination of experience made him the perfect 'impresario' for the home

---

[126] Summerson, 'Bread & Butter Architecture', p.237.

exhibits of UK industry and commerce at the exhibition. It elucidates his conception of the 'Arts of Display'—spatial and design coordination at the exhibition undertaken by his expansive network of architectural patronage. The young architects he championed were modern and progressive, including figures like Edward Maufe, Clough Williams-Ellis, Percy Morley Horder, and Joseph Emberton. Through intimate connections between design reform, architecture, and the changing nature of the advertising industry, Weaver was at the vanguard of an important paradigmatic shift in architectural culture: architects would need to market their services more effectively to the consuming public through strategic allegiances and demonstration of their range. Chapter 2 picks up this theme by showing how techniques of publicity matured into a recognition that the architectural profession needed to master public relations, ranging from advertising to developing a more sophisticated relationship with the state and its institutions. 'Slump' argues that the catalyst for this paradigm shift was the economic turbulence created by the Great Depression and its acute impact on the construction industry. The creation of the Special Committee for Public Relations of the newly established Building Industries National Council led directly to the establishment of a public relations function at the RIBA. The context of the first two chapters provides the framework for a new reading of the RIBA's new headquarters at 66 Portland Place. This building is significant for two reasons: first because it was the culmination of a series of material and spatial transformations and modernizations of the profession's governance intended to establish it as a pseudo-public institution; second because it is a building whose previous readings have exemplified the perils of an overemphasis on style. 66 Portland Place is normally taken as an exemplar of Art Deco—a phrase jettisoned in this book. Here it is read in terms of 'Machine-Craft'—a term used by the critic John Gloag to express a particular strand of the design reform movement—to align Arts and Crafts with industrial production and the machine. Gloag had been much influenced by Lawrence Weaver, and both men knew Grey Wornum, the appointed architect of the RIBA's new building. But the imbrication of the RIBA with design reform was more substantial and to elucidate my reading of 66 Portland Place I draw on hitherto unexplored connections between this project and the establishment of the Building Centre in 1932. I also discuss one of the first exhibitions held at the new headquarters, 'Everyday Things', a phrase common in the progressive design reform movement propagated by Weaver, Gloag, and others, and which showed how deeply these ideas had permeated the professional institute. 66 Portland Place was the culmination of the

46   DESIGNS ON DEMOCRACY

new conception of public relations discussed in the opening chapters, and a vehicle for architects to publicize their re-energized public role.

The third and fourth chapters interrogate two 'watchwords'—Vigilance and Manners—to explore ideas of public proprietorship and public propriety. Chapter 4, 'Vigilance', discusses the centrality of what I term a Georgian imaginary which exerted a strong influence on architectural culture at this time, not just in neo-Georgian design, but also through a socio-political imaginary which informed preservationist debates. It looks at a series of connected episodes, from the rebuilding of Regent Street in the 1910s and 1920s, to the Carlton House Terrace controversy of the 1930s, to the establishment of the Georgian Group in the late 1930s and the origins of statutory listing. At the core of this chapter is the repeated declaration of the need for democratic instruments of lay supervision of architectural practice and preservation. In retelling the early and pre-history of the Georgian Group, specifically through an organization called the Londoners' League and their campaign to save the working-class 'village' of Portland Town on the periphery of St John's Wood, the chapter tackles the epistemes of preservationism, later enshrined in the Town and Country Planning Acts (1944, 1947). The demands of a proprietary public were articulated through the associational culture of civil society, and the chapter also interrogates how a public opinion was constructed and weighted, and then used to exert pressure on government and non-governmental organizations. The importance of associations to architectural culture in this period is made manifest in the fifth chapter, 'Manners', which provides the first substantial account of the Hundred New Towns Association, a campaigning vehicle led by Trystan Edwards. Edwards was a highly vocal and subtly influential critic and campaigner, specifically on the subject of working-class housing. The issue of housing—in particular, private speculation, social housing, and slum clearance—was fundamental to the new claims the profession was making about its revivified obligations to the community and the wider public. Trystan Edwards was the most significant reformer challenging the orthodoxies of housing policy in this period, both the low-density, low-rise peripheral cottage estates, and the increasingly higher-rise tenement blocks in central areas. Underpinning my reading of Trystan Edwards is the idea of public propriety—codes of acceptable behaviour of buildings and people in public spaces—which Edwards and contemporaries expressed as 'good manners'. Manners drew on civilizing rhetorics. Edwards's ethos of social obligations to the wider community led him to forge significant connections in the worlds of Liberal Anglicanism, heterodox economics and monetary reform, and—more problematically—of positive eugenics. The principle of manners was also another facet of the Georgian imaginary introduced in Chapter 4. Edwards's early writings and design propositions, both of which informed his housing campaign, drew heavily on principles extrapolated from his reading of the late Georgian and Regency periods.

By using the conceit of the architectural mind to pull together the themes of the book, we can revisit how the profession devised its designs on democracy in light of the keywords and constructs examined. If the archetypal architect of the interwar years is normally characterized as small-minded and parochial, here the architectural mind is characterized by its breadth, encompassing and crucially connecting the intellectual, practice, and imaginative aspects of professional practice. It also allows us to revisit the architecturally minded public, a kind of architectural Pygmalion. The architectural mind and its architecturally minded public were often concentrated on a very particular topography in interwar London, namely the central portion of riverside between the edges of Westminster and the City and the area now known as the South Bank, and the making of the physical public realm through improved planning and amenity. The chapter looks at three connected projects, therefore, bringing together a cast of characters encountered through the earlier episodes of the book. The first of these is Waterloo Bridge, comprising the structural failure of John Rennie's bridge of 1817, its 'unbuilding', and then its reconstruction to the designs of Giles Gilbert Scott between 1937 and 1942. Bound up in the demolition of the old bridge and Scott's two designs for its replacement were attitudes to the Romantic, the representational, and the presence of history. On the surface a simple, 'streamlined' design, in fact Scott's bridge is read as an attempt at creating a modern urban amenity while negotiating the city's historical context. The bridges controversy extended beyond merely the architectural design of individual monuments; it was really a question of planning. Architects remained deeply involved in planning; it was core to their professional identity. The second part of the chapter discusses the various plans and proposals for a new bridge at Charing Cross, but encompassing a wider perspective; the bridge was one part of a much bigger and longer conversation about cross-river communication, riverside development, and the expansion of the metropolis into its 'Surrey side'. The traffic circus—an essential instrument in the planner's armoury—was a motif which united much of the serious thinking about urban improvement in this period. The narrative arc of the final chapter takes us from the 1910s to the 1940s and another reconstruction debate during another world war, in particular the

48 DESIGNS ON DEMOCRACY

contributions of the Royal Academy Planning Committee first chaired by Edwin Lutyens, succeeded after his death by Giles Gilbert Scott. The eventual development of the South Bank for the Festival of the Britain in 1951 is seen not simply as the triumph of post-war Modernist hegemony but in terms of the dawn of a new political economy in which architects would play a central role. This ambition for the hearing of an architectural voice built on new ways of training, articulating, and transmitting its cadences in the interwar period. Professional values were embedded in a transformed sense of public purpose.

1
Propaganda

Publicity and the Arts of Display at the British Empire Exhibition, Wembley

Introduction

Architecture has its political Use; Public buildings being the Ornament of a Country; it establishes a Nation, draws People and Commerce; makes the People love their native Country, which Passion is the Original of all great Actions in a Common-wealth.[1]

In the first decades of the twentieth century Christopher Wren remained to the architectural profession a figure of totemic importance. He influenced design: the pomp of Edwardian Baroque, the 'Wrenaissance' as Lutyens christened it, amounted to an 'Imperial Style' that owed much to his precedents. And by the 1920s and 1930s in particular he was also a model of prolific public service and professionalism. Despite his pioneering auto-didacticism, and the wider context of gentlemanly amateurism in the early modern period, it was Wren as an office-holder and the scale of his ambition which secured his place as a paragon of architectural professionalism into the twentieth century. The quotation above from Wren's first tract, published posthumously in *Parentalia*, stakes a claim for architecture as a political and economic instrument in the binding together of 'a Common-wealth'. To contemporaries in the interwar years, this notion anachronistically connected a seventeenth-century imaginary with the burgeoning of the Commonwealth as a new political entity, an idea formalized through the early twentieth-century Imperial Conferences. It was quoted by Lawrence Weaver (Fig. 1.1), the civil servant and former architectural editor of *Country Life*, in his short bicentenary biography of Wren published in

---

[1] Christopher Wren, 'Tract 1', *Parentalia; or Memoirs of the Family of the Wrens* (1750).

Designs on Democracy: Architecture and the Public in Interwar London. Neal Shasore, Oxford University Press.
© Neal Shasore 2022. DOI: 10.1093/oso/9780192849724.003.0002

Fig. 1.1 Portrait of Sir Lawrence Weaver by Walter Stoneman (1920), NPG x28057, © National Portrait Gallery, London

1923.[2] The quotation was perhaps in his mind as Weaver simultaneously organized the United Kingdom exhibits for the British Empire Exhibition (BEE) at Wembley, an initiative also intended to develop 'the family estate', to draw together people and commerce.[3]

This quotation from Wren's first tract was also deployed by Sir Herbert Baker, the favourite architect of Cecil Rhodes and the torch-bearer of 'Imperial Classicism' in the interwar years. In a draft paper, 'Architecture in Relation to the Empire', intended for the journal *Round Table* (which promoted the idea of the Commonwealth), Baker used it to open his argument for the development of a symbolical architecture: 'if on the full realisation of full Imperial Union, we have, as is to be hoped, an Imperial Capitol, let it consist of a building which with its surroundings may be truly expressive of all that is best in the Empire, in the past as well as in the present of the Empire'. It was the higher mission of the Architect as of the Poet to give outward expression to national ideals, '"To turn them to shape and give them a local habitation and a name" throughout the Empire', he concluded,

---

[2] Lawrence Weaver, *Sir Christopher Wren: Scientist, Scholar and Architect* (1923).

[3] 'Developing the Family Estate' was George V's expression upon opening the exhibition in 1924. Daniel Stephen, *The Empire of Progress: West Africans, Indians, and Britons at the British Empire Exhibition, 1924–25* (New York, 2013).

PROPAGANDA 51

quoting Carlyle.[4] Significantly too, the quotation from Wren prefaced a section on 'Building' in an anthology of texts, *Craftsmen All* (1926), collated by Arts and Crafts design reformer and proprietor of Dryad Cane Furniture, Harry Hardy Peach, one of the founding members of the Design and Industries Association (DIA) in 1915.[5]

The varied deployment of this quotation shows how significant Wren was both to proponents of increasingly formal Imperial Classicism and also to adherents of the later Arts and Crafts movement; he provided inspiration for both 'the Grand Manner' and craftsmanship of the 'lesser arts'. These of course had common origins: Baker and Lutyens both had classical 'conversions' at the turn of the century, but both were Arts and Crafts architects by origin with an enduring interest in craft and vernacular forms. This apparent tension carried through to the generation that followed them, particularly architects patronized by Weaver at the Empire Exhibition. Furthermore, Wren's statement gestures towards the ways in which architects in the 1920s and 1930s understood the 'political use' of their practice. Lawrence Weaver was, like Peach, active in the DIA, a body profoundly engaged with the twentieth-century imperialist project of forging close links in trade and commerce, in particular with the emergent white settler Dominion nations. Although postcolonial readings of the British design reform movement have been lacking, this chapter suggests a framework for one. The citation of Wren encapsulated how nation/empire-building was connected with the commercial imperative of trade under the aegis of industrial design, a practice—it was widely argued by design reformers— that itself sat within the ultimate purview of the architect.

The BEE's emphasis on trade and commerce—not, as some design histories have emphasized, on popular and mass entertainment—is the locus of an architectural history of British imperialism. Architects engaged with the serious commercial purpose and political ambition of Wembley, which could seem to be belied by the Orientalizing or primitivizing performativity of the colonial and national pavilions.[6] The manufacturing displays were centred in the Palace of Industry under the control of the director-general of United Kingdom exhibits, Sir Lawrence Weaver, and his network of architectural patronage. It is through foregrounding this element

---

[4] RIBA, Sir Herbert Baker Papers, BaH/64/1: draft for article entitled 'Architecture in Relation to Empire'.

[5] Harry Hardy Peach, *Craftsmen All: An Anthology* (Leicester, 1926).

[6] Crinson, *Modern Architecture*, pp.72–92; cf. Crinson, 'Imperial Modernism' in Bremner (ed.), *Architecture and Urbanism*, pp.198–235.

52   DESIGNS ON DEMOCRACY

of the exhibition that we can see how the 'political uses' of architecture for the furthering of intra-imperial trade were made tangible. Weaver himself codified these ideas in what he called the 'Arts of Display'.

Lawrence Weaver, Design Reformer

Lawrence Weaver was a significant patron of architecture and design in the interwar years. A prominent member of the DIA, serving as president from 1926 to 1927, his activities extended into architectural journalism, the Civil Service and public administration, as well as commercial enterprise and advertising.[7] Through his patronage he inculcated in a generation of modernizing architects new ideas about publicity and public relations, just as Frank Pick's design reform ideals were expressed through Charles Holden for the London Underground. All three figures were active in the DIA. Weaver, like Pick, promoted the skills, methods, and paradigms of architectural design and craft as a framework through which he pursued diverse professional and personal passions and interests throughout a varied career.

Superficially—and this may be why he is now little-known—Weaver appears on first inspection to be the quintessential early twentieth-century establishment figure, representative of the insularity and parochialism of British architectural culture; he had written extensively about country houses, in particular those of Lutyens and the gardens of Gertrude Jekyll; he had obscure connoisseurly interests, including the history of English lead-work and other traditional crafts; and he was a well-connected civil servant. These, however, set in their context in fact reflected progressive interests. And Weaver was far from conventional; born in 1876, he had begun his professional life taking articles with an eccentric Bristolian architect, the elusive 'Mr Youlton'.[8] Youlton was involved in a number of unconventional enterprises, including holding a number of patents for construction techniques which Weaver helped to administer. The period after leaving Youlton's office is obscure—it was in part an unhappy time professionally,

---

[7] Christopher Hussey (rev. Catherine Gordon), 'Weaver, Sir Lawrence Walter William (1876–1930), civil servant and architectural writer', *ODNB* (September 2004), https://doi.org/10.1093/ref:odnb/36792 [accessed 25 April 2019]; John Gloag, 'Sir Lawrence Weaver: An Appreciation', *AJ* (15 January 1930), p.118; Albert Richardson, 'Sir Lawrence Weaver, KBE, FSA, Hon Associate RIBA', *JRIBA* (25 January 1930), pp.206–7.

[8] Clough Williams-Ellis, *Lawrence Weaver* (1933), p.17.

PROPAGANDA 53

the one period of his life 'about which he spoke a little bitterly'.[9] He was at some point rescued by a fortuitous appointment as office manager of the Victoria Agency Ltd, established by Malcolm McAlpine as the London arm of the construction firm Robert McAlpine and Sons. The companies McAlpine Hennebique Ferro-Concrete Company (registered in 1907) and BHB Patents (registered the following year) were part of the same enterprise.[10] McAlpine was later responsible for the construction of Wembley Stadium.

Weaver tapped into a number of progressive circles and initiatives throughout this career. He was a nonconformist, a member of the Irivingite or Catholic Apostolic Church, and politically reformist, participating in the Rainbow Circle of Liberals and Fabians.[11] He was a close friend of Stafford Cripps.[12] It was Weaver who earnt *Country Life*'s epithet as 'keeper of the architectural conscience of the nation'.[13] He secured its architectural editorship in 1910, and later served as a director of the magazine. Although Edward Hudson, one of its proprietors, had been a longstanding friend and patron of Lutyens, until Weaver's arrival 'the magazine showed little commitment to contemporary architecture'.[14] Building on the work of his predecessor H Avray Tipping, Weaver produced articles on domestic architecture, including the design and repair of small houses and cottages: 'With his enthusiasm, *Country Life* championed architects associated with the Arts and Crafts movement, and it sponsored architectural competitions with informed architectural critique.'[15] A National Competition for Cottage Designs was launched in December 1913, and intended to rebuff St Loe Stratchey's earlier competition for 'cheap' cottages through an emphasis on design quality and regional traditions of material and construction.[16] This competition brought Weaver into contact with Clough Williams-Ellis, who became a good friend and collaborator over the following decade or so.

---

[9] 'Lawrence Weaver: Some Memories', *Architect and Building News* (17 January 1930), p.101.

[10] Glasgow U, ASC: Victoria Agency Ltd, GB 248 UGD 254/11; BHB Patents Ltd, GB 248 UGD 254/13; McAlpine Ferro-Concrete Co Ltd, GB 248 UGD 254/18.

[11] Michael Freeden (ed.), *Minutes of the Rainbow Circle, 1894–1924* (1989), p.367.

[12] Richard Stafford Cripps and Clough Williams-Ellis, 'Sir Lawrence Weaver', *Journal of the Royal Society of Arts*, 78.4039 (18 April 1930), pp. 635–7. Weaver's children, orphaned after his untimely death in 1930, were effectively adopted by the Cripps family.

[13] Roy Strong, *Country Life 1897–1997: The English Arcadia* (1996), p.27.

[14] Ibid.; John Cornforth, *The Search for a Style*: Country Life *and Architecture 1897–1935* (1988), pp.52–4.

[15] Ibid.

[16] Mark Swenarton, 'Rammed Earth Revival: Technological Innovation and Government Policy in Britain, 1905–1925', *Construction History* 19 (2003), pp.107–12.

54 DESIGNS ON DEMOCRACY

Weaver's work in and around *Country Life* made it an epicentre of design reform. An examination of his career more broadly shows what an important 'missing link' he has been in describing shifts in architectural culture in the early decades of the twentieth century. Elizabeth Darling has exposed the 'mischievous' Pevsnerian myth that England had simply 'lapsed into a stylistic backwater in the two decades after 1910' as a gross over-simplification.[17] She has argued persuasively that organizations like *Country Life* and the DIA in particular became battlegrounds for design reformers and in some cases the avant-garde. Christopher Hussey, who succeeded Weaver in the architectural editorship of *Country Life*, for example, gathered together influential progressive thinkers and practitioners in the mid-1920s.[18] This was undeniably the case, but it is important to contextualize these later developments; Weaver had established *Country Life* as a modernizing force from the early 1910s and continued to use his patronage of emerging architects in the Civil Service and then subsequently at Wembley. Many of these 'young guns', as we shall see, had close connections to Lutyens's office, unsurprisingly given *Country Life*'s promotion of his practice, and Weaver's particular role in securing his reputation in this period as the preeminent contemporary British architect.

Having left his position at *Country Life* to serve in the war as a Royal Naval Volunteer Reserve, Weaver's considerable organizational talents were recognized by Sir Arthur Lee, later Viscount Lee of Fareham, then director general of food production within the Board of Agriculture. He quickly rose up the ranks, moving from unpaid Controller of Supplies in the Food Production Department to Commercial and Second Secretary to the Board of Agriculture in 1918. When the board became the Ministry of Agriculture in 1919, Weaver remained, taking on responsibility for the Land Settlement programme, the fulfilment of a promise to serving soldiers that the state would provide smallholdings upon their return to a 'Land Fit for Heroes'. Smallholdings involved the provision of housing, and here Weaver was able to develop his earlier work in cottage design, encouraging experimentation with regional construction techniques, such as 'rammed earth' and concrete.[19] Swenarton has described the land settlement programme as 'effectively the national rural housing programme', 'ranked second only to the housing programme in its political importance'.[20] While at the Ministry, Weaver also founded the National Institute of Agricultural Botany, established as a

---

[17] Darling, 'Institutionalising English Modernism', pp.299–320, p.300.
[18] Ibid., pp.301–4.   [19] Swenarton, 'Rammed Earth Revival', pp.107–26.
[20] Ibid., pp.112–13.

'research institute for plant breeding with a company for the development and distribution, on a commercial scale, of new and improved varieties of farm crops'.[21] Even this enterprise was informed by design reform ideas. As with so much of DIA thinking in this period, it owed much to the example of Sweden; Weaver had used the Swedish Society for the Improvement of Seeds based in Svalov as his model.[22] Morley Horder, the architect charged with designing the headquarters of the Institute, was also asked to include a community of smallholdings for ex-officers and their families appended to the site. The Institute buildings themselves used 'the classical vernacular of Wren, with steep roofs and bold chimneys' using local brick (Fig. 1.2). This was typical of Weaver's holism.[23]

Fig. 1.2 Buildings for the National Institute of Agricultural Botany, commissioned by Lawrence Weaver, by Percy Morley Horder (1921), photographer and date unknown, NIAB

[21] 'Research for the Farmer', *Times* (8 October 1921), p.5; PS Wellington and Valerie Silvey, *Crop and Seed Improvement: A History of the National Institute of Agricultural Botany, 1919 to 1996* (Cambridge, 1997); Clive Aslet, 'Architecture and Agriculture', *Country Life* (14 January 2015), pp.58–61.
[22] 'Research for the Farmer', *Times* (8 October 1921), p.5.
[23] Ibid.; cf. WH Parker, 'The National Institute of Agricultural Botany', *Journal of the Ministry of Agriculture* 28 (May 1922), pp.1072–7.

56 DESIGNS ON DEMOCRACY

Weaver's tenure as commercial secretary is significant. Historians of public relations have shown how in Britain the development of the profession was closely linked to the need for propaganda campaigns and large-scale commercial interventions necessitated by the war.[24] The expansion of the Board of Trade and the patronage of powerful civil servants such as Hubert Llewellyn Smith were crucial to this success. Llewellyn Smith patronized Stephen Tallents, considered to be the first professional public relations expert in the country, and later secretary to the Empire Marketing Board.[25] Arguably wherever the state was involved in any form of commercial practice or interventionism, new techniques of publicity and public relations followed, fostered by progressive attitudes to public administration. At the Ministry of Food, where Tallents later worked, there were pioneering publicity campaigns. Ulick Wintour had been permanent secretary at the Ministry, and notably he was later appointed as general manager of the BEE. Wintour had previously been British Commissioner-General for the Exposition Universelle et Internationale at Ghent in 1913. There he had hosted Llewellyn Smith, who had been overseeing the British government's presence at overseas exhibitions since 1909, and Cecil Harcourt Smith, the director of the Victoria and Albert Museum who had a longstanding interest in modern industrial design. This early meeting eventually led to the establishment of the British Institute of Industrial Arts.[26] Later, at the Ministry of Food, Wintour attracted the talents of EF (Frank) Wise as principal assistant secretary, and Wise and Weaver were friends.[27] Wise, a socialist and later Labour politician, invited Weaver to address the Society of Civil Servants in 1921 on the subject of 'The State as Trader' in which he called for the state to provide consumer protection, corporate intelligence for industry collectives, and market information and developed 'consular services' for overseas trade, pre-empting precisely the sorts of arguments that would inform the founding of the Empire Marketing Board later in the decade.[28] The worlds of agricultural commerce, industrial design, and international exhibitions naturally intersected within the Civil Service. They also

---

[24] Jacqui L'Etang, *Public Relations in Britain: A History of Professional Practice in the Twentieth Century* (Mahwah: Lawrence Erlbaum, 2004), pp.20–5.

[25] Scott Anthony, *Public Relations and the Making of Modern Britain: Stephen Tallents and the Birth of a Progressive Media Profession* (Manchester, 2012), p.5.

[26] Yasoku Suga, ' "Purgatory of Taste" or Projector of Industrial Britain? The British Institute of Industrial Art', *Journal of Design History* 16.2 (2003), p.5.

[27] Lawrence Weaver, 'The State as Trader: Practical Difficulties' in *The Development of the Civil Service: Lectures Delivered Before the Society of Civil Servants, 1920–21* (1922), pp.60–82.

[28] 'The State as Trader', *Times* (22 October 1921), p.5.

contextualize Weaver's interest in and ambitions for the Empire Exhibition as well as placing him clearly within a reforming and progressive network of civil servants in the early 1920s, many of whom were directly or indirectly involved with Wembley.

In September 1922 Weaver relinquished his post at the Ministry of Agriculture to take up a role initially as director of the Art and Agricultural sections of the Empire Exhibition, eventually assuming responsibility as director of United Kingdom exhibits over significant sections of the site.

Empire and Advertising

The exhibition opened on an 88-hectare site in Wembley Park on St George's Day in 1924 (Fig. 1.3). Many of the 17 million visitors who attended the exhibition over its first season, which lasted until October, reached the exhibition grounds by rail, pulling into Wembley Park Station. Thereafter some will have boarded the 'Never Stop Railway' to the east of the site, alighting near the large amusement park appended to the exhibition. Others,

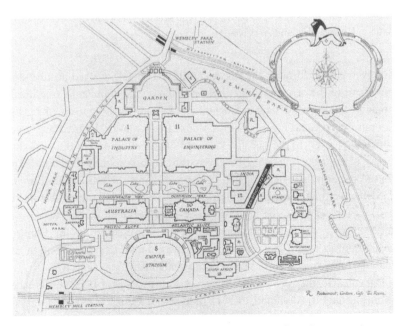

Fig. 1.3 'A General Plan of the British Empire Exhibition', *AR* (June 1924), p.209, RIBA Collections, courtesy of the *Architectural Review*

58 DESIGNS ON DEMOCRACY

Fig. 1.4 The east quadrant of the garden just inside the north entrance to the exhibition site, photograph by Katherine Jane Macfee (1924), MCF01/02/0815, Source: Historic England Archive

however, passed through the north entrance (Fig. 1.4), walked around the quadrants of the ornamental garden, and then up the grand axial tree-lined boulevard, Kingsway, terminating in the Empire Stadium framed by its famous twin towers (Fig. 1.5). Either side of the boulevard loomed two large concrete 'palaces': to the east, the Palace of Engineering; and to the west, the Palace of Industry (Fig. 1.6). These were the two largest individual buildings on the site, and they encapsulated the primary purpose of the exhibition to stimulate 'voluntary preferential trade between Britain and constituent parts of the empire'.[29] For the purpose of intra-imperial trade the Palace of Industry was of paramount importance, the nerve-centre of the Empire Exhibition; its main function was to display the variety and strength of manufacture, wholesale, and retail in the United Kingdom (Fig. 1.7).

Attached to the rear of the Palace of Industry was a large conference facility (Fig. 1.8), designed to host industry or trade conventions, up to

---

[29] Stephen, *The Empire of Progress*, p.5.

Fig. 1.5 Aerial view of the exhibition site showing the main boulevard, Kingsway, from Wembley Park to the twin towers of the Stadium, photography by Aerofilms Ltd (1925), EPW012752, © Historic England

Fig. 1.6 Crowds in front of the Palace of Industry at the British Empire Exhibition in Wembley Park, with a 'Railodock' electric bus in the foreground, photograph by Katherine Jane Macfee (1924), MCF01/02/0806, Source: Historic England Archive

Fig. 1.7 Palace of Industry, British Empire Exhibition, photograph by Campbell Gray, published by Fleetway Press (1924), 0985, Courtesy Brent Museum and Archives

Fig. 1.8 The 'Gate of Harmony', entrance to the Palace of Industry, by John Simpson and Maxwell Ayrton, photograph by Walter Benington (1924), *AR* (June 1924) 55.331, p.207, RIBA Collections, courtesy of *Architectural Review*

PROPAGANDA 61

eighty in the first season of the exhibition,[30] and a neighbouring Palace of Arts, where related temporary displays could be shown alongside the permanent exhibits of handicrafts and artworks.[31] The first of these trade conferences, held in July 1924, was the International Advertising Convention organized by the International Exhibit Committee of the Advertising Clubs of the World, a primarily American organization. It was the first of its annual conventions to be held outside North America, and London had been selected to honour the formation of the organization's newest European chapter, District 14, the coordinating body for advertising clubs in the United Kingdom.[32] On 12 July, the convention was formally opened by the Prince of Wales (Fig. 1.9), presided over by Viscount Burnham, the newspaper proprietor still then in possession of the *Daily Telegraph* and chair of the Empire Press Union, a trade organization which strengthened 'the friendship and solidarity of the Newspaper Press throughout the Empire by close companionship and mutual understanding.'[33] William H Lever, Viscount Leverhulme, was another president of the convention and active in the programme. The theme of the convention was 'Truth in Advertising' (Fig. 1.10), and the event attracted some 4,000 delegates, over half of whom had travelled from the USA.[34] Such was the high profile of the event that the opening ceremony of the convention was broadcast by the BBC.[35]

The General Sessions opened in the afternoon, and after an introduction by Lou E Holland, the president of the Associated Advertising Clubs of the World, the convention was addressed by Lawrence Weaver on the subject of 'Exhibitions and the Arts of Display.'[36] Weaver, *The Times* reported, treated his subject 'with authority, for the BEE is itself the most ambitious and most highly-conceived advertising project ever launched.'[37] Exhibitions, Weaver claimed, were 'among the most potent instruments in the advertiser's hands, and the background of a score or even a hundred methods of promoting the

[30] 'British Empire Exhibition—Origin and Embodiment', *The Times Trade and Engineering Supplement: British Empire Exhibition Section* (3 May 1924), p.173.
[31] Jiyi Ryu, 'Visualising and Experiencing the British Imperial World: The British Empire Exhibition at Wembley (1924/25)', Ph.D. thesis, University of York, 2018; Jiyi Ryu, 'The Queen's Dolls' House within the British Empire Exhibition: Encapsulating the British Imperial World', *Contemporary British History* 33.4 (19 October 2019), pp.1–19.
[32] Stefan Schwarzkopf, 'Respectable Persuaders: The Advertising Industry and British Society, 1900–1939', Ph.D. thesis, Birkbeck, University of London, 2008, pp.42–50.
[33] Robert Donald, *The Imperial Press Conference in Canada* (1921), p.xiii.
[34] 'Opening of World Congress', *Daily Telegraph* (15 July 1924), p.7.
[35] 'Convention Programme', *Daily Telegraph* (12 July 1924), p.7.
[36] 'Opening of World Congress', p.7.
[37] 'Modern Advertising', *Daily Telegraph* (14 July 1924), p.10.

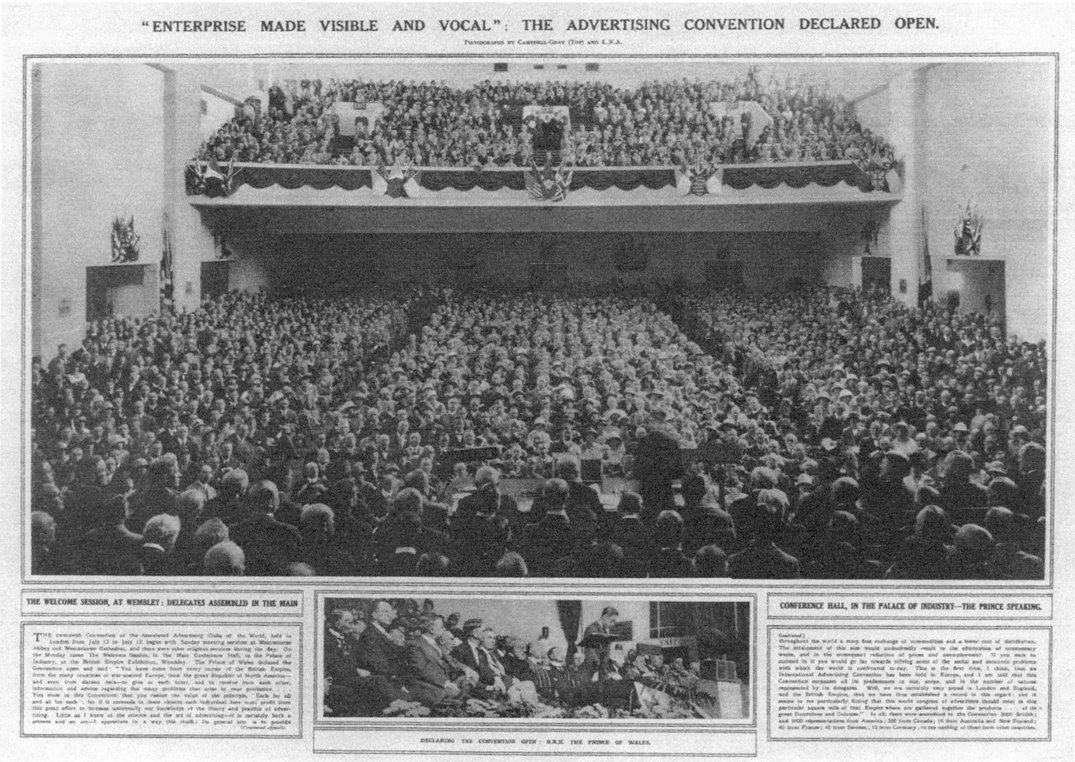

"ENTERPRISE MADE VISIBLE AND VOCAL": THE ADVERTISING CONVENTION DECLARED OPEN.

Photographs by Campbell-Gray (Top) and L.N.A.

THE WELCOME SESSION, AT WEMBLEY: DELEGATES ASSEMBLED IN THE MAIN CONFERENCE HALL, IN THE PALACE OF INDUSTRY—THE PRINCE SPEAKING.

THE twentieth Convention of the Associated Advertising Clubs of the World, held in London from July 13 to July 17, began with Sunday morning services at Westminster Abbey and Westminster Cathedral, and there were other religious services during the day. On the Monday came The Welcome Session, in the Main Conference Hall, in the Palace of Industry, at the British Empire Exhibition, Wembley. The Prince of Wales declared the Convention open and said: "You have come from every corner of the British Empire, from the many countries of war-scarred Europe, from the great Republic of North America—and even from distant Asia—to give to each other, and to receive from each other, information and advice regarding the many problems that arise in your profession. . . . You show in this Convention that you realise the value of the principle, 'Each for all and all for each'; for if it succeeds in these objects each individual here must profit from this great effort to increase universally our knowledge of the theory and practice of advertising. Little as I know of the science and the art of advertising—it is certainly both a science and an art—I appreciate in a way this much: Its general aim is to provide

[Continued opposite.

DECLARING THE CONVENTION OPEN: H.R.H. THE PRINCE OF WALES.

Continued.]

throughout the world a more free exchange of commodities and a lower cost of distribution. The attainment of this aim would undoubtedly result in the elimination of unnecessary waste, and in the consequent reduction of prices and unemployment. If you were to succeed in it you would go far towards solving some of the social and economic problems with which the world is confronted to-day. This is the first time, I think, that an International Advertising Convention has been held in Europe, and I am told that this Convention surpasses all its predecessors in size, scope, and in the number of nations represented by its delegates. Well, we are certainly very proud in London and England, and the British Empire, that we have thus established a record in this regard; and it seems to me particularly fitting that this world congress of advertisers should meet in this particular square mile of that Empire where are gathered together the products . . . of its great Dominions and Colonies." In all, there were accredited to the Convention 3000 British; and 1600 representatives from America; 300 from Canada; 16 from Australia and New Zealand; 40 from France; 40 from Sweden; 12 from Germany; to say nothing of those from other countries.

Fig. 1.9 '"Enterprise Made Visible and Vocal": The Advertising Convention Declared Open', *ILN* (19 July 1924), pp.134–5, photograph by Campbell Gray, published by Fleetwood Press, 13419361/ILN, © Illustrated London News Ltd/Mary Evans

PROPAGANDA 63

Fig. 1.10 'Truth In Advertising', lithograph poster designed for use in connection with the Advertising Convention, designed by Frederick Charles Herrick (c.1923–4), E.144-1976, © Frederick Charles Herrick/Victoria and Albert Museum, London

sort of trade most needed to-day—the trade between nations'.[38] With fitting hyperbole, Weaver described how:

> The great Exhibition was the platform on which could be most fruitfully discussed that greater interflow of commodities which would do more than anything to dissipate animosities, to correct the tragedy of shattered exchanges, to remove the social menaces of unemployment, and to offer the shrewd, adventurous spirits of the world the occasion for harnessing natural forces and develop the dormant heritage of mankind. He was not putting the case too high in saying that the association of Exhibition and Convention created the most highly dynamic condition for the improvement of trade that the world had yet seen.[39]

Weaver was promoting 'beauty in relation to salesmanship', arguing that although elements of advertising were an 'offence against the amenities of our cities and still more of the countryside', it could and should aspire not

[38] 'Business Ideals and Advertising', *Daily Telegraph* (15 July 1924), p.7.
[39] Ibid.

64　DESIGNS ON DEMOCRACY

only for 'truth in advertising' but also 'for truth in beauty'. Fundamentally, the devotion of 'art to the service alike of manufacture and salesmanship'—through industry and commerce—was the greatest hope 'for the correction of some evil aspects of the industrial revolution'. Finally, the great patrons of the arts would, in the future, 'be the men who were making or distributing the commodities or directing the public services like gas and transport, and the men who commended to the public those universal necessities of our everyday lives'.[40]

These statements place Weaver, along with figures like Frank Pick, firmly within an 'informal network of individuals whose common influences, associations, and views about the unity of art and life qualify them as a recognisable avant-garde'.[41] This world-view was characterized as 'Medieval Modernism' in a now classic account of Pick and the London Underground by Michael T Saler. The ideas of Fry and Bell's 'significant form' merged with a Ruskinian and Morrisian conception of craft now harnessed to the realities of industrialization. 'Medieval Modernism' was a descriptor for these views 'expressed by government officials at the Boards of Trade and Education, critics, educators, artists, businessmen' as well as media organizations like *The Times*, *The Guardian*, and the BBC, many of whom were active participants in the DIA.[42] The DIA had been established in 1915 as a response to the Deutchser Werkbund Exhibition (1914) which, in times of war, seemed to encapsulate Germany's advances in commercial and industrial design and what seemed like Britain's frustrating adherence to a quaint 'Arts and Crafts' institutional and design culture. The DIA was intended as a modernizing force.

'Medieval Modernism' as a phrase, however, is limited; it suggests a coherent style or visual language when in fact the impulses behind it generated diverse formal expression across different media. The phrase also implies a compromised or qualified 'Modernism', whereas much scholarship since has asserted the multiplicity of modernity, and British or English responses as valid on their own terms. Finally, the status of proponents of 'medieval Modernism' as an 'avant-garde' is problematic, implying oppositional practice when in fact they were seeking to make these

[40] Ibid.
[41] Michael T Saler, *The Avant-Garde in Interwar England: Medieval Modernism and the London Underground* (Oxford, 2001), p.15.
[42] Ibid., p.16.

ideas mainstream, or least widely acceptable, in the interwar years.[43] Saler's other expression for these manifestations—results of the 'DIA point of view'—serves us better in encapsulating the early twentieth-century British design reform movement. Subsequent scholarship has uncovered how much more pervasive the 'DIA point of view' was. Yasuko Suga has shown in detail how many of these design reform ideas were circling around the British Institute of Industrial Art (BIIA), established by Herbert Llewelyn-Smith (also a DIA man) and Cecil Harcourt Smith. The BIIA's influence was felt not only through a programme of exhibitions but also in, among other things, the General Post Office's selection of a design for new telephone kiosks by Giles Gilbert Scott and the Royal Mint's Standing Committee on Coins, Medals and Decorations.[44]

The Palace of Industry

In 1925, Weaver published *Exhibitions and the Arts of Display*, a record of his experiences at Wembley, developing the theme he had first addressed at the International Advertising Convention.[45] This book was a reflection of Weaver's experience in organizing the exhibition. His responsibilities as director of United Kingdom exhibits extended to control over not only the Palace of Industry but also the Palace of Art and some limited influence over the Palace of Engineering. For the second season of the exhibition, the Palace of Engineering was replaced by the Palace of Housing and Transport, and Weaver had total jurisdiction over these displays too. He was therefore in the higher reaches of the exhibition administration.

The primary message of Weaver's book was around coordination and group advertising with sections and stands designed to the highest quality *by architects*. To Weaver and his contemporaries this was felt to be a new departure in British exhibition design, and it served the additional function of advertising architects' services for marketing products to industrial clients. The professional service of architectural design was supposed to guarantee a

---

[43] Clement Greenberg, 'Avant-Garde and Kitsch', *Partisan Review* (1939), pp.34–39, and Thomas Crow, *Modern Art in the Common Culture* (New Haven, 1996).

[44] Yasuko Suga, '"Purgatory of Taste"', pp.174–5; Gavin Stamp, *Telephone Boxes* (1989).

[45] Lawrence Weaver, *Exhibitions and the Arts of Display* (1925).

66 DESIGNS ON DEMOCRACY

higher quality of exhibit, distinct from stand-fitting. As Weaver pleaded in a private circular to the architects engaged by various industry bodies:

> In defending the arrangement whereby architects and not stand-fitters are responsible for exhibitors' stands in the Palace of Industry, I have claimed that speed and punctuality as well as artistic success are amongst the great justifications. PLEASE DO NOT LET ME DOWN.[46]

John Simpson and Maxwell Ayrton were the chief architects to the exhibition, with Owen Williams as consultant engineer, designing the concrete infrastructure of the site including the Stadium and the large hangars which became Weaver's 'palaces'. With the scale of the work and the short timeframe, however, it was not feasible that they could control the design of individual sections and stands, and so, as Weaver wrote to the architect Edward Maufe, 'it has been arranged for Mr Clough Williams-Ellis to be associated with them in superintending the decorative treatment of the exhibitors' stands in the Industrial and Machinery Halls' (Fig. 1.11).[47] A panel of twenty-five architects was invited to take part. As Williams-Ellis himself described in his biography of Weaver:

> To them, severally, were allotted various sections of the exhibition— Morley Horder this, Curtis Green that, Joseph Emberton the other. [HPG] Maule was responsible for the Bakery and Railway sections, [HD] Hendry brought order and seemliness into the Silk and Paper galleries, whilst Oswald Milne showed what could be done to make even linoleum look enticing.[48]

Weaver's Wembley Panel of up-and-coming architects comprised a significant section of his network of patronage. It reveals something about the nature of progressive architectural practice and design in the 1920s. Many of these architects, who were known in their early careers for their domestic architecture, had some association with Lutyens and were closely

---

[46] RIBA, Sir Edward Maufe Papers (hereafter, Maufe Papers), Ma/E/24/2, Job Correspondence File for British Empire Exhibition at Wembley, letter from Lawrence Weaver to Edward Maufe (10 March 1924).

[47] RIBA, Maufe Papers, Ma/E/24/3: letter from Lawrence Weaver to Weaver Maufe (9 December 1922).

[48] Williams-Ellis, *Weaver*, p.53.

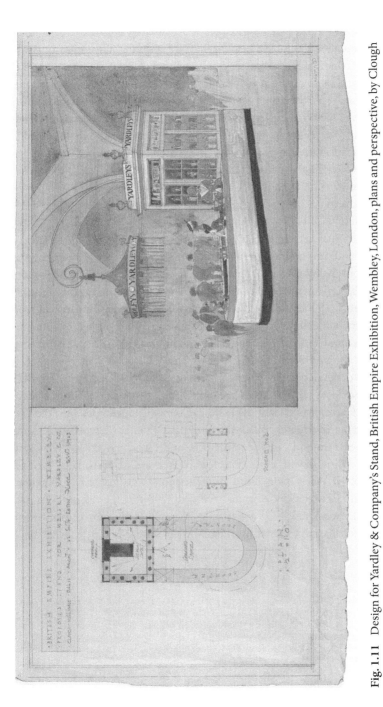

Fig. 1.11 Design for Yardley & Company's Stand, British Empire Exhibition, Wembley, London, plans and perspective, by Clough Williams-Ellis (1923), RIBA126425, RIBA Collections

68 DESIGNS ON DEMOCRACY

linked with the later Arts and Crafts more broadly. For this reason, many were proponents of the last gasps of the 'Wrenaissance', albeit in a more subdued language. Hubert Worthington, for instance, later taught a course at the Royal College of Art in which students produced designs for the fictional eighteenth-century country town of 'Wrenworthy';[49] HD Hendry edited the volumes of the Wren Society with AT Bolton. And this, of course, tallied not only with Weaver's own interests in Lutyens, whom he had championed at *Country Life*, but also with Wren. These architects also had reputations for employing high-quality craftsmanship on their buildings, the care and attention given to Arts and Crafts detailing for this reason also found its place in formal, Classical and neo-Georgian commercial work in the 1920s and 1930s.

Morley Horder, another member of the Wembley Panel, was clearly a close friend; not only did he live on Hamilton Terrace, the same road as Weaver in St John's Wood, but he also redesigned Weaver's house whose interiors, particularly the music room, were well known among this milieu.[50] They were both members of the Rainbow Circle.[51] Morley-Horder had been a member of the Art Workers' Guild and built an early reputation for designing Arts and Crafts houses. After the war, he was engaged by the Housing Association for Officers' Families (of which organization Weaver was treasurer) to design a portion of a significant estate at Morden. Morley Horder's two large closes separated by a belt of existing trees, were set within a larger site of 26 acres leased from the London County Council (LCC) for the Earl Haig Memorial Homes, which comprised 123 homes designed by George Grey Wornum and Louis de Soissons, and for which Weaver was also client.[52] Wornum was another protégé of Weaver's who also later lived on Hamilton Terrace. Oliver Hill, a family friend of Lutyens, briefly shared an office with George Grey Wornum in Piccadilly before the war and was part of this network too. Also active at Wembley was William Curtis Green, known for his finely crafted work at Wolseley House (1922–3), originally a

---

[49] 'Sir Hubert Worthington' *Times* (27 July 1963), p. 10; 'Our Presidents', *AJ* (17 August 1932), p.204.

[50] Randal Phillips, *The House Improved* (1931), pp.46–51; Lawrence Weaver, *Gas Fires and their Settings* (1929), pp.51, 56, 59, 61, 63. Cf. Williams-Ellis, *Weaver*, p.57.

[51] Martin Briggs (rev. Catherine Gordon), 'Percy Richard Morley Horder (1870–1944), architect' *ODNB* (January 2011), https://doi.org/10.1093/ref:odnb/33984 [accessed 25 April 2019].

[52] 'The Offices' Homes at Modern', *ABN* (5 June 1931), pp.323–5; 'The Early Haig Memorial Homes, Morden', *ABN* (29 May 1931), pp.284–5.

car showroom, Westminster Bank, and Stratton House, all on Piccadilly. When Lutyens first went to New Delhi, Curtis Green took over the management of his practice.[53] Oswald Milne—who developed particular expertise in schools and hotels—had also briefly been in Lutyens's office, having originally been articled to Sir Arthur Blomfield. Hubert Worthington had likewise worked as an assistant to Lutyens for two years before the Great War. His friend, the wood-engraver Margaret Pilkington, praised him as 'an architect of the older school for an intimate knowledge of materials and methods of stone-cutting, wood-carving, and carpentry and he combined the care for such details with an understanding and appreciation of the skill of the men who worked under him'.[54] Joseph Emberton, an architect who was later an active proponent of British Modernism (demonstrated by his prodigious Royal Corinthian Yacht Club and Simpsons on Piccadilly) was particularly favoured by Weaver. And on the other hand, so was Edward Maufe, who was known for his admiration of Lutyens, and whose work embraced the ideals of Swedish Grace. The association of Maufe, derided as a rather safe architect of the establishment in later years, with this progressive coterie shows how catholic conceptions of modern architecture were in the mid-1920s. HPG Maule, an architect now little known, had been headmaster of the Architectural Association School between 1903 and 1913, and after the war served as chief architect to the Ministry of Agriculture and Fisheries before returning to private practice in 1923. He also worked on the Douglas Haig Memorial Homes for Ex-Soldiers at Birmingham and Newcastle,[55] and he too espoused Arts and Crafts ideals; in a lecture in Manchester in 1925 he called for the education of the architect to be 'as far as possible, linked together with that of builders and craftsman...He believed the medieval spirit of craftsmanship was not dead'.[56] There were others in Weaver's network of patronage—Maxwell Ayrton, for instance, had also worked under him at the Ministry of Agriculture on the Small Holdings Scheme.

[53] Hubert Worthington (rev. Catherine Gordon), 'William Curtis Green (1875–1960), architect', *ODNB* (September 2004) https://doi.org/10.1093/ref:odnb/33535, [accessed 25 April 2019].
[54] Margaret Pilkington, 'Sir Hubert Worthington', *Times* (3 August 1963), p.8.
[55] 'Major HPG Maule', *Times* (16 May 1940), p.9.
[56] 'Houses and Social Problems: An Architect's Diagnosis', *Manchester Guardian* (5 February 1925), p.11.

70 DESIGNS ON DEMOCRACY

Collectively, these architects demonstrated the vitality of late Arts and Crafts ideals among progressive practitioners in the 1920s. Weaver sat at the centre of this network of patronage, providing them with important commissions not only in domestic work for the voluntary sector and the Land Settlement programme but also in forging closer links with the realms of industrial and commercial design. These two spheres—progressive social housing and design reform—were, in Weaver and the DIA's formulation, the new defining features of modern architectural practice in the post-war period.

The Palace of Industry itself was organized around three main thoroughfares (Fig. 1.12): the South Walk (Fig. 1.13), running south to north, intersected with the East Walk (Fig. 1.14), connecting in turn to a North Walk (Fig. 1.15) at its eastern end. There were multiple points of entrance and egress, but most visitors would enter through one of the larger ceremonial entrance ways. From Craftsmens Way—an appropriate name for Kipling to settle on given the DIA underpinnings—you could enter South Walk through the Gate of Plenty, surrounded by large restaurant areas either side (Fig. 1.16). From Kings Way you would enter East Walk via the Gate of Harmony, and the North Walk terminated in the West Gate. A subsidiary thoroughfare, the South West Walk, terminated in the Postman's Gate. As Weaver commented in the *Architectural Review*: 'Tiresome streets of individual stands have been done away with, and the exhibitors have grouped themselves in sections under the title of their various industries, such as *Chemicals, Pottery, Food,* etc.' The main thoroughfares were punctuated by large kiosks; at the intersection of East and South Walks, for instance, was the famous Lion Kiosk featuring Percy Metcalf's sculptural interpretation of FC Herrick's exhibition symbol (Fig. 1.17). On the outside of the parapet circling the open podium were advertisements for Lipton. In the centre at the base of the cenotaph-like structure was an official publications stand (operated by Fleetway Press), surmounted by Metcalf's lion (Fig. 1.18). The kiosk was made of 'Ten-Test' Fibre Board, with a stone facing of 'Lapidosus' (Fig. 1.19).

Along with these kiosks, Weaver's team was responsible for the overall wayfinding system; lettering was designed by FC Herrick based on the inscriptions on Trajan's column, and this was taken up by the 'Sign King', Frank Harris, for use on sign-posts in the gangways and on section porticoes.[57] Decorative columns, 24 feet tall, coloured and gilded, were also erected at intervals, designed by Clough Williams-Ellis in November 1923. Section

---

[57] RIBA, Maufe Papers, Ma/E/24/2, Job Correspondence File for British Empire Exhibition at Wembley, Circular from Lawrence Weaver to Committee of Architects (25 October 1923).

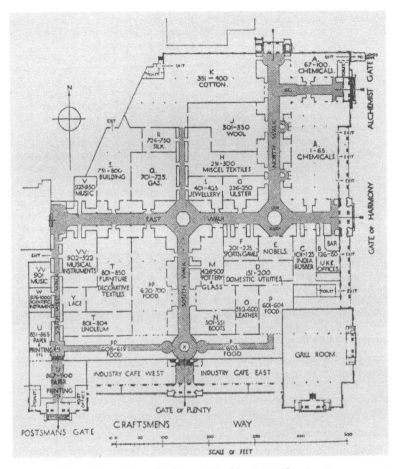

Fig. 1.12 'Plan of the Palace of Industry, Wembley 1924, Showing Arrangement of Sections', reproduced in Lawrence Weaver, *Exhibitions and the Arts of Display* (London, 1925), p.9, Wellcome Collection

architects were responsible for designing an appropriate device with which to crown them.[58]

For the design of specific industry sections, conferences of Weaver's architects' panel were convened occasionally from September 1923 onwards to discuss design issues and ensure coordination, and though Clough Williams-Ellis was 'superintending', Weaver's correspondence with just one

---

[58] RIBA, Maufe Papers, Circular from Lawrence Weaver to Committee of Architects (11 November 1923).

Fig. 1.13 'South Walk, Palace of Industry, Wembley, 1924', reproduced in Lawrence Weaver, *Exhibitions and the Arts of Display* (1925), plate ix, Wellcome Collection

of the panel—Edward Maufe—shows how engaged he was in the minutiae of planning throughout.

Coordination was paramount. To this end, Weaver described how he encouraged the formation of informal trade associations if none had been established. There were, in Weaver's experience, various means of achieving coordination. The first, and most preferable, was through the complete subordination of individuality to present an industry—for instance, a widespread public utility. This was evidenced by Austen Hall's designs for the gas industry. Group exhibits might have overarching decorative schemes, while retaining the individuality of firms, shown by Oliver Hill in the Pottery section. In other instances, an association would supervise individual leases from the exhibition management. Here the architect might take on a coordinating role while working simultaneously on individual briefs for respective firms. Clough Williams-Ellis did this for the chemical industries. And finally, in particular where no trade association existed or could be cobbled together, individualized stand design could be linked by uniform

Fig. 1.14 The interior of the Palace of Industry building at the British Empire Exhibition in Wembley Park, showing people standing near the Cauldon China stand, MCF01/02/0824, Source: Historic England Archive

colour and lettering, as demonstrated in the Building section. These were all strategies for overturning what Weaver repeatedly asserted as an innate British sense of individualism in commerce. Group exhibits served as a kind of spatial metaphor for collective advertising. Collective advertising was seen as an effective means of boosting intra-imperial trade.[59]

Various craft traditions in the graphic and plastic arts came together for the animation of the stands and sections: the architect and designer Oliver Bernard designed friezes for the Pacific Café restaurant operated by Lyons;[60] Clive Gardiner produced painted friezes for Rubber Industries Hall, designed by Morley Horder, depicting the 'co-operation between Art and Commerce' painted on canvas by students from Goldsmiths' College.[61] These friezes showed the cultivation, production, and manufacture of

---

[59] Weaver, *Exhibitions*, pp.24–45.
[60] Alan Powers, 'Oliver Percy Bernard (1881–1939), architect and designer', *ODNB* (September 2004), https://doi.org/10.1093/ref:odnb/37186 [accessed 2 April 2019].
[61] *Design in Modern Life and Industry: The Year Book of the Design and Industries Association 1924–25* (1925), pp.106–11.

Fig. 1.15 'Porticos to Cotton and Wool Sections, North Walk, Palace of Industry, Wembley, 1924', reproduced in Lawrence Weaver, *Exhibitions and the Arts of Display* (1925), plate xxxiii, Wellcome Collection

Fig. 1.16 People on the tea balcony at the British Empire Exhibition in Wembley Park, photography by Katherine Jane Macfee (1924), MCF01/02/0811, Source: Historic England Archive

PROPAGANDA 75

Fig. 1.17 The 'Wembley Lion', lithograph poster, designed by Frederick Charles Herrick for the Baynard Press (c.1923–4), Twentieth Century Posters Ltd

rubber as an imperial enterprise, spanning jungle scenes and plantations, 'natives felling and burning the jungle in preparation for planting', preparation for export, transportation, and unloading, and arrival at a London factory where the rubber was 'machined'.[62] Decorative incidents such as these serve to show how the Palace of Industry's United Kingdom exhibits reinforced a technocratic vision of the 'workshop of the world'. Similarly, part of the Cotton section was arranged by the Empire Cotton Growing Association, the British Cotton Growing Association and the Liverpool and Manchester Cotton Associations; in the approach to the Cotton Machinery Hall, 'bales of commercial grown and experimental crops from the Sudan, Uganda, British West Indies, Nyasaland, Queensland, Nigeria, etc.' were displayed, with samples available for interested parties.[63]

Cotton Textiles occupied a significant portion of the display space, organized by a representative committee of Lancashire cotton interests, with exhibits of manufacturing process and products covering some 32,187 square feet. They were second only to the Chemical Industry, occupying some 37,500 square feet including a central 'exhibit of research in pure

[62] Ibid.
[63] *The Business Features of Wembley (Compiled by the Investors' Chronicle)* (1924), p.5.

(a)

(b)

Fig. 1.18 (a) Steel, glass, and concrete construction in the Palace of Industry 'hangar' (November 1923) and (b) East Walk, Palace of Industry, looking east, reproduced in Lawrence Weaver, *Exhibitions and the Arts of Display* (1925), plate v, Wellcome Collection

Fig. 1.19 The Lion Kiosk, Palace of Industry, designed by Joseph Emberton, sculpted by Percy Metcalfe (1924), reproduced in Lawrence Weaver, *Exhibitions and the Arts of Display* (1925), plate LXV, Wellcome Collection

chemistry' facilitated by the Royal Society in conjunction with the section organizers, the Association of British Chemical Manufacturers. Northern Ireland was also represented within the industrial sections; Ulster and its industries took up 6,187 square feet of space with displays of shipbuilding and the production of flax, linen, and beverages.[64] The Ulster Pavilions

[64] *Metro-Land: 1924 Edition* (2004), p.14.

(Fig. 1.20) occupied slightly awkward sites, including one to the north-west of the Lion Kiosk. Here, Clough Williams-Ellis negotiated the corner by effectively splaying the entrances with whimsical pavilions characterized by Serlian entranceways and roofs which, 'instead of finishing with a parapet [employed] a treatment which led to an amusing sort of volute treatment where the portico dies back into the slope of the roof'.[65] Section entrances were generally marked by porticos on the main thoroughfares—larger sections would have multiple entrances with different porticos. As the *AR* noted, 'each industry forms a little town of its own which approached through the great porticoes that flank the three main avenues'.[66] The Pottery section featured two by Oliver Hill; one, a classical arch with decorative ceramic panels, was for Wedgwood (Fig. 1.21), incorporating its 'house style'. Another, also by Hill and Orientalist in tone, was for Pilkington and Twyford (Fig. 1.22). Elaborate fretwork punctuated the parapet, and the

Fig. 1.20 'Ulster Pavilion, Palace of Industry, Wembley, 1924', reproduced in Lawrence Weaver, *Exhibitions and the Arts of Display* (1925), plate XXI, Wellcome Collection

---

[65] Lawrence Weaver, 'Exhibitors' Architecture', *AR* (June 1924), p.227.
[66] Ibid., p.223.

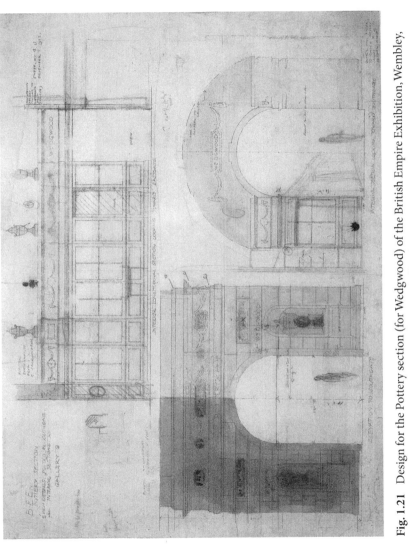

Fig. 1.21 Design for the Pottery section (for Wedgwood) of the British Empire Exhibition, Wembley, London, by Oliver Hill (1924), RIBA20238, RIBA Collections

Fig. 1.22 Porticos, showrooms, and galleries for the Pottery section designed by Oliver Hill, reproduced in Lawrence Weaver, *Exhibitions and the Arts of Display* (1925), plate LXXXVIII, Wellcome Collection

PROPAGANDA 81

lower portion was tiled, no doubt celebrating the lustrous glazes which had make Pilkington famous. For Staffordshire firm Moorcroft, Maufe produced a simple, broad, and monumental entrance-way.

Energy providers, competing anxiously to capture an increasingly crowded domestic market, were highly visible in the Palace of Industry. The section for the Electricity Development Association (EDA), formed in 1919, was largely designed by the firm of Imrie and Angell, architects with whom Weaver also had a longstanding relationship.[67] The EDA display included two pavilions—the north pavilion was essentially a villa with a large open front porch 'used as a lounge', and the south, following the same theme, was used 'as a two storey house fitted electrically throughout', including an upper storey loggia with a recessed garden space (Fig. 1.23). There were, in addition, kiosks displaying labour-saving devices like vacuum cleaners, and sample shop windows for electrical products.[68]

The exhibits of the EDA's main rival, the British Commercial Gas Association, are particularly instructive. The gas industry had close connections with the architectural profession, and these were carefully looked after by Weaver. In June 1924, for instance, the British Empire Gas Exhibit Committee, chaired by Francis Goodenough, hosted a lunch for the Royal Institute of British Architects (RIBA), the Society of Architects, the Architectural Association, and the Architecture Club at the exhibition. The lunch was to celebrate the success of the gas industry's display.[69]

The exhibit committee had engaged the services of Herbert Austen Hall, who designed a Classical entrance portico which led into a lavishly furnished lounge. This lounge or rest-space led into smaller sub-sections. An Industrial Gas section displayed 'continuous domestic and industrial processes...to illustrate the use of gas for melting aluminium, firing hand-made pottery, etc.'[70] Here was also a 'miniature sweet factory', including a 'standard size gas-heated sugar-boiler, using gas at ordinary pressure and air-blast...used to boil the sugar required in sweet manufacture', as well as a 'gas-heated caramel toaster and a Uno pea-nut roaster.'[71]

The centrepiece of the display, however, was 'The Seven Ages of Women' in chambers coming off the central lounge furnished by Heal's. Ethel Wood,

---

[67] 'Park Ways and Ribbon Roads: Building Site Control', *Times* (28 August 1929), p.13.
[68] Weaver, *Exhibitions*, p.27.
[69] 'Many Advantages of Gas', *Financial Times* (24 June 1924), p.3.
[70] *Business Features of Wembley*, p.11.   [71] Ibid.

Fig. 1.23 Pavilions for the Electricity Development Association, by Imrie and Angell, reproduced in Lawrence Weaver, *Exhibitions and the Arts of Display* (1925), plate XXVIII, Wellcome Collection

a director of Samson Clark advertising, was the design consultant. Each chamber represented 'a feminine stage of life, from the girl-child in the cosy nursery, to the schoolgirl cleaning up after a hockey-match, to a young working woman efficiently managing her own business, ending up with the mature matron relaxing at home. Every room came fitted with the appropriate

PROPAGANDA   83

gas appliances and fixtures' (Figs. 1.24 and 1.25).[72] This display showed vividly the alignment of a modern domestic arena with 'feminine stages of life', which included employment in commerce and productive leisure. Ann Clendinning has shown how the gas exhibit at Wembley 'was designed with the consumer in mind, and, in particular, the female consumer'.[73] Her work places the BEE exhibit in a wider context, showing how the industry and its leading companies engaged in a range of strategies to raise standards of design and display to compete with new energy provision like electricity. Under David Milne-Watson, the governor and managing director of the Gas Light and Coke Company (GLCC), then the largest gas concern in the country, a new emphasis had been placed on sales of labour-saving devices and domestic appliances in showrooms and dealers, and this was reflected in the domestic displays of the Empire Exhibition. A programme of modernization led to the updating of showrooms under Austen Hall and Walter Tapper.

Goodenough was a key figure in this process, and was closely linked to Weaver and the engagement of architectural and design talent. Significantly he was also involved with the DIA. He was the first sales manager of the GLCC, and a proponent of education in salesmanship and sales management more widely; he chaired the Government Commission on Education for Salesmanship and was president of the Sales Managers' Association. He was closely associated with Reginald Sykes, founder and chairman of the London Press Exchange (LPE)—'it was in conjunction with him that the first great effort was made in the field of cooperative advertising'[74]—and this alignment with Weaver's ideals no doubt led to his appointment as a director of that company. Indeed, the LPE ran the advertising account for the GLCC. Goodenough was also the founding executive chairman of the British Commercial Gas Association (1911–36), a body which pioneered the advocacy of cooperative advertising championed by Weaver. It was this role that had led him to organize the exhibition displays at Wembley.

Goodenough's advocacy of salesmanship also brought him into touch with the forces changing the advertising industry, encapsulated by the International Advertising Convention. He chaired the Public Utilities section of the programme.[75] At a meeting of the British Commercial Gas

---

[72] Ann Clendinning, *Demons of Domesticity: Women and the English Gas Industry, 1889–1939* (Aldershot, 2004), pp.212–55, p.212.

[73] Ibid., p.12.   [74] 'Obituaries', *Times* (20 January 1940), p.9.

[75] FW Goodenough, 'Why the Public Utilities Need Advertising', *Advertiser's Weekly* (11 July 1924), p.110.

Fig. 1.24 Six of the seven tableaux of 'The Seven Ages of Women': gas exhibit, reproduced in Lawrence Weaver, *Exhibitions and the Arts of Display* (1925), plate XXIII, Wellcome Collection

PROPAGANDA 85

Fig. 1.25 The seventh tableau and other images of the gas exhibit, reproduced in Lawrence Weaver, *Exhibitions and the Arts of Display* (1925), plate XXIV, Wellcome Collection

86 DESIGNS ON DEMOCRACY

Association in October 1924, to mark the close of the exhibition, Goodenough declared that 'as a public utility service it was their duty to advertise'.[76] Weaver spoke at the same event on the subject of 'Art in Industry', arguing for the imbuing of 'beauty and seemliness' into not only 'things that were made' but also 'services that were rendered'.[77] Gas took on an additional prominence at the second session of the exhibition, when it was placed in the Palace of Housing and Transport. The displays were split into two parts—one on the place of gas in modern housing, the other on the broad 'revitalization of the gas industry'.[78] Weaver's advocacy of the gas industry extended beyond the exhibition, however; he gave a paper on 'Beauty and Industry as Partners' at the Gas Industry Annual Conference in 1928,[79] and, aping Goodenough's language, on 'The Art of Salesmanship' in relation to modern gas lighting the following year.[80]

The display of gas at Wembley under the aegis of Weaver's broader programme and patronage network is significant; accounts of British Modernism have gestured to the 1930s as a seminal moment in the patronage of avant-garde design. Elizabeth Darling has shown how in 1933 the GLCC convened a design consultancy panel chaired by Walter Tapper's son Michael, and a number of *moderne* architects, including Grey Wornum, Charles Holloway James, and Robert Atkinson, alongside Max Fry and the housing consultant, Elizabeth Denby. This group took over the process of designing modern showrooms for gas appliances, and an internal competition resulted in Denby and Fry's collaboration on Kensal House.[81] But once again, developments of the 1930s in which Modernists participated had earlier precedents and were part of well-established modernizing impulses. The alignment of Weaver and Goodenough's ideals of cooperative advertising in the early 1920s are expressed clearly in Austen Hall and Ethel Wood's display designs.

Weaver's activity across the Empire Exhibition was varied. Though primarily responsible for the Palace of Industry, he also had jurisdiction over the Palace of Arts. Here, close collaboration was fostered with the British Institute of Industrial Art—its director, Major AA Longden, and secretary, WT Mitchell, were effectively seconded to the exhibition to organize the Applied

---

[76] 'Commercial Gas: Fuel of the Future', *Daily Telegraph* (2 October 1924), p.7.

[77] Ibid.; Saler, *The Avant-Garde in Interwar England*, pp.78–84.

[78] 'British Empire Exhibition', *Times* (21 April 1925), p.11.

[79] *Times* (5 January 1931), p.iv; Weaver, *Gas Fires*.

[80] 'Modern Gas Lighting', *Financial Times* (30 October 1929), p.11.

[81] Darling, *Re-forming Britain*, pp.138–43.

PROPAGANDA   87

Arts sections.[82] In February 1924, Weaver was involved in a competition for an exhibition of domestic arts there which resulted in a number of period rooms, the winning design in an Adamsesque vocabulary by Gerald Wellesley and Trentwith Wills.[83] In the Engineering sections his broader network was also closely involved. There Lutyens designed a temple-like pavilion for steel contractors Dorman Long. Weaver was also involved in the 'Anglo-Swedish Court', organized by the Swedish Chamber of Commerce and Anglo-Swedish Society, no doubt engaging his extensive and influential contacts made from a visit to the Gothenburg Exhibition of 1923, whose influence over Wembley Weaver readily acknowledged.[84] In July 1924 it was announced that Weaver would chair a series of informal conferences over September and October 'to further the development of trade within the Empire as the result of the British Empire Exhibition'.[85] Seventeen such meetings were held involving principal associations of manufacturers who had organized sections in Weaver's palaces and who were given the opportunity to meet representatives of overseas industries and exhibition commissioners of Dominion and colonial administrations with a view to discussing 'methods of improving inter-Imperial trade'.[86]

Weaver also promoted an Exhibition of British Advertising Art displayed in the Palace of Art over a month-long period spanning July and August (Fig. 1.26). This was co-organized by the Arts Council of the BEE and the convention organizers. Weaver initially chaired the committee, which also included Albert Richardson and the illustrator Percy Bradshaw. The display included drawings, paintings, show cards, catalogues, labels, cartons, and other ephemera produced by British artists for advertising purposes, as well as press advertisements produced by agents, consultants, and advertisers. A second gallery space was created in the front part of the Stadium for similar displays of American Advertising Art and Printing. The two displays toured provincial centres in the months following the convention. Additionally, along a narrow strip separating the Palace of Art from the Palace of Industry, Weaver created a 'Poster-Street', a 250-feet model hoarding designed by Joseph Emberton (Fig. 1.27), featuring the work of British poster designers

---

[82] 'Maj AA Longden', *Times* (21 September 1954), p. 10; 'Royal Academy Banquet: Prince of Wales and British Art. Importance of Wembley', *Daily Telegraph* (5 May 1924), p.9.

[83] Weaver, *Exhibitions*, p.43.

[84] See 'Sweden at the Exhibition', *Daily Telegraph* (1 May 1924), p.18; 'Gothenburg Exhibition', *Daily Telegraph* (23 May 1923), p.9; Lawrence Weaver, 'The Gothenburg Exhibition', *AR* (December 1923), pp.201–7.

[85] 'Empire Trade', *Times* (25 July 1924), p.11.   [86] Ibid.

Fig. 1.26 A gallery in the Advertising Art Exhibition, Palace of Arts, reproduced in Lawrence Weaver, *Exhibitions and the Arts of Display* (1925), plate LXX, Wellcome Collection

Fig 1.27 Poster Street, designed by Westood and Emberton, reproduced in Lawrence Weaver, *Exhibitions and the Arts of Display* (1925), plate LXX, Wellcome Collection

90   DESIGNS ON DEMOCRACY

and printers, including figures like McKnight Kauffer and Spenser Pryse who were later involved with the Empire Marketing Board. There were works too by William Orpen, Frank Brangwyn, and Adrian Stokes.[87]

The overlap of architectural design with commercial art was explored in other parts of Weaver's brief. Joseph Emberton's kiosks, peppered around the exhibition site, were conceived as three-dimensional adverts.[88] He 'refused to design buildings which would have to be labelled. His design was its own label. Taking as his starting-point the advertising poster or the trade device or package of the firm for which he was working, he proceeded to design a poster in three dimensions.'[89] ENO Fruit Salts had a white, domed kiosk, the counter-opening surrounded by trellis and covered with vine leaves and bunches of grapes, aping its posters and packaging. Sharp's Toffee Kiosk, advertising its 'Super Kreem' toffee, had a semi-nautical theme with a ship's mast at the rear, and giant tins of toffee featuring the company's two brand mascots: a parakeet and Sir Kreemy Knut, the latter adopted in 1919.[90]

The Advertising Exhibition at Olympia

Despite a small and slowly growing body of work on the Empire Exhibition at Wembley, relatively little attention has been paid to its impact and legacy. Its role in promoting the idea of intra-imperial trade was superseded by the Empire Marketing Board (EMB), established in 1926, picking up an earlier resolution from the Imperial Economic Conference of 1923. In fact, both should be seen in a much wider context of strategies, some official, others less so, to promote intra-imperial trade in this period. The links between the BEE and the EMB have been oddly unexplored. Clearly contemporaries noted the influence Wembley had had on the new body's work—in describing the establishment of the EMB, *The Times* noted that 'it was amazing to find how great an effect Wembley had had on the demand for Empire goods throughout this country. This work must be followed up.'[91] JH Thomas, the former Labour Colonial Secretary, also later reflected that 'there was no

---

[87] 'Opening of World Congress', *Daily Telegraph* (15 July 1924), p.7; 'Art and Commerce', *Daily Telegraph* (26 June 1924), p.14.

[88] Ibid., pp.83–5.

[89] Hector Bolitho, 'Commercial Art at Wembley', *Commercial Art: A magazine devoted to art as a selling force* (June 1924) 3.2, p.48.

[90] Richard Hornsey, '"The Penguins Are Coming": Brand Mascots and Utopian Mass Consumption in Interwar Britain', *Journal of British Studies* 57.4 (October 2018), pp.812–30.

[91] 'Trade in Empire Produce', *Times* (1 October 1926), p.7.

PROPAGANDA 91

greater fillip given to the cause we are now promoting [intra-imperial trade under the auspices of the EMB], and no greater advertisement could have been conceived than that which was given by the old Wembley Exhibition.[92] Certainly there were significant links: one was the Department of Overseas Trade (and its Comptroller-General, William Clark), which had overseen state participation in the exhibition and which went on to work closely with the EMB.

Another indirect consequence of the Empire Exhibition was the establishment of the Advertising Association of the United Kingdom, which had grown out of the success of the International Advertising Convention. The new body promoted the ideals of the EMB; at the second British Advertising Convention in Blackpool (1926), the theme was 'Selling British Goods.'[93] Here Weaver discussed the work he had done for the UK at the Leipzig Exhibition in conjunction with William Crawford, who along with Frank Pick was heavily involved with Stephen Tallents. Weaver also took up a directorship of the London Press Exchange,[94] and this agency was often used by the EMB for press advertisements.

The Advertising Association took the decision to hold an Advertising Exhibition at the Olympia Exhibition Hall in 1927, the first major industry exhibition since the International Advertising Exhibition at White City in 1920.[95] Weaver was appointed as chairman of the exhibition committee, and the committee in turn selected Joseph Emberton as sole architect. Through close cooperation with Weaver, the lessons derived from Wembley could be applied to the Advertising Exhibition with even greater clarity, such that the exhibition was felt to mark a departure in coherent exhibition design: 'It is well known what an influence Sir Lawrence Weaver has had on exhibition design. One seemed to trace many of his ideas in the planning of the present scheme.'[96] A general scheme for stands brought unity to some 300 individual exhibitors, and, as Leo Amery described it, 'it had been both "town-planned" and artistically constructed.'[97] The layout comprised a grid of exhibition stands from the main entrance leading up to the central

[92] 'The State & Advertising', *Daily Telegraph* (22 July 1927), p.6.
[93] 'British Advertisers', *Daily Telegraph* (26 April 1926), p.7.
[94] Lawrence Weaver, 'The London Press Exchange and its Outlook on Commercial Art', *Commercial Art* (September 1928) 5.27, pp.129–30.
[95] James Taylor, '"A Fascinating Show for John Citizen and his Wife": Advertising Exhibitions in Early Twentieth-Century London', *Journal of Social History* 51.4 (2018), pp.899–927.
[96] 'What Impressed us at the Advertising Exhibition', *Commercial Art* (September 1927) 3.15, p.98; 'The Advertising Exhibition', *AJ* (24 August 1927), p.259.
[97] 'The Advertising Exhibition: Aladdin's Cave of Treasures', *Times* (19 July 1927), p.11.

92 DESIGNS ON DEMOCRACY

display of the show—the Empire Marketing Board—occupying some 10,000 square feet. The EMB stand comprised a staircase bracketed by two large pylons and display cases, leading up to a gallery with further display stands for Dominion produce. Posters and their architectural setting were once again a feature of the exhibition design; Reginald Blomfield was enlisted to design 'ideal hoarding' for the British Poster Association. A stand in the centre of the great hall was also accessed by a stairway up each side, 'and from the bridge on the top visitors get a panoramic view of the hundred selected posters arranged round the galleries on specially-erected hoardings'.[98]

The Advertising Exhibition was, in many senses, Weaver's swansong; it was the last major public event or project in which he took an active and central role. The final years of his career were occupied by directorships of various commercial concerns, not only the London Press Exchange but also incidentally Eno. Weaver died suddenly of a heart attack in early 1930 at the age of fifty-three. His continuing influence will be seen in subsequent chapters, however; in Chapter 3, for instance, we will see how his particular brand of design reform inspired John Gloag, Grey Wornum, and the development of the RIBA's new headquarters at Portland Place. Such was Weaver's importance to the DIA, it was described as 'his Heir' in an epilogue to his biography written by Clough Williams-Ellis.[99]

Weaver influenced a paradigmatic shift in architectural culture towards publicity and public relations. In the introduction to *Exhibitions and the Arts of Display*, Weaver quoted a leader in *The Times* on the International Advertising Convention, which welcomed the convention's assertion of 'the value of advertising as the creator of public standards in business' and encouraged further consideration of advertising as 'a potential creator of public standards in good taste'.[100] Weaver described these words as 'salutary' in relation to advertising and in relation to the built environment—to the desecration of amenities in cities and the countryside—but they had 'wider and deeper implications'.[101] The arts of display should strive, as Weaver emphasized in his own speech to the convention, 'not for truth only, but for truth in beauty'.[102]

---

[98] 'British Advertising', *Daily Telegraph* (14 July 1927), p.12.
[99] See ch. 12, 'The DIA as his Heir – a Postscript by Several Hands' in Williams-Ellis, *Weaver*, pp.99–111.
[100] Weaver, *Exhibitions*, p.v.   [101] Ibid.   [102] Ibid.

PROPAGANDA 93

Important shifts were taking place in the advertising industry from the turn of the previous century to the eve of the Second World War. Advertisers were becoming 'respectable persuaders'; seeking 'credibility and authority as a commercial persuader within a mass democracy that consisted of diverging social and political interests'.[103] To do this, leading figures within the industry developed better strategies to turn 'the advertising industry from an adjunct to the newspaper and publishing sector into a central player within the wider system of the governance of consumption in Britain in the twentieth century'.[104] Stefan Schwarzkopf identifies innovations like the formation of the Advertising Association and participation in the Empire Exhibition through the International Advertising Convention as part of this earlier legitimizing strategy.

This broader shift in the strategies and techniques of the wider advertising industry provides important context for Weaver's arguments about the nature not only of industrial design but also of commercial art. His deep understanding of and implication in these shifts—through commercial experience and public administration—demonstrate his pioneering role. His advocacy for the role of architectural design was not merely incidental, but the result of a sophisticated and perspicacious analysis of the ongoing processes of industrialization as a committed design reformer. As advertising grew more respectable, architects, as the most professionally oriented of industrial designers and craftspeople, were best placed to ally themselves with industry. To do so, they themselves needed to demonstrate the value of their professional services more clearly not only to industry but to the public and its institutions more widely. Architect-designed exhibitions presented an increasingly valuable opportunity to do this, as Wembley demonstrated. As James Taylor has shown, advertising exhibitions in particular were reoriented towards catering for public audiences, to mass consumers or 'John Citizen and His Wife', as the *Daily Mail* described them in relation to the 1927 exhibition which Weaver organized.[105]

Conclusion

This shift in the presentation of professional services to a mass public had important consequences for architectural practice itself. In July 1923,

---

[103] Schwarzkopf, 'Respectable Persuaders', p.2.   [104] Ibid.
[105] Taylor, '"Fascinating Show"', pp.899–927.

94   DESIGNS ON DEMOCRACY

William H Lever, Viscount Leverhulme—one of the presidents of the International Advertising Convention—opened an exhibition of architectural drawings at the Liverpool School of Architecture. He recited to the students a few clunky lines of verse loosely inspired by Henry Wadsworth Longfellow's popular poem 'A Psalm of Life':

> Lives of artists all remind us
> That if architects are wise,
> They will fling their modesty behind them
> And will boldly advertise[106]

Leverhulme was a patron of the Liverpool School and its head, Charles Herbert Reilly. He was a significant patron of architecture more generally; he had built one of the earliest model industrial villages at Port Sunlight, and as a young man had in fact harboured desires to become an architect himself.[107] As proprietor of Lever Brothers he had pioneered new techniques of advertising for 'Sunlight Soap', the bedrock of his extensive business interests.[108] In 1923 he was described by the *Daily Telegraph* as 'Britain's biggest advertiser'. The *Telegraph's* proprietor Lord Burnham was also heavily involved in the organization of the advertising convention at the BEE in Wembley.[109]

It was, therefore, glib of the *Architects' Journal* to fear that 'his lordship is no better skilled in advising architects than he is in adapting poetry'.[110] Leverhulme's advice ought to have been heeded. HB Cresswell, writing under his pseudonym Karshish, was truculent in his response: any engagement with advertising required a flinging out not of mere 'modesty', but of 'self-respect'. Advertisement would generate 'hypocritical blather about "desiring to serve the public," which is a common-place of the advertisement agent'.[111] The public 'would know that architects were no longer serving them, but serving themselves, and the status of the profession would fall'.[112]

Two years earlier, Reilly had himself spoken on the subject of 'Propaganda and Publicity' at the RIBA's inaugural provincial conference in Liverpool. His advice to the profession was tentative, if not ambivalent: 'Do we want propaganda...in connection with architecture at all? I venture to suggest

---

[106] 'Architects and Advertising', *AJ* (18 July 1923), p.82.
[107] William Percy Joly, *Lord Leverhulme: A Biography* (1976), p.7.
[108] Jules Marchal, *Lord Leverhulme's Ghosts: Colonial Exploitation in the Congo* (2008).
[109] 'Worlds Advertising: The Wembley Convention', *Daily Telegraph* (30 November 1923), p.5.
[110] 'Architects and Advertising', *AJ* (18 July 1923), p.82.
[111] 'Corresponding: Architects and Advertising', *AJ* (25 July 1923), p.141.   [112] Ibid.

we do not.' Architects could not, in fact should not, 'proclaim the virtues of ourselves or our buildings in the mass. Propaganda we must leave to the market-place and those who work there. But that does not mean that we cannot do anything to educate the public as to what is good architecture, and having educated it, let those who are fit to benefit.'[113]

By the 1930s, however, the idea that the architectural profession needed to understand and master the techniques not only of publicity but also of public relations was no longer controversial, even if there remained lingering questions over its ethical integrity. This chapter and the next trace this changing attitude to publicity and public relations in architectural culture. Publicity in its most fundamental definition describes the quality of being public and being subject to public scrutiny—in this sense it speaks directly to the wider theme of this book. It is, though, a word which in particular from the late nineteenth and early twentieth centuries had strong associations with the bogey of advertising. Advertising goods and services in the market for the purpose of trade had enduring negative connotations for the professional classes, who considered themselves aloof from these base activities. Architecture was no exception—as Reilly's tentativeness and Creswell's scepticism showed, there was an uneasy relationship between the disinterested claims the profession was making for its public importance and the growing necessity to master the techniques of mass media and advertisement to reach a mass democracy.

Synonymous with publicity was the word 'propaganda'. Propaganda held a range of connotations for contemporaries. Not only did it suggest the dissemination of information by the state (for good or for evil), it also spanned the production of publicity material through advertising and the use of that material as a technique of salesmanship, but more capaciously, as an expression for public relations, which included any relations with the state, through advocacy and lobbying as well as with the public and its institutions. The flexibility of meaning is important: the interchangeability of the terms 'propaganda', 'publicity', and 'public relations' is 'historically more authentic... contemporary rhetoric and discourse are clearly traceable to a range of activities early in the twentieth century'.[114] It was only later on in the century that public relations professionals sought to distance themselves from the fascistic connotations of 'propaganda', which suggested state-controlled

---

[113] Charles Herbert Reilly, 'Propaganda and Publicity', *AJ* (6 July 1921), pp.11–12.
[114] Jacqui L'Etang, 'State Propaganda and Bureaucratic Intelligence: The Creation of Public Relations in 20th Century Britain', *Public Relations Review* 24.4 (1998), pp.413–41, p.414.

96 DESIGNS ON DEMOCRACY

disinformation. Nevertheless, these first two chapters argue that within architectural discourse, and certainly in the institutional contexts they examine, there was a discernible movement from a range of activities which came under the umbrella of 'publicity', associated with advertising and salesmanship in the 1920s, to a more ambitious and capacious conception of 'public relations' from the early 1930s.

Publicity and public relations became paradigmatic; they became concepts through which architects increasingly understood their place in the wider political economy, and they opened up new prospects for practice and professionalism. Publicity in particular was a tool of commerce and a technique of salesmanship; in this sense, the chapter has explored how the architectural profession set out to understand its 'consumers', not only the public but also industry and indeed the state.

The BEE at Wembley was the most significant exposition of imperial trade and commerce in the early twentieth century. For Lawrence Weaver, connected to a wider world of design reform, these shifts were understood also in relation to the place of architectural and artistic design and the enduring ideals of Arts and Crafts as they reconciled with the forces of industrialization. The next chapter will explore another post-Ruskinian aspect of architectural practice in the interwar years, specifically its relationship with the wider building industry, and how this intersected with the new paradigm of publicity and public relations, having been sanitized by advertising's 'respectable persuaders'.

2
Slump
Public Relations and the Building World

Introduction

The first chapter showed how advertising underwent significant development in the early twentieth century, refining its own messages and diversifying its techniques of publicity and propaganda. It showed how figures in architectural culture—journalists and public servants like Weaver—were implicated in this aspect of design reform, not least because of architecture's profound connections with the worlds of industrial art and commercial art. The 'DIA Point of View', which encapsulated these links, was pervasive among the generation of architects who enjoyed Weaver's patronage.

This chapter looks at how the architectural profession, and indeed the wider construction industry, themselves began to mobilize techniques of publicity and public relations explicitly for their own interests. It contextualizes how public relations crept up the professional agenda over the course of the 1920s in particular, stimulated by the growing prominence of advertising and publicity signalled by events such as the British Empire Exhibition (BEE) and the Advertising Exhibition. Strategies employed by the profession and wider industry were not explicitly modernist or 'avant-garde' per se (at least in architectural terms), but rather grew out of the increasing acknowledgement of the need to market professional service. In this respect, questions about professional publicity (in particular, collective advertising) and public relations intersected with broader debates about professional status, namely the campaign for statutory registration and the growing claims of salaried architects to have their interests represented at institutional level.

The overwhelming factor in catalysing these public relations strategies, however, was the Great Slump and resulting financial crisis which struck in 1929. The construction industry was affected acutely; not only was unemployment particularly high in the sector, drastically increasing from

Designs on Democracy: Architecture and the Public in Interwar London. Neal Shasore, Oxford University Press.
© Neal Shasore 2022. DOI: 10.1093/oso/9780192849724.003.0003

98 DESIGNS ON DEMOCRACY

264,123 in September 1931 to 368,172 in September 1932,[1] but the resulting political impact led to an economy campaign promoted by the National Government in the early 1930s which insisted on budgetary rectitude and eschewed public works. These factors profoundly affected the construction industry, and consequentially the architecture profession. A growing scarcity of work amplified anxieties among private practitioners that a swollen state apparatus was robbing them of opportunities in public projects. At the same time, the curtailment of capital expenditure inordinately affected salaried employees. The Slump thus threw into sharp relief questions about the relationship of the profession to the state, especially the state as client and developer.

On the one hand, the cliché of the impact of the Slump on architecture and construction has been often invoked but subjected to relatively little scrutiny. On the other, economic histories have not engaged with the impact of the Slump on the building industry in a systematic way. In Marian Bowley's study of the British building industry—a history written in the 1960s which, for the interwar years, has not been much updated—the 1920s and 1930s are characterized by their inertia:

> Between the First and Second World Wars there were no important changes in the ways in which the design and production of buildings were organised. The essential rightness of *the system* was not queried by the government, by public bodies, by the wealthy or by other large property owners. Within *the system* relations between professions continued to be conceived in terms of competition and demarcation rather than mutual co-operation; it was still *the establishment* against the rest with probably on the whole *the establishment* winning.[2]

There is some consensus that Britain's economic recovery in the 1930s was 'largely based on the growth of the consumer goods sector and the construction industry', in other words it took place through the stimulation of production for the home market.[3] The implications of this have been

---

[1] BINC, *The Case Against 'Economy' (revised edition), Memorandum No. 1 'Economy and its Results'* (May 1933), p.12.

[2] Marion Bowley, *The British Building Industry: Four Studies in Response and Resistance to Change* (Cambridge, 1966), p.362; Peter Scott, 'The *Evolution* of Britain's Urban Built Environment' in Martin Daunton (ed.), *The Cambridge Urban History of Britain, 1840–1950*, 3 vols. (Cambridge, 2001), 3, pp.495–515.

[3] Forrest Capie and Michael Collins, 'The Extent of British Economic Recovery in the 1930s', *Economy and History* 13.1 (1980), pp.40–60, pp.40–1.

SLUMP 99

explored in relation to housing, which gained renewed impetus in the mid-1930s. There has, however, been relatively little discussion of remedial efforts undertaken by the construction industry itself, let alone the architecture profession, which fed into the housing boom. Belying Bowley's characterization of the intractability of 'the system' and 'the establishment' (themselves contestable terms), there were initiatives which sought to recalibrate industrial relations and shifting conceptions of how to solve structural issues in the sector.

The Building Industries National Council

One such initiative—notably absent from Bowley's account—was the establishment of the Building Industries National Council (BINC) in 1932, which grew out of a series of conferences on unemployment in the construction industry convened by Raymond Unwin as president of the Royal Institute of British Architects (RIBA). It brought together a number of professional interests as well as representatives from the industry trade union, the National Federation of Building Trades Operatives, and its counterpart organization for employers. The materials manufacture and supply part of the sector was also represented. Though forgotten now, the BINC endured into the post-war period but ultimately faded from view, according to one observer, 'because it was in advance of its time'.[4] With the benefit of hindsight, however, it was among the earliest institutions to formalize interactions between various sections of the building trades and professions, and was arguably more ambitious than the post-war Building Trades Parliaments and other *ad hoc* industrial councils of the 1920s. The economic impact of its attempts at rationalization and the provision of industry information is beyond the scope of the present analysis. Instead the BINC is examined more through the lens of cultural economics, through understanding the architectural cultural dynamics of the financial crisis and their interaction with wider professional and industry concerns. The BINC is particularly instructive because it was highly attentive right from the start to the importance of effective public relations in the conception of its work.

---

[4] 'Sir Jonah Walker-Smith', *The Times* (2 March 1964), p.15. John Summerson recognized its significance, however, penning two articles on the 'Building Boom' and citing its role in it. See John Summerson, 'Building Boom—1', *The Listener* (29 December 1937), pp.18–20; Summerson, 'Building Boom—2', *The Listener* (5 January 1937), pp.20–2.

100 DESIGNS ON DEMOCRACY

Public relations represented a new institutional response to major political and economic events like the Great Slump. Coordination and collaboration became a *sine qua non* of relations with the state. By 1931, the economic crisis had become a full-blown political crisis. In summer 1931, in response to the contraction of the economy, the second Labour government, propped up by Liberal support, shifted its economic policy. The May Report of the Committee on National Expenditure was published in July, calling for extensive public spending cuts, primarily targeted at social services and public works schemes. The Unemployment Fund and the Roads Fund should both, it concluded, be discontinued as part of a general reduction in expenditure by national and local government.[5] Even working-class housing, although acknowledged as fundamentally important, was euphemistically to be kept 'steadily in view'.[6] The Committee's underlying principle of retrenchment sought to return the country to budgetary rectitude and, it argued, pre-war prosperity.[7] The essential argument, as Philip Williamson has described it, was that the 'budget had been unbalanced, and the economy burdened by what was assumed to be largely unnecessary, wasteful, and counter-productive expenditure upon improving working-class living conditions'.[8]

By August 1931, however, Labour's attempts to push through a package of cuts acceptable to Parliament had failed, and the administration fell, leaving Ramsay MacDonald, now ostracized from his party, to form a National Government with Conservatives and Liberals. In September, the government began to issue Economy Circulars encouraging local authorities to make savings, some of which were vocally resisted in particular by Labour-run councils. One of its primary targets had been highways infrastructure, but local authorities were also encouraged to make savings where possible. This in turn led to the institution of a Ministry of Health Committee on Local Expenditure, chaired by Sir William Ray, resulting in a report published in 1932 which recommended *inter alia* the reduction in numbers of local authority staff and discouragement of major capital expenditure.[9] Other capital projects, such as large-scale house building programmes, also inevitably suffered. It was estimated at the time that some

---

[5] 'The Economy Report', *The Times* (1 August 1931), p.15.   [6] Ibid.
[7] Philip Williamson, *National Crisis and National Government: British Politics, the Economy and Empire 1926–32* (Cambridge, 1992), p.3.
[8] Ibid., p.267.   [9] BINC, *Case Against 'Economy'*, p.31.

£70–80 million worth of construction work was abandoned as a result of the economy campaign.[10]

The economic and political crises of the late 1920s and early 1930s had, therefore, a significant impact on architectural culture, in large part through the debate about public works and housing. MacDonald's economic policy under both the second Labour government and then the National Government went against not only Keynesian economic thinking as it was coalescing but also a fairly widespread view in the interwar years that capital outlay and investment in public works in periods of slump were essential to economic recovery. Peter Sloman has described the Liberal Party's attitude to public works from the late 1920s, citing Lloyd George's famous pamphlet, 'We Can Conquer Unemployment' (1929) as a 'landmark in the development of Keynesianism as a practical policy option. It launched into British political debate the possibility that a large-scale public works programme, financed by public borrowing, could resolve the seemingly intractable problem of mass unemployment.'[11] Indeed, such an economic approach sat within a 'current of interest in national development and public works which had existed at least since the Edwardian period.'[12] In the context of the 1931 crisis, however, a programme of public works was not seen as particularly viable; 'Experience had shown MacDonald that public works were primarily a political rather than an economic exercise.'[13] Furthermore, although there were ready advocates of a public works programme, there was no clear sense of the size or scope of such a programme, and concern that its economic effects might '"distort" the course of investment.'[14]

In policy terms, therefore, the argument for 'budgetary rectitude' prevailed, but this 'victory...obscured important shifts in monetary, commercial, agricultural, and industrial policies towards state assistance and stimulus to private enterprise. Outside the government, more explicit *dirigiste* ideas, of state management and planning, became deeply entrenched, while Keynes moved towards the full development of his theory and policy prescriptions.'[15] One of the consequences of the political and economic crisis was that unemployment became accepted as a political fact: 'high unemployment

---

[10] *BINC Year Book* (February 1936), p.56.

[11] Peter Sloman, 'Can We Conquer Unemployment? The Liberal Party, Public Works and the 1931 Political Crisis', *Historical Research* 88.239 (February 2015), p.163.

[12] Ibid.   [13] Williamson, *National Crisis*, p.267.

[14] Ross McKibbin, 'The Economic Policy of the Second Labour Government 1929–31', *Past and Present* 68 (August 1975), pp.95–123, p.106.

[15] Williamson, *National Crisis*, p.3.

102   DESIGNS ON DEMOCRACY

had become as politically tolerable as it seemed economically unavoidable.[16] In the context of this particular policy vacuum, industry was forced to take proactive steps.

In March 1932, the Abbey Road Building Society opened its expanded headquarters at Baker Street. Having been extended by one of the leading commercial architects of the day, Delissa Joseph, in the late 1920s, the company now boasted premises on the same site of almost three time its original size, including a 150-feet 'Lighthouse' clock tower, designed by JJ Joass and Daniel Warry. There to cut the ribbon was the Prime Minister, Ramsay MacDonald. In his opening remarks, he praised the building society for promoting the ideal of homeownership: 'Here was the building society's moral foundation, its spiritual existence—its ability to provide that essential extension of personality which included home.'[17] The state, MacDonald continued, was concentrating on providing assistance for cheap working-class housing for let. His comments on the wider economic situation were also revealing. 'He wished', the *Daily Telegraph* reported, 'he could impress on everybody in the country that economy did not merely mean cutting down expenditure.'[18] The 'proper and necessary objects of personal retrenchment' were 'useless expenditure; expenditure that one cannot afford; expenditure that does nothing for the activity of production and the reduction of unemployment in our own country.'[19] MacDonald's comments on the surface counteracted the strict adherence to the idea of 'economy' then so prevalent in political discourse. They in turn help to nuance our understanding of National Government policy during this continuing crisis period, not least in relation to architecture, development, and the building industry.

Although there was no mention of loan-financed public works, in the context of the building society, MacDonald was appealing primarily to private enterprise to help stimulate house-building aided by local authorities. The building societies had grown in size and significance after the end of the war, partly contingent on the growth of the housing market. In triumphalist accounts of the wider Building Society movement, the chairman of Abbey Road, Harold Bellman, stressed not only the role of the friendly societies in promoting new notions of citizenship based on homeownership but also the importance of 'thrift' through the promotion

---

[16] Ibid., p.495.   [17] 'Every Man His Own Landlord', *The Times* (19 March 1932), p.9.
[18] 'Hoard is Not Economy', *Daily Telegraph* (19 March 1932), p.10.   [19] Ibid.

SLUMP 103

of savings for 'small capitalists'. In his history of the Abbey Road society, Bellman quoted Keynes:

> The building societies...have done splendid work since the war, because they have organized saving on the one hand and have at the same time organized ways of using the thrift on building houses on the other hand. To them the two complementary activities have gone hand in hand.[20]

Though 'thrift' was complementary to the National Government's economy campaign, MacDonald's speech warned on the other hand against 'stocking' or hoarding by private individuals in particular. Capital, in other words, should be put to some good use for money to circulate in the economy. In MacDonald's words, it should be put 'freely at the disposal of labour so that it may fructify'.[21]

This speech was not the first time that MacDonald had made such comments tempering the National Government's economy campaign. In December 1931, he made remarks in the House of Commons to similar effect. 'There are too many people,' he suggested, 'both private individuals and public authorities, who imagine that simply by cutting down expenditure they are doing a service to the nation':

> There are circumstances under which a cutting down for the sake of cutting down is, especially at this moment, the greatest disservice that people can do to the nation. The most uneconomic place for money is as stocking, and the most uneconomical use for capital is to fail to find employment for the working man. Therefore, the policy of public authorities and private individuals, while economical and while following the same rules that we have had to lay down for ourselves, must always have regard to the relative value of cutting expenditure and reducing demands for labour, and unless every public authority proposing to cut down examines its proposals from that point of view, it may not be giving the assistance to the nation which we all wish it to give.[22]

---

[20] Harold Bellman, *The Thrifty Three Millions: A Study of the Building Society Movement and the Story of the Abbey Road Society* (1935).

[21] 'Every Man His Own Landlord', p.9.

[22] Hansard, HC Deb. 09 December 1931 vol.260 cc.1885–2006, cc.1915–16.

104 DESIGNS ON DEMOCRACY

In direct response to MacDonald's speech, Raymond Unwin, as the president of the RIBA, wrote to the Prime Minister thanking him for his comments, and asked for them to be disseminated to relevant government departments. The RIBA had been disturbed by the quick cessation of building operations, which had resulted in 'hundreds of architects being flung out of employment'.[23] As a result Unwin had formed a joint council including the RIBA, the Association of Assistant Surveyors, Technologists and Architects (AASTA), and the Architects Benevolent Society to establish an unemployment fund for the profession. This resulted in the formation of the RIBA Unemployment Committee, which worked with the London Society to produce a survey of London and make suggestions for slum clearance and development opportunities. An exhibition marking the culmination of this work was held in 1934.[24]

The scope of such activity, however, was limited. Immediately prompted by MacDonald's speech at the Abbey Road Building Society, Unwin embarked on a more ambitious course of action. He convened a meeting to assemble a deputation on 'Unemployment in the Building Industry' to 'consider what further steps should be taken to endeavour to bring about an increase in work'.[25] The meeting included representatives of the Building Materials Manufacturers' and Suppliers Committee, the Clay Industries Employees, the National Federation of Building Employers, the National Federation of Building Operatives, the Surveyors' Institute, and the Building Industry Council of Review (BICR), a pre-existing body chaired by Alfred Bossom, a Conservative MP who had made his fortune designing skyscrapers in Manhattan. The BICR had been appointed in January 1929 to report on industry cooperation and rationalization.[26] In its interim report of November 1929, Bossom's review indeed proposed a permanent joint council for the building industry.[27] The RIBA was represented by Unwin, who chaired the meeting, and by Harry Barnes and Sydney Tatchell, who also sat on Bossom's Council. Significantly, the conference concurred that 'an extensive campaign of propaganda and publicity was desirable to try

---

[23] 'The Architectural Profession and Unemployment: An Appeal by the President', *JRIBA* (19 December 1931), p.137.

[24] 'The Work of the RIBA Unemployment Committee', *JRIBA* (23 June 1934), pp.781–805.

[25] RIBA, SCM (9), (30 March 1932), 'Unemployment in the Building Industry: Meeting of the Deputation', fo.391.

[26] Alfred Bossom, *Building to the Skies: The Romance of the Skyscraper* (1934).

[27] Sydney Tatchell, 'How the Council Came to be Formed', *BINC Year Book* (February 1936), p.15; *Building Industry Council of Review: Interim Report* (London, 1930).

SLUMP   105

and educate the private owner of the importance of the building industry and the desirability of proceeding with building operations'.[28]

Publicity and propaganda were 'essential in the present state of the building industry', and as a result a representative sub-committee was appointed in March and formally constituted in May.[29] This committee occupied a special role because it represented a profound shift in the way that the industry saw itself and understood its position in the wider political economy. As Sydney Tatchell would later reflect, it grew out of what was felt to be a new need 'to invoke public opinion in a manner calculated to influence the Government'.[30] The Committee was 'charged with the function of endeavouring to enlighten the public concerning the economic advantages of a fully employed building industry'.[31] Government, industry had realized, would only deal with bodies which spoke with a clear and single voice.

The Committee, initially known as the Joint Sub-Committee on Propaganda—funded by the RIBA, the National Federation of Building Trades Employers, and a number of leading building materials manufacturers— was chaired by Howard Robertson (representing the RIBA), with HB Bryant, secretary of the BICR, acting as committee secretary. The representative committee of six also included Richard Coppock, secretary to the National Federation of Building Trades Operatives. By July 1932, the committee had produced its initial report showing how public relations and propaganda would be key to any remedial efforts made by the industry to reduce unemployment and bolster trade in the construction industry.[32] Some of its publicity activities were important but perfunctory; the committee had drafted a letter to the Prime Minister to thank him for this Abbey Road speech, and had produced articles for the specialist and general press. It had also begun to develop a lobbying position, road-tested in a deputation to the Ministry of Health's Committee on Local Expenditure in September 1932.

The fundamental conclusions drawn by the Joint Sub-Committee were the need for the institution of a Publicity Committee or Panel for the construction industry on a permanent basis; the formation of an Information Bureau catering to different major stakeholders in the industry (those interested in speculative work, industrial and commercial projects, and public

---

[28] RIBA, SCM (9), 'Unemployment', fo.391.   [29] Ibid.
[30] *BINC Year Book* (February 1936), p.17.   [31] Ibid.
[32] RIBA, SCM (9), 'Report of the Sub-Committee appointed by the Conference on Unemployment in the Building Industry held at the Royal Institute of British Architects, on 30th March 1932' (July 1932), inset fo.421.

106 DESIGNS ON DEMOCRACY

building); the management of parliamentary delegations; and contact with appropriate bodies of industry.

The committee's attempts to define different types of propaganda suitable for its purposes is noteworthy for its perspicacious analysis.[33] The first was propaganda to appeal to the public spirit and public opinion through an economic case. The building industry, it argued, was one of the largest employers in the country, and therefore responsible for the livelihood of a substantial proportion of the population. Savings made by the curtailment of building work would, therefore, be disproportionate to expenditure on unemployment benefits and public assistance. Propaganda was directed at building owners, exhorting them to develop sites and properties while building costs were low and construction efficiency was high. In addition, there was propaganda to influence those responsible for the finance of construction, both public bodies and private enterprise. Manufacturers were targeted to show how construction work (implicitly including architectural design) could aid industry and commerce through 'better planned buildings'.[34]

Each of these types of propaganda required different 'methods' or techniques: the production of pamphlets and technical information; the provision of advice and case studies for building owners and developers; the establishment of 'an Information Bureau or Centre' to gather information on wage rates, materials costs, construction techniques, site availability, and transport; and the establishment of a properly funded publicity organization acting on behalf of the industry as a whole rising above narrow professional or sectional interests.[35]

In Robertson's view, focus was best placed on twin campaigns of 'salesmanship' for industrial and domestic buildings. Industrial development could be improved through 'possession of adequate buildings and equipment', which lowered costs and increased 'facilities in production'.[36] Robertson proposed a publication with comparative evidence of businesses before the Depression and then those after which had invested in new premises, along with plans and sections. For housing development, he recognized that 'small house building of the popular kind' tended not to use architects' services, and that architect-designed houses were beyond the reach of most. To that end he proposed a lowering of design fees as well as standardization in

---

[33] Ibid., p.4.   [34] Ibid.   [35] Ibid.   [36] Ibid.

SLUMP   107

construction and equipment using panels of architects, quantity surveyors, and builders, akin to the American Small House Service Bureau.[37]

It was largely as a result of this memorandum that the proposal emerged to establish a 'Central Council for the Building Industry', formally suggested by Sydney Tatchell.[38] This body would provide the 'machinery for the purpose of facilitating joint consultation and co-operative action where these would conduce to the greater usefulness and the greater prosperity of the industry'.[39] By October 1932, the Conference on Unemployment had transmuted into the provisional BINC and preparations were in hand for the absorption of the existing Building Industry Advisory Council, chaired by Maurice Webb, and Bossom's BICR. Two memoranda making the economic case for the building industry were issued in September and October, and the first formal meeting of the BINC was held in February of 1933.[40]

The inaugural president of the BINC was Raymond Unwin, supported by a senior vice-president, Sydney Tatchell, who succeeded him in 1935. The Council's patrons were industrial arbiter and Labour peer Lord Amulree and Alfred Bossom, and there were four vice-presidents, including Maurice Webb. HB Bryant was carried over from the BICR as secretary. The original public relations committee remained at the heart of the BINC's early activities as one of four committees of Council, initially chaired by Howard Robertson.[41]

The work of the BINC in the 1930s can be split roughly into two phases, speaking to the shifting economic and political context. In its first years, the focus was on mitigating the effects of the economy campaign, primarily through presenting the merits of building to not only the government 'but the public, and the investing public'.[42] In this sense, the focus was primarily on private enterprise, but also on challenging the economy narrative for local authorities. The second phase, from 1935, focused on the development of a long-term public works policy to counteract the effects of periodic economic boom and bust. In 1938, the BINC could boast that it had had some success in pressing 'upon the Government the need to develop a reserve of capital works, to be brought into operation on the basis of a concerted

[37] Ibid.
[38] RIBA, SCM (9), (27 July 1932), Meeting of the Conference on Unemployment in the Building Industry.
[39] Ibid., 'Suggested Propositions to be Laid Before the Conference on Unemployment in the Building Industry on 10th August at the Royal Institute of British Architects'.
[40] The first two memoranda are reprinted in Case Against 'Economy'.
[41] BINC Year Book (February 1936). Robertson was also eventually succeeded by Tatchell.
[42] 'National Importance of the Building Industry', Financial Times (29 October 1932), p.7.

108   DESIGNS ON DEMOCRACY

policy when the volume of private investment recedes'.[43] The long-term public works policy was also Keynesian in spirit, though these basic ideas, as we have seen, were in relatively common currency. The public relations committee alluded to the influence of the politician and academic, Arthur Salter, the economist AC Pigou and the Royal Institute of International Affairs (Chatham House) and its report on the 'Future of Monetary Policy'.[44] Again, much of this thinking was canalized by the Special Committee for Public Relations, which had held a conference at the RIBA in July 1935 to develop policy and a lobbying position. Here also the need for a centralized information service (and establishment of a headquarters) was discussed: 'In these respects the Special Committee for Public Relations, on behalf of the Building Industries National Council, could act in an increasing capacity as the articulate voice of the entire industry.'[45]

The establishment of the BINC, therefore, was a bold and ambitious attempt at promoting industry rationalization, economic stimulation, and the development of long-term policy in the 1930s. Fundamentally, this initiative was driven by a burgeoning sense of the need for effective public relations, encapsulating propaganda and publicity, targeted messaging and cooperative action, but also through lobbying and the production of an evidence base for policy formation.

The BINC also reveals something about the relationship between architects and the wider 'building world', as Brian Hanson has described it.[46] In the political economy of the twentieth century, these relationships were brokered not just 'on site' but also at an institutional level. The Council's work was underpinned by two important strands of architectural and economic thought. The first was essentially Ruskinian. As we have seen, the driving force behind the establishment of the BINC was Raymond Unwin. In the early 1930s he was increasingly concerned with issues relating to professional practice as well as housing and regional-scale urban planning, having developed the government housing programme after the First World War. However, he had never abandoned his socialist ideals influenced by Edward Carpenter, Ruskin, and Morris in relation to design, craft, and political

---

[43] *BINC Year Book 1938* (London: 1939), p.30.

[44] O Healing, 'Development of Public Works', *Building Industries Survey* (March 1935), pp.67–9.

[45] 'Conference on the Building and Allied Industries (May 1935)', *Building Industries Survey* (July 1935), pp.134–6, p.135.

[46] Brian Hanson, *Architects and the 'Building World' from Chambers to Ruskin: Constructing Authority* (Cambridge, 2003), pp.1–21.

economy.[47] His presidency of the RIBA in 1932–4 afforded opportunities to promote new initiatives which held true to these ideals, albeit subtly at times. He was an important ally in the growing clamour for recognition by salaried and official architects, having served as one in the Ministry of Health, brokering a policy of compromise in February 1932.[48] This was expressed through 'collaboration' whereby officials could bring to bear technical expertise aided by the input of private practitioners for elevations and architectural setting.

The BINC can also be viewed in terms of post-Ruskinian ideas about architects' relationships with the wider building team. After the publication of the *Seven Lamps of Architecture* in 1849, Ruskin's conception of the architect—detached, aloof, and superior—had changed. He increasingly advocated 'descent' by the architect into the building world, among the craftsmen engaged in construction.[49] Unwin's conception of the BINC partially drew on this ideal, albeit at an institutional scale, whereby the architectural profession engaged with the building world supposedly on equal terms in a joint enterprise. This is exemplified by the inclusion of the National Federation of Building Trades Operatives and its secretary, Richard Coppock. Coppock had started his working life as a bricklayer and trade union official who, after the First World War, became a leading syndicalist and Guild Socialist. The movement for Guild Socialism had been evangelized by Unwin's one-time collaborator AJ Penty.[50] Coppock had been an early member of the National Guilds League and promoted the National Building Guild, a combine of building trade unions in London, Manchester, and elsewhere 'with the purpose of collectively tendering for local authority housing contracts at cost price', and which had also championed the concept of 'continuous pay'.[51] It is telling from the language that Coppock used that he understood his presence on the BINC in Ruskinian terms, writing in the Council's publication, *The Building Industries Survey*, that 'In the last resort, the quality of the products of the building industry rests on the skill of the craftsmen. However skilled or inspired the architect may be, the execution of his designs and the realisation of his inspiration depend on the

---

[47] Mark Swenarton, *Artisans and Architects: The Ruskinian Tradition in Architectural Thought* (Basingstoke, 1989), pp.126–66.

[48] RIBA, Official Architecture Committee Minutes (1) (17 June 1926–8 February 1935), (24 June 1929), fo.31. Unwin continued to advocate for this policy into the 1930s.

[49] Hanson, *Architects and the 'Building World'*, pp.163–90.

[50] Swenarton, *Artisans and Architects*, pp.163–90.

[51] 'Sir Richard Coppock', *The Times* (31 February 1971), p.12.

110 DESIGNS ON DEMOCRACY

craftsman...So far as the corporate spirit in industry is concerned, I venture to say that nowhere is this spirit more developed than in the building craftsman.'[52] The BINC was profoundly linked to late Arts and Crafts ideals tempered by experience and a shifting understanding of the modern economy; Penty's medievalism here gave way to a modern vision of industrial organization inspired by medieval values. In this sense, there was a traceable line of descent from the Building Guilds to the Industrial Council for the Building Industry (the Building Trades Parliament), and the BINC.

This was, however, still a professional enterprise in the Soanian mould: the professional architect retained due prominence in and authority over the building world. The BINC—as in other projects and initiatives we will encounter—represented a compromise with the consensus view of professionalism earlier described. These ideals are expressed by the prominence of Sydney Tatchell, a significant figure in modernizing professional practice in the 1920s and early 1930s. Tatchell had played a prominent role on the RIBA Registration Committee, chaired the Institute's Practice Committee, was the first chairman of the Joint Contracts Tribunal which had published the RIBA Standard Form of Contract in 1931, and went on to chair the Architects Registration Council (ARCUK) from 1935 to 1951.

The second strand running through the work of the BINC was Keynesian economic theory. The BINC's essential economic arguments were Keynesian in spirit; a reissue of the Council's early memoranda in 1933 cited Keynes, 'an economist of international repute', and his series of articles advocating a public works policy published in *The Times*, which later formed *The Means to Prosperity* (1933).[53] Certainly, the BINC was keen to demonstrate that its economic arguments had had some tangible effect: at Kingston-Upon-Thames the local authority was induced to spend £150,000 on new municipal offices, a town hall, and police courts, eventually manifesting itself as Maurice Webb's Guildhall opened in 1935. At Somerset, the council rescinded a decision to postpone its new county offices at Taunton in 1933.[54] The Public Relations Committee claimed not only that the building industry supported the home industry of raw materials but that it enabled 'the largest weekly circulation of money of any single industry' through weekly wages.[55] The sophisticated engagement with serious economic thought and nuanced readings of the political context of the day are noteworthy. By analogy with

---

[52] Richard Coppock, 'The Point of View of the Building Operative (June 1935)', *Building Industries Survey* (28 August 1935), pp.166–7.
[53] *Case Against 'Economy'*, p.5. [54] Ibid., p.6. [55] Ibid., p.11.

SLUMP   111

the BEE, in which ideals of cooperation and public relations were being tested, and notions of craft and architecture's relationship to industry and commerce were being explored, the BINC was a 'particular form of collective action', in Sydney Tatchell's phrasing, a 'collective endeavour' on a 'much higher plane than any form of mass advertising', but using the advantages of cooperation and common action.[56] The Public Relations Committee drove this: 'Competitive advertising and publicity still have their place, and are carried out by the particular concerns and special organisation, but are rendered more effective by the educative influence of the central machinery.'[57]

The BINC claimed that it was the first such industry body to have a developed public relations function. That is arguable, but at any rate it helped to give an impression of coherence and shared purpose, implanting 'in the public and official mind the conception of the industry as an industrial entity.'[58] In its 1938 *Yearbook*, the BINC claimed that 'Since its inception almost every Government Department—and certainly every Government spending Department—has appointed its Public Relations Officer. Many of the Associated Bodies of the Council have now appointed one or more of their Officers to undertake, to the extent available to them, the duty of Public Relations Officer. This development is one of the essentials of industry generally to meet modern needs.'[59] Whether or not it was the first, the BINC was certainly among the vanguard of institutions to develop a public relations function. As we have seen the RIBA and the architect members of the BINC played a crucial role in this development. In turn, the RIBA itself formalized its public relations function, building on earlier attempts at devising effective means not only of advertising professional services but also governmental lobbying and public education. To these efforts we now turn.

RIBA Public Relations

The final section of the chapter traces the emergence of a developed and comprehensive public relations function at the RIBA in 1933. We have seen how sections of architectural culture and indeed architectural thought were closely aligned to movements in industrial and commercial art. We have seen too how architects gave physical, three-dimensional expression to new

---

[56] *BINC Year Book* (1936), p.72.   [57] Ibid., p.73.
[58] *BINC Year Book 1938* (1939), p.32.   [59] Ibid.

112 DESIGNS ON DEMOCRACY

notions of 'truth in advertising' and commercial display at the BEE and Advertising Exhibition. But advertising and professional service were often unnatural bedfellows. Indeed, a nineteenth-century conception of advertising as related to the base and unseemly practices of the market, as individualistic and self-interested, persisted in professional quarters in the early twentieth century. This was, to some extent perversely, expressed by the BEE's 'Poster Street' and Joseph Emberton's designs for hoardings earlier discussed. Outdoor advertisements—posters, bills, and hoardings in particular—were a scourge which the profession had vociferously resisted. The Society for Checking the Abuses of Public Advertising (Scapa) had been established in 1893, in part stimulated by Alfred Waterhouse's public statements on the spoliation of the street through such prevalent methods of advertising, indeed as much as the rural landscape which in due course became the movement's focus. Waterhouse described it, in a letter to *The Times* in 1892, as 'The Advertising Plague'.[60] Scapa's functions were effectively absorbed by Guy Dawber and Patrick Abercrombie's initiative in the mid-1920s, the Council for the Preservation of Rural England (CPRE).[61] Despite anxieties about outdoor advertising and unsightly hoarding, architectural control, it was implicitly argued in 'poster-street', could sanitize these ills through well-mannered design.

Advertising and marketing were also felt to sully the credentials of professionals, including architects, and their articulated role of protecting the public interest. The RIBA Code of Professional Practice stipulated that an architect 'must not advertise nor offer his service by means of circulars or otherwise, nor may he make paid announcements in the press'.[62] This was, however, an increasingly contentious issue: the inability of architects, as individuals and as a corporate body, to market their professional services to clients and to the public was felt, in the changing cultural context in which increasingly sophisticated techniques were emerging, to be holding the profession back. Charles Woodward, chair of the Practice Standing Committee in the early 1930s, commented in the Institute's centenary history that 'In recent years probably the most difficult task has been to distinguish between advertisement by an architect (which is prohibited) and legitimate propaganda which is necessary for the advancement of the profession'.[63]

---

[60] 'The Advertising Plague', *The Times* (18 November 1892), p.10.

[61] David Matless, *Landscape and Englishness* (1996), pp.46–93.

[62] *Kalendar of the Royal Institute of British Architects* (November 1934–October 1935), p.20.

[63] Charles Woodward, 'Professional Practice' in Gotch (ed.), *Growth and Work of the RIBA*, p.125.

SLUMP   113

Architects had been concerned with questions and methods of 'public education' in the nineteenth century, an expression which captures the Victorian rhetoric of professional expertise. Notions of 'propaganda' and 'publicity', however, emerged as meatier themes in professional discourse in the post-war years. 'Public relations' as a phrase entered into common usage in the early 1930s, quickly reifying as an institutional function through the establishment of Public Relations Departments in large business concerns, trade associations, and government departments, and with the appointment of specialized public relations officers.[64] These departments fulfilled a range of responsibilities including lobbying, market research, development and monitoring of advertising, editorial content and publicity, internal communications, and industrial relations. As PA Wilson noted in 1937, in these departments rested the 'right, at any rate, to be consulted on any matter which might in any way affect the prestige of the firm'.[65]

A substantial body of work on the history of the emergence and professionalization of public relations in Britain anchors its development in changes in the administration of local government and public services. As Jacqui L'Etang has shown, public relations officers involved with the National Association for Local Government Officers were instrumental in establishing the Institute of Public Relations. 'Public relations' was a frequent subject in the journal *Public Administration*, initially in the form of articles on publicity and propaganda in the context of reconstruction, and from 1923 dealing with 'general relations with the public'. In this context, sound public relations were posited as a prerequisite of 'smooth administration': 'Achieving better understanding between the populace and local government began to be seen as intrinsically important to the job of administration and to the improvement of democracy.'[66]

It is perhaps partly for this reason that these new conceptions of public relations entered into architectural culture so early. The department responsible for local government was the new Ministry of Health. Its political priority in the years immediately following the war was the institution of a state-funded housing scheme. The housing division was led by Raymond Unwin, and included young assistant architects such as Manning Robertson

---

[64] PA Wilson, 'Public Relations Departments' in Arnold Plant, *Some Modern Business Problems* (1937), pp.123–55.

[65] Ibid., p.123.

[66] Jacqui L'Etang, *Public Relations in Britain: A History of Professional Practice in the 20th Century* (2004), p.25.

114 DESIGNS ON DEMOCRACY

and Arthur Trystan Edwards.[67] Having left the Civil Service, these became powerful voices in advocating for and participating in publicity initiatives in the 1920s. The other significant governmental department delivering housing on a large scale was the Ministry of Agriculture, specifically the Land Settlement programme through the granting of small holdings, led by Lawrence Weaver before he moved to the BEE. Weaver worked very closely not only with Clough Williams-Ellis but with others such as Maxwell Ayrton, Hugh Maule, and Oswald Milne, all of whom Weaver worked with at the BEE at Wembley. Williams-Ellis in particular developed a reputation as an effective propagandist in the 1920s through publications like *England and the Octopus* which supported many of the arguments of the CPRE.[68]

Of course, there had been a longer tradition of propagandizing for better housing conditions, in particular for the working classes. The popularity of Unwin's own early publications and practice had led to his *de facto* leadership of the Garden City movement. What was markedly different about wartime and post-war developments was the institutionalization of propagandizing activity and the establishment of a highly effective political lobby.[69] Unwin's continuing mastery of these practices was, as we have seen, codified in the initial activities of the body that became the BINC.

The project of social housing, and the resulting immersion in questions of public administration, showed to an influential group of propagandists the need for more systematic articulation of architecture and architects' importance to the public, using proper techniques of publicity and public relations. In 1926, for instance, Manning Robertson, formerly Deputy Chief Architect to the Ministry of Housing, wrote a letter to the RIBA on the subject of architecture and publicity. Having moved back to his native Ireland, he was establishing a career as a writer and critic, publishing *Everyday Architecture* in 1924, which discussed *inter alia* housing schemes and advertisements in public places, and *Laymen and the New Architecture* in 1926, which reflected on the new relationship between the architect and democratized community of laymen—the language was always strongly gendered—to which he was now increasingly answerable.[70] Writing to

---

[67] 'Forty-eighth annual report of the Local Government Board, 1918–1919' (HMSO, 1919), comd.413, p.150.

[68] Clough Williams-Ellis, *England and the Octopus* (1928); Matless, *Landscape and Englishness*, pp.46–93.

[69] Mark Swenarton, *Homes Fit for Heroes: The Politics and Architecture of Early State Housing in Britain* (1981).

[70] Manning Robertson, *Everyday Architecture: A Sequence of Essays Addressed to the Public* (1924); Manning Robertson, *Laymen and the New Architecture* (1925).

MacAlister, he suggested that 'at present when there is a question of architectural moment upon which the Institute wishes to pursue a definitive policy, there exists no channel for the persuasive advocacy in the Press'.[71] He suggested the employment of a press agent—a journalist 'interested in architecture, to act as a liaison between us and our public'.[72] Robertson's suggestion led the Executive Committee to establish a short-lived 'Publicity Committee' of architects and lay journalists. This committee concurred with Robertson's basic suggestions—a 'Press Secretary' supported by a 'Press Advisory Committee', was endorsed by the Executive Committee but in the end amounted to no concerted action.[73]

The Publicity Committee included not only the London editor of the *Manchester Guardian*, James Bone, brother of the etcher Muirhead Bone with whom he often collaborated on architectural subjects, but also JC Squire, the editor of the *London Mercury* and founder and first president of the Architecture Club in 1922.[74] Indeed, the Architecture Club had been established precisely to bridge the gap between architect and layman through a small but influential membership of 300, half of whom had to be architects, the other half of whom included writers, journalists, clients, and other marshals of public opinion. The Club held its first exhibition in 1923 with displays of 'Twenty Years of British Architecture' in the galleries of the Duke of Westminster's Grosvenor House. The displays eschewed plans and diagrams—considered too difficult for the lay public—instead favouring large-scale photographs and models, not only of contemporary architecture such as the new Peter Robinson department store on Oxford Street but also historical fantasies, such as LCC architect George Topham Forrest's reconstruction of the Old Globe Theatre or a model of sixteenth-century Cardiff. One section was devoted to recent housing and town planning schemes, including a display of housing by the Ministry of Agriculture arranged with *Country Life*.[75] Lawrence Weaver undoubtedly supported this initiative, offering a paper to the accompanying lecture series on 'Fashion and Styles in Domestic Architecture'. Notably, Weaver succeeded Squire as president in 1927.[76]

---

[71] RIBA, ECM (1), (19 February 1926), record of a letter from Manning Robertson to Ian MacAlister, fo.153.

[72] Ibid.   [73] RIBA, PCM (1), (7 July 1926), fo.1.

[74] Patrick Howarth, *Squire: Most Generous of Men* (1963), pp.160–91.

[75] 'Living Architecture', *Daily Telegraph* (6 March 1923), p.5; 'Twenty Years of British Architecture', *The Times* (28 February 1923).

[76] 'Obituary: Sir Lawrence Weaver: Architecture and the Land', *The Times* (11 January 1930), p.12.

116　DESIGNS ON DEMOCRACY

These early essays by the profession and its lay supporters show that publicity and propaganda had been established as desiderata on an institutional scale by modernizers in the late 1910s and 1920s. This initial activity also gestures towards the importance of a vital world of architectural criticism not just in the specialist press but also in the general or lay press.

Public relations became an increasingly pressing issue in the late 1920s because of four interrelated professional anxieties previously discussed: firstly, the growth of salaried practice, in particular by local authorities, which was felt to suppress architectural skill through the subjugation of the architect beneath a borough engineer, or through the denial of the skills of the private practitioner; secondly, the broader context of the recognition of architectural qualification through the campaign for statutory registration, increasingly predicated on making an effective public interest case; thirdly, campaigns, and specifically conservation campaigns, including the CPRE but also other preservationist battles which required governmental intervention; and finally, as we have seen, in relation to the wider construction industry. All of these increasingly necessitated sophisticated governmental relations and coherent lobbying positions.

In relation to the campaign for statutory registration, a Joint (Publicity) Committee was formed by the Councils of the RIBA, the Surveyors' Institution, and the Institute of Chartered Accountants in 1928.[77] The RIBA was represented by Banister Fletcher, Edwin Stanley Hall, and a provincial architect, Reginald Rix. The aim of this body was to establish the credentials of professionals with chartered status over other membership or professional organizations; in the case of the RIBA, this was to counter the effects of the establishment of the Incorporated Association of Architects and Surveyors and the Faculty of Architects and Surveyors discussed in the Introduction and to bolster its position as potential statutory registrar of qualified architects. The Joint Committee briefly engaged the services of the 'publicity expert' Barrington Hooper who, significantly, had succeeded the short tenure of Sir William Crawford as controller of publicity for the BEE in June 1923, and who had cut his teeth previously on the Victory Loan and Good Economy campaigns during the First World War. Crawford left to devote his

---

[77] RIBA, ECM (1), (8 October 1928), fo.347, inset 'Report of Joint (Publicity) Committee, 24 July 1928'.

SLUMP 117

energies not only to his own agency, but also to organizing the programme for the International Advertising Convention at Wembley.[78]

The Joint Committee's proposals amounted to no definitive action, partly because of the late realization that many of the provincial members of the Allied Societies were not, in fact, chartered. This short-lived committee, however, put the idea of organized publicity back on the professional agenda. It also galvanized Reginald Rix, president of the Berks, Bucks and Oxon Architectural Association (1927–9), who had piloted a resolution by the Allied Societies' Conference to impress on the RIBA Council the need to institute a publicity committee.[79]

Prompted by this local action, therefore, a new Publicity Committee was reconstituted by the RIBA in October 1929 under the chairmanship of Clough Williams-Ellis.[80] The Committee included Rix, FR Yerbury, the secretary to the Architectural Association (AA), and the 'warring' critics Frederick Towndrow, the first editor of *Architectural Design and Construction*, and Arthur Trystan Edwards, an erstwhile colleague of Manning Robertson's in the government housing department, who had also written extensively on the new relationship between the architect and what he called the 'average man'.[81] Rix was particularly active on this group, preparing a detailed memorandum with important observations on collective advertising and public education. 'The public', he wrote, 'generally is profoundly ignorant of the functions of an architect.'[82] The inability of the RIBA to look after the interests of its members, and of its members to look after themselves, in this regard was because professional ethics prevented individual advertising, and collective advertising by the professional association was seen as overly commercial. Sustained and 'well-directed' propaganda would, however, Rix argued, not only promote the public appreciation of architecture and architectural practice but also enhance the reputation of the RIBA and 'help the passing of the Registration Bill by stimulating public interest.'[83] The

[78] Crawford's was a significant patron of modern design and architecture. Its headquarters on High Holborn was designed in part by Frederick Etchells, whose translation of *Vers Une Architecture* was published in 1927, the same year the building was completed.

[79] 'Obituary: Reginald Rix', *JRIBA* (March 1949), p.243; MI Batten, 'Personalia VII—Reginald A Rix, ARIBA', *Architectural Design and Construction*, pp.76–7.

[80] RIBA, PCM (1), (22 October 1929), fo.4.

[81] Neal Shasore, ' "A stammering bundle of Welsh idealism": Arthur Trystan Edwards and Principles of Civic Design in Interwar Britain', *Architectural History* (2018), pp.175–204.

[82] RIBA, PCM (1), (22 October 1929), inset memorandum of Reginald Rix entitled 'Architects and Publicity' (2 October 1929), fo.4.

[83] Ibid.

118   DESIGNS ON DEMOCRACY

Committee's report, submitted to Council in 1930, was, however, rejected in substance; though the premises of Rix's analysis were right, the repeated suggestion of a paid official and supervisory committee was deemed impractical 'in view of the large expenditure with which the Institute is faced in connection with new premises'.[84]

These abortive attempts to develop a publicity machine were nevertheless valuable in developing a case for a coherent policy. They demonstrate a persistent concern by powerful voices in the membership of the RIBA and from lay supporters. They are also evidence of some of the ethical issues at stake in cooperative action and collective advertising. They were, however, necessarily lower priorities than the first phase of the registration campaign and the increasingly imminent need for enlarged Institute premises. Significantly, the arguments advanced in favour of developing publicity and propaganda for architecture emerged as fundamentally linked to professional service rather than the promotion of any architectural style. Discussions of style were entirely absent in these early RIBA committees; in this regard public relations was part of a broader phenomenon of modernization, rather than promoting Modernism per se.

The origin of the RIBA's public relations function as it emerged was, in fact, an aspect of the 'consensus' culture earlier described and marked a profound paradigm shift in architectural professionalism and in the modernization and technocratization of its management. Not only has this aspect of institutional history been largely overlooked, certainly compared to developments in the 'Modernist Academy' (as Crinson and Lubbock defined it) during this period, it also exemplifies how seemingly *de novo* 'Modernist' initiatives in fact built on earlier work and wider conversations in architectural culture.[85]

The establishment of the BINC, and the Public Relations Committee which sat at its heart, made a convincing case for the Institute to develop its own analogous function, not least because the RIBA was the main promoter of the new body. It demonstrated a recognition of the wider construction industry to develop sophisticated means of publicity, both propaganda activity to potential developers, but also public affairs with governmental bodies. Both Ramsey and Robertson, central figures in the BINC, were inaugural members of the Public Relations Committee, established in May 1933.

---

[84] RIBA, PCM (1), (21 May 1930), recording a letter from Ian MacAlister to Clough Williams-Ellis (2 May 1930), fo.16.

[85] Crinson and Lubbock, *Architecture, Art or Profession?*, pp.89–156.

SLUMP   119

The BINC was one stimulus, but, as we have seen, questions about collective advertising and architectural publicity had recurred at the RIBA since the mid-1920s. In 1933, the Practice Standing Committee produced a memorandum on 'Advertising and Publicity', under three headings: Direct or Indirect Personal Advertisement by Members, which remained in the eyes of the Committee 'unprofessional and forbidden'; Direct Collective Advertisement by the RIBA and other bodies; and Indirect Collective Advertisement through lectures, publications, exhibition, and awards. The Committee recommended pursuing this line of activity in particular, and in collaboration with the CPRE. As previous reports and committees on this issue had suggested, the Memorandum recommended the establishment of a committee and a paid official to consider the issue of collective advertisement and propaganda, and the pursuit of an 'agreed line of policy for the sake of architecture, the RIBA and all its members'. Among the first actions of the new Public Relations Committee was to recommend the appointment of Eric Bird (1894–1965) as public relations officer and technical editor of the *Journal of the Royal Institute of British Architects.*[86]

Bird had been a student at the AA in the early 1920s, and then in private practice with Hubert Clist, the latter of whom would in time join the Committee. Having taught briefly back at the AA from 1928 to 1930, he then worked as assistant editor (along with Summerson) at the *Architect and Building News* before moving to the RIBA in this new and relatively senior office. His appointment was perspicacious; Bird was clearly sympathetic to the younger generation of architects entering the ranks of the RIBA—he was part of it, in fact—and his experience in private practice and architectural journalism also set him apart, along with the Institute's librarian and *Journal* editor Bobby Carter, as embodying the shift towards a more technocratic management of the Institute.

The new Committee he was taken on to administer was drawn from the progressive ranks of the profession—committed Modernists like Max Fry, RA Duncan, and later Basil Ward all participated. The coincidence of the establishment of Wells Coates' Modern Architectural Research Group (MARS) in April 1933 is notable, not least because Fry and Ward were active members.[87] Certainly this was a moment of maturation of British Modernism, but it would be mistaken to see the institution of the Public

---

[86]   RIBA, PRCM (1), fo.1.
[87]   William Whyte, 'MARS group (act.1933–1957)', *ODNB* (October 2007), https://doi.org/10.1093/ref:odnb/96308 [accessed 9 June 2020].

120   DESIGNS ON DEMOCRACY

Relations Committee as in some sense a knee-jerk reaction to this. It was anchored, as we have seen, in a much longer trajectory of professional debate, and built on the work of bodies like the BINC. The BINC was home to a number of *modernes* and modernizers; Howard Robertson was one, and on the RIBA Public Relations Committee he was joined by the likes of Charles Holloway James and John Alan Slater. Significantly, Grey Wornum, the architect of the RIBA's new premises, would also participate in the group's work. All of these men had been senior figures in the AA. John Dower was also particularly active on the group. He had been involved with the CPRE, later championing a scheme of National Parks, and at this time was a member of Political and Economic Planning group (more commonly known as PEP), along with Max Fry, and an established specialist in housing and town planning. The Committee, however, was a broad church, accommodating more established Institute figures, some of whom were representatives or chairs of the standing committees *ex officio*. These included figures such as T Alwyn Lloyd, the Garden Suburb architect, AL Roberts, 'Official Architect' to the County of Hampshire, Arthur Knapp-Fisher, newly installed Professor of Architecture at the Royal College of Art and outgoing president of the AA, and Stanley Ramsey, who had designed the pioneering Duchy of Cornwall estate in Kennington with Stanley Adshead. In this respect, the Committee's composition represented the emergent diversity of practice as a deliberate policy. Influential lay members, sympathetic to the emerging forces of British Modernism, were co-opted too, including Frank Pick and Elizabeth Denby, both of whom had experience in publicity and public relations. What united almost all of the members of the new Public Relations Committee was a specialism in social housing and planning, and this informed a great deal of their early work.

The group very quickly demonstrated a willingness to find new and effective ways of working. Max Fry submitted a report on areas 'in which architects have lost ground from a variety of causes, financial, practice, etc.'[88] RA Duncan stressed the need for the collation of 'Data and Statistics' to underpin their work. And Stanley Ramsey, showing the need for political sensitivity, produced a memorandum on the 'Detail of Operation'; the new Committee were 'Not Missionaries, Writers, Or Speakers—their chief work will be to initiate policy, watch events and inspire action in others',

---

[88] RIBA, PRCM (1), (28 June 1933), fo.5a, appended 'Memorandum by Mr E Maxwell Fry: List of subjects in which architects have lost ground from a variety of causes, financial, practical, etc.'

SLUMP   121

working through existing committees and collaborating with other bodies to effect change.[89]

There was a deliberate policy of decentralizing the work of the Committee—an innovation in the RIBA's governance. The Committee also had an effective honorary secretary in the form of Stanley Ramsey, who worked with Bird to liaise with MacAlister, the Executive Committee and the Council. By December, the Committee had organized itself into a number of standing working-groups with clear terms of reference for distinct areas of concern, led by a 'convenor' (not a chair as was conventional) who reported formally back to the main Committee. The Professional Services Sub-Committee, led by Dower, was to 'collect information on why architects' services are only utilized for a small part of the building work of this country';[90] a 'Publicity Sub-Committee', convened by RA Duncan and including Elizabeth Denby among its number, to supervise propaganda;[91] a House Design Sub-Committee, convened by Ramsey, to 'study and report on methods of improving general design, planning and layout of houses in urban and suburban areas', and a 'Panels' Sub-Committee to act as a 'liaising sub-committee between the RIBA and the CPRE.'[92] The 'panels' in question were local schemes whereby a panel of architects could be consulted for house-building programmes.[93]

The Committee pursued a number of objects through these sub-committees besides monitoring general policy. Representative of their wide-ranging remit was the taking up of the campaign for the Statutory Registration of Architects. As we have seen, this campaign was previously pursued by the Registration Committee, chaired by Harry Barnes. It was only really by the late 1920s that this committee, prompted by MacAlister, had begun to articulate and promote the public interest case for statutory protection of title, which contributed to its eventual passage into law in the 1931. It is symptomatic of the publicity paradigm shift that occurred in the early 1930s that this campaign was continued by the new Public Relations Committee. Indeed, from spring 1934, the Committee began to develop a blueprint for statutory protection of function. The Architects Registration

---

[89]   RIBA, PRCM (1), (28 June 1933), fo.6, appended memorandum by Ronald Avery Duncan, 'Data and Statistics' (25 July 1933).

[90]   RIBA, PRCM (1), (1 December 1933), fo.44.

[91]   Elizabeth Darling, '"To induce humanitarian sentiments in prurient Londoners": The Propaganda Activities of London's Voluntary Housing Associations in the Inter-War Period', *London Journal* 27.1 (1 May 2002), p.46.

[92]   RIBA, PRCM (1), (1 December 1933), fo.44.

[93]   Cf. Chapter 4.

122   DESIGNS ON DEMOCRACY

Act of 1931 had been a first step in the statutory protection of title, namely 'Registered Architect'. This meant that only architects subscribed to the register, administered by ARCUK, were legally entitled to style themselves as 'Registered Architects'. There were three remaining objectives in the Registration Campaign after this, however.

The first related to control of the register. ARCUK had been established as an independent body by Parliament with proportional representation for architectural associations, and then a number of *ex-officio* seats for other interested bodies (e.g. architecture schools and universities). The RIBA, however, had initially sought to own the register and had only ceded to the insistence of an independent registering body to quell opposition within Parliament and get the legislation passed. Privately it had a definite long-term policy of pursuing amending Acts until it achieved its original goal of total control. In the short term it sought vicarious control of the register by bolstering its membership through ensuring the largest number of seats by proportional representation and that as many of the other seats as possible (the architecture schools, etc.) were also occupied by RIBA members to ensure voting *en bloc* in the Institute's interests. The second objective was to gain statutory protection of the title 'Architect', and this was secured by the amending Act of 1938. Only qualified architects registered through ARCUK could style themselves as 'Architect'. But there was a third ambition—statutory protection of function. There were no provisions in the Architects Registration Act of 1931 (nor, as it eventuated, in 1938) enshrining the mandatory use of architects on any type of design or construction project. Architects were—and are still—not legally necessary to put up buildings, and this made—and continues to make—the professional status of the architect inherently vulnerable, in particular for public works which are either state-funded or state-aided.

The Public Relations Committee therefore proposed to lobby for the engagement of qualified architects to design and superintend all significant building works, particularly those for which public authorities were building owners, or for which they provided financial assistance by loan or subsidy. To establish the legislative principle, the Committee attempted to introduce amending clauses into the 1935 Housing Bill to make provision for large-scale public housing schemes to be supervised by 'qualified' (i.e. registered) architects. Tabled by Alfred Bossom, these were rejected.[94]

---

[94] The Housing Act 1935 was aimed at slum demolition and programmes of mass rebuilding by local authorities. It marked the reassertion of local authorities to deliver housing, and

SLUMP   123

Nevertheless, the Committee persisted, lobbying the Minister of Health and circulating letters to local authorities. Although these early efforts had little practical effect, they clearly show that the campaign for statutory protection of function for qualified architects in private practice or salaried employment was part of RIBA policy in the mid-1930s. The Public Relations Committee in 1935, indeed, circulated questionnaires to build up reliable data on how many architects were local authority employees and what the nature of their working practices was.[95] This built on earlier work by the RIBA's Official Architecture Committee, periodically revived in the early 1930s under the chairmanship of Raymond Unwin to drive forward RIBA policy in this area. Because the Architects Registration Act (1931) had defined common standards of qualification, the RIBA was in the mid-1930s able to argue more convincingly for the employment of architects of all types who had achieved those qualifications to practise.

While the campaign for statutory protection of function went no further, despite attempts by Alfred Bossom to pursue a more substantial private members bill in 1935, it was superseded by the more achievable goal of securing the protection of the title of 'Architect' in the 1938 Architects Registration Act.

Another area of growing interest in the committee was the use of broadcast media, including film and television, which sat within the province of the Publicity Sub-Committee chaired by Basil Ward. Film had been a feature of architectural communication in Britain from the early 1920s; it had been used as propaganda by voluntary housing associations, like the St Pancras House Improvement Society and the Kensington Housing Trust in which Denby had been involved. By the early 1930s, with the emergence of the documentary film movement, progressive architects and planners were also beginning to explore the use of film, and this was carried through into post-war reconstruction.[96] Film had been a subject of discussion in the

the relative diminution of housing associations. James Alfred Yelling, *Slums and Redevelopment: Policy and Practice in England, 1918–45* (1992), pp.102–5.

[95] RIBA, PRCM (2), (7 June 1935), fo.36.

[96] Toby Haggith, ' "Castles in the Air": British Film and Reconstruction of the Built Environment, 1931–1951', Ph.D. thesis, University of Warwick, 1998; Nicholas Bullock, 'Imagining the Post-War World: Architecture, Reconstruction and the British Documentary Film Movement', in François Penz and Maureen Thomas (eds.), *Cinema and Architecture: Méliès, Mallet-Stevens, Multimedia* (1997); John Gold and Stephen Ward, 'Cinematic Representations of Urban Planning and the British New Towns', in Stuart C Atiken and Leo E Zonn (eds.), *Place, Power, Situation, and Spectacle: A Geography of Film* (1994); Gold and Ward, 'Of Plans and Planners: Documentary Film and the Urban Future, 1935–1952', in David B Clarke (ed.), *The Cinematic City* (1997).

124   DESIGNS ON DEMOCRACY

Public Relations Committee from its earliest meetings, specifically by the Publicity Committee, which in February 1936 changed its name to the 'Film, Broadcasting and Television Sub-Committee'.[97] In October 1935 it had appointed a sub-committee convened by Basil Ward to work with Gaumont-British to produce five magazine films on architecture. At this time, Stanley Ramsey was also in dialogue with the British Film Institute on 'general possibilities of educational films in architecture'.[98] This culminated in Ramsey's participation in a 'Social Service Panel' at the Institute. The Publicity Committee was more broadly concerned with broadcasting in all media; Thornton White raised the issue of television in January 1936 as broadcasts 'in a vastly improved form, will soon be available'.[99] The BBC's regular television service launched in November 1936, and the Publicity Committee had initial ambitions for a half-hour programme every fortnight or twelve talks a year including exhibition photographs and specially commissioned diagrams. There was a convenient link to the television service—Gerald Cock, director of BBC Television from 1935, had a brother who was on the staff of the recently established Building Centre and known to FR Yerbury. Cock worked closely with Eustace Robb, an early experimental television producer.

Around the same time, in early 1936 the complexion of the Film, Broadcasting and Television Sub-Committee began to change. Ward proposed the documentary film maker Paul Rotha for co-option, and later Serge Chermayeff to advise on publicity literature.[100] Alongside this project, Ward, Rotha, and the Sub-Committee produced a more substantial memorandum for a 'Documentary and Instructional Film Programme', presented to the Public Relations Committee in May 1936.[101] It has been suggested that this was largely authored by Rotha, and the working-group that produced it included co-opted members from the RIBA Board of Education, among them Lionel Budden. The memorandum was essentially a pitch by the Association of Realist Film Producers, a collective which included Rotha and John Grierson. It showed how other public organizations and industrial concerns had developed documentary film content, and proposed the production of one feature-length film for the RIBA of thirty to

[97] RIBA, PRCM (2), (14 February 1936), fo.99, appended 'Report of the Publicity Sub-Committee'.

[98] RIBA, PRCM (2), (11 October 1935), fo.53.

[99] RIBA, PRCM (2), (10 January 1936), record of a letter from Thornton White to Eric Bird, fo.88.

[100] Ibid.

[101] RIBA, PRCM (3), (8 May 1936), fo.5, appended 'Memorandum for the Production of a Programme of Documentary and Instructional Films on Architecture'.

forty minutes (three to four reels) intended for public exhibition, and then a series of shorter films about architecture, the construction industry, and the built environment for private use by organizations, schools, architecture departments, the RIBA, and other affiliated bodies.[102] This initial scheme was left unfulfilled, partly because of the reluctance of HB Bryant and the BINC to provide finance for the programme, although by late 1939, Ward had secured funding for a film project from the gas industry.[103]

Conclusion

In this chapter, we have looked at two aspects of the RIBA Public Relations Committee's work in the mid- to late 1930s, the continuing campaign for statutory recognition, specifically through protection of function on publicly funded building schemes, and documentary film production. These represent both ends of the spectrum of public relations, which spanned lobbying to broadcast media. The work of the Public Relations Committee permeated the administration of the RIBA, holding significant control over important areas of policy which had previously been treated as ad hoc and assuming significant status within the Institute hierarchy. We will revisit its activities in succeeding chapters, in particular its work in promoting a 'panel' system for architects with the CPRE and the development of a bold exhibitions policy. Indeed, of all of Ward's unfulfilled grand ambitions for the use of documentary film, one idea did come to fruition. In 1936, he worked with Gaumont-British on a film which would describe the work of the RIBA itself in its new building by George Grey Wornum. Ward produced a spoken commentary with Wornum and Carter, and it was narrated by the then president of the RIBA, Percy Thomas.[104]

The emergence of the RIBA's public relations function in the mid-1930s was a significant episode in the development of the Institute, and in professional practice more widely. This brief account has placed it in its full context. It was not conceived as a Modernist reform programme per se. Although it coincided with the maturation of a number of impulses in British Modernism, it was in fact connected to a much wider set of modernizing

---

[102] Ibid.; cf. Haggith, '"Castles in the Air"', pp.45–52.   [103] Ibid., p.187.

[104] 'The RIBA Film', *JRIBA* (8 August 1936), p.960. Earlier film had been taken on the building's opening. See RIBA, PRCM (1), (9 November 1934), fo.108. It has not been possible to locate footage from either film.

126 DESIGNS ON DEMOCRACY

tendencies, a much longer series of discussions not only about the nature of professional status but also about the nature of publicity and public relations themselves. It is striking that the history of the Public Relations Committee has been by-passed in Modernists' own accounts of architectural culture in the 1930s, despite the fact it brought them right to the heart of the architectural establishment. This hardly coincidental omission underlines that the oppositional language between Modernists and Traditionalists was over-played for rhetorical effect.

3

Machine-Craft

Forging Public Institutions

Introduction

The *Architectural Review* had shown little interest in the competition for the new premises of the Royal Institute of British Architects (RIBA) concluded in May 1932. The magazine's June issue was devoted largely to Elisabeth Scott's recently opened Shakespeare Memorial Theatre at Stratford, and included a dismissive overview of the competition in its 'Marginalia' section. Reluctantly, if not sarcastically, congratulating the winner Grey Wornum and the other premiated competitors on their designs, it also quoted a number of press sources picked out for being particularly bland and non-committal in their analysis. It reproduced Wornum's statement to the *Sunday Times*: 'I sought to create something that would be a bridge between the extreme modern and the classic examples of architecture';[1] and to the *Daily Mail*: 'I have tried to compromise between the traditional and the modern.'[2] It further undermined the competition by including quotations from figures such as the arts and literature critic Raymond Mortimer, who remarked on seeing the submitted designs: 'I knew that contemporary architecture was in a bad way, but I had not realized quite how bad.'[3] There were private condemnations too; a young William Holford wrote to his contemporary, the planner Gordon Stephenson, that 'the RIBA comp [*sic*] has been won, (as you will have seen), by a building which complies with the bye-laws and hasn't a damn thing else to recommend it unless it be a staircase on which the high officials of the RIBA will cut important figures on their way to and from their epoch-making discussions.'[4]

---

[1] 'Marginalia', *AR* (May 1932), p.258.   [2] Ibid.   [3] Ibid.
[4] University of Liverpool Archives, D147/P17/1/1, William Holford to 'Robert' [Gordon Stephenson] (2 May 1932). I am grateful to Patrick Zamarian for drawing my attention to this quotation.

Designs on Democracy: Architecture and the Public in Interwar London. Neal Shasore, Oxford University Press.
© Neal Shasore 2022. DOI: 10.1093/oso/9780192849724.003.0004

128   DESIGNS ON DEMOCRACY

These disparaging comments, Holford's in particular, reflected not just a stylistic or formal dislike of the design, but also a cynicism about an Institute which could be remote, haughty, and 'oligarchical'.[5] In all of this, as the *AR*'s initial review of the competition suggested, *style*—and certainly the idea of stylistic compromise—was an important but second-order issue. To de-centre style and discuss not only the design but also the wider processes and discourses which brought the building into being, is to understand the project's significance to the development of the architectural profession in Britain during this period, and its role in defining a new relationship with the public.

The tone of the *AR*'s coverage might well be taken as representative of the increasingly zealous Modernism of its editorial policy in the early 1930s. At the time of the building's opening, however, the *Review* gave over its entire December issue of 1934 to the Institute's new headquarters. What had caused this *volte-face*? The special issue was bold and thorough in its coverage. It included a foreword by the incumbent RIBA president, Giles Gilbert Scott,[6] a short history of the Institute by Maurice Webb, chairman of the RIBA New Premises Committee and son of the late Aston Webb,[7] and an account of the new building by Charles Herbert Reilly.[8] Elaborate headpieces to the articles were designed by the architectural draughtsman Myerscough-Walker, and the issue was richly illustrated with photographs by the notable partnership of Dell & Wainwright, who had become the *Review*'s photographers in 1930.[9] Twenty-seven of their photographs were used for a series of twenty-five plates (thirty-four photographs in total) of the new building and its interior in the centre of the issue.[10] An editor's note at the beginning encouraged the reader 'to imagine that he is behind a movie camera mounted on a truck which is making a photographic record of the building…Read as a consecutive series rather than as isolated shots, they should give something of the effect of a film, so that those who have not seen the building can get a reasonably accurate idea both of the different parts and relation of each part to the other.'[11]

---

[5] Alexander Morris Carr-Saunders and Paul Alexander Wilson, *The Professions* (Oxford, 1933), p.185.

[6] Giles Gilbert Scott, 'Foreword', *AR* (December 1934), p.189.

[7] Maurice Webb, 'A Century of Progress', *AR* (December 1934), pp.190–1.

[8] Charles Herbert Reilly, 'Grey Wornum and His Building', *AR* (December 1932), pp.192–4.

[9] Robert Elwall, *Photography Takes Command: The Camera and British Architecture 1890–1939* (1994), pp.66–77.

[10] *AR* (December 1934). All the photographs used in the sequence were by Dell & Wainwright, except for plates viii (A), x (B), xi (C), xiv (B), xix (B), xx (B), xxv (C) (as noted on p.195 of the *AR*), and are located between pp.202 and 203.

[11] *AR* (December 1934), p.202.

This quasi-filmic experience of the new building was a conceit which drew both on newsreel and documentary. It was deployed to heighten the essentially modern attributes not only of the building and the magazine but also of the Institute itself. The first plate (Fig. 3.1) was a view looking 'down Portland Place', approaching from north of the site, showing the main

Fig. 3.1 *AR* (December 1934), plate ii, image courtesy of the Museum of Domestic Design & Architecture, Middlesex University, http://www.moda.mdx.ac.uk

130   DESIGNS ON DEMOCRACY

façade of the building. The façade to Portland Place, three bays wide, dominated by a large central window above the doorway, is flanked by a pair of castellated pylons (borrowed from the RIBA badge), each surmounted by a primordial sculpted figure by James Woodford—a creative architectural force—woman on the left, man on the right, with drawing equipment by their feet. The building was of four storeys above a basement: a rusticated ground floor, a tall *piano nobile*, and a further two storeys above. At the level of the upper storey, beneath the shallow, simple projecting cornice, the monumental carved figure relief of 'Architectural Aspiration' by Bainbridge Copnall stretches upwards.

The camera then 'swings round' to the upper part of the Weymouth Street elevation. The large gap between the second- and third-floor fenestration, so stark on the Portland Place façade, was here alternated with figures in carved relief on the central bays, representing the archetypal figures of the Sculptor, the Painter, the Architect (in the form of Sir Christopher Wren), the Mechanic, and the Artisan, all carved by Copnall. The balcony and three of Copnall's figures, including Wren, are picked out by the particularly cinematic photograph on Plate v of the *AR*'s sequence (Fig. 3.2), showing a dramatic view from the roof-top of a neighbouring building to the south of the site. The camera then moves back to the Portland Place façade, zooming in on the pair of large cast-bronze entrance doors (Fig. 3.3), each 12 feet by 6 feet, designed by James Woodford, and depicting, as contemporary press accounts described, 'London's river and its buildings'. The Thames snakes up both doors, its flow interrupted by superimposed depictions of monuments such as Guildhall, the Palace of Westminster, John Rennie's Waterloo Bridge, the former RIBA headquarters on Conduit Street, St James's Palace, St Paul's Cathedral, Charing Cross Railway Bridge, Horse Guards, a tube tunnel, and a London County Council tenement. The careful linear designs of the buildings were rendered by the draughtsman and perspectivist JDM Harvey. The door handles carry the arms of the Borough of St Marylebone and Lord Howard de Walden, the ground landlord.

Focus then switches to the interior of the building, to two shots of the entrance hall (Fig. 3.4). The first looks back to the entrance, showing the four plate-glass inner doors, and the Perrycot stone-lined walls of the entrance hall, now inscribed with the names of past presidents and gold medallists in lettering designed by Percy Smith. The second looks towards the two electric lifts, with the main staircase off to the right. After a look around the Henry Jarvis Memorial Hall (Fig. 3.5)—the entrance on the half-storey down to the basement—the camera returns to the entrance lobby before ascending the main staircase (Fig. 3.6). Lit by illuminated

Fig. 3.2 *AR* (December 1934), plate v, image courtesy of the Museum of Domestic Design & Architecture, Middlesex University, http://www.moda.mdx.ac.uk

glass coffers, the staircase is bounded by four enormous star-plan columns, steel stanchions cased in dark Ashburton marble which rise up to the second floor of the building. 'From worm's eye to a bird's eye',[12] Dell & Wainwright's sequence switches, characteristically, from a dramatic look

---

[12] *AR* (December 1923), plate xvi.

Fig. 3.3 *AR* (December 1934), plate vii, images courtesy of the Museum of Domestic Design & Architecture, Middlesex University, http://www.moda.mdx.ac.uk

up to a vertiginous look down the staircase void (Fig. 3.7). The camera proceeds into the Florence Memorial Hall, giving a glimpse of Woodford's plaster reliefs on the ceiling, showing various building trades employed in the construction and ornamentation of the building, and incorporating portraits of known craftspeople (Fig. 3.8). Exiting the hall, it stops again at the side staircase that carries visitors to the upper floors of the building

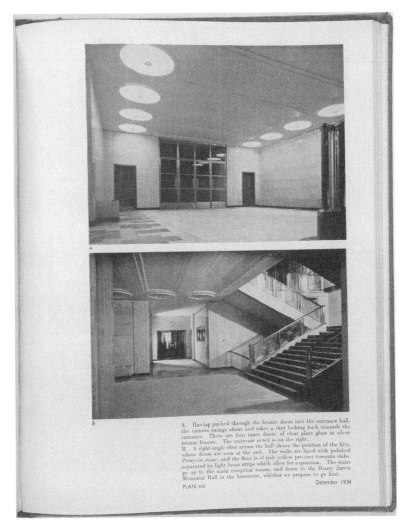

Fig. 3.4 AR (December 1934), plate viii, image courtesy of the Museum of Domestic Design & Architecture, Middlesex University, http://www.moda.mdx.ac.uk

(Fig. 3.9), splicing between day- and night-time views, showing off the new and easy capability of electric lighting, reflected also in the specially designed floodlighting of the main façade by Waldo Maitland.[13] Round the

---

[13] Ruth Hommelen, 'Building with Artificial Light: Architectural Night Photography in the Inter-war Period', *Journal of Architecture* 21.7 (November 2016), pp.1062–99.

134   DESIGNS ON DEMOCRACY

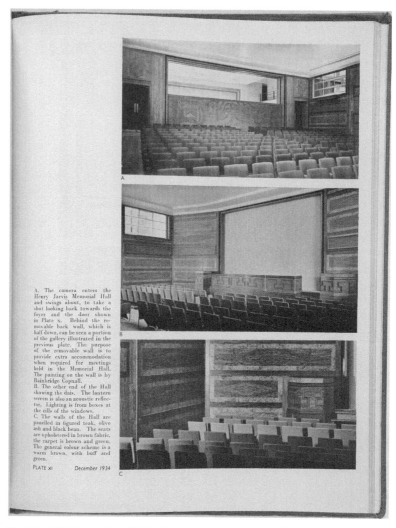

Fig. 3.5 *AR* (December 1934), plate xi, image courtesy of the Museum of Domestic Design & Architecture, Middlesex University, http://www.moda.mdx.ac.uk

jamb and soffit of the opening are representations of the tools and machinery used to construct the building in cream lap with gold leafing. Thenceforth, the camera shows the rest of the main interior spaces—reception rooms, the leather-panelled Aston Webb committee room, the Library (Fig. 3.10), the upper-floor landing, including glass etchings by

Fig. 3.6 *AR* (December 1934), plate xiv, image courtesy of the Museum of Domestic Design & Architecture, Middlesex University, http://www.moda.mdx.ac.uk

Raymond McGrath's office,[14] before three concluding views of the wood-panelled Council Chamber on the upper storey of the building, the heart of the Institute's governance (Fig. 3.11).

---

[14] Apocryphally, these are said to have been executed by Gordon Cullen, then working for McGrath.

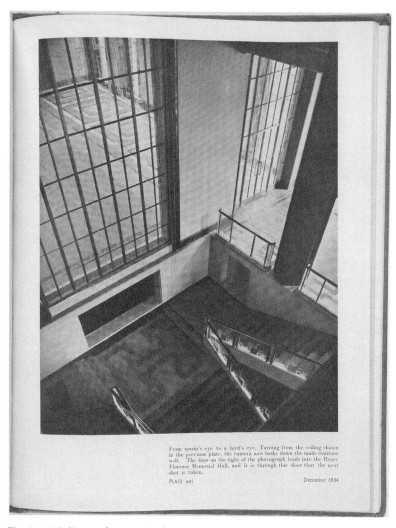

Fig. 3.7 *AR* (December 1934), plate xvi, image courtesy of the Museum of Domestic Design & Architecture, Middlesex University, http://www.moda.mdx.ac.uk

The sequence featured many of the hallmarks of Dell & Wainwright's photographic style;[15] the transparency of the building's interiors, the quality of the plan, and the variety of functions it accommodated were all shown to

---

[15] Elwall, *Photography Takes Command*, pp.66–77; Valeria Carullo, 'Image Makers of British Modernism: Dell & Wainwright at the *Architectural Review*', *Journal of Architecture* 21.7 (November 2016), pp.1012–32.

Fig. 3.8 *AR* (December 1934), plate xvii, image courtesy of the Museum of Domestic Design & Architecture, Middlesex University, http://www.moda.mdx.ac.uk

great effect. The coverage of the RIBA building reflected the *AR*'s experimental editorial policy, enlivening text with ambitious photography, typography, and layout to accentuate the modernity of both the subject matter and the *Review*'s own way of seeing it. Readers were not to look through the photographs as isolated shots, but instead to imagine a sequence of moving

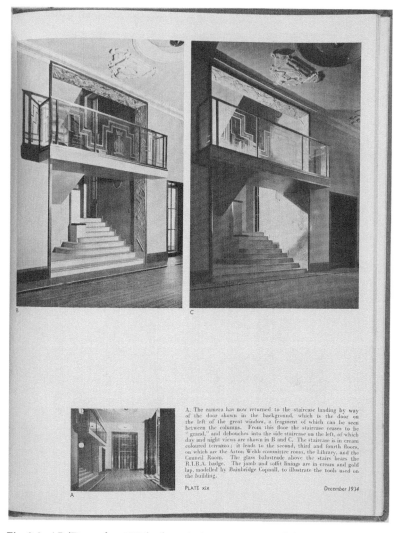

Fig. 3.9 *AR* (December 1934), plate xix, image courtesy of the Museum of Domestic Design & Architecture, Middlesex University, http://www.moda.mdx.ac.uk

pictures: the use of the film sequence motif was a visuospatial metaphor, seemingly without precedent. Notice, for instance, how the viewer was asked to imagine not that they were merely watching a film, but rather that 'he is behind a movie camera mounted on a truck'—in other words, part of the making of the film, loosely quoting the opening scenes of Vertov's *Man*

Fig. 3.10 *AR* (December 1934), plate xxi, image courtesy of the Museum of Domestic Design & Architecture, Middlesex University, http://www.moda.mdx.ac.uk

with a Movie Camera (1929). The sequence presumes a filmic imagination, inviting the reader actively to fill in the gaps between the static shots, drawing on and heightening known tropes of film construction and allowing smoother and more ambitious leaps and movements from one tableau to another.

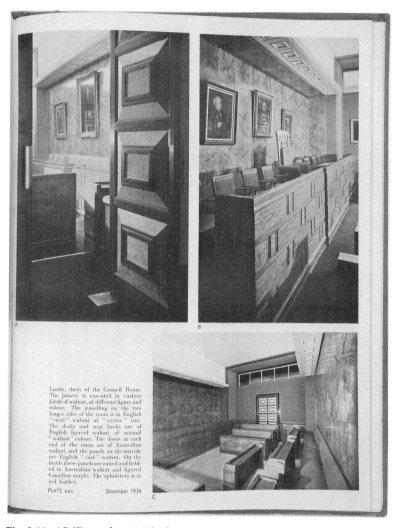

Fig. 3.11 *AR* (December 1934), plate xxv, image courtesy of the Museum of Domestic Design & Architecture, Middlesex University, http://www.moda.mdx.ac.uk

The motif of the film sequence was connected to something much more significant happening not just in the editorial strategy of the *AR*, but in the policy and development of the RIBA itself. The *AR* was careful to express a note of thanks to Eric Bird, the RIBA's recently appointed public relations officer.[16] The answer, then, to what had changed between the derisory coverage of the RIBA's competition, and the lavishness afforded to the building's opening, was that the Institute had started to take control of its image and messages, in short to understand the increasingly sophisticated language and techniques of public relations and propaganda. The design and construction of its new headquarters presented a particularly rich opportunity to present the Institute and its workings to a wide professional and lay audience.

By the mid-1930s the RIBA had begun to engage fully with the possibilities of documentary film in close consultation with the documentary filmmaker Paul Rotha. Rotha had connections with the *AR*, but these had almost certainly developed through his interaction with the DIA. The DIA had championed documentary film-making a little earlier in order to enhance the medium's role in developing techniques of salesmanship and public relations, pioneered by Tallents's and Grierson's relationship first at the Empire Marketing Board (EMB) and then at the General Post Office.[17] A still from Rotha's *The Face of Britain* was used as the cover for the Design and Industries Association's (DIA) revived publication, *Design To-Day* in January 1935, and included an article by Rotha on the film.[18] He contributed a further article on 'The Rise of Documentary' in August of the same year. The documentary film motif used by the *AR* therefore connects the RIBA, its new premises, and public relations function, to the progressive wing of the DIA, particularly figures like John Gloag, an intellectual disciple of Lawrence Weaver, who by this time was one of the editors of *Design To-Day* and who had a long association with the DIA. The RIBA building expressed, in subtle ways, the 'DIA point of view' discussed in the first chapter with important links to the design reform movement.

Artifex

'Machine-craft' was coined by the journalist and public relations expert John Gloag (Fig. 3.12).[19] A design reformer, Gloag had received some

---

[16] *AR* (December 1934), p.195.   [17] Anthony, *Public Relations*.

[18] Paul Rotha, 'The Face of Britain', *Design for To-Day* 3.21 (January 1935), pp.13–19; Rotha, 'The Rise of Documentary', *Design for To-Day* 3.28 (August 1935), pp.313–17.

[19] Despite Gloag's significance, he has received very little scholarly attention. Glenn Hooper, 'English Modern: John Gloag and the Challenge of Design', *Journal of Design History* 28.4 (November 2015), pp.368–84; Julian Holder, '"Design in Everyday Things": Promoting

Fig. 3.12 John Gloag, photographer and date unknown, PP.8.17.1, Pritchard Papers, University of East Anglia

architectural training at the Regent Street Polytechnic before the war, although he never practised, and later worked as a buyer for Heal's before editing the *Cabinetmaker*. The expression 'machine-craft' appeared prominently in his essay for the *To-day and To-morrow* series, *Artifex, or the future of craftsmanship* (1926).[20] Here, Gloag argued that the nineteenth-century Ruskinian critique of labour had created a 'false idea of a war between craftsmanship and machinery'.[21] Initially this led to the eschewal of the machine in Arts and Crafts discourse. The twentieth-century reaction had been to suggest 'that civilisation might dispense with craftsmanship altogether'.[22] In fact, this antagonism was a falsehood: 'both the hand craftsman and the manufacturers are craftsmen'.[23] Gloag therefore proposed the idea of 'machine-craft' as a future synthesis of the qualities of handcraft and the efficiency of manufacture to describe a new ideal for industrial design. This was an English interpretation of the ideals of the Svenska Slöjdföreningen and the Deutscher Werkbund:

Modernism in Britain 1912-1944' in Paul Greenhalgh (ed.), *Modernism in Design* (1990), pp.123-44.
[20] John Gloag, *Artifex; or, The Future of Craftsmanship* (1926). [21] Ibid., p.39.
[22] Ibid. [23] Ibid.

The practically progressive nations, such as Sweden and Germany, may set an example to the rest of the world by solving industrial problems, and achieving perfect compatibility between handcraft and machine-craft.[24]

'Machine-craft' was a phrase Gloag continued to deploy in his writings into the 1930s. In 1934—the same year that 66 Portland Place opened—he published *Industrial Art Explained*, in which he again decried the disunion of handcraft and manufacture, and the failure of the promise of machine-craft in furniture design.[25] The phrase articulated the enduring but modernising Arts and Crafts conception of architectural practice in the increasingly technocratic political economy of the twentieth century, expressing a distinctive set of attitudes to design and professionalism. The 'lesser arts', as Morris had defined them, continued to be sublated into architecture in this discourse; this was indeed part of the design reform paradigm discussed in relation to the British Empire Exhibition (BEE).[26] Gloag, like Weaver, was therefore active in—though often respectfully critical of—the DIA in the 1920s and 1930s, serving as its chairman in 1926, and proselytizing for its causes, 'the liveliest of activists on the Council' as Noel Carrington would later recall.[27] Gloag was also closely connected to progressive architectural culture; he had a friendship with Wornum, no doubt in part born of their mutual admiration of Weaver, but with many others too in and around the RIBA and later the Modern Architectural Research Group (MARS). His ideal of 'machine-craft' encapsulated a shared ambition among professional modernizers of this period.

Industrial Art Explained was, as Gloag explained in its introduction, 'directly and indirectly concerned with putting a case for the employment of architects in far more departments of design than building'.[28] Gloag argued that industrialization had had three primary influences on the practice of design broadly conceived: firstly, on industrial architecture, i.e. the accommodation of industry, which in turn had profoundly 'influenced modern architectural design', which we might interpret as 'functionalism'; secondly, on industrial arts, i.e. the products of industry, which we would now term 'industrial design'; and finally, on commercial art, the distribution of these products to the public through advertising materials, packaging, etc.[29] In all

---

[24] Ibid., p.57.
[25] John Gloag, *Industrial Art Explained* (1934).
[26] Saler, *Avant-Garde in Interwar England*, pp.61–91.
[27] Noel Carrington, *Industrial Design in Britain* (1976), p.91.
[28] Gloag, *Industrial Art*, p.24.   [29] Ibid., p.33.

144   DESIGNS ON DEMOCRACY

of these activities, Gloag argued, architects had a central role to play, and this conception was made manifest through Lawrence Weaver's 'arts of display' at the Empire Exhibition and Olympia.

'Machine-craft' therefore encompassed a view of the world of design prevalent within an influential and progressive milieu of architects and designers, a number of whom were in Weaver's network of patronage and on the RIBA Public Relations Committee. Grey Wornum was one of many involved in a series of spatial and material transformations undertaken by the RIBA in the 1920s and 1930s, culminating in its new premises at 66 Portland Place. The expanded 'DIA point of view', in other words, permeated the commissioning, designing, construction, and use of the RIBA's new headquarters. Portland Place exemplifies this aspiration; indeed, it was praised by contemporaries as cathedral-like in its holistic integration of architecture, the building crafts, and decoration, a familiar trope in Arts and Crafts discourse.

'Machine-craft' captured this aspiration to marry handcraft and the artistic expression of the craftsman with a technical and economic understanding of the role of the machine in manufacture—of buildings and their construction, but crucially also the things inside buildings, their interior decoration, ornamentation, furniture, fixtures, and fittings. As is well known, contemporaries across the Continent felt themselves to be living through a 'machine-age', and the metaphor of the machine invoked efficiency and functionalism, in terms of both the production and use of the objects of industrial and architectural design.[30] 'Machine-craft', therefore, expressed an English conception of a transnational practice and discourse attempting to reconcile design with the possibilities afforded by late industrialization and growing consumer culture.

But it did yet more than that. Progressive thought for the generation of architects active in the last decade of the nineteenth century had also centred round the contested notion of 'craft', significantly in relation to a wider conversation about professionalization. The Memorialists, led by Norman Shaw and TG Jackson, defended the value of 'art' in architectural education and practice. Art for these dissenters was 'both the facility of design and the ability to foster the building crafts', rather than a defence of the architect as the 'fount of fine art expression: the Soanian type'.[31] In the

---

[30] Reyner Banham, *Theory and Design in the First Machine Age* (1960).
[31] Mark Crinson and Jules Lubbock, *Architecture: Art or Profession?* (Manchester, 1994), p.62.

MACHINE-CRAFT 145

volume of essays they published in 1892, *Architecture: A Profession or an Art?*, marking their disapproval of the campaign for statutory registration and examined standards of qualification, WR Lethaby discussed the 'rejoining of the intellectual and manual aspects of architecture', lamenting the divorce of craft from design and its relationship 'with real processes and materials'.[32]

Although their immediate objects failed, the Memorialist channelling of this Ruskinian theme continued to influence debate, practice, and professionalism as well as education and curriculum in the early twentieth century. Significantly for our purposes, it contextualizes Gloag's invocation—even reclamation—of 'craft' as no longer inimical to professionalism. 'Machine', meanwhile, evoked modernity, efficiency, and technical proficiency, and 'machine-craft' an attempt at reconciling the art of architecture to its new technocratic and industrial professional demands. This apparently oxymoronic phrase of Gloag's therefore captures both the technocratic and the mechanistic as well as the material and decorative. There was no longer a choice between 'a profession or an art', as the Memorialists had seemed to suggest (indeed, if ever such a binary meaningfully existed),[33] but a rhetorical imperative for the architect to articulate this resolution in practice. Grey Wornum's education and career were reflective of this perceived, indeed sometimes awkward, resolution and it is expressed—not always entirely successfully—in the design, construction, ornamentation, and use of 66 Portland Place. This tension defined the practice of Grey Wornum and his circle much more than any stylistic dilemma expressed in the language of the 'middle-line'.

This chapter explores 66 Portland Place and Wornum's practice through this tension first and foremost. The intellectual connections between Gloag and Wornum were strong, in part mediated by personal and professional collaborations with Weaver. Wornum lived on the same road as Weaver, and later asked him to act as godfather to his youngest daughter. Weaver gave Wornum an important early commission in designing the Haig Homes in Morden, and after his death Wornum designed the Lawrence Weaver Memorial Hall on that estate.[34] Clearly, Wornum was interested in the late Arts and Crafts; he met Oliver Hill at an Architectural Association (AA)

---

[32] Ibid., p.63.
[33] Alan Powers, 'Architectural Education in Britain 1880–1914', Ph.D. thesis, University of Cambridge (1982), p.35.
[34] 'The Lawrence Weaver Institute, Morden', *ABN* (6 January 1933), pp.10–13.

146   DESIGNS ON DEMOCRACY

visit to Lutyens's Deanery Gardens, Sonning in 1909—a commission for Edward Hudson of *Country Life*.[35] Both Wornum and Weaver admired and wrote on ornamental plasterwork.[36] Wornum's master at the AA was Hugh Maule, who worked closely with Weaver on the Land Settlement programme. Gloag and Weaver's relationship was also clearly a significant one; Gloag wrote his obituary and spoke of his influence in *Industrial Art Explained*.[37] Gloag and Wornum themselves later collaborated on a book about prefabrication, *House Out of Factory*, in 1946.[38]

Wornum was clearly in sympathy with the new currents of thinking in industrial design and their implications for architecture, which was Gloag's theme in the 1920s and 1930s. Here he is quoted at length, discussing decoration and furnishing in terms closely analogous to Gloag's conception of 'machine-craft', though proposing a different relationship between standardization and high specification:

> We have in this country some of the finest craftsmen in the world, and in their executive ability they are no less able than at any period of our island history. They want organising, and encouraging. You can help the organising by demanding a higher standard of taste from the mass producers. You can get in touch with these craftsmen through your architect who should control and co-ordinate them. You can encourage them by giving orders for specially designed articles in your 'made to measure' homes.[39]

He discussed the importance of the possibility of the machine for these purposes and its saturation in contemporary life:

> ...contact with machinery in some form is constant in our daily life. This contact is so close and so frequent that actual sentiment is aroused in us by geometric forms suggesting machine parts, whether a wheel, a nut, or a discarded safety razor blade.[40]

---

[35] RIBA, Grey Wornum Papers, WoG/1, Miriam Wornum, *Grey Matter: Book II*, p.2.
[36] George Grey Wornum, 'Mr George P Bankart and his Work', *AJ* (12 October 1927), pp.470–2; Wornum, 'Mr George P Bankart and his Work', *AJ* (26 October 1927), pp.536–8. Lawrence Weaver, *Tradition and Modernity in Plasterwork* (1928).
[37] Gloag, *Industrial Art*, p.84.
[38] John Gloag and George Grey Wornum, *House out of Factory* (1946).
[39] WFPC, Typescript of lecture: 'Decoration and Furnishing' (22 February 1930), p.8. From a series of lectures at the AA.
[40] Ibid., p.5.

Although there are other ways of reading the building, 'machine-craft' allows us to explore how these ideas and tensions relating to both design practice and professionalism were embedded in Wornum's design paradigm and encoded in Portland Place's spaces, functions, and surfaces. If the previous chapter established a discursive context, the present one maps this onto a particular case study. What emerges is a much richer and historically located understanding of the RIBA and the new home it built for itself.

The next sections of the chapter look at these two aspects of Wornum's practice. The first is his profound interest in 'craft' and the decorative, in particular for a set of interiors in the 1920s. The second picks up the 'machine' side through an excursus on the establishment of the Building Centre in 1932, which has hitherto unexplored rich connections to the RIBA's new premises. Having grown out of the AA Materials Bureau, established in 1928, the Centre's Board of Directors comprised largely AA men, counting among their number Robert Atkinson, Maurice Webb, and Grey Wornum—in other words, competition assessor, client liaison, and lead designer for 66 Portland Place. This is a crucial coincidence which has never been explored.

The Centre itself was a quintessential example of the tension evoked by 'machine-craft': on the one hand, technocratic and functional, providing data and analysis to inform the architect and his client, and on the other, celebrating craft and materiality. It exhibited a set of carefully composed displays of building and finishing materials and techniques, some of which were designed by Wornum himself, which sought to extend notions of craft to relative technological novelties like neon lighting design. It also hosted important revivals of what were felt to be dying handcrafts like hand-painted inn signs in 1936, initiated as part of a wider move towards rejuvenating rural amenities, championed by luminaries like Sir Guy Dawber, Sir Edwin Lutyens, and the public house architect Basil Oliver.[41]

Wornum reflected this tension in his designs for the RIBA's new premises at Portland Place. Machine-craft manifested itself literally in the symbolism of the ornamental programme he devised with a team of sculptors, but also in the construction and furnishing of the building itself. The chapter also looks at the building in use, focusing on the administrative functions which coalesced around the Library, intended as a tool of the new technocratic management of the profession. The concluding section looks briefly at the

---

[41] 'Famous Inn Signs', *The Times* (22 October 1936), p.19 and 'Inn Signs Old and New', *The Times* (3 November 1936), p.8. Cf. 'Designers of Inn Signs', *The Times* (26 June 1937), p.11.

second major exhibition to be held at Portland Place, 'Everyday Things' in 1936. This was another DIA theme which John Gloag popularized through wireless broadcasts and publications. Crucially, both Wornum and Gloag were involved in the exhibition organization. The chapter closes by reflecting on the emerging discourse of 'everyday things' in progressive architectural circles in the 1930s.

Chinese Papers

Grey Wornum (Fig. 3.13) met his American wife Miriam Gerstle (Fig. 3.14) in the summer of 1922 at a *thé dansant*. In her recollection, as she crossed a room to present her hostess Julie Hunter-Gray with a gift, she dropped a bundle of Chinese papers—'emerald green, vermillion and gold'—scattering them across the parquet flooring. Perhaps procured from the thriving Chinese community in her home city of San Francisco, they could also have

Fig. 3.13 George Grey Wornum, photograph by Bassano Ltd (1934), NPG x151237, © National Portrait Gallery, London

Fig. 3.14 Miriam Wornum painting the fixed shutters in the Members' Room of 66 Portland Place, photographer unknown (c.1934), Wornum Family Private Collection

been acquired during a visit to China and the Far East earlier that year. Wornum leapt to her assistance and this serendipitous first encounter led to a further meeting over tea the following day to look at more sample papers. In late August 1922, she sent another bundle for Wornum's perusal, presumably for use on a project.[42]

In the early 1920s, Wornum's burgeoning independent practice had led to a series of interior decoration projects which used Chinese papers, chinoiserie, and other eighteenth-century-inspired panels and mural decorations. He developed a particular speciality in the interior design of dance halls, an emerging typology associated with the 'dance craze' of the 1920s, itself part of a wider post-war 'democratisation of pleasure'.[43] At Derby,

[42] WFPC, Letter from Miriam Gerstle to George Grey Wornum (25 August 1922). Cf. *JRIBA* (November 1934), p.85.
[43] James Nott, 'Dance Halls: Towards an Architectural and Spatial History, c.1918–65', *AH* 61 (2018), pp.205–33, p.213.

150 DESIGNS ON DEMOCRACY

Wornum redecorated the Palais de Danse in 1921, creating a 'colourful and "refined" interior' demonstrating 'the level of glamour in leading dance halls'.[44] Wornum used eighteenth-century-style panel decoration, applying 'hand-made marble and other papers, and water-colour life-size costume figures painted on drawing-paper, cut out, pasted to the walls, and then sized and varnished'.[45] He collaborated with the interior designer Walpole Champneys, who had worked with Robert Atkinson on the interiors of his celebrated Regents Cinema, Queen's Road, Brighton. At Derby, the deep blue of the ceiling was punctuated by painted stars, echoing—even anticipating—the 'atmospherics' of contemporary cinema design, the 'night sky' motif in particular popularized by Gunnar Asplund's Skandia Cinema in Stockholm opened in 1923.

Two years later, Wornum redesigned the King's Hall Bournemouth, a dance hall adjoining the Royal Bath Hotel. Here once again decorative papers, including chinoiserie, were used extensively. As Wornum described:

> I have obtained from East and West a collection of fancy papers, nearly all hand-made or hand-printed, which for richness and transparency of colour cannot be equalled in any way by stippled paint. I first made use of these papers two years ago [at Derby], because I found tempera and distemper not strong enough for the wear and tear of entertainment places, and their use is by no means prohibitive in cost.[46]

Bournemouth was another rich interior: the lounge and waiting room were 'composed in the form of large tapestry panels based on a study of French seventeenth-century designs' and the lobby included 'red marble paper broken with gold and black', with 'large cartouches of pale yellow marble paper'.[47] Figure decoration in the main hall was designed by 'Miss Penrose-Thackwell and Mr Gilroy. A good deal of trouble was taken in the study of costumes and pastimes of the eighteenth century, though definite period work was not strictly adhered to.'[48]

In 1925, Wornum once again used 'the application of coloured printed papers, assisted by hand-printing' for the redecoration of a house in the West End.[49] A decorative panel in the drawing room—seemingly in the

---

[44] Ibid., p.224.
[45] George Grey Wornum, 'An Essay in Decoration: A Ballroom by G G Wornum', *AR* (July 1923), p.25; *The Architect* (25 April 1924), pp.299, 301, 302, 309.
[46] Wornum, 'Essay in Decoration', p.30.   [47] Ibid., pp.26, 30.   [48] Ibid., p.30.
[49] PL Dickinson, 'Some Thoughts on Modern Architecture', *The Architect* (30 October 1925), pp.313–16.

hand of Miriam Wornum—depicted two herons on a craggy rock, with stylized waves lapping at its base in a chinoiserie style.[50] Miriam also painted a safety curtain for the proscenium of Welwyn Garden City Theatre in 1928, designed by Wornum's former partner Louis De Soissons with AW Kenyon. A parochial fantasy—it showed 'a house on a cliff with an adaptation of the Welwyn crest, a fish in the sea'[51]—it nonetheless also invoked Chinese wallpapers.

Wornum's early interiors exemplify the 'modern Swedish rococo' taste of neo-Georgian interiors recently described by Clare Taylor.[52] That expression was coined by Christopher Hussey in relation to the decoration of Virginia Courtauld's bedroom at Eltham Palace. As Taylor suggests, 'The Classical, chinoiserie and rococo were all pressed into service' of the neo-Georgian interior, 'sometimes with apparent authenticity of copies or actual salvaged examples, and sometimes by reinterpreting eighteenth-century aesthetic devices in new finishes and materials.'[53] Jane Stevenson has also recently discussed 'Chinese Wallpaper' as exemplary of rococo taste in the interwar years, noting its use at Knole and at the Courtaulds' London townhouse on North Audley Street.[54]

Two important aspects of Wornum's practice are demonstrated by this early work: firstly, the importance of the partnership with his wife, and secondly, the centrality of interior design and craftsmanship to his work, which were later made manifest in his designs for the RIBA. Both problematize assumptions about gender and architectural design in the interwar years. Taylor and Stevenson have explored the associations of camp and effeminacy in relation to chinoiserie and the rococo of interwar interiors. Understanding Wornum's practice in this context counteracts a perception that these were somehow secondary to the housing developments or larger-scale public works which typified his later practice; they were in fact fundamental, and indeed enriched these projects. But whereas Miriam Wornum has been acknowledged because of her gender as the author of the interiors and fittings of buildings designed by her husband, in fact these were collaborations, and work in which Wornum was himself profoundly interested. For Miriam Wornum the injection of humanity into interior spaces was a necessary

---

[50] Ibid., p.314.   [51] '40-ft. picture by a woman', *Daily Mail* (7 April 1928), p.11.
[52] Clare Taylor, '"Modern Swedish Rococo": The Neo-Georgian Interior in Britain, c.1920–c.1945' in Julian Holder and Elizabeth McKellar (eds.), *Neo-Georgian Architecture 1880–1970: A Reappraisal* (Swindon, 2016), p.156.
[53] Ibid., p.157.
[54] Jane Stevenson, *Baroque Between the Wars: Alternative Style in the Arts, 1918–1939* (Oxford, 2018), pp.168–96, p.187.

152 DESIGNS ON DEMOCRACY

challenge to the increasingly ascetic—and implicitly, masculine—architecture of Le Corbusier and his followers: 'They give us a plain box and ask us to believe it is the "last word" of the Spirit of the Age. I don't think it is. I think this age is as rich in romance, beauty, colour, and subtlety, in living and thinking, as any age that came before it. Richer in fact...'[55] It is a consummate irony that the building has over several decades been 'masculinized' to conform to notions of a Modernist machismo in the stripping out of much of the Wornums' decorative detail.

We know from Wornum's published writings how fundamental decoration and ornament were to his practice. In this he had much in common with Oliver Hill, with whom he briefly shared an office and then maintained a lifelong friendship—Wornum later wrote that the 'quality and ambition of his work put me under a kind spell'.[56] Wornum, like Hill, had a tendency toward the exuberant, revelling in colour and material. In 1928, for instance, he addressed the AA general meeting on 'Modern Decoration', in which he stressed the importance of lighting and ornament, and defined what he described as 'the "representational idea"' of decoration, determined by what the 'public wants'.[57] Indeed, he also stressed the imperative for the architect to understand 'the potentiality of the observer'; 'his psychology and reaction should be very carefully studied'.[58]

It was striking that Wornum avoided examples of British design, demonstrating rather a catholicity of taste, praising the Austrian and Soviet pavilions of the Paris Expo, by Hoffman and Melkinov respectively, aspects of the work of Le Corbusier, Erich Mendelsohn's Einstein Tower, and the Palace of Culture at Leningrad (the Lensoveta in St Petersburg). He also singled out the interior decoration in the house of Fritz August Breuhaus, known for his wallpaper designs and wall decoration, and of the Russian Jewish architect Michael Rachlis (who later lived at Jack Pritchard's Lawn Road flats, 1935–6), whose Villa Zissu included a living room which Wornum described as an 'exhibition of colour decoration'.[59] He also discussed interiors by BJ Klotz and a bedroom in Berlin incorporating painted decoration by Cesar Klein and Rudolf Belling, both German Expressionists

---

[55] Miriam Wornum, 'Houses—Ancient and Modern: A Home to Live in, not a Mansion for "Occasions"' in Irena Žantovská Murray (ed.), *Le Corbusier and Britain: An Anthology* (Abingdon, 2009), p.43.

[56] RIBA, George Grey Wornum Papers, WoG/1/1, Box 16, Folder 1, Typescript: 'Grey's Friends: Oliver Hill'. This document was intended for his unpublished memoirs, *Grey Matter*.

[57] 'AA General Meeting January 2nd, 1928: Modern Decoration', *AAJ* (January 1928), p.237.

[58] Ibid., p.245.   [59] Ibid., p.239.

MACHINE-CRAFT 153

and members of the November Group. Wornum's outlook, therefore, was broad; he was abreast of continental developments, as well as Japanese interiors, North American cliff-dwellings, and South American Spanish colonial vernacular, all of which were referenced in his paper.[60]

Wornum, like Weaver and the DIA, was also a close follower of developments in Swedish architecture and design, visiting Stockholm with the AA in 1923. Swedish craft—both industrial design and the decorative arts—was highly influential on Wornum's practice. That these practices, tastes, and sources collided and overlapped in sometimes surprising ways is neatly expressed in a reception Wornum put on as president of the AA in connection with the Exhibition of Swedish Industrial Art held at Dorland Hall in 1931, organized under the auspices of the DIA and Svensk Form, the successor body to the Svenska Slöjdföreningen.[61] The *Architectural Association Journal* was impressed by 'how strong upon the designers is the influence of the late eighteenth century.'[62] The AA Library was given over to a large party including Swedish royalty; both Prince Eugen, an established painter and muralist, and Prince Sivgard (Sivgard Bernadotte), an industrial designer, attended. The Library was given 'a festive air contributed to by a gay display of modern hand printed Chinese Papers, lent by the President, and which hung in squares on screens around the walls'.[63]

Materials and Manufacture

The Building Centre, established at 158 New Bond Street in 1932 (Fig. 3.15), was intended as a permanent space for changing exhibits of the latest materials and manufacturing processes in construction, including furnishing, fixtures, and fittings. It symbolized what Katie Lloyd Thomas has described as the 'proprietary turn' in architectural practice in the interwar years, whereby architects began to act as 'shoppers' for their clients: 'Whilst previously, with only a few exceptions, architects had specified building materials by generic names—brick, plaster, glass and so on—by the mid-1930s they were selecting and naming *specific products* and *brands* for their

---

[60] 'AA General Meeting January 2nd, 1928: Modern Decoration', pp.235–50.
[61] Gillian Naylor, 'Swedish Grace', pp.164–84; Lucy Creagh, Helena Kåberg, and Barbara Miller Lane (eds.), *Modern Swedish Design: Three Founding Texts* (New York, 2008), in particular Gregor Paulson's essay 'Better Things for Everyday Life', pp.72–125; Charlotte Ashby, *Modernism in Scandinavia: Art, Architecture and Design* (2017).
[62] 'The AA Reception', *AAJ* (April 1931), p.331.   [63] Ibid., p.333.

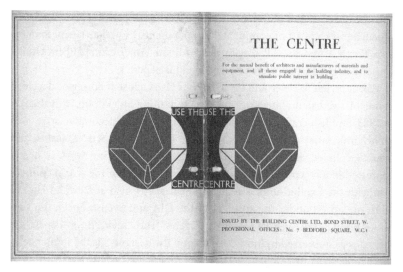

Fig. 3.15 Cover of a prospectus for the Building Centre (1932), F203A, Architectural Association Archive

contractors...'[64] The Building Centre provided a physical space for the display for these brands and their products. It attested to the growing power in the sector of materials manufacturers, energy suppliers—both electricity and gas—and industrial designers expanding into the domestic market with labour-saving devices. All were on display at New Bond Street.

This proprietary turn was another facet of the broader publicity paradigm shift in architecture and the construction industry described in the previous chapter. Its effect—of making the architect a shopper, or concierge, on behalf of their client—also carried the risk of making them the salesperson on behalf of manufacturers, which posed risks to the integrity of their professional status. It was for this reason that the Centre was not positioned as a saleroom or retail space: 'whilst manufacturers applied and paid to have their products on display, goods were not on sale to visitors'.[65]

The establishment of the Building Centre is germane to the RIBA's development of new premises in particular because of Grey Wornum's involvement in the enterprise. Not only was he one of the directors of the

---

[64] Katie Lloyd Thomas, 'The Architect as Shopper: Women, Electricity, Building Products and the Interwar "Proprietary Turn" in the UK' in Hélène Frichot, Catharina Gabrielsson, and Helen Runting, *Architecture and Feminisms: Ecologies, Economies and Technologies* (2017), pp.54–65, p.57.

[65] Ibid., p.58.

Centre, he also contributed to the design of its exhibition spaces, on which he then subsequently drew in the specification for the new premises at Portland Place.

The Centre had begun life as the Architectural Association Materials Bureau, set up in August 1928 as a 'museum of buildings materials', originally confined to the use of students and members.[66] It was run by a former student, JK Winser, who in October 1929 became the Bureau's permanent curator. LH Bucknell, one of the AA's principal tutors, chaired the committee responsible for the Bureau, which also included Charles Holloway James, Arthur Knapp-Fisher, Humphrey Packington, Howard Robertson, and the Association's secretary, FR Yerbury.[67] By 1930, the Bureau was receiving on average 46 enquiries per week, amounting to 2,172 in total that year, with over 2,000 samples representing 850 firms. As the enterprise expanded, it moved from the basement of 36 Bedford Square to 28 Bedford Square, the former premises of the Society of Architects. It is notable that at this point, Yerbury made approaches to Richard Allison, chief architect to the Office of Works, Frances Goodenough, in his capacity as president of the Incorporated Sales Managers' Association, and Stephen Tallents, secretary to the Empire Marketing Board. The Bureau felt that these connections were important to maintain; the following year they were consulted as to how the AA could make the Bureau more useful to their work.

It was in November 1931 that Robert Atkinson wrote to Yerbury about establishing the Bureau as a financially independent enterprise. As it had continued to expand, it needed ever-larger premises, and the Bedford Estate, ground landlords on Bedford Square, were reluctant to allow the increasingly commercial purposes of the Bureau to continue there. Meanwhile, brothers Vincent and Sidney Gluckstein, directors of the contractors Bovis, had visited the Architects' Samples Bureau in New York in 1929 which was operated by an American technical journal. Upon their return, they 'invited a number of leading architects to a lunch at the Carlton House Hotel' to discuss the possibility of a similar enterprise in London.[68] Those in attendance included Bucknell, Knapp Fisher, Robert Atkinson, Louis de Soissons, and Grey Wornum. Also present—apparently at Wornum's suggestion—was Yerbury, then unknown to the Glucksteins, but

---

[66] AA, BMB, 1928–1931, Box 1991, 18, Memorandum entitled 'The Architectural Association Building Materials Bureau' (undated).

[67] Ibid., Memorandum entitled 'Report of the Work of the Architectural Association Building Materials and Technical Service Bureau up to March 19th, 1931'.

[68] Peter Cooper, *Building Relationships: The History of Bovis 1885–2000* (2000), pp.59–60.

156 DESIGNS ON DEMOCRACY

who around the same time had visited Berlin and been impressed by the Bauwelt Musterschau, established on more commercial lines than the AA's Materials Bureau.[69] These coincidences set in train the establishment of a new commercial Bureau, untethered from formal institutional affiliation to the AA and financially supported by the Glucksteins, who not only provided seed capital but also seem to have leased the premises at New Bond Street and underwritten a programme of alterations. A Board of Directors was convened, with Maurice Webb acting as chair.[70] Atkinson was one of the prime movers in selling the idea to Yerbury and, crucially, MacAlister and the RIBA.[71] A meeting was called at Conduit Street in December 1931 to discuss the proposed 'Architectural Bureau', and it was out of this meeting that the name 'Building Centre' emerged.[72] In March 1932, a lunch was held at Claridge's to launch the Centre, which its promoters hoped would be open by June.[73]

In fact, it took a little longer; over the course of 1932, the directors set about transforming the former French Gallery at 158 New Bond Street. Mayfair was selected in the hope that 'the public (which includes the usual Bond Street shoppers) by visiting the Centre, will tend to become "building conscious" and be urged by contact with fine and new materials and up-to-date equipment, to a sense of the desirability of building, decorating and re-equipping as well and as often as possible'.[74] Lloyd Thomas has argued compellingly that the Centre's exhibits also 'actively developed a new market for building products—women'.[75]

The works were under the general direction of Robert Atkinson, with various other architects and design consultants dealing with the overall schemes for each floor (Fig. 3.16): PD Hepworth was occasional consultant; Raymond McGrath created settings for the electrical section on the ground floor, and had also been asked initially to design the shop windows,

---

[69] Ian M Leslie, '40 Years On: The Building Centre Success Story 1932–1971', *Building Centre Intelligence Report* no. 5 (1971), p.2.

[70] The other directors were Robert Atkinson, LH Bucknell, E Guy Dawber, Sidney Gluckstein, Vincent Gluckstein, Louis de Soissons, G Grey Wornum and FR Yerbury, with Yerbury also acting as honorary secretary. He was later appointed as manager of the Building Centre in 1932.

[71] AA, BMB, 1928–1931, Box 1991, 18, Robert Atkinson to FR Yerbury (23 November 1931), and Robert Atkinson to FR Yerbury (27 November 1931).

[72] Leslie, '40 Years On', p.3.

[73] 'The Building Centre: A Permanent Exhibition in London', *JRIBA* (19 March 1932), p.398.

[74] 'The Building Centre', *AAJ* (September 1932), p.80.

[75] Lloyd Thomas, 'The Architect as Shopper', p.58.

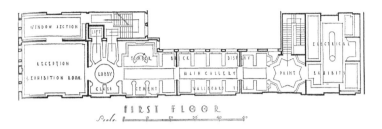

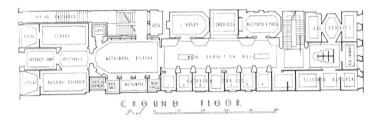

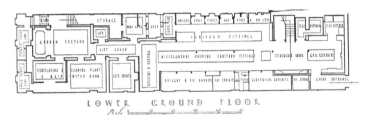

Fig. 3.16 'Plans of the Building Centre', *AAJ* (September 1932), p.81, Architectural Association Archive

producing designs in the end deemed too modern for the purpose; Waldo Maitland served as lighting consultant; LH Bucknell designed the first floor; Walpole Champneys—who had worked with Wornum on the interiors at Derby—here partnered with JC (Jock) Shepherd (of Scott, Chesterton and Shepherd), another former AA student, on the lower-ground floor and staircase.[76] Significantly, Wornum and Atkinson collaborated on the ground

---

[76] Ibid., p.81.

floor, though *Country Life* ascribed the 'major share in the design of the interior' to Wornum, 'whose vivacious sense of design and colour has found a most happy expression'.[77] The Centre opened on 7 September 1932, and the *AAJ* unsurprisingly stressed its immediate success; on the opening day there were 3,000 visitors, and somewhere between 1,500 and 2,000 daily visitors were recorded on average in the first month of operation.[78]

For all its celebration of the standardization of materials and manufacture, the Centre itself offered a carefully choreographed, almost bespoke service. The launching prospectus outlined the process of the 'scheme in practice'.[79] Open from 9.30 to 7 p.m., Monday to Saturday, an architect could arrive at the Centre with their client, whereupon they would be issued with two guides from the 'Enquiries' counter (Figs. 3.17 and 3.18), one outlining type of exhibit and exhibitors, the other an alphabetical list of exhibitors with location codes. Visitors would also be provided with an

Fig. 3.17 View of the main entrance hall of the Building Centre with the enquiries desk to the left, photographer unknown (c.1932), © Building Centre

[77] 'Building and the General Public', *Country Life* (17 September 1932), p.xxx.
[78] 'The Building Centre', *AAJ* (September 1932), p.79.
[79] AA Archives, F203A, Building Centre Prospectus.

Fig. 3.18 Enquiries counter at the Building Centre, photographer unknown (c.1932), © Building Centre

'enquiry card' on which they could note the numbers of exhibits which interested them. The architect could then take their client round the exhibits (Fig. 3.19). Expert advice was available to professional visitors from the Technical Enquiry Department on the second floor, with ready access to a 'great mass of data, library of catalogues, and information generally upon materials, where and by whom they have been used'.[80] Led by a technical manager, a role first occupied by the former Bureau curator, JK Winser, additional technical assistants were available on each floor.[81] At the end of the visit, the enquiry card was returned to the ground-floor Bureau—signed and addressed—and thereafter would follow by post a package of standardized information sheets collated by the Centre delivered to the architect or client, providing a complete catalogue of their desired materials and products. It was initially proposed that these standardized sheets would 'be handed to the architect or enquirer in a special wrapper'.[82]

[80] Ibid., p.80.   [81] Ibid., p.79.
[82] AA Archives, F203A, Building Centre Prospectus.

Fig. 3.19 View of paint section on the first floor of the Building Centre, photographer unknown (c.1932), © Building Centre

Wornum's scheme for the entrance and ground floor was highly decorative, consistent with his early interior work for dance halls, restaurants, and domestic spaces. An entrance lobby was sandwiched between the external window displays, originally including backcloths designed by the theatre and interior designer George Sheringham, leading to a vestibule.[83] The vestibule, with a cloakroom and building research display off to either side, was a striking introduction to the building's interior. In the middle of the vestibule, which was floored with marble terrazzo, a sculpted figure sat on a base of Hopton Wood stone, which was also used for the architrave of an elaborate doorway leading to the metalwork display. Beyond this was the main exhibition hall, off which sat the Library or Periodicals Room, and the enquiries counter. Opposite was a suite of example building cubicles, and beyond were the gas industry exhibits and an electrical kitchen. The Enquiry Office, signalled by illuminated suspended signage, featured glass display

---

[83] For an image of one of Sheringham's backcloths, see 'News and Topics', *AR* (7 September 1932), p.274.

MACHINE-CRAFT 161

cabinets and extensive shelving for the standardized information sheets. The Periodicals Room was a space with a deliberately domestic feel; the wood panelling and fireplace served as exhibits themselves.

There were three types of display in the Building Centre which had significant bearing on Wornum's approach to the RIBA commission. The first of these was light and lighting, which was praised by contemporaries: 'The finest bit of instructive design is the lighting, which has been carried out to the designs of Mr. R. W. Maitland'—'the building is not so much "lighted" as in a state of being light, with fittings disposed (as well as the main scheme) to produce decorative interest'.[84] The careful integration of electric lighting was not accidental. In March 1930, the AA Materials Bureau had forged an important link with the Electrical Lamp Manufacturers' Association (ELMA), based at Elma House nearby at 25 Bedford Square. ELMA had recently formed a Lighting Service Bureau (LSB) on Savoy Street and appointed Ralph Waldo Maitland, himself a former student of the AA, as its consultant architect.[85] The LSB was keen to establish Maitland as a 'liaison between the managements of the two Bureaux', acting as an illumination consultant. This was an important first foray into institutionalizing a link between illuminating engineers and architects, culminating in the Joint Committee of Architects and Electrical Lighting Experts in September 1932 and coinciding with the opening of the Building Centre that month. The panel of architects included LH Bucknell, Howard Robertson, and Grey Wornum.[86] Significantly, Maitland worked particularly closely with Wornum on the lighting scheme for Portland Place. In the vestibule of the Building Centre (Fig. 3.20), the ceiling was fitted with 'Sunlight' neon tubes, semi-concealed and 'specially suitable for indoor use', which, as the *Electrical Age* noted, 'reproduces natural sunlight as nearly as possible, and provides at the same time a warm and practically shadowless system of lighting'.[87]

Connected to light was glass, a material extensively displayed at the new Building Centre. As the *Electrical Age* reported: 'In their search for materials which have beauty as well as practical efficiency, designers have rediscovered one of the old building materials—Glass—and in the Building Centre it can be seen in profusion. Plain and decorated glass, moulded and

---

[84] 'News and Topics', *AJ* (7 September 1932), p.274.
[85] AA, BMB, 1928–1931, Box 1991, 18, Letter from CW Scully (Director of the Electric Lamp Manufacturers' Association) to FR Yerbury (25 May 1930).
[86] 'Architects and Electrical Engineers', *Electrical Times* (8 September 1932), p.285.
[87] *Electrical Age* (October 1932), p.415.

Fig. 3.20 Ceiling lights in the vestibule of the Building Centre, photographer unknown (c.1932), © Building Centre

coloured, all play their part in the modern home.'[88] Glass was used extensively and in novel ways at the RIBA, often combined with experiments in illumination.

And finally timber. The use of timber in Wornum's architecture and interior design is significant. With de Soissons he had designed the secretary's office for the plywood manufacturer, Venesta, at Vintry House, panelled in birch plywood (Fig. 3.21). The partnership's interior for Bellometti's Restaurant in Soho, also designed in 1930, had featured plywood panels with small decorative motifs painted by Miriam (Fig. 3.22). Jack Pritchard, the progenitor of Isokon with Wells Coates was, of course, a director of Venesta. His brother, Fleetwood Pritchard, was a director of the advertising agency Pritchard Wood and Partners. In the mid-1930s the agency held the account for the recently established Timber Development Association (TDA).[89] In 1936, none other than John Gloag was appointed as director of

---

[88] Ibid.
[89] For a wider survey of the TDA's activities and relationship to modern architecture, see Alan Powers, 'A Popular Modernism? Timber Architecture in Britain 1936–39', *Architectural Theory Review* 25.1–2 (2021), pp.245–66.

Fig. 3.21 Venesta Ltd, Vintry House, London: the secretary's office panelled in birch plywood, designed by Lois de Soissons and Grey Wornum, photograph by Dell & Wainwright (1930), RIBA72582, Architectural Press Archive/RIBA Collections

public affairs with a remit to drive forward plans for 'wood consciousness'. Gloag had a longstanding interest in the use of timber for furniture and architecture, dating back to his editorship of the *Cabinetmaker*. Wornum himself addressed the TDA in 1935, speaking on 'The Application of Timber in Modern Architecture' and praising wood 'as the only material available for work to-day which can beautify with age'.[90]

'Wood consciousness', as the *Timber Trades Journal* named it, had been developing over the course of the previous decade.[91] The EMB had initiated, for instance, a campaign to promote the use of Empire woods in construction from the early 1930s, and first the Materials Bureau and then Building Centre were instrumental in aiding it. Empire woods were considered an untapped resource: 'The Empire embraces some 2,000,000 square miles of forest, and many of the chief timber trees of the world flourish within its

[90] WFPC, 'Lunch originally arranged as an address to Timber Merchants in St Paul's Yard'.
[91] 'A Lively New Year for the TDA', *Timber Trades Journal* (4 January 1936), p.7.

Fig. 3.22 Bellometti's Restaurant, Soho Square, London: detail of the wall decoration, photograph by Sydney Newberry, RIBA72003, RIBA Collections

borders.'[92] Whereas the United Kingdom derived about 10 per cent of its imported supplies of wood from the Empire, it was estimated 80 per cent of its timber furniture was made from American Oak. The EMB's campaign aimed at the popularization of Empire woods through 'the creation of an appetite by, and the education of, the public which would lead to a demand at present non-existent'.[93] A cornerstone of this campaign was to cultivate a sense of responsibility among architects and engineers to specify the use of Empire timbers and to ensure their uses had been properly tested and the material properly treated. At the Building Centre, therefore, not only was a display of empire timbers featured (Figs. 3.23 and 3.24), but the Building Research Station (BRS) and the Forest Products Research Laboratory included information about testing they had conducted on use, including the prevention of disease. The display itself comprised fifty woods contained in a 'semi-circular display rack of the Empire Marketing Board, wherein is housed in bookcase fashion a specimen of every Empire timber described

[92] *Handbook of Empire Timbers* (1932), p.3.
[93] 'Empire Wood for Furniture', *The Times* (7 September 1932), p.9.

in their recent handbook'.[94] Within the semi-circular floor space of the stand, EF Ebner, a firm known for the production of woodblock flooring, laid 'a fancy parquet flooring which shows the possibility of Empire woods for decorative floor covering'.[95] In addition, specimen miniature floors of hardwood strips were laid by Hollis Bros & Co., 'the well-known firm which has for many years devoted tremendous energy and solid hard work to the advancement of Empire woods on the floors of British buildings'.[96] Empire timbers in particular were a feature of Portland Place; clearly, Wornum's insistence not only on the extensive use of wood but specifically on Empire timbers grew out of this connection at the Building Centre, and not—as has been presumed—out of the generic 'Buy British Campaign', aimed directly at consumers, run by the EMB in 1931.[97]

Fig. 3.23 Empire Timbers Exhibit on the first floor of the Building Centre, photographer unknown (c.1932), © Building Centre

[94] 'New "Building Centre"', *Timber and Plywood* (10 September 1932), p.473; *A Handbook of Empire Timbers* (1932), p.56.
[95] 'New "Building Centre"', p.473. [96] Ibid.
[97] Stephen Constantine, 'The Buy British Campaign of 1931', *European Journal of Marketing* 21.4 (1987), pp.44–59.

Fig. 3.24 Empire Timbers Exhibit, showing the parquet flooring laid by Hollis Brothers & Co. and EF Ebner, photographer unknown (c.1932), © Building Centre

The Building Centre project was an important immediate precursor to Wornum's work for the RIBA, and seems to have informed many aspects of the design and perhaps even the design process. We have no evidence for Wornum taking MacAlister or indeed Webb round New Bond Street with an enquiry card, but the presence of Webb and Atkinson in the enterprise suggests that aspects of the RIBA specification were generated by this process.

The timing at least was highly coincidental; in the second half of 1930 the RIBA New Premises Committee had appointed a Jury of Assessors, including Atkinson, and was preparing a detailed brief. In April 1931 the competition was launched, with the deadline for entries in March 1932. Wornum was announced as winner in May. And so the months following the competition were also the months during which the Building Centre was under construction.

Although Wornum's winning design for the RIBA competition received a mixed reaction, there was a degree of consensus that, whatever the merits or demerits of the design, he was 'the right man for the job'.[98] Indeed, Maurice Webb went as far as to suggest that the assessors 'must have tried to get behind the paper work to the man who put it onto paper, if all competitions could be assessed on the same basis it would be good for architecture'.[99] This view was echoed by Frederick Towndrow, who noted that 'what we are out to get is not the peculiar expression of one fortunate individual, but a man who will deputize for us and give us the best building of our time, representative not merely of himself, but of every good contribution that can be made by the best brains in the profession'.[100] Wornum's involvement with Webb on the Building Centre certainly contextualizes this endorsement. But more than this, Wornum showed an attitude to architectural design and practice—engaged with industrial design and craftsmanship, with standardization and high specification—which encapsulated wider professional aspirations.

The Building Centre's directors and designers, moreover, help to situate Wornum's practice and ethos in the early 1930s; we see echoes of the Building Centre in 66 Portland Place, quite literally in the ornamental scheme and specification, but more capaciously in the vision of the profession it implied. The opening of the Building Centre also coincided with the establishment of the Building Industries National Council (BINC) and its remedial attempts to alleviate unemployment in the wider construction industry. The name, the 'Building Centre'—*not* the Architectural Bureau, as mooted at one point[101]—spoke to a renewed sense in the interwar years of architects understanding themselves as deeply implicated in the 'building world' at an institutional level, and to the processes of construction and to the possibilities and limitations of 'craftsmanship'. There was later a brief flirtation by the RIBA New Premises Committee, which Webb chaired, with the idea of 'adding two extra floors of offices in which various Societies already associated with the RIBA or of a similar character could be accommodated as tenants of the RIBA',[102] an idea which had received general approval from the Institute's Council. Writing to the then president, Giles Gilbert Scott, Webb noted that

---

[98] Margaret Richardson, *66 Portland Place: The Headquarters of the Royal Institute of British Architects* (2004), rev. Charles Hind, p.14.

[99] 'The RIBA Competition: Some Opinions iii', *AJ* (25 May 1932), p.687.

[100] Ibid.   [101] Leslie, '40 Years On', p.3.

[102] RIBA, New Building Committee Minutes and Papers, 1932–1938, 'Minutes of New Building Committee, Wednesday 4 October 1933', fo.99.

168 DESIGNS ON DEMOCRACY

The Sculptors and the Stained Glass people both want to come in provided that we can take them…our top floors could be built now instead of waiting for a problematical number of years, and I feel sure that it would very much strengthen the prestige of the RIBA if they could house all these different people—as [JC] Squire expresses it, a sort of 'Burlington House' for the Architectural Societies and others working in the same or allied fields.[103]

These ideals informed Wornum and powerful figures within the RIBA in the design of 66 Portland Place. It became a test-case for these maturing, modernizing impulses.

A Conduit to Progress

By the late 1920s, the RIBA—with an increased membership and expanding functions—was outgrowing its headquarters at 9 Conduit Street, a late-eighteenth-century townhouse designed by James Wyatt (Fig. 3.25). The building had originally been purchased in 1859 by the Architectural Union Company (AUC), which made a number of interventions to the rear of the site, primarily the creation of three gallery spaces—a series of ribbed iron structures, centrally top-lighted, for the display of architectural drawings, materials, and products. A fourth 'North' gallery was essentially a corridor leading to an entrance in neighbouring Maddox Street.

The RIBA had initially let small apartments at Conduit Street, but as its size and functions expanded, it began to take up more and more space. Plans to develop a large meeting room on the second floor were put forward by the RIBA in the late 1870s, but were ultimately rejected by the membership.[104] As the RIBA began to develop closer links with the 'Allied Societies', however, the Institute grew significantly in the 1880s. As a result, in the 1890s the RIBA began to spread beyond the first floor. The Library, which had doubled as the Institute's main meeting room, was given additional accommodation to the front and rear, so that by 1897, the RIBA had taken over the second and ground floors for member accommodation and administrative purposes. In 1910 a committee of Institute eminences, including

---

[103] Ibid., 'Letter from Maurice Webb to Giles Gilbert Scott, 25 September 1933', fo.101.
[104] 'Institute Premises Improvement Scheme', TRIBA 31 (1877–8), pp.139–43. These were rejected in 1878. See 'Report of the Council', TRIBA 32 (1878–9), pp.87–8, 109–12.

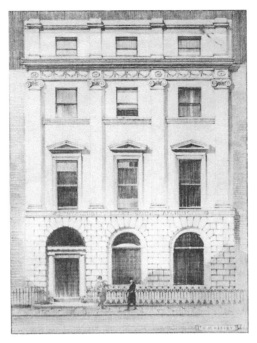

Fig. 3.25 9 Conduit Street, 1920s. Drawing by Walter Monckton Keesey, RIBA114066, RIBA Collections

Reginald Blomfield, Edwin Lutyens, and Ernest George, and chaired by the honorary secretary, Henry T Hare, was appointed to rationalize the Conduit Street premises, completed in time for the RIBA international Town Planning Conference that year.[105] The changes, designed and supervised primarily by Hare, were facilitated by the RIBA buying out the AUC in 1909.[106]

By 1924, however, a further set of renovations were in hand, led by Hare's successor as honorary secretary, Arthur Keen. In 1922, a strip of land adjoining the Maddox Street Corridor (the former North Gallery) was purchased freehold. This allowed Keen to double the size of the main meeting room (Fig. 3.26) and to reorganize the office accommodation.[107] In the large front room of the original townhouse, which had been used as the Council Room, Keen created a front office divided into two compartments for the

---

[105] 'The New Rooms at the Institute', *ABJ* (5 October 1910), p.336.
[106] *JRIBA* (24 September 1910), p.767.
[107] 'The RIBA Meeting Room', *JRIBA* (22 March 1924), p.312.

Fig. 3.26 9 Conduit Street, Meeting Room, photograph by Herbert Felton (c.1934), RIBA113992, RIBA Collections

secretary and assistant secretary, adjoining a general office for the clerks (Fig. 3.27). The Council Room had by this time migrated to the old East Gallery.

Keen's alterations and those before his reflected the expanding scope and structure of the RIBA, which were made clear in a number of spatial and material manifestations at Conduit Street. By the time the RIBA left in 1934, it resembled little the townhouse into which it had moved in 1859. The periodic re-makings of Conduit Street—these projects were often referred to as a 'new premises'—also tell a story about how professional associations started to see themselves; less the dilettantish clubs of the Victorian and Edwardian years, and more as organized bureaucracies with semi-public functions. Significantly, over this period we see the reification of 'the membership' as distinct from the executive operations of the Institute itself, initially in the allotting of a tea room on the second floor, then a common room and a meeting room. In the first four decades of the twentieth century, the Institute changed from an institution largely managed by its own members, to one increasingly run by a distinct executive function, which

Fig. 3.27 9 Conduit Street, general office towards counter, photograph by Herbert Felton (c.1934), RIBA114064, RIBA Collections

combined the membership and a new breed of bureaucrats and managers overseen by the secretary.

In all, over 300 sites were considered by the Premises Committee between 1926 and 1929, and sketch-plans prepared for serious contenders.[108] By May 1928, the Committee had reported to the Finance and House Committee that, having considered a number of sites, they now firmly advised the Council against rebuilding on the present site. The Portland Place site, on the north-east corner where it meets Weymouth Street, was duly acquired from the Howard De Walden Estate on 4 March 1929.

Despite suggestions of a limited competition or direct appointment, it was eventually resolved that the architect be selected by means of a competition open to all members, Empire- and worldwide.[109] The assessors for the

---

[108] 'The Buildings of the RIBA 1834–1934', *JRIBA* (6 November 1934), p.19; 'The "Old Lady" of Conduit Street: A Fantasy', *AJ* (6 June 1923), p.951.

[109] RIBA, Council Minutes (10 June 1929–11 May 1931), Minutes of Meeting (10 June 1928), fos.2–5, Memorandum by President (Walter Tapper) re Selection of Architect for New Premises.

172   DESIGNS ON DEMOCRACY

competition, appointed on 21 July 1930, were Giles Gilbert Scott, Percy Worthington, HV Lancaster, Robert Atkinson, and Charles Holden.[110] The RIBA published widely and regularly about the competition conditions and planning requirements. The 'Schedule of Accommodation' included a 'dignified entrance hall with spacious and well-planned staircase'; committee rooms of various sizes; 3,500 square feet for the Library; space for exhibition galleries-cum-examination rooms of 6,000 square feet (with 'moveable screens'); a Council Club Dining Room of 1,000 feet; members' accommodation of at least 1,700 square feet; a Council Room of 1,500 square feet; as well as ample accommodation for various administrative and support staff.[111] The difficulty of the site and complexity of these stipulations was appreciated by the appointed assessors. Robert Atkinson acknowledged that a 'most unusual building was demanded of them [the competitors]— with accommodation which was very heavy for the site, of a character very complicated in its structure and difficult to describe in the conditions'.[112] He described the building really as five in one: a meeting hall with adjoining cloakrooms; exhibition galleries with a banqueting hall for its services; a library with stackrooms and workspaces; council rooms, committee rooms, and offices for the administration of the Institute; and additional office accommodation for letting.[113]

Despite the awkwardness of the site and the complex schedule of accommodation, submissions duly came in; 284 designs were submitted, of which only two were disqualified.[114] Writing in the *AR* special issue, Giles Gilbert Scott praised the Institute's initiative, 'at a time when not only the profession but the whole country was deep in economic depression...The gesture is not merely symbolic. By embarking on the scheme when it did and by means of an Empire-wide competition, the RIBA made the greatest practical contribution in its power to the welfare of the profession and the Building Industry.'[115] His claim that the Institute had 'thereby definitely helped to overcome the depression' may be an overstatement but reflects the broader policy instigated by the BINC and its campaign to stimulate capital investment discussed in the previous chapter.

Such was the volume of submissions that a special exhibition in order to review the designs was held at Frank Baines's recently opened Thames

---

[110] RIBA, NPCM (9 October 1930).
[111] 'The RIBA's New Building', *AJ* (15 April 1931), pp.562–3.
[112] Robert Atkinson, 'The New RIBA Premises Competition', *JRIBA* (5 December 1932), p.81.
[113] Ibid.   [114] Ibid., p.83.   [115] Scott, 'Foreword', *AR* (December 1934), p.189.

MACHINE-CRAFT   173

House, the second of his buildings for Imperial Chemical Industries on the north side of the river just east of Westminster Bridge; 140 designs came from London, 54 from elsewhere in England, 20 from Scotland, 2 from Ulster, 23 from Australia, 16 from Canada, 5 from New Zealand, 3 from India, 9 from South Africa, 5 from the United States, and 1 each from Kenya, France, and Sudan.[116] The overwhelming sense from the contemporary press was that the competition was compromised by the awkwardness of the site and the problematic stipulation of having separate office accommodation for another organization. Some competitors sought to express this difference architecturally, which made for a number of unhappy designs. In May 1932, the assessors nevertheless awarded the commission to Wornum, with Verner Rees awarded second place, and O'Rorke and Peacock third equal with Percy Thomas and Ernest Prestwich, and Frank Roscoe and Duncan Wilson.

Construction began at 66 Portland Place in April 1933. The build lasted eighteen months, and the new Institute was opened by the king and queen on 8 November 1934. The arrangements, jointly coordinated by the Public Relations Committee and a Centenary Committee convened to arrange the RIBA's hundredth anniversary celebrations, were fastidious. They demonstrate vividly how the Institute increasingly perceived itself as a semi-public institution. A press preview was arranged a week before the opening ceremony; 130 of the leading technical and popular titles were invited to view the building, with members of the design team, artists, and consultants, alongside committee members, present to field questions. Visitors were directed to the Florence Hall where they were given typewritten notes of the building, details of the consultants and artists, and a 'route card showing them how to circulate round the building'.[117] Refreshments were provided in the members' rooms, with free copies of photographs taken for the *Journal* available.[118]

At the opening ceremony itself, twenty-five papers and agencies 'most likely to effect desired publicity' were given seats in the Florence Hall.[119] The Hall had a special platform at its rear to allow six photographers to capture the event. Another temporary platform was erected outside the building for moving and static shots. A shorthand writer was deployed in the Jarvis Hall to capture the king's remarks—the notes were immediately

[116] Ibid.
[117] RIBA, PRCM (1), (7 December 1934), fo.111, appended report entitled 'RIBA Public Relations Committee: Report on Press Work During the Centenary Celebrations'.
[118] Ibid.   [119] Ibid.

174   DESIGNS ON DEMOCRACY

run downstairs to the typists' office and a stencil made, so that 'copies were available on the enquiry counter before the end of the ceremony'.[120] Provincial papers, like the *Yorkshire Post*, also published commentary on the new building:

> It is meant as a demonstration of modern architectural practice and as an invitation to the public to stop, look and criticise. The Council of the RIBA could, no doubt, have been content with a quietly conventional building which would have been accepted with luke-warm approval. Rightly, they decided instead to celebrate the Institution's centenary by challenging public opinion with a new policy of bold experiment.[121]

The RIBA's hired press agent, Philip Jordan, concluded in his report to the Committee that 'It would appear that partly by accident and partly by design the Institute and the profession as a whole have been brought before the public notice to an extent that the Public Relations Committee a few months ago would have considered a satisfactory result of several years of persistent propaganda.'[122]

The opening of the centenary exhibition and an impromptu visit by the Prince of Wales to Portland Place also afforded opportunities for further publicity of the Institute and its new building. Volumes of press cuttings were arranged according to each event to show the result of the press work and the extent of the coverage. The BBC's *Radio Times*, with a circulation of 3 million, included a note on the opening ceremony.[123] Charles Herbert Reilly, writing in the BBC's other flagship publication, *The Listener*, used the opportunity to ruminate on 'What the Architect Stands for Today', concluding that the architect 'is indeed becoming a leader of community instead of the servant of an individual'.[124]

This was a view echoed by the king at the royal opening, which was also widely reported: 'To-day', he said, 'as the importance of co-ordination in the whole field of building becomes even more clearly recognised, it is the great task of the Royal Institute to make the profession of architecture

---

[120] Ibid.
[121] RIBA, Centenary Committee—Boxes, Press Cuttings, File B, 'Architects at Home', *Yorkshire Post* (8 November 1934).
[122] RIBA, PRCM (1), (7 December 1934), fo.111, appended Report entitled 'RIBA Public Relations Committee: Report on Press Work During the Centenary Celebrations'.
[123] Ibid.
[124] CH Reilly, 'What the Architect Stands For To-Day', *The Listener* (7 November 1934), p.12.

MACHINE-CRAFT   175

increasingly useful to the community.'[125] The Prince of Wales was hailed by the profession for his comments two weeks later at the centenary banquet:

> To-day we are not the race of individualists which we were in Victorian and Edwardian times...Wealth is more evenly distributed throughout the country than it has ever been and the interest of professional men, in common with the interest of commercial men, is being directed to a great consideration of the mass of the people and their requirements than it is to the individual client or the more selective group we commonly call society.[126]

The building effectively became a monument to the articulated ideals of statutory registration, endorsed at the highest levels.

The public or semi-public nature of 66 Portland Place was amplified in this orchestrated public relations campaign, but it was also made manifest in the design of the building. Not only was it less grandiose in ornamentation and scale than conventional professional institute headquarters; it was also the most open to the new public constituency. It differed from austere and remote nineteenth- and early twentieth-century buildings such as John Belcher's grandiose urban palazzo in an exuberant Arts and Crafts Baroque for the Institute of Chartered Accountants in collaboration with Beresford Pite (1893), the former's disciple JJ Joass's Royal Society of Medicine (1912), and James Miller's building for the Institution of Civil Engineers in Westminster (1913).

Amongst the frequently commented-on aspects of the building in the 1930s were the freedom of circulation, the transparency of the design, and the lack of corridors (Fig. 3.28). These were fundamental to the modernity of the plan, and key features of what was called by several newspapers 'The Perfect Building'.[127] The absence of corridors was felt to be a particularly noteworthy achievement because of the extent of administrative function which needed to be in easy communication. Corridor passageways were

---

[125] RIBA, Centenary Committee—Boxes, Press Cuttings, File C, 'Architects' New Home', *Evening Chronicle and Evening News* (8 November 1934).

[126] Ibid., File E, 'Mass-Produced Houses: Prince Points the Way to End Slums' (23 November 1934).

[127] Ibid., File A, 'The Perfect Building at Last for Architects Only', *Manchester Event News* (3 November 1934); 'Perfect London Building', *Yorkshire Post* (3 November 1934); 'London's Most Perfect Building', *Northern Despatch* (3 November 1934); 'Architects' New Home: Starting Sculpture on the "Perfect Building"', *News of the World* (4 November 1934); 'The Perfect Building', *News Chronicle* (3 November 1934).

176 DESIGNS ON DEMOCRACY

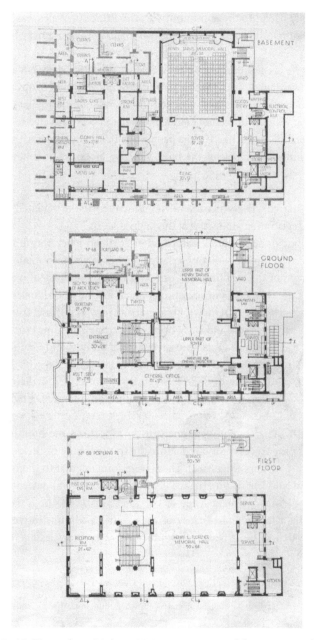

Fig. 3.28 *AR* (December 1934), p. 199, image courtesy of the Museum of Domestic Design & Architecture, Middlesex University, http://www.moda.mdx.ac.uk

MACHINE-CRAFT 177

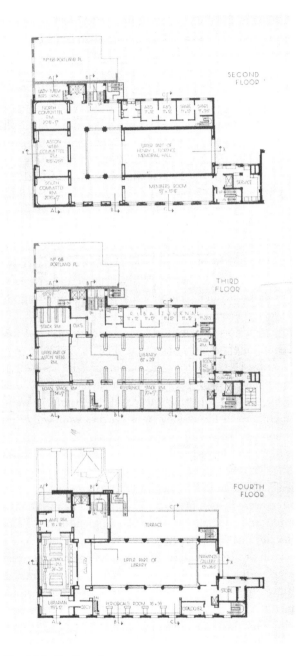

Fig. 3.28 *Continued*

178   DESIGNS ON DEMOCRACY

increasingly common in offices and buildings for public administration in the nineteenth and early twentieth centuries, often deliberately commented upon and labelled in plans as architectural features. Wornum avoided corridors through cleverly arranged interlocking volumes and this was aided by a relatively small site. But it was also about attitude: the doubling up of functions, and the connectivity of rooms without corridors, meant a more democratic and less hierarchical arrangement of space, made all the more interesting by the general layering of functions—administrative staff on the ground floor, public areas on the first, members on the second, and a co-mixing of all three on the third where the Library was housed. Service functions were still relatively concealed at the rear of the site with separate circulation, but office administrative staff were now felt to be distinct from service staff, and administration spread across common areas too. The transparency and lack of corridors meant that different constituents could see and be seen by others, in particular around these common areas. Freer circulation and an enfilade constituted a typically eighteenth-century approach to domestic architecture, which Wornum probably deliberately wanted to evoke.

The transparency of some of the principal public spaces was counteracted by the relishing of craft and ornamental detail. It is easy to forget what a highly decorative set of interiors Wornum's practice created at Portland Place, producing 'an effect of permanent decorative value, governed by quality of available materials and practical considerations'.[128] The walls on either side of the entrance hall had long inset benches with leather-upholstered scarlet cushioning. The enquiries counter, which ran between the assistant secretary's room and the general office, was cut from English walnut. The cream of the Perrycot marble lining the entrance hall contrasted with the dark veined Ashburton and Demera marble of the staircase. There etched glass balusters were lighted green by fittings concealed in the bases of the silver-bronze frames. On the first-floor landing and in the Florence Hall, the lustrous curtains, a medley of greens, browns, creams, and golds, in a curved chevron or fishtail pattern, were specially adapted for the commission from an earlier design for Crosby Hall by Alec Hunter at Warner Textiles in Braintree (Fig. 3.29). On the second floor, the main committee room, named for Aston Webb, was lined with cream kid leather panels of uneven colouring. The large horseshoe table—the original Council Room

---

[128] Anthony Charles Tripe, 'The Building in Detail', *AR* (December 1934), p.210.

Fig. 3.29 Royal Institute of British Architects, 66 Portland Place, London: incised sculpture by Bainbridge Copnall in the Henry Florence Memorial Hall depicting Maurice Webb, Grey Wornum, and Ragnar Ostberg, photograph by Dell & Wainwright (1934), RIBA15119, Architectural Press Archive/RIBA Collections

table at Conduit Street (Fig. 3.30)—was given a new leather top of light olive green, picked up by the curtains in the same colour with an elaborate shaped, braded, and tasselled pelmet. The green contrasted pleasingly with the chairs upholstered in tan moquette and the terracotta and pale-brick carpet.

The Members' Room, running much of the length of the Weymouth Street side of the building, had a particularly bold scheme (Fig. 3.31). The warm beige of the walls was contrasted with a darker tone on the ceiling beams. The panels around the windows were enlivened with brown, beige, and 'off-pink', picking up the brown and 'faded rose' stripes of the curtains. The sofas and seating were horizontally stripped in green and 'old rose' on a pastel ground. The Women's Members' Room, tucked away in the corner by the lift, had more elaborate decoration. Here (Fig. 3.32), Miriam Wornum painted directly onto polished plaster 'a dozen fair-size panels showing the

Fig. 3.30 Royal Institute of British Architects, 66 Portland Place, London: the Aston Webb committee room, photograph by Dell & Wainwright (1934), RIBA15112, Architectural Press Archive/RIBA Collections

fashions of the British Empire', among them 'a Victorian Englishwoman, mannered and decorative; a little Burmese girl; and a bright-skirted African twirling her hair into the long horns that are a fashion in that part of the British Empire'.[129] The room also featured needlework cushions with geometrical instruments as their design, such as T-squares, compasses, rulers, and pencils. The RIBA's Women Members Committee, convened by Gertrude Leverkus from 1932 onwards, was engaged by Wornum to advise on the layout of the women's cloakrooms, described by *The Listener* as 'a revolutionary innovation for a "learned body"'.[130] For these, Miriam Wornum painted 'a series of colored sketches...representing fashions throughout the ages...Round mirror-frames she is putting amusing little sketches of rouge-pots, hairpins and other paraphernalia of beauty through the centuries.'[131]

---

[129] WFPC, 'A Mother's Part in a New London Building: Artist-Wife of the Designer', *Evening News* (22 August 1934).
[130] 'Week By Week', *The Listener* (7 November 1934), p.12.
[131] WFPC, *Daily Herald* (24 January 1935), 'Goatskins for Walls: Architect's Wife Decorates New Wonder-Building'.

Fig. 3.31 Royal Institute of British Architects, 66 Portland Place, London: the Members' Room on the second floor, photograph by Dell & Wainwright (1934), RIBA15091, Architectural Press Archive/RIBA Collections

The significance of some of this detailing was obscured by its omission in the male-dominated technical press—and much of it has since been physically erased. Its mention in 'women's interest' columns of popular daily newspapers reinforced its marginalization as part of the core architectural concept. The *Daily Herald*'s 'Woman Writer' described Miriam Wornum, who showed them round, as a 'modest little woman artist'.[132] Wornum noted that the white walls and ceilings had 'a touch of pink in their coloring, taking off the hardness of dead white. To have them so colored she had to battle with those responsible for the building. They were up in arms at the idea of what they thought would be un-masculine rosy walls.'[133] The *Herald* also described the interior decoration of the library, another collaboration between Grey and Miriam, here noted for breaking away from stereotypes 'by having a delicate shade, mingling lapis lazuli blue and sea-green as the keynote of its decorative scheme'.[134] These colours were used for the stove-enamelled curved book-case ends, with concealed lighting and heating. The library issue-desk had a blue linoleum cover to complement them.

[132] Ibid. [133] Ibid. [134] Ibid.

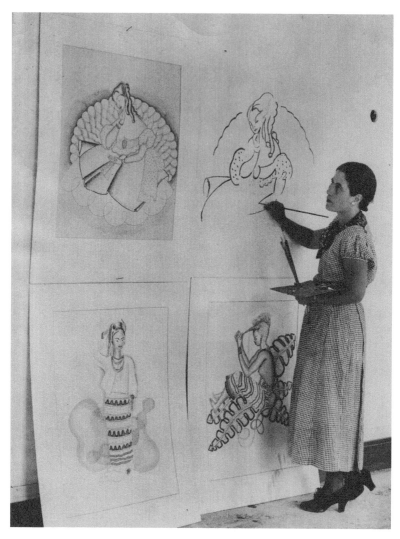

Fig. 3.32 Miriam Wornum painting at 66 Portland Place, photographer unknown (c.1934), Wornum Family Private Collection

In the Council Chamber, English and Australian walnut polish veneers were complemented by beige fabrics ('sound-absorbing tapestry', according to the *Cabinet Maker*) and seats upholstered in 'faded red', with a rich brown carpet.[135]

---

[135] WFPC, Newspaper clipping of *The Cabinet Maker and Complete House Furnisher* (10 November 1934), p.222.

MACHINE-CRAFT 183

On the mezzanine leading down to the basement was the Institute's main lecture theatre, the Henry Jarvis Hall, divided into raked seating facing a stage, and a foyer which doubled as overspill for crowded meetings. The main space was panelled in figured teak, olive ash, and black bean, and the pioneering tubular steel tip-up auditorium seating by Cox & Co. was upholstered in mohair of varying shades of brown, dark to light from back to front.[136] The carpets were mottled brown with green borders in three shades.[137] The foyer, with painted cork walls to facilitate the pinning of drawings, could be separated from the lecture hall through the raising of a motorized screen, a partition of canvas stretched over an iron frame otherwise submerged in the basement (Fig. 3.33).

This 'disappearing wall' provided acoustic absorption but also further opportunity for decoration; Bainbridge Copnall, assisted by Nicholas Harris, painted a mural depicting the 'Empire-wide scope of the RIBA' (Fig. 3.34). At its centre was a loose evocation of the stepped seating and raised dais of the building's Council Chamber, with faceless, grey tiers of councillors in conference. Above their heads to the right floated a row of terraces in Bedford Square, the home of the AA, and to the left, the recently completed Leverhulme Building of the Liverpool School of Architecture by Lionel Budden and Charles Herbert Reilly, a recognition of the importance of the Liverpool School to the development of the Institute's place in architectural education. Surrounding them were perspectives of other spaces of governance and administration, and other institutions of state: above, the Palace of Westminster and Herbert Baker's new Bank of England; below, Stormont, the Irish Parliament Building, and Cardiff City Hall. The nation of Scotland was represented by Sir Robert Lorimer's National War Memorial in Edinburgh Castle. Round the periphery were placed government buildings of colonies and dominions—the domes and towers of Lutyens's Viceroy's House and Herbert Baker's Secretariat blocks in New Delhi, Baker's Union Buildings in Pretoria, the Canadian Parliament Buildings, etc. More problematically, Orientalizing and primitivizing depictions of subjugated indigenous peoples were placed next to them; men, women, and children from the First Nations, Aborigines, others from the African colonies and Asia, all in tribal dress and gesture, jarring with the colonialist architecture of the Empire, from whose governance they were excluded. These found their

---

[136] The firm had also produced furniture for Coates and Chermayeff's interior at BBC Broadcasting House. See 'Cox & Co.' in Jonathan Woodham (ed.), *Oxford Dictionary of Modern Design* (Oxford, 2016), https://www.oxfordreference.com/view/10.1093/acref/9780191762963.001.0001/acref-9780191762963-e-195 [accessed 9 June 2020].

[137] WFPC, Newspaper clipping of *The Cabinet Maker*, p.224.

184 DESIGNS ON DEMOCRACY

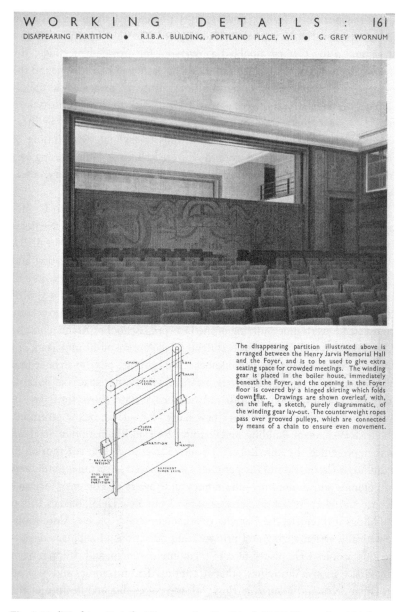

Fig. 3.33 'Working Details: Disappearing Partition', *AJ* (22 November 1934), p.783, RIBA Collections

Fig. 3.34 Bainbridge Copnall (seated) and his assistant Nicholas Harris (standing) at work on the Henry Jervis Memorial Hall screen, photographer unknown (c.1934), Leeds Museums & Galleries (Henry Moore Institute Archive), part purchased and part presented by Jill Copnall Neff

echoes in Miriam Wornum's depictions of women's fashion and beauty in the Empire described earlier.

Copnall's mural is a bombastic expression of the centrality of the RIBA and its Council to the governance of the architecture profession throughout the Empire. It certainly emphasizes the supremacy of the Council in the eyes of the Institute, in particular over the Allied Societies Conference, the associations and branches in the nations, provinces, dominions, and colonies of the Empire which had federated with the Institute since the 1890s.

The subject of institutional governance—not a naturally engaging theme—in the Institute's large meeting hall was, however, also a visible claim for a place in the imperial polity. This is a theme that ran throughout the building's symbolic programme. It was reflected explicitly in the ornamentation; the coats of arms of the Dominions etched into the glass balustrading, and their flora and fauna depicted on a screen at the rear of the Florence Hall. This was also expressed in materials, owing much to the

Fig. 3.35 Royal Institute of British Architects, 66 Portland Place, London: the Henry Florence Memorial Hall, photograph by Dell & Wainwright (1934), RIBA15087, Architectural Press Archive/RIBA Collections

Empire timbers campaign run by the EMB and aided by the Building Centre. The Dominion Screen was carved in Quebec Pine (Fig. 3.35). Indian Silver Grey Wood was used extensively, on the flooring of the Florence Hall, and in the furniture and fittings of the Library. English and Australian walnut, as well as Canadian Maple, faced the walls and doors of the Council Chamber. The use of black bean, ash, and teak in the Jarvis Hall has already been noted. The sliding doors of the reception room on the first floor were veneered in walnut, teak, and laurel. All these woods were advertised by the EMB, and it seems clear that Wornum was keen to incorporate their use into Portland Place as a showcase. The *Evening News* reported that 'architects from all over the country who have been viewing their new temple during this week are making excited inquiries now about certain Empire woods and marbles'.[138]

---

[138] RIBA, Centenary Committee—Boxes, Press Cuttings, File B, *Evening News* (7 November 1934). The article commented that Wornum 'had been studying Empire materials for many years, and knew a lot about them long before we became Empire-conscious'.

MACHINE-CRAFT 187

There was, therefore, a strong emphasis on craft and ornament, but it is important to emphasize that Wornum understood this as profoundly Modern, and meaningfully English at the same time. His Presidential Address to the Architectural Association gives a snapshot of his design philosophy and understanding of architectural Modernism in the early 1930s.[139] He concluded that 'This new Architecture has shown itself in so many fields and so many countries that it cannot be ignored, nor can its attractions be resisted in one way or another by any of us, because it is part and parcel of our life to-day.'[140] Nonetheless, he warned against the excesses of functionalism: 'The modern Architect's work touches life in every part and he has got to work as a biologist with living material and not as a chemist at work on synthetic creations.'[141] Wornum later alluded to an 'institute in Moscow'— probably the Russian Constructivist school Vkhutemas or one of its splinter organizations, such as the OSA Group—'a united and clear-headed body set on making a synthetic world':[142]

> The impulse of their movement will be hard to resist. England is about the only country who can stand up to it. When I say stand up to it I do not mean that we have to resist the thrill of living in an immediate present, and miss indulging in sincere creative effort to serve our own age. I do mean, however, that we should stand up against casting ourselves on to a hypothetical future. Stand up against accommodating ourselves to a synthetic world. We have to fight against this also, that as a nation we do not take to philosophy, we do not get moved 'en masse' by theories, though we have always been to the fore with representations of modern thought and Science, we have no great national backing behind us to support our pioneers, until their enterprise has proved itself and become absorbed in national life.[143]

Wornum, albeit obscurely, was reiterating his criticism of high functionalism through the rejection of what he called a 'synthetic world'. At the same time, he defended national characteristics in architectural form, described in the language of the time as 'racial inheritance'. Elsewhere Wornum had asserted that 'Our Architecture Must be English'. The 'Englishness of English Architecture' in Modernist theory and polemic in this period has been provocatively reviewed. William Whyte has shown that, though recent

---

[139] 'AA General Meeting: Diagonal Views', *AAJ* (November 1930), pp.151–66.
[140] Ibid., p.153.   [141] Ibid., p.157.   [142] Ibid.   [143] Ibid.

188   DESIGNS ON DEMOCRACY

scholarship has 'been more sympathetic to modernism and keener to establish its English identity' situated 'within discussions of modernity, citizenship, and social reform...They have not, however, explored the way in which modernists sought to defend and define modernism as English.'[144] 'Machine-craft' was one such strategy.

Wornum's argument should be read as an attempt to talk about a native architecture that was pioneered in England, albeit not yet proven and 'absorbed in national life',[145] but one that could contend with foreign architecture, in this case Russian Constructivism, on its own terms. Craft tradition was one way in which architecture was supposed to 'stand up' to some of what Wornum described as the dangerous tendencies towards the 'synthetic world', towards extreme functionalism. It was partly through carefully executed ornament by a team of craftsmen working collaboratively on site that Wornum sought to humanize his architecture and to invest it with meaning.

'Machine-craft' and Wornum's exploration of the possibilities of decoration and industrial art thus open up new ways of reading the interior design and ornamentation of Portland Place. As suggested in the Introduction, these fall broadly into three categories. The first is metaphorical, the use of machine or machine-craft motifs in the ornamentation. The second, perhaps subtler use is manifest in the interiors, fixtures, and fittings. The third was embedded in the design and construction processes themselves.

The metaphorical exploration of machine-craft is particularly apparent in James Woodford's plaster reliefs in the Henry Florence Hall. Here smoothly modelled panels were set into the lower parts of the ceiling. They depicted the building industry trades at work on the building. The north side of the hall, opening onto the garden terrace, included the electrician, plumber, radiator-fitter, carpenter, and engraver. To the south, lining Weymouth Street, were the slater, glass-cutter, steel-erector, plasterer, and bricklayer. As was recorded at the time, some of these depicted known craftspeople; Jan Juta was depicted as the glass-cutter, executing one of the panels for the building's staircase. Curiously, Woodford depicted himself as the electrician, holding bunches of cabling and examining a lightbulb. This was perhaps a play on the idea of a 'lightbulb moment', common to cartoon and comic book visual culture of the period. Rather than the illuminated

---

[144] William Whyte, 'The Englishness of English Architecture: Modernism and the Making of an International Style, 1927–1957', *Journal of British Studies* 48.2 (April 2009), p.444.

[145] 'AA General Meeting: Diagonal Views', *AAJ* (November 1930), p.157.

lightbulb hovering above the craftsman's head, he instead is holding it just above eye-level with a furrowed brow and quizzical expression. These gestures were perhaps poking fun at the fetishization of artistic inspiration. More pertinent is the invocation of electric light, and the casting of an electrician as a craftsman. The plaster reliefs are in quasi-heraldic arrangements—the bricklayer is shown assembling a grained brick wall, balancing a mortar board in his left hand with a trowel. Two baskets of bricks on either side of the figure act as 'supporters', and a giant trowel behind the composition acts almost as a crest. The carpenter kneels in front of an enormous handsaw, whilst stripping a beam of wood. Two metallic cutting-disks with teeth act as supporters.

These reliefs are significant because of their depiction of craftspeople in the act of labour, with construction trades mixing with finishing trades. Machine tools and their products are set alongside those of handcraft. Their value was recognized by contemporaries—Richard Coppock noted that 'the commemoration of craftsmen in buildings such as that for the Royal Institute of British Architects, are all instances of the recognition accorded to the building world'.[146] We know Wornum to have been an admirer of English decorative plasterwork, particularly that of the Leicester craftsman George P Bankart who had worked with Gimson, Lethaby, and others of the late Arts and Crafts architects. In a review of his work, Wornum praised Bankart's technique of what he called 'direct modelling', analogous to direct carving for stone sculpture. He also admired 'The play of surface against surface as an expression of simple but powerfully decorative form...superseding the old tastes for multiplicity of moulding and motifs.'[147] Seeing the Florence Hall reliefs in this context elucidates the shared vision of architect and sculptor. Decorative plaster work, or stucco, was prevalent in the exemplary buildings of Swedish Grace which Wornum admired, not only at Stockholm Town Hall but also at Tengbom's Concert Hall. The entrance foyer, with splayed piers and plaster relief work by Nils Olsson and Robert Nilsson, bore a striking resemblance to the Florence Hall (Fig. 3.36), and the building in general was a strong influence on 66 Portland Place, both in its general massing and in its detail, far more so than Asplund's Public Library with which comparisons have been more often drawn.

---

[146] Richard Coppock, 'The Point of View of the Building Operative', *Building Industries Survey* (28 August 1935), p.166.

[147] George Grey Wornum, 'Mr George P Bankart and his Work', *AJ* (26 October 1927), pp.537–8.

Fig. 3.36 Entrance foyer to Ivar Tengbom's Konserthuset, photograph by August Malmström (1926), SSM D2367, Stadsmuseum, Stockholm

Machine-craft was also on display on the first-floor landing, round the jamb and soffit of the side staircase leading visitors to the upper floors. Towards the base of the jambs were tools and machinery for the superstructure of the building; beams and cement-mixers, rising up to equipment for interior construction, bags of plaster, electric cabling, and at the summit the tools of the finishing trades, paint-brushes, paint-pots, and lightbulbs. In both this decoration and the reliefs on the Florence Hall, the ornament was intended to draw attention to the construction and craft processes operating on the building themselves. In the Jarvis Hall, the acoustic panels on the back wall were decorated by Bainbridge Copnall, one of which depicted a repeat motif of three T-squares and drawing boards, with two incongruous cogs above and below. This motif also appeared on an early cover of the DIA journal.[148]

The possibilities of electric lighting were explored to maximum effect at Portland Place, with Waldo Maitland serving as lighting consultant, building on his earlier relationship with Wornum through the Building Centre.

[148] *DIA Quarterly Journal* (December 1928).

Fig. 3.37 Royal Institute of British Architects, 66 Portland Place, London: the Henry Florence Memorial Hall, photograph by Dell & Wainwright (1934), RIBA15101, Architectural Press Archive/RIBA Collections

Maitland was a pioneer of integrated architectural lighting design. In a co-authored paper with Howard Robertson he described light not only as 'illuminant' but as a 'combined illuminant and element of decoration', imbuing his practice with the status of craftsmanship.[149] The architect today, they wrote, 'is conscious of the importance of artificial light as a contribution to the final interior'.[150] Whereas electrical contractors had customarily been employed to install fittings at the end of the construction process, the aim of modern lighting is to 'eliminate the excessive use of small suspended light sources, and to distribute the light over comparatively large areas'.[151] At Portland Place, Maitland and Wornum collaborated closely on the lighting provision; over the staircase, twenty coffers were fitted with 75-watt lamps and reflectors. In the Florence Hall (Fig. 3.37), different lighting

---

[149] RW Maitland and Howard Robertson, 'The Specification Writer: Electric Light in Architecture', *AJ* (30 September 1931), p.441.
[150] Ibid.   [151] Ibid.

Fig. 3.38 Royal Institute of British Architects, 66 Portland Place, London: the main elevation by night, photograph by Dell & Wainwright (1934), RIBA15097, Architectural Press Archive/RIBA Collections

systems were used for different modes; fourteen direct lights were used for exams, whereas a decorative scheme could be used for evening receptions. There were ten glass bowls in saucer domes and tubular lamps covered by thick-cut glass in bronze flames which up-lighted the curtains. A similar type of fitting was used for the external floodlighting of the Portland Place façade, where four project units of 300 watts were placed beneath flat glass slabs set into the plinth (Fig. 3.38).

Machine-craft was evident in the design and construction processes themselves. Having appointed Bainbridge Copnall as lead sculptor, Wornum commissioned a large-scale clay model of the building, and in his memoirs Copnall recalled the difficulties of keeping the model wet enough to change fenestration patterns and details at Wornum's whim (Fig. 3.39). This particularly sculptural approach to model-making as a tool of composition contrasts strikingly with the orthogonal façades and the efficient overlapping of functions in the plan. Again, in the furnishing and ornamentation this tension between handcraft and machine production was evident; the Warner Textile curtains were handwoven for the production of samples, but produced by power-loom in keeping with the design philosophy of production designer Alec Hunter, incidentally later a president of the Society of

Fig. 3.39 Royal Institute of British Architects, 66 Portland Place, London: clay model made by Bainbridge Copnall (c.1933), photographer unknown, RIBA113984, RIBA Collections

194   DESIGNS ON DEMOCRACY

Industrial Artists. Copnall's technique for the incised Perrycot stone splayed piers in the Florence Hall also answers Wornum's call for the combination of handcraft and efficient production. Here Copnall engaged semi-skilled labour to produce his designs, first producing full-size chalk drawings which were then traced onto the stone: 'The work was carved and polished by a firm who employed thirty-five carvers and ordinary masons to do the job. The work was fast and accurate and it can be seen...that this is a most useful method of employing a number of assistants.'[152]

Information Bureau

The Library, perhaps the most visible part of the RIBA's administrative function, also exemplified the 'machine-craft' tension, as both a collection of prints, drawings, and other antiquarian objects, as well as a vehicle for efficient practice and a repository of technical knowledge.

At Conduit Street, the Library—with a small but highly significant collection of books, prints, and drawings—had been a pressing concern, its 'vitality...restrained by the inflexible corsetry of insufficient room.'[153] It was rarely used—a 'pleasant elderly institution', without a comprehensive catalogue and with a labyrinthine storage structure such that members were unable to retrieve items without assistance. Furthermore, lit by candles and heated by open fires, it presented serious risks which expedited the need for new premises.[154] For Portland Place, the Library was reconceptualized as a machine for learning. The transformation of the library function had begun with the merging of the librarianship and editorship under Rudolf Dircks in 1921. Dircks's priority, however, was 'to establish more surely the library in scholastic esteem.'[155] His successor, Bobby Carter, who inherited the challenge of collaborating with Wornum on the new premises, had by contrast an altogether more technocratic vision. He saw the Library not as an academic resource, but as a technical service to the profession. The new Library was effectively divided into a reference section, of around 50,000 volumes, and a loan library (which included a postal service for members). The reference library comprised printed materials including books and periodicals,

---

[152] Edward Bainbridge Copnall, *A Sculptors' Manual* (Oxford, 1971), p.10.
[153] Edward J Carter, 'The Royal Institute of British Architects Library', *Library Association Record* 2 (January 1935), pp.4–15, p.4.
[154] Ibid.
[155] RIBA, NPCM (1), (11 December 1930), fo.5, 'Memorandum on the Library', p.2.

but also a renowned collection of early works and rare books, as well as prints and drawings. But the Library also included a nascent 'Information Bureau', 'still in its infancy' in 1935 but intended to develop 'the service as a clearing house service for all architectural enquiries of every kind', enabled by the rationalized and expanded accommodation at Portland Place.[156] This work had been initiated not only through the systematic cataloguing of the Library's holdings but also by the production of 'information files', to collect 'all odd pieces of information worth keeping' in a standardized format.[157]

Information was key. We have seen already how the BINC, the Building Centre, and the RIBA public relations function—populated by modernizers like Carter—all articulated the need for an information centre. Once again, the Building Centre seems to have been an immediate stimulus and had a significant impact on Carter's aspirations; preliminary conferences were held not only with JK Winser of the Building Centre but also with the librarians of the AA, the Science Museum, and the BRS to ensure there was proper coordination with other architectural libraries and information services. This was part of the new ideal of 'research', the 'most popular and widespread manifestation of scientific thinking in architecture', whose introduction as a serious activity Andrew Saint credits to the maturation of Modernism, namely the establishment of Lubetkin's Tecton in 1932 and MARS the following year.[158] In fact, these ideals were embedded institutionally with the appointment of Carter from 1931.

Carter's library was, therefore, more than just a repository for books; it was the nerve-centre of a whole set of additional administrative functions and professional services. Overall, the design of the Library was guided by the principle that the Centre was not a museum of 'learned society', but rather 'an institution of professional men and its library a workshop for practising architects and architectural students'.[159] It was designed to be free of clutter—the heating system, famously, was concealed in the stove-enamelled book-case ends—and open access—even the drawings were easily accessible in special roller-front presses made by Roneo. Supervision was kept to a minimum, freeing up staff time for other activities.[160]

The 'machine-craft' efficiency is most effectively summed up by the design of the Issuing Desk, a 'functional' piece of custom furniture designed

---

[156] Carter, 'RIBA Library', p.6.   [157] Ibid., p.14.
[158] Andrew Saint, *Towards a Social Architecture: The Role of School-Building in Post-War England* (New Haven, 1987), p.10.
[159] Carter, 'RIBA Library', p.7.
[160] Ibid.

by the architect's practice to standardize and bring together multiple tasks. Despite its rather analogue functions—an attendance register, issuing slip files, shelves for returned books, and correspondence files—in its design and context, surrounded by recessed catalogue drawers strip-lighted from above, it resembled an Arts and Crafts version of a power station control room. Indeed, it could easily have doubled for one of the recent studio interiors for Broadcasting House opened only two years previously. The gallery 'decks' and streamline curved book-case ends, as well as the blue-green colour theme, deliberately conjured up the ocean liner (Fig. 3.40).

Here, then, was a professionalised library and information service; evidence of yet another process of professionalization besides that of the practice of architecture and the management of administration. Carter's technocratic vision of professional service was enabled by the new building. His library shows how closely the building design developed in cooperation with administrative staff for the provision of professional service, as much as it was guided by the requirements solely of the membership. MacAlister congratulated Carter warmly upon the building's completion, writing: 'You cannot image how it has sustained me through all those worrying months

Fig. 3.40 Royal Institute of British Architects, 66 Portland Place, London: the Library, photograph by Dell & Wainwright (1934), RIBA15090, Architectural Press Archive/RIBA Collections

MACHINE-CRAFT 197

to know that you were up there all the time, giving the very best of your mind + energy + imagination to these two big jobs.'[161]

The journal, also the responsibility of the librarian, occupied the offices adjoining the Library. Shortly after his arrival in 1930, Carter had commissioned a redesign of the journal; Stanley Morrison was asked to overhaul the typography, and Eric Gill was commissioned to design a new version of the Institute badge to adorn the bookplates and the cover. The staff also included Carter's new technical editor, from 1933, Eric Bird, the public relations officer. His appointment occasioned further 'development' of editorial policy, widening its scope to 'touch every side of architectural work, including the technique of planning, structure, and the use of materials', while maintaining the 'more general aspects of architectural design and scholarship' that had characterized it previously. Carter and Bird also instigated regular reviewing of current buildings (including detailed technical analysis); a review of current information on construction and materials (liaising with the BRS and the Building Centre); a review of current problems in professional practice, including law, business methods, and practice policy; and a digest of current architectural periodicals (a forerunner of the Architectural Periodical Index).[162] Through Bird, this capacious library function therefore also included responsibility for public relations, an expression of the wide reach of the Public Relations Committee. Exhibitions, also within that body's remit, came to be seen increasingly as an essential tool of public information.

'Everyday Things'

On the floor of the entrance hall at Portland Place, Bainbridge Copnall designed three decorative marble panels with carborundum mastic inlay. The panel in front of the lifts showed a rotary dial telephone and rolled-up letters. Nearby, in front of the typists' office another panel included quills dipped in an inkpot with more rolled-up letters and pamphlets. To the right of the hall, in front of the enquiries counter and general office was a seemingly exploded typewriter, with three prominent keys (bearing the letters 'MGW', presumably for Miriam and Grey Wornum), a platen with carriage release lever, envelopes, and books. These panels signalled the primarily

---

[161] RIBA, EJ Carter Papers, CaE/2/5, Correspondence files, letter from Ian MacAlister to EJ Carter (26 November 1934).
[162] 'The Development of the RIBA Journal', *JRIBA* (14 October 1933), p.841.

198　DESIGNS ON DEMOCRACY

administrative function of the ground floor, and all described methods of communication. They depicted the 'everyday things' of office life, and the contrast between the panels in front of the typists' and general office in particular was deliberate; on the left were the 'everyday things' of the office of the 1830s, and on the right, those of the 1930s. This method of comparison—between contemporary and historical design—was familiar in the visual culture of the time. For the RIBA's centenary celebrations in late November 1934, coinciding with the building's opening, Raymond McGrath was commissioned to design a 'Programme for Reception' (Fig. 3.41).[163] It featured two images: at the top, a carriage pulling up to the pilastered doorway of 16 Grosvenor Street, the RIBA's first permanent home (1837–59), and at the bottom a saloon car drawing up to the new building at Portland Place. The vehicle motifs were strikingly similar to those designed by McGrath for a 'Progress and Period Chart' in the *AR* of July 1933 (Fig. 3.42), an issue in honour of the Exhibition of British Industrial Design for the Home at Dorland Hall, a display of 'everyday things' in domestic use. The chart showed furniture (chairs, sofas, fireplaces, tables, beds, and other fittings) and transport (carriages, planes, trains), 'intended to show at a glance the evolution of the design of familiar objects' from the 1500s to the present day.[164]

This display (and contrast) of 'everyday things' through time was a well-established trope by the 1930s for design reformers and architects. As Julian Holder has shown, writers such as JM Richards, Noel Carrington, Anthony Bertram, WR Lethaby, and, significantly, John Gloag often discussed 'what was variously termed "everyday life" or "everyday things", the obvious focal point for Modernists committed to harnessing industrialisation to the cause of social equality'.[165] The phrase had been popularized by CHB and Marjorie Quennell's 'Everyday Life' series, the last volume of which was published in 1934. Gloag had referenced the expression in his *DIA Yearbook* of 1925–6, 'Design in Everyday Life and Things', and a series of broadcasts for the BBC and resulting publications in the mid- to late 1930s, in which Gloag participated, also made use of the phrase.[166]

The production of high-quality 'Everyday Things' for mass consumption, therefore, was a central plank of design reform discourse in the interwar

---

[163] RIBA, CCMP (8), 'Programme of Reception' (21 November 1934), signed by Raymond McGrath.

[164] Raymond McGrath, 'Progress and Period Charts of English Design', *AR* (July 1933), plate ii; reproduced as fold-outs in John Gloag (ed.), *Design in Modern Life* (1934).

[165] Holder, 'Design in Everyday Things', p.125.　　　[166] Ibid., p.134.

MACHINE-CRAFT 199

Fig. 3.41 Programme for RIBA Centenary Celebration Reception, cover designed by Raymond McGrath (1934), AA/02/05/03/13, Architectural Association Archive

period. 'Everyday Things' were not merely for the upper and middle classes, made by 'the figure of the hairy hand-craftsman—William Morris brand— voluble unpractical, proudly unbusinesslike, but brilliantly picturesque'.[167] Instead, it would require the 'marriage of convenience between hand- and

[167] Gloag, '"Everyday Things"', p.481.

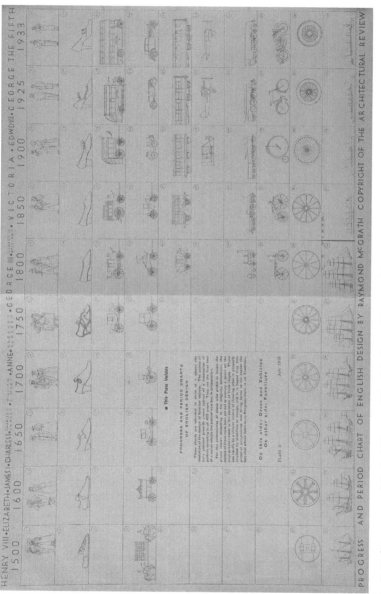

Fig. 3.42 'Progress and Period Charts of English Design' designed by Raymond McGrath, *AR* (July 1933), plate ii, image courtesy of the Museum of Domestic Design & Architecture, Middlesex University, http://www.moda.mdx.ac.uk

machine-craft' advocated by Gloag and other design reformers in his milieu;[168] everyday things were intended for 'everyday people'. This more often than not was in theory rather than practice, as Robin Schuldenfrei's examination of 'luxury modernism' in 1930s Germany has discussed.[169]

For the second major exhibition at Portland Place in 1936, the Committee alighted on the subject of 'Everyday Things', building not only on the Dorland Hall exhibition of 1933, which Oliver Hill had designed, but also on the Royal Academy Exhibition of Art in Industry held in early 1935 (Fig. 3.43). Hill participated in the design of this exhibition too, as did Edward Maufe and Grey Wornum, who was asked to design the plastics room. As Miriam Wornum recalled, 'Grey's interest in new materials and eagerness to use them, made it natural for him to see from the very

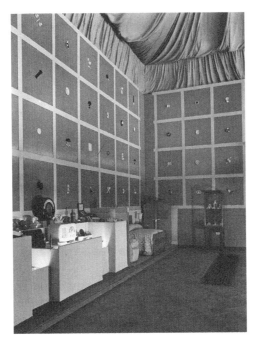

Fig. 3.43 British Art in Industry, Royal Academy, Burlington House, Piccadilly, London: the Plastics Gallery, photograph by Sydney W Newbery (1935), RIBA73645, RIBA Collections

---

[168] Ibid.
[169] Robin Schuldenfrei, *Luxury Modernism: Architecture and the Object in Germany, 1900–1933* (Princeton NJ, 2018).

Fig. 3.44 Dressing table equipment exhibited at the 'Everyday Things' exhibition, 66 Portland Place, photograph by Herbert Felton (1936), RIBA60662, RIBA Collections

beginning that plastics were going to play a very important part in the building material of the future.'[170] He lined his exhibition space with yellow plastic sheeting, and then collected 'as many different small plastic pieces used in industry as we could find', slicing them to a uniform thickness and then screwing them onto the walls in an abstract pattern.[171]

Both Gloag and Wornum participated in the putting together of the 'Everyday Things' exhibition. An ambitious revived exhibition programme for the RIBA had been made possible by the multifunctional space of the Florence Hall. Latterly exhibitions had tended to be organized ad hoc at Conduit Street, with no definitive or particularly ambitious scheme. In 1932, however, it was decided to formalize the exhibition policy to appeal to the lay public, primarily building on the biennial exhibition instituted in 1929. This came under a sub-committee of the Arts Standing Committee. This work was paused in November 1932 because of financial stress, but public

---

[170] RIBA, Grey Wornum Papers, WoG/1, Miriam Wornum, *Grey Matter: Book II*, p.44.
[171] Ibid.

initiatives of this kind were seen as part of economic recovery.[172] The Public Relations Committee carried this work forward in conjunction with the Centenary Committee already alluded to. This spawned the building's inaugural exhibition of 'International Architecture, 1924–1934.' The Exhibition Sub-Committee, convened on a more permanent basis after the success of this exhibition, was yet another function of the RIBA's new public relations operation.[173] Administrative support was provided by Bird. The exhibition also carried forward the 'kernel' of the idea that public education should focus as much if not more on the various roles and services of the architect, particularly in relation to the client and community, rather than solely on design, and certainly more than on style. Most importantly, however, it led to the instigation of a longer-term policy for exhibitions, and the establishment of a new exhibitions department with a permanent staff member in the form of George Marfell (who succeeded Eric Bird as public relations officer after the war). Along with Ronald Avery Duncan, later secretary to the Exhibitions Committee, this led to the formulation of a more focused exhibitions policy, published in the *Journal* in 1935.[174]

This policy emphasized the centrality of the public, rather than exhibitions for related trade and industry: 'the patronage and control of building have passed into the hands of the people, in a large measure through their elected representatives, the local authorities'.[175] It was thus necessary to explain the functions of the architect, as the International Exhibition had done. Secondly, the policy would eschew style because of the public's lack of interest in abstract theories of architecture: '"traditionalism" or "modernism" as creeds leave them cold, though very occasionally the popular press tries to make a minor sensation of these'.[176] And finally, exhibitions should be seen as part of the public service of architecture, distinct from collective advertising, which was still seen as expensive and overly commercial in tone.[177]

The 'Everyday Things' exhibition was, therefore, an opportunity for the architectural profession to show the public its engagement with the objects of industrial design. As the *Journal of the Royal Institute of British Architects* explained:

---

[172] RIBA, Exhibition Officer's Papers, 11/2/3, Box 3 (1932–1953), Memorandum entitled 'Exhibitions', Memorandum dated 11 November 1932, and Memorandum entitled 'Preliminary Notes for Preparation of: Proposed Memorandum on Proposed Policy and Programme for RIBA Exhibitions'.

[173] RIBA, PRCM (1), (11 January 1935), fo.116, appended RA Duncan, 'Report of the Exhibition Sub-Committee: Policy for Future Exhibitions' (8 January 1935).

[174] 'Public Education in Architecture', *JRIBA* (12 October 1935), pp.1145–7.

[175] Ibid., p.1145.   [176] Ibid.   [177] Ibid., p.1146.

204 DESIGNS ON DEMOCRACY

The Exhibition inevitably reveals the architect in his capacity as selector. The things shown are of kinds which the architect normally selects both for his own and for his clients' houses. It also, in some cases, shows him as actual designer, either as a practising architect occasionally designing for industry, or as an architect-trained man or woman working solely for the trade.[178]

What is particularly striking in this articulation of the ambitions of the exhibition is how closely aligned it is to the ideals of the Building Centre. The architect as selector is a clear expression of the 'proprietary turn'. The exhibition broke from convention in presenting *things* rather than predominantly photographs, the conventional mode of display by the RIBA thitherto. Exhibits were arranged into sections, which were then organized by architects or designers (Fig. 3.44). They included furniture, silverware and cutlery, plastics, glassware, china, dressing-table equipment, church furnishings, textiles, kitchen equipment, building equipment, and building finishes. Section organizers included LH Bucknell, RA Duncan, Max Fry, Murray Easton, Gordon Cullen, Noel Carrington, Cachemaille Day, Betty Scott, Raymond McGrath, Geoffrey Jellicoe, Rowland Piece, both Miriam and Grey Wornum, and John Gloag.[179]

For Gloag, the implicit argument, just as he had articulated in *Industrial Art Explained* two years previously, was for the architect to direct the design of 'everyday things', and that this conformed to a traditional professional role which had been lost in the Victorian period. It is worth quoting at length:

...the designer, the man whose taste and judgement are trained and who can direct and select design, is fundamentally different from the man who has his spiritual roots in the Morris period: the real designer has his intellectual kinship with the eighteenth century; the real designer, the arbiter of taste, should be the architect. In the Georgian age he was in control of all design—he influenced the form of every object made by workers in metal, wood and glass; and the Georgian age was the golden age of taste. The Exhibition of Everyday Things at the RIBA suggests that when the architect once again assumes the responsibility for every branch of design, we shall enjoy a gracious and urbane period, comparable with the eighteenth century.[180]

---

[178] '"Everyday Things": The RIBA Exhibition', *JRIBA* (22 January 1936), p.416.
[179] ML Anderson (ed.), *'Everyday Things' 1936: Catalogue to the Exhibition Arranged by the Royal Institute of British Architects* (1936).
[180] John Gloag, '"Everyday Things"', p.481.

This non-stylistic articulation of the Georgian period shows how expansive the neo-Georgian sensibility could be in the interwar period. This was indeed a paradigm shared by Grey Wornum, who argued that the 'eighteenth century manner has outlasted its own attempted revivals, though this may sound paradoxical. But the truth is that the feathers and trappings have been given the revival rather than the creative impulse and ideal that were behind its original manifestation.'[181]

The exhibition, then, had an important function in making the case for 'machine-craft' to the buying public: 'For the public this exhibition is the first official proof that an architect is not merely the man who puts up a house, but is the trained mind who is capable of helping people to fill a house with well-chosen things.'[182]

Conclusion

The design of the RIBA headquarters—through both the Institute as client and Wornum's practice—enacted these new roles which Gloag, Weaver, and others were arguing should define progressive practice. The RIBA became once again the locus of critical engagement with the nature of architectural practice and professionalism across the board—this was not just the terrain of self-identifying Modernists. Wornum was famously disbarred from membership of the MARS Group by Wells Coates for not being sufficiently Modernist in the mould of the Congrès Internationaux d'Architecture Moderne.[183] But institutional lines were thin and permeable; Gloag was a founding member of MARS, and, through an exploration of his concept of 'machine-craft', this chapter has shown how close these interactions could be outside institutional definition. Wornum was not a conviction Modernist of the International Style, but nor was he an unthinking Traditionalist. He was working within an enduring stream of Arts and Crafts progressivism, in which 'Arty-craftiness', as Betjeman put it,[184] was jettisoned in favour of a more robust 'machine-craft' aspiration. Ornament and decoration were still fundamental markers of craftsmanship, and craft continued to be fundamentally constitutive of architectural meaning and architectural practice.

---

[181] 'AA General Meeting: Diagonal Views', *AAJ* (November 1930), p.154.
[182] Gloag, '"Everyday Things"', p.481.
[183] Darling, 'Institutionalising British Modernism', p.315.
[184] John Betjeman, 'There and Back 1851 AD to 1933 AD: A History of the Revival of Good Craftsmanship', *AR* (July 1933), p.8.

206   DESIGNS ON DEMOCRACY

The exhibition of 'Everyday Things' in 1936 draws together the cognate themes of these opening chapters. 'Everyday Things' were the products of 'machine-craft', and 'machine-craft' was expressive of a tension that defined architectural practice and professionalism to a significant group of mainstream reformers in the 1920s and 1930s. The subject of 'Everyday Things' also demonstrates how profoundly the 'DIA point of view' had penetrated the heart of architectural professional culture by the early 1930s; it was manifest in the BEE at Wembley; in the architecture profession's conception of its place in the wider building industry, both the BINC and the Building Centre; and at the RIBA, particularly in the design and construction of its new premises and in the new uses and services it facilitated. As Charles Holden observed in the introduction to the exhibition catalogue: 'twenty years of enthusiastic work among that little band of [DIA] pioneers has not been without result, and its influence will be seen today in this exhibition which has been organised to illustrate the present-day tendencies of design in "Everyday Things".'[185]

66 Portland Place was not just a 'building commissioned by architects, for architects'.[186] Architecture is constituted not just by monuments, but also by a set of discursive practices and representations, and the RIBA amounted to much more than a society or club for architects in this period. 'Architecture', in this analysis, stands for all the social processes involved in bringing a building into being and use. This includes the complex factors leading to the development of a brief, the procurement of design and construction services, the execution of that design, the set of procedures and conventions used to inaugurate it and disseminate its images, and the use of the building both as intended and against intentions, by its occupants and visitors. The RIBA and 66 Portland Place operated for at least three different constituencies and basic purposes: to house a growing bureaucracy administering and pursuing policies on the profession's behalf; for the benefit of its professional membership; but most of all to serve a newly articulated public interest and to establish the architect's place within the wider polity. 66 Portland Place was a temple to the victory of statutory registration and the establishment of the semi-public nature of the profession. It sought triumphantly to enact this performative function.

---

[185] Charles Holden, 'Everyday Things' in 'Everyday Things' 1936, p.9.
[186] Margaret Richardson, 'The RIBA Building' in Gavin Stamp (ed.), AD Profiles: Britain in the Thirties (1979), pp.60–9, and Richardson, 66 Portland Place: The London Headquarters of the Royal Institute of British Architects (1984); cf. Richardson, 66 Portland Place: The Headquarters of the Royal Institute of British Architects (2004), rev. Charles Hind.

4
Vigilance
Preservationism and a Proprietary Public

Introduction

In the interwar years, time and time again architects and their allies asserted the proprietary right that the public had over their built and natural environment. Architectural discourse was reframed in terms of democratization and community interest by a range of figures in architectural culture. There are a number of familiar episodes in the early twentieth-century preservationist movement, particularly those that centred on the defence and loss of Georgian monuments in towns and cities, which culminated in the institution of statutory listing in post-war planning legislation. But the theme is here explored from unfamiliar perspectives, in order to shine a light on the wider cultural imaginary of the Georgian, through the lenses of associational culture and the role of the architect as campaigner.

The defence of Regent Street's Quadrant and later Carlton House Terrace, both well-known episodes in early twentieth-century Georgian preservationism, is addressed explicitly in terms of an underlying argument about the proprietary right of the public over the built environment, and more specifically its heritance of the historic environment. Similar arguments were mobilized in the defence of rural England often by the same activists.[1] These controversies became significant battlegrounds in a war between the claims of public proprietorship and perceived vested and individualistic interests. This was, as the Introduction argued, a tactic of the liberal professional consensus which emerged in this period. Other divisions into opposing camps which have lain beneath many existing interpretations of the period—preservationism versus commercialism, or Traditionalism versus Modernism—in many respects describe only proxy or perhaps phoney wars.

---

[1] Matless, *Landscape and Englishness*, pp.46–93.

Designs on Democracy: Architecture and the Public in Interwar London. Neal Shasore, Oxford University Press.
© Neal Shasore 2022. DOI: 10.1093/oso/9780192849724.003.0005

208   DESIGNS ON DEMOCRACY

That is not to say that stylistic and formal questions were of no relevance at all. These campaigns and controversies often intersected with diverging, and shifting, tastes: from Wren and the English Renaissance, to the classical and vernacular of domestic Georgian, to civic design in the Regency, or to the monumentality of the Greek Revival and its own subsequent revival as neo-Grec. Within the span of what we now call the long eighteenth century there were a number of competing imaginaries of aesthetic, social, and political ideals which influenced serious architectural thought among late nineteenth- and early twentieth-century architectural practitioners.[2] Aspects of these imaginaries will be explored further in the next chapter in relation to 'manners' and ideals of public propriety. There was, as Elizabeth McKellar has recently suggested, a 'Georgian or even a Neo-Georgian London before [John Summerson's] *Georgian London*, but it is one that we are only just beginning to uncover.'[3]

There was a complex interweaving of the antiquarian and the modern in design which in contemporaries' minds went beyond mere revivalism. There were contested ideas about 'The Past in the Future', as Summerson later described it when reflecting on the principles which codified early listing criteria.[4] This narrative—which avoids strict distinctions or high contrast between preservation of historic monuments and principles of architectural design and planning—is full of ambiguities and ambivalences which have subsequently been smoothed over or disaggregated in more triumphalist accounts of preservationism and the conservation movement.

Without understanding these subtleties, however, actors in the interwar period can appear to have taken at times strangely contradictory positions. Reginald Blomfield serves as an instructive example, a figure who emerges as both hero and villain in a number of preservationist skirmishes in this period. On the one hand, Blomfield vociferously defended the saving of Wren's City Churches in the late 1910s and early 1920s, and in the case of Rennie's Waterloo Bridge in the early 1930s fought not just for its preservation but for its adaption to modern needs, drawing up a detailed scheme for the bridge's widening. Yet on the other hand, Blomfield—whose generation had been taught to regard the stucco façades of Nash as 'the last

---

[2] Alan Powers, 'Quality in Quality Street: Neo-Georgian and its Place in Architectural History' in McKellar and Holder (eds.), *Neo-Georgian Architecture*, pp.13–24.

[3] Elizabeth McKellar, 'Georgian London before *Georgian London*' in McKellar and Holder (eds.), *Neo-Georgian Architecture*, p.49.

[4] John Summerson, 'The Past in the Future' in *Heavenly Mansions* (1949), pp.219–41.

VIGILANCE 209

word in vulgarity and ridiculous building'[5]—was complicit in the felling of old Regent Street in the first decades of the twentieth century, and attracted particular opprobrium for his interventions into Carlton House Terrace in 1932. These vacillating positions are explained not only by shifting tastes but also by differing motivations for development, and the growing efficacy of the preservationist lobby.

Architects mobilized rhetorics of public proprietorship and public propriety with similar motivations to those identified in the opening chapters; invoking the public was a means of asserting the architect's place in serving the needs of mass democracy. Nevertheless, the public they invoked and with whom they worked was drawn from a limited pool of expert and lay publics. More often than not a public opinion was formed among members of 'Society', a social category which cut across the middle and upper classes, but whose membership 'required an acceptable mix of breeding, education, wealth, and cultural assumptions'.[6] Society was often canalized into campaigns and associations; these actors were often distinct from, but equally often in interaction with, state power. In some circumstances, however, invocation of public proprietorship did indeed refer to 'the masses', or to specific sections of the working classes, though normally as the *subjects* of action and agitation, rather than fully participant in it. How to incorporate 'the average man', however, was a recurrent concern in the discourse of the 1920s and 1930s, especially for the architect-planner and critic Arthur Trystan Edwards, whose writing and campaigning features heavily in this and the following chapter.

Associational culture and civil society were the mediators of public proprietorship. Campaigning found expression in and direction from the institution of 'the committee' and its bureaucracy as a technique of governmentality. The writer and founder of the Georgian Group, Douglas Goldring, wrote sardonically of 'England's Committees' in his memoir *Odd Man Out*:

> This urge to remedy abuses, to 'get something done', to 'call public attention to the matter' and generally speaking, to waste time and money on wholly unprofitable forms of patriotic endeavour, sweeps over many of us before we reach fifty, and when it does it usually survives all other passions.

[5] Reginald Blomfield, *Memoirs of an Architect* (1932), p.212.
[6] Ross McKibbin, *Classes and Cultures: England 1918–1951* (Oxford, 1998), p.2.

210   DESIGNS ON DEMOCRACY

Hence the enormous numbers of Committees, Councils and Societies which England contrives to support.[7]

Public intervention relied on those whom Eve Colpus has identified as 'busybodies', often a misogynistic euphemism for women involved in voluntary and philanthropic activity.[8] This was a trope in architectural writing too: in *England and the Octopus*, Clough Williams-Ellis wrote of 'Beneficent Busybodies'.[9] These were characters like Gertrude Freemartin, a protagonist in Osbert Sitwell's novel *Those Were the Days*,[10] an intrepid participant in committee work to uphold civil society, whom Goldring cited as typical of this tendency:

> God has created them to the life and death of Committees. Committees are their vocation, their hobby, their natural means of self-expression... Most Committees arise out of newspaper controversy. Someone writes to the Press pointing out that a valuable invention, such as the Iron Lung, ought to be made available to every hospital and clinic etc etc...Inevitably, Freemartins, scenting the quarry from afar, turn up to see if they can help.[11]

Civil society and associational culture—campaigns and committees—were vital to the thriving of architectural culture in the interwar years, partly because there was an ambivalence about the role of the state and its institutions, often felt to be subject to powerful vested interests. In a mass democracy, the public needed to be vigilant, and vigilantism—watchfulness by the public for the public to preserve that which was most valuable—was a frequent refrain in discourses of preservation and development in the interwar years.

The word 'vigilance' evokes a sense of watching and being watched. It conjures up, much like the word 'propaganda', an Orwellian image of the interwar period—of surveillance and misinformation. In fact, vigilance committees were an American phenomenon in origin; in the mid-nineteenth century, groups of vigilantes sprang up to enforce justice and

---

[7] Douglas Goldring, *Odd Man Out: The Autobiography of a 'Propaganda Novelist'* (1936), p.31.

[8] Eve Colpus, *Female Philanthropy in the Interwar World: Between Self and Other* (2018).

[9] Williams-Ellis, *England and the Octopus*, ch. 10.

[10] Osbert Sitwell, *Those Were the Days: Panorama with Figures* (1938).

[11] Goldring, *Odd Man Out*, p.32.

VIGILANCE 211

order where it was felt the law and the state had failed, most famously perhaps in San Francisco in the 1850s where a 'junta of private citizens' rose up against pervasive criminality and corruption.[12] In Britain, the need for 'vigilance' related largely to the defence of public morality; the National Vigilance Association, formed in 1885, was primarily concerned with the protection of women and children from prostitution and the international trafficking trade. A Central Vigilance Society was established not long after for 'the promotion of social purity'.[13] This association with sex, morality, and propriety prevailed in the twentieth century. The National Vigilance Association campaigned against Jacob Epstein's sculptural programme on Charles Holden's British Medical Association completed on the Strand in 1908. An Oxford Vigilance Committee was revived in 1916, enlisting all-women patrols around the city to monitor and report on licentious behaviour.[14] 'Vigilance', canalized through 'vigilance committees', then, was associated with extrajudicial intervention and with self-appointed, self-righteous citizens taking matters into their own hands—with 'busybody' Freemartins serving on committees. But vigilance was also linked to dissidence; vigilance committees were established during the Siege of Paris in 1870 and in Cape Colony, where the South African Vigilance Society was formed by imperial loyalists against the Boer Republics at the turn of the nineteenth century. They were also later a feature of American commercial life; in the developing advertising industry, vigilance committees were supposed to promote consumer protection and advertising standards. In Britain, a 'National Vigilance Committee' was established by the Advertising Association following the International Advertising Convention at the BEE in 1924. Chaired by Horace Imber, it championed the 'Truth in Advertising' campaign (see Chapter 1).[15]

These essentially moral connotations are important because 'vigilance' and 'vigilance committees' were phrases recurrent in polemical architectural discourse of the period, especially in reaction to any threat to historical towns, buildings, and monuments and, as importantly, proactively in relation to the need for the 'right' development of the city. In 1903 a London

---

[12] 'The State of California', *The Times* (25 September 1851), p.5.

[13] 'National Vigilance Association', *The Times* (5 November 1891), p.6.

[14] Stephen Barker, 'The Oxford Vigilance Committee Report of November 1916 and Fears over Declining Moral Values in the City', http://ww1centenary.oucs.ox.ac.uk/?p=3614 [accessed 25 May 2020].

[15] History of Advertising Trust, Advertising Association Archive, AA/2/6, records of the National Vigilance Committee and successor bodies. See 'Mr Horace S Imber', *Daily Telegraph* (14 January 1929), p.13.

212   DESIGNS ON DEMOCRACY

Architectural Vigilance Committee was instigated by the editor of *The Builder*, H Heathcote Statham, to challenge the London County Council (LCC) designs for a new Vauxhall Bridge.[16] This short-lived committee's stated primary objectives were to influence public opinion and to create a consultative body to advise public bodies on projects of this kind. Many of those prominent in it were involved in the pioneering civic society, the London Society, founded in 1912—Robert Windsor-Clive, Lord Windsor (later the Earl of Plymouth), had been the chairman of the Vigilance Committee and went on to be the new body's first president. Lord Crawford, Aston Webb, and WD Caröe were also deeply involved in both ventures. In the 1920s, the critic and architect-planner Trystan Edwards wrote of the need for 'the exercise of public vigilance upon architectural developments' through 'a roving committee of lay critics especially chosen for their harsh and unsympathetic minds' to 'catechise' design work in architecture schools.[17] Douglas Goldring claimed to have advocated for 'vigilance committees' publicly from the early 1930s 'to supplement the work of the SPAB [Society for the Protection of Ancient Buildings] by enlisting the co-operation of the general public'.[18] And in 1938, in a controversial inaugural speech as president of the Royal Institute of British Architects (RIBA), Goodhart-Rendel spoke of the need for an 'architectural vigilance committee made up of competent persons outside the profession' who 'could do an enormous amount of good by securing the early publications of designs for prominent buildings and their exposure to public criticism'.[19] 'Watchfulness' was needed not only for the preservation of monuments and ensembles but also, in theory, to guide principles of development and control of elevations through democratic means, what we would now call 'design review' and 'public consultation' in the planning process.[20]

'Vigilance' is, therefore, a useful way of understanding important shifts in architectural culture in the early twentieth century and of capturing

---

[16] Eileen Chanin, *Capital Designs: Australia House and Visions of an Imperial London* (Melbourne, 2018), p.57.

[17] Arthur Trystan Edwards, *Good and Bad Manners in Architecture* (1924), p.38.

[18] Goldring, *Odd Man Out*, p.49.

[19] 'President's Address', *AJ* (10 November 1938), p.751.

[20] Matthew Carmona and Andrew Renninger, 'The Royal Fine Art Commission and 75 Years of English Design Review: The First 60 years, 1924–1984', *Planning Perspectives* (2017), pp.577–99; John Punter, 'A History of Aesthetic Control: Part 1, 1909–1953: The Control of the External Appearance of Development in England and Wales', *TPR* 57.4 (October 1986), pp.351–81; Raymond Unwin, 'Architectural Control of Building Plans', *TPR* 13.3 (May 1929), pp.152–4; Patrick Abercrombie, 'The Preservation of Rural England', *TPR* 12.1 (May 1926), pp.5–56.

VIGILANCE 213

attitudes to public participation in development and preservation. It spoke first and foremost to a proprietary right of the community to buildings and the physical and natural environment as a whole. There was an obligation on citizens to take control where the state, local authorities or private interests were being negligent or doing deliberate harm. In this sense, 'vigilance' evoked the richness of associations and volunteerism in architectural culture of the interwar years. Civic societies in particular played a crucial role at municipal and national level. This was especially needed in the absence of robust legislation for planning and preservation, a frustration repeatedly expressed in the campaigns and controversies of the interwar years. The demand for vigilance was a call to arms for the public; in all the examples above, the proposed vigilance committees were to be comprised of lay members (or have some lay presence), though invariably with professional supervision.

Regent Street and the Quadrant

The rebuilding of Regent Street, which spanned the first three decades of the twentieth century, receiving a royal opening in 1927, was one architectural controversy in which claims to public proprietorship became a leitmotif of the preservationist campaign. Although a centre of commerce, Regent Street served an important parallel function as a public space, not only because of the public interest it attracted, and in its role as 'first street of the Empire', but also in terms of ownership. Regent Street was built on Crown land which was, in the words of the Committee on Crown Lands and Government Lands of 1922, a possession of the Crown 'surrendered to the public for the term of life of the Sovereign'.[21]

Controversy had first been aroused by the rebuilding of the Quadrant, the curving blocks running north from Piccadilly Circus, initiated by the destruction of St James's Hall and construction of the Piccadilly Hotel to the designs of Norman Shaw in its middle portion. The profitability of St James's Hall had been hit by its rival music hall, the Queen's Hall, next to All Souls Church on Langham Place, and there was a feeling that the site was ripe

---

[21] H Frank, 'Interim and Final Reports of the Committee on Crown Lands and Public Lands' (1922), p.7, *House of Commons Parliamentary Papers Online*, http://gateway.aa1.proquest.com/openurl?url_ver=Z39.88-2004&res_dat=xri:hcpp&rft_dat=xri:hcpp:rec:1922-025497 [Cmd. 1689] VII.225 [accessed 8 July 2015].

214   DESIGNS ON DEMOCRACY

for more lucrative redevelopment. The P and R Syndicate—the name presumably alluding to the site which bridged Piccadilly ('P') and Regent Street ('R')—acquired the plot in 1902. One controlling interest was Polydore Weichand de Keyser, nephew of the late Sir Polydore de Keyser (1832–1898),[22] a former Mayor of London, who had commissioned the Royal Hotel in Blackfriars. The Syndicate consulted the Commissioners of Woods and Forests as to whether they would be obliged to keep the façades of the existing Quadrant; they intended to build a hotel with a restaurant and retail units considerably higher than the existing fabric. Hotels had proven lucrative opportunities in the West End, exemplified by the recent success of the Ritz Hotel on Piccadilly, commercially and architecturally. The P and R Syndicate eventually transmuted into the Piccadilly Hotel Company in early 1905.[23] The ambitious project of the new hotel awoke the Commissioners of Woods and Forests to the broader issue of the rebuilding of the Quadrant, as other leases were due for imminent renewal. As Hobhouse notes, the Treasury was also increasingly aware of the potential public outcry over any radical intervention or rebuilding of the Quadrant and, detecting public sensitivity, insisted on designs being submitted to an Advisory Committee under the RIBA president. After the Crown's architect Arthur Green, who had been asked to produce initial designs, died, the task of seeking a new architect fell to the Advisory Committee made up of Aston Webb, John Belcher, and Sir John Taylor, consulting architect to the Office of Works. The Committee, reporting to the Treasury in 1904, recommended a new advisory architect outside of the Office of Woods and Forests, and put forward three names: Richard Norman Shaw, Macvicar Anderson, and HT Hare.

Shaw accepted within a month, and quickly produced designs for the new hotel, the rebuilding of the surrounding Quadrant and a new scheme for Piccadilly Circus. In fact, he produced three designs for Piccadilly Circus between April 1905 and March 1906 (Fig. 4.1), with various proposals to mask the unsightly entrances of Haymarket and Shaftesbury Avenue, late-nineteenth-century 'improvements' which had ruined the balance of Nash's circus, and to move the Shaftesbury Memorial to a more suitable position, forming a piazza out of the chaotic street arrangements and subsequent development (Fig. 4.2). Testament to the awkwardness of the site spatially and politically then and ever since, Shaw's proposals quite literally to square

---

[22] The speculation and furore surrounding the rebuilding of the Quadrant contributed to De Keyser's ruin.

[23] The address for both companies was listed as 120 Bishopsgate-street Within.

the circle were ultimately fruitless. For the Hotel, Shaw tinkered with various ideas in the months following his appointment, many of which were met with resistance by the hotel company and its architects, who sought to maximize height and revenue. Indeed later, when the Piccadilly Hotel Company was in liquidation, de Keyser would attribute 'the failure of the company to the alterations in the plans and designs of the building insisted upon by the Crown'.[24]

In April 1906, with St James's Hall now demolished, Shaw's designs were displayed at the Royal Academy. The Quadrant designs were closely modelled on John Carr's crescent at Buxton with ground-floor arcades, a giant engaged order above with clusters of half-blocked and engaged columns, a high cornice at 65 feet, and tall chimneys in the steeply pitched roof.[25] The designs were deemed too expensive to be carried out in Portland Stone, too high for adequate provision of light and ventilation, and the design of the shop windows was also problematic. Set back at some depth, they reflected a trend in shop design that had recessed shop fronts to allow perusal away from the mainstream of pedestrian traffic; it was felt in this case, however, that they would obscure the goods on display to casual passing trade. In fact, as the *Daily Express* pointed out, shop fronts would only be recessed 15 inches from the piers, not halfway back as was the common misconception propagated by illustrations of Shaw's scheme. The height of the shop fronts would be 13 feet, the units would be 30 feet deep, and the arches offered 17 feet of clear frontage between piers for the display of goods.[26]

A fundamental mismatch of expectations between architects and shopkeepers had emerged in commercial architecture of the late nineteenth and early twentieth centuries. Shopkeepers increasingly desired large plate-glass windows to display products and ensure maximum visibility. With the advent of steel-framed construction, wide expanses of plate glass were now possible on the ground floors of large shop buildings, with masonry cladding for the upper floors. For many architects, however, the semblance of heavy masonry façades resting on insubstantial supports between expanses of plate glass was deceitful in Ruskinian terms.[27] The seemingly dark and dingy shop spaces in Shaw's Palazzo design were therefore unacceptable to the shopkeepers. Spurred on by support from the Hotel, they eventually

---

[24] 'The Piccadilly Hotel (Limited)', *The Times* (7 August 1909), p.3.

[25] Saint, *Shaw*, p.404.

[26] TNA, CRES35/3609, 'Merits of the New Quadrant: Artistic Triumph of the Regent Street Shops', *Daily Express* (September 1906).

[27] Julia Scalzo, 'All a Matter of Taste: The Problem of Victorian and Edwardian Shop Fronts', *JSAH* 68.1 (March 2009), pp.52–72.

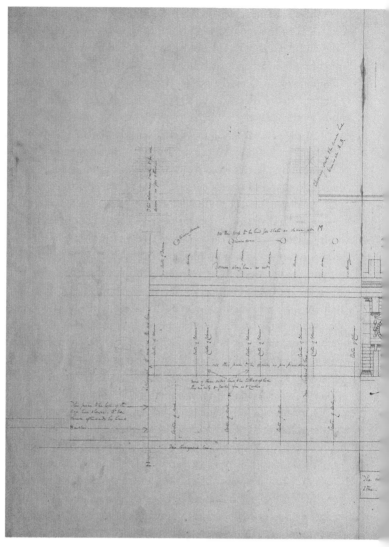

Fig. 4.1 Design for Regent Street Quadrant, London W1: part-elevation, Richard Norman Shaw (c.1905), 11/4302, © Royal Academy of Arts, London; photographer: Prudence Cuming Associates Limited

Fig. 4.2 32–4 Regent Street, London, photograph by Bedford Lemere & Co. (1910), RIBA7796, RIBA Collections

formed the Regent Street Rebuilding Committee in 1907 to put pressure on the Commissioners to alter the scheme.[28]

Indeed, resistance by the shopkeepers persisted and prevailed. The Commissioners had considered abandoning Shaw's scheme earlier, but were unhappy at their characterization as meretricious in the press. The *Standard* went so far as to accuse the Commissioners of disregarding leaseholders' rights. It was 'every British citizen's…right to take an active interest in any scheme for beautifying the metropolitan city of the empire'.[29] And as Erika Rappaport notes, it was London's imperial status that transformed the Quadrant, and by extension Regent Street, 'from private property into a public place that should be controlled by the public'.[30] The Piccadilly Hotel was put up by the end of 1908, work having commenced in 1905, but resistance to Shaw's scheme for the rest of the Quadrant showed no signs of

[28] Saint, *Shaw*, pp.385–6.
[29] Quoted in Erika Rappaport, 'Art, Commerce, or Empire? The Rebuilding of Regent Street, 1880–1927', *History Workshop Journal* 53.1 (April 2002), p.106.
[30] Ibid.

VIGILANCE   219

slowing—the Hotel company was made bankrupt in August of the same year and this, according to the *Survey of London*, 'strengthened the agitation against the completion of the rebuilding of the Quadrant to Shaw's designs'.[31]

In 1912 opposition to Shaw's scheme was still simmering. Elderly and ailing, he resigned all association with it in March that year. In mid-1912 there was a notable shift in the commentary on Regent Street from some corners of the press that was prescient in terms of articulating a new discursive relationship between architecture and public opinion in the 1920s and 1930s, especially in relation to high-profile, preservationist battles. The *Pall Mall Gazette* and *Daily Telegraph* were particularly vociferous in their agitations against the Commissioners of Woods and Forests. In late May of 1912, the *Gazette* issued its clarion call: 'It is time for Londoners to take a hand in the deliberations upon which the fate of one of their greatest thoroughfares is to depend…If the conjoined interests of art and commerce are to be saved from the pedantic and meretricious instincts of Woods and Forests, the weight of public opinion should be thrown without delay into the scale of sense, taste and propriety.'[32] Siding with the shopkeepers, it argued that if the Quadrant plans proceeded it would be a 'mishandling of valuable public property'.[33] Crucially, the onus was on the mobilization of democratic instruments: 'The public responsibility for great artistic heritage is the more immediate because the means of public control are unusually direct.'[34]

One of the more articulate voices of protest came from Stanley Adshead, in a letter published in the *Telegraph*. Echoing the *Gazette*, he argued: 'If we are to retain the present delicate charm of Regent Street, popular indignation must be voiced and an inquiry instituted.'[35] He concluded by praising the recently founded London Society, evidence that 'public interest is at last being aroused in architectural matters…But to insure success the lead given by your valuable paper must be followed by the co-operation of the whole of the Press.'[36] Later that year the *Gazette* would once again refer to the 'scandal of public importance', arguing that 'Up to this point, the

---

[31] 'The Rebuilding of Piccadilly Circus and the Regent Street Quadrant', in FHW Sheppard (ed.), *Survey of London: Volumes 31 and 32, St James Westminster, Part 2* (1963), pp.85–100; *British History Online*, http://www.british-history.ac.uk/survey-london/vols31-2/pt2/pp85-100 [accessed 10 June 2020].
[32] TNA, CRES 35/3610, 'The Ruin of Regent Street', *Pall Mall Gazette* (6 April 1912), newspaper-cutting.
[33] Ibid.
[34] TNA, CRES 35/3610, 'A Nobler London', *Pall Mall Gazette* (28 May 1912), newspaper-cutting.
[35] TNA, CRES 35/3611, 'Regent-street: Prof. Adshead's Protest', *Daily Telegraph* (30 May 1912), newspaper-cutting.
[36] Ibid.

220 DESIGNS ON DEMOCRACY

question is one which ranges the modern architect and the public interest upon one side against the ineptitude of our public organisation.'[37] It is this mobilization of public opinion, and the language of public proprietorship of the street, by the non-specialized press that is striking. The rebuilding of the Quadrant and the consequent rebuilding of the rest of Regent Street became a public matter, and is early evidence of a trope that would become increasingly common in the post-war years through to the 1930s. As the *Gazette* contended, 'The making of London's exterior is the concern of London, and in a very considerable sense, of the nation at large.'[38] Architecture was understood as inherently political in this regard.

The study of 'public opinion' has been of recent concern in the new political history. James Thompson has unpacked the uses and meanings of 'public opinion' in the late nineteenth and early twentieth centuries, many of which have continuing relevance for public discourse of the 1920s and 1930s. The 'political public', in Thompson's formulation, links the 'consuming public' and the 'participatory public', literate, educated, and politically engaged.[39] It was this group whose political views were designated 'public opinion', and moments of high controversy such as the Quadrant debacle elevated architectural and planning discourses to a level of public comment. Thompson's analysis of 'public opinion' traced changes in the meaning of the phrase, and in particular 'the interaction between ideas about the public and public opinion, and ideas about labour.'[40] The growth of the labour movement 'had important implications for inherited unitary, consumerist and intellectualist conceptions of the political public.'[41] The reputation of public opinion remained high and influential in public debate, expressed on 'the political platform, the press, and in petitions', where 'opinions were *weighed* rather than *counted*'; reasonable opinions 'should be privileged in the identification of true public opinion', and reasonableness was supported by 'volume, persistence and intensity' rather than by sheer force of numbers.[42] The idea of the 'weighting' of public opinion in the hyperbole of the *Telegraph* and other media for the preservationist lobby led to the altering of the design of the Quadrant and stimulated longer-term changes in the administration of Crown land.

---

[37] TNA, CRES 35/3611, 'A Scandalous Muddle', *Pall Mall Gazette* (26 September 1912), press-cutting.

[38] TNA, CRES 35/3610, 'A Nobler London', *Pall Mall Gazette* (28 May 1912), newspaper-cutting.

[39] James Thompson, *British Political Culture and the Idea of 'Public Opinion', 1867–1914* (Cambridge, 2013), p.27.

[40] Ibid., p.23.   [41] Ibid.   [42] Ibid.

VIGILANCE 221

The strength of the claim of public proprietorship, and the centrality of public opinion to directing the thoroughfare's future development, was asserted in particular because there was a feeling that Regent Street was a more democratic shopping market, and that it was reflective of imagined social ideals of the age that built and developed it. The *Telegraph* had remarked in 1907 that the 'thoroughfare is no longer exclusively devoted to catering for the wants of wealthy customers...Regent-street has become very largely a middle-class shopping centre.'[43] Trystan Edwards described it as 'an assemblage of buildings designed to serve the commonalty...here imbued with aristocratic grace.'[44] Beresford-Chancellor would claim in 1927 that in fact 'Regent Street always seems to be the particular hunting-ground of all. It is the most cosmopolitan thoroughfare in London—perhaps in the world.'[45]

In the interventions by the *Gazette* and the *Telegraph*, in the marshalling of 'public opinion', there was no explicit contest over who constituted the public, but implicitly there were a number of different characterizations. First, there was the public opinion that the Commissioners of Woods and Forests had to represent—the land was owned by the Crown but surrendered to the public. Some, such as Aston Webb, indeed contended that this 'extensive scheme, which in its making transformed the district of London through which it passed, was carried out on Crown land with great foresight and public spirit by the managers of the Crown property.'[46] Second, there was the preservationists' appeal to public intervention to protect the existing architecture. And thirdly, and unusually mixed up in the preservationist appeal, there was the consuming public interest, represented by the shopkeepers' desire for larger shops and bigger displays.

The largely rebuilt Regent Street was opened on 19 June 1927 (Fig. 4.3). After initial resistance (fearing a charge of preferment over other commercial centres), it was given an informal royal ride through by the king and queen. Writing in *The Observer*, Stanley Adshead reflected that 'Few reconstruction schemes have created so much public interest...Criticism has appeared in the Press on many occasions, and it has become a commonplace to describe its facades as being typical of the deplorable state of architecture at the present time.'[47] But, he insisted, fair judgement could not be passed until the

---

[43] TNA, CRES 35/3608, *Daily Telegraph* (April 4 1907), newspaper-cutting.

[44] Edwards, *Good and Bad Manners*, 1st edn., p.68.

[45] Edwin Beresford Chancellor, 'A Century of Regent Street—Yesterday', *AR* (December 1927), vol.62, p.202.

[46] TNA, CRES 35/3607, Aston Webb, 'Improved Shop Architecture for London', *Nineteenth Century* (July 1906), p.166.

[47] SD Adshead, 'Royal Drive Through Regent Street', *The Observer* (19 June 1927), p.18.

Fig. 4.3 67–71 Regent Street, Westminster LB: redevelopment, photographer unknown (1925), 136641, image © London Metropolitan Archives (City of London)

whole street had been completed: 'Let us rejoice that it finished better than it began.'[48]

There were, however, more equivocal and even negative responses. In a volume of caricatures of architectural personalities, Hubert de Cronin Hastings depicted Goodhart-Rendel hunched, almost menacingly, over a lectern, smirking, with the caption: 'The new Regent Street is perhaps a trifle…(long pause).'[49] The caption suggests that obloquy toward the new Regent Street had become Goodhart-Rendel's familiar theme, the reader imputing the tension in the pregnant long pause. Perhaps de Cronin Hastings had made the drawing at Goodhart-Rendel's Presidential Address to the Architectural Association in October 1924. Entitled 'Yesterday and To-morrow', Goodhart-Rendel complained that:

---

[48] Ibid.
[49] Hubert de Cronin Hastings, *Caricatures* (1925), p.28.

VIGILANCE   223

Whatever its faults there is nothing that is imitation antique about the new Regent Street; nothing exactly like it has ever been seen before, and it is to be hoped that nothing like it will ever been seen [*sic*] again. I return to this thoroughfare because it seems to me in spite of its novelty to be peculiarly representative of those things of yesterday upon which we must try to ensure that to-morrow turns its back. Foremost among these things I put its utter insincerity.[50]

This quotation captures a sense among contemporaries that the loss of old Regent Street was the loss of something authentic—antithetical to the 'utter insincerity' of commercial architecture of the day. Furthermore, there was a sense that Regent Street—despite its close connection to the Regency and whimsy of Prince George—was somehow a manifestation of a social order in which commerce was subjugated by a democratic ideal. We will return to these themes in the next chapter.

Crown Lands and Carlton House Terrace

Lessons were never fully learnt from the Regent Street debacle. Five years after the new street was 'opened', further redevelopment at its southern end reignited preservationist passions. How had techniques of mobilizing public proprietorship in the preservationist cause shifted? In 1932, the uniformity of Nash's Carlton House Terrace and Carlton Gardens was threatened by an unwieldy proposal by Reginald Blomfield. The situation was uncannily similar to the earlier Quadrant debacle in which Blomfield had played such an active role; Carlton House Terrace, at the foot of Regent Street, was administered by the recently formed Commissioners for Crown Lands, successors to the Commissioners of Woods and Forests, and the proposals, submitted by a firm of wholesale paint manufacturers, Pinchin, Johnson and Company Ltd, was for a tall steel-framed building clad in Portland stone at No.4 Carlton Gardens, incidentally home of the late Arthur Balfour.

The *Architects' Journal* certainly saw the roots of the debacle in the handling of the rebuilding of Regent Street twenty years earlier, which 'suffers from a huge, haphazard, piecemeal rebuilding, in which architects, buildings, contractors, and, one might think from a glance at the street as it is

---

[50]   HS Goodhart-Rendel, 'Yesterday and To-morrow', *AAJ* 150.453 (November, 1924), p.96.

224   DESIGNS ON DEMOCRACY

today, enthusiastic and semi-inspired amateurs, were given a free run.[51] The *Architect and Building News* too saw the origins of the present controversy in the 'blundering policy of Regent Street'.[52]

The scheme was approved by the Royal Fine Art Commission in July 1932, though the ease with which it was gained was 'somewhat embarrassing' given that Blomfield sat on it.[53] No.4 was promptly pulled down before protest had coalesced and it was replaced with Blomfield's tall and incongruous steel framed building in a simplified Classical style. As Fellows recounts, it soon emerged that the intention was that Carlton House Terrace, like Regent Street, would be replaced wholesale with modern commercial buildings. Blomfield's intervention was just a trial run.[54] Press opposition flared up—*The Times* was particularly critical, and the *Architects' Journal* and the *Architectural Review* were especially vociferous in campaigning against the scheme: 'Their rôle was not impartial, but aggressively pro-Nash and anti-Blomfield.'[55]

As Elizabeth McKellar has recently shown, the defence of Carlton House Terrace has long been associated with British Modernists' interest in the preservation of Georgian architecture. JC Squire's famous letter to *The Times*, which announced the formation of the Carlton House Terrace Defence Committee, included a number of Modern Architectural Research Group (MARS) members such as Max Fry, and Peter and Roger Fleetwood-Hesketh. The support of the titles of the Architectural Press—the *AJ* and the *AR*—also expressed Modernist-preservationist concern. As McKellar notes, however, membership was far wider than just Modernists, 'it included all the leading architectural figures of the time as signatories not to mention the massed ranks of the establishment'.[56]

In January 1933, the *AR* published a number of responses to a questionnaire it had issued entitled 'Carlton House Terrace: What Public Opinion Says'.[57] Respondents included Osbert Sitwell, Robert Byron, Max Beerbohm, and Aldous Huxley, as well as a number of professional figures. Banister Fletcher commented that he did not 'believe that His Majesty's Government, or even public opinion, would countenance such a disastrous commencement'.[58]

---

[51] 'Vandalism and High Rents: Lessons from Regent Street and Carlton House Terrace', *AJ* (1 April 1933), p.12.

[52] 'Marginalia', *AR* (January 1933), p.47.

[53] Richard Fellows, *Sir Reginald Blomfield: An Edwardian Architect* (1985), p.135.

[54] Ibid., pp.133–8.   [55] Ibid., p.136.

[56] McKellar, 'Georgian London before *Georgian London*', p.38.

[57] 'Carlton House Terrace: What Public Opinion Says', *AR* (January 1933), pp.11–15.

[58] 'Carlton House Terrace: Professional Views', ibid., p.16.

VIGILANCE 225

Giles Gilbert Scott wrote that he would 'be very reluctant to see these buildings demolished...a magnificent terrace in a position of unrivalled importance'.[59] It was the channelling of public opinion that would prevent its demolition. The writer Osbert Burdett demanded a public inquiry and railed against AS Gaye, Commissioner for the Crown Lands, and Blomfield for their misplaced and 'unlimited faith in the passivity of the only public that cares for the beauties of London, especially when they can confront us stealthily with an accomplished disaster'.[60]

The weight of public opinion indeed ultimately halted the wider redevelopment scheme for Carlton Gardens and Carlton House Terrace. The debate and furore has been well charted. What has been less considered is the episode's impact on the administration of Crown land. As early as February 1933, while the *AJ* and *AR* continued to publish pages and pages of 'Public Opinion' against the rebuilding, AS Gaye was writing to Sir Donald Vandepeer, permanent secretary of the Ministry of Agriculture and Fisheries (the Minister of Agriculture was the other ex-officio Commissioner), in order to propose names for a new Advisory Committee for the Commissioners for Crown Lands.[61] The decision for the formation of the standing committee had been made at Cabinet on 8 February 'to advise the Commissioners of Crown Lands on questions involving aesthetic and similar considerations in connection with the Crown's urban estates'.[62]

The Committee was intended essentially as a public relations strategy to protect ministers and Commissioners from criticism. The Crown Commissioners had been subjected to much public opprobrium; they were, as one journalist described them, 'mysterious'—with 'mysterious methods, and their mysterious absence of any apparent feeling of public responsibility'.[63] Gaye had come in for particular criticism—one document in the Treasury papers regarding the matter is entitled 'Alternative ways of saving Gaye's face'.[64] Further reform of the administration of the Crown lands was clearly needed. Proposals to merge the Crown lands with the Office of Works were mooted, but found to be politically unworkable.[65]

---

[59] Ibid.

[60] Osbert Burdett, 'Carlton House Terrace: The Chance for the Defence', *AR* (February 1933), p.49.

[61] TNA, CRES 35/3911, Letter from AS Gaye to Vandepeer (14 February 1933).

[62] Ibid., Letter from Walter Elliot to Ramsay MacDonald (22 February 1933).

[63] 'Vandalism and High Rents: Lessons from Regent Street and Carlton House Terrace', *AJ* (1 April 1933), p.12.

[64] TNA, T161/1030, Handwritten memorandum entitled 'Alternative Ways of Saving Gaye's Face' (12 December 1932).

[65] Ibid.

226 DESIGNS ON DEMOCRACY

Gaye was rather sceptical about the Committee's potential to help, writing to a Treasury official that: 'Every new building in London affects town planning interests and public or private amenities to some extent. Hitherto the Commissioners of Crown Lands have proceeded on the same principles as the other great London landowners, but in future that policy is not going to satisfy "educated public opinion".'[66] The Committee was to be made up of experts, though it was suggested that the chairman should be 'someone, not an architect, on whom the public can rely not to lose sight of the aesthetic side, but who will at the same time keep the Committee on the rails and take a broad and common sense view'.[67] With his position threatened, Gaye wrote to Walter Elliot, the recently appointed Minister of Agriculture, complaining that

> ...recent agitation in Parliament and the press had caused a splash utterly out of proportion to its real weight. The attack on this Office is based on ignorance of the law and misrepresentation of the facts. So far as I have been able to gauge the opinion of the educated man in the street, there is more support for the views expressed by Sir Reginald Blomfield than there is for attitude of 'The Times'.[68]

The Committee was appointed for an initial period of four years. As notes from a meeting with the Carlton House Defence Committee—set up to canalize the preservationist protest—show, it was designed with satisfying public opinion in mind. Members served as individuals rather than representatives of bodies; they were there to represent the 'point of view of the interested and instructed man in the street', 'to advise only on important questions of public interest'.[69] It was chaired by Lord Gorrell, a design reformer, and included Lord Jessel, president of the London Municipal Society, Frank Pick, who had been a prominent voice in the Carlton House Terrace Defence League, Raymond Unwin, Sir John Oakley, a past president of the Surveyors' Institution, and the writer and publisher EV Lucas.

'Public opinion' in the architectural sphere, therefore, had successfully coerced the government into forming the Advisory Committee as a public relations mechanism. Somewhat tellingly, 'What Public Opinion Says', the results of the *AR*'s questionnaire, took as representative of the public

---

[66] TNA, CRES 35/3911, Letter from AS Gaye to James Rae, Treasury (28 March 1933).
[67] TNA, CRES 35/3911, Letter from Walter Elliot to Ramsay MacDonald (22 February 1933).
[68] TNA, T161/1030, Letter from ASG to Walter Elliot (5 January 1933).
[69] TNA, T161/1030, Memorandum of meeting with Carlton House Defence Committee.

members of the intelligentsia such as Osbert Sitwell, Robert Byron, Aldous Huxley, Clive Bell, and Kenneth Clark; establishment figures, such as the president of Magdalen College, Oxford and The Slade Professor of Art; and members of the aristocracy, such as the Countess of Oxford and Asquith, the Duchess of Roxbrughe, and Viscount Weymouth. Certainly this reinforces James Thompson's argument about the 'weighting' of public opinion—here a network of well-informed, powerful figures were able to manipulate the power of 'public opinion' to their own advantage.

To observe the consequences of the Committee, we might briefly consider Rex House (1937-9) on Lower Regent Street (Fig. 4.4), one of the last rebuilding projects of the interwar years. Designed by the cinema architect Robert Cromie, it was intended as a cinematograph theatre with office accommodation above. It came before the Advisory Committee's consideration in 1937, by which time Giles Gilbert Scott had been appointed as an additional member. He had previously acted as a special adviser to the Committee on the design of the foreground and façades to the new Adelphi, not in fact on Crown land, but the project was probably referred to them because of their experience with Georgian preservationists in the face of strong public

Fig. 4.4 Rex House, Lower Regent Street, London, Rex Cromie, photograph by Charles Borup (1939), RIBA23481, RIBA Collections

228   DESIGNS ON DEMOCRACY

opposition. It was felt that in spite of Scott's membership, 'the Crown Lands Advisory Committee would still remain a "Plain Man's" Committee as distinguished from the Royal Fine Art Commission which is predominantly an "Expert" committee'.[70]

Rex House was a plain, stripped classical commercial office-block with the Paris Cinema in its basement. It perhaps demonstrates that the victory for public opinion was not necessarily a victory for ambitious design. Rather as AS Gaye had feared, invention and creativity were stifled: the public face was staid. The advice offered by the Advisory Committee through design review was pedantic: as indicated by the limp suggestions that 'the central entrance on the Regent Street front might be made more significant if the architectural treatment could be carried up to the level of the first floor', or that the appearance of the building might be improved if the number of visible supports was increased.[71]

In the controversies surrounding Regent Street and Carlton House Terrace, public opinion and public proprietorship were mobilized for the preservationist cause. The offence to public proprietorship was a more widespread concern than formal or stylistic divisions. The consequences of a vociferous public opinion and the increasingly frequent challenge of the claims of public proprietorship did not necessarily make for successful design outcomes. This is expressed in the uncertainty about the new Regent Street, and shown by the banal observations and bland results of the Crown Lands Committee's intervention into Rex House. A similar process beset Stanley Hamp's New Adelphi put up by the G&D Development Company which, under Section 33 of the Adelphi Estate Act, also required consultation with the Crown Lands Committee for its river frontage. Where the relatively new practice of design review was increasingly effective in domestic and public buildings, in the commercial sector the results were less than impressive.

Nash's ensembles were high status *causes célèbres*; highly visible relics in an imperial capital being visibly remade. Cumulatively, by the mid-1930s, they led to the institutionalization of Georgian preservationism. There was, however, another side to this story which has been less frequently told, in which domestic architecture and more modest ensembles began to make claims on public vigilance and canalize preservationist feeling. Furthermore,

---

[70] TNA, T161/1030, Beresford to Sir James Rae, Treasury (9 March 1937).
[71] RIBA, Giles Gilbert Scott Papers (hereafter, Scott Papers), ScGG/278/1, 'Crown Lands Advisory Committee: Proposed Cinematograph Theatre on the site of Nos 4–12 Regent Street', 'Supplementary References', fo.36viii.

the significance of these campaigns was amplified by a growing fascination with the 'everyday lives' of working-class communities and 'slum-dwellers,' intersecting with the wider housing question and the consequences of universal franchise which expanded the political category of 'the public'.

Shutters up in Portland Town

In August 1936, the critic and architect-planner Arthur Trystan Edwards wrote to *The Times* on the subject of 'Architecture and Slum-Dwellers', arguing that the democratization of architecture should not only include the widening of opportunity for architectural training to diverse social classes but also expand the conception of the architectural client to acknowledge the new 'patrons of art': 'It would surely be a beneficial development if those living in the little streets of cities would assume a proprietary interest in the whole field of town-planning.'[72] Lay working-class opinion, he argued, would compute the importance of the social life of the street with the theory and practice of civic design. The housing campaign which he organized from 1933, the Hundred New Towns Association, advocating low-rise high-density compact New Towns strategically developed across the country, was predicated on this premise; the Association was convened by a committee of 'ex-servicemen', of ordinary veterans who had served in the Great War, in the service of their 'slum-dwelling' communities. Moreover, Edwards posited that refinement of street architecture was the enduring legacy of the Georgian and Regency periods, and he alluded to recent campaigns to preserve eighteenth- and early nineteenth-century ensembles in north-west London, including a row of terraces in Haverstock Hill, Belsize Park, to which Stanley Adshead had also drawn attention in the correspondence columns of *The Times* a few weeks earlier, and 'a meeting called to protest against the erection of luxury flats on a site near St John's Wood, now occupied by terraces for wage-earners', a network of streets known as Portland Town.[73]

Edwards's letter outlined three interlinked areas of concern: first, an increasingly accepted view that architecture was undergoing a process of democratization, and that this included a proprietary and participatory

---

[72] Arthur Trystan Edwards, 'Architecture and Slum-Dwellers', *The Times* (12 August 1936), p.15.

[73] SD Adshead, 'Town Planning in Hampstead', *The Times* (6 August 1936), p.6.

230 DESIGNS ON DEMOCRACY

claim by the public over the built environment, including by working-class 'slum-dwellers'; second, that this proprietary sense extended to preservation of built heritage, in particular that of the Georgian and Regency period, typified not necessarily by public monuments but by domestic ensembles and town planning; and finally, that the principles underlying that period were germane to contemporary architectural and planning challenges, namely the provision of housing on a large scale and the creation of sustainable communities to populate them. It is to the first two of these areas we now turn, before developing the third in the next chapter.

Earlier that year, in January 1936, the young developer Rudolph Palumbo ordered the demolition of a house he had acquired on Maida Vale.[74] The semi-detached Regency villa—122 Maida Vale—was next door to the home of Dorothy Warren Trotter and her husband Philip Trotter. With the house at 120 it formed a typical pair of suburban villas in St John's Wood, stucco with a shared pediment and an oculus in the tympanum, the symmetry of which would be interrupted by Palumbo's proposed replacement block of flats (Fig. 4.5).[75] The Trotters fought to resist the development, while also drawing up contingency plans to make the façade of their half appear detached. These proposals were rejected by Palumbo, and the development proceeded.

In Mrs Trotter, Palumbo had found a formidable opponent. Born Dorothy Warren, she was the daughter of the Arts and Crafts architect Edward Prioleau Warren, and an interior designer in her own right, most notably working on Studio 3D for BBC Broadcasting House 'designed in the character of a Regency Library'.[76] She had opened the Warren Gallery, latterly run with her husband, which gained a reputation for daring exhibitions of modern art, including an early show for the sculptor Henry Moore and a controversial display of paintings by DH Lawrence in 1929 which resulted in a prosecution for obscenity. The same year, the Trotters had bought the house on Maida Vale and did 'much to enhance its period atmosphere' thereafter.[77]

The *Daily Telegraph* was a valuable ally in arousing public interest in the plight of the Trotters. Richardson, Lutyens, and later Giles Gilbert Scott

---

[74] 'Georgian House Doomed', *Daily Telegraph* (7 January 1936), p.10.
[75] 'Obituaries of Buildings—Nos 120 and 122 Maida Vale (no 45)', *ABN* (3 January 1936), supplement n.p.
[76] Edward Nehls (ed.), *DH Lawrence: A Composite Biography* (Madison, 1958) vol.2, p.695.
[77] 'Georgian House Doomed', p.10.

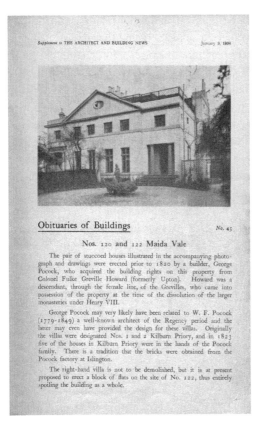

Fig. 4.5 'Obituaries of Buildings: Nos 120 and 122 Maida Vale', *ABN* (3 January 1936), RIBA139645, RIBA Collections

wrote with concern over 'The Pickaxe in Maida Vale'.[78] Reginald Blomfield's solution was to instil principles of 'good taste' in the articulation of public opinion, and to embed questions of public amenity into 'the ethics of citizenship'.[79] Others decried the 'Sentence on Old Villas', noting that their ruin was an offence to public amenity. The art historian Robert Witt—co-founder of the National Art Collections Fund and the Courtauld Institute—was careful to record the wider public interest in the case and others like it: 'it is mainly on the vigilance of members of the public that the hope of a

[78] 'The Pickaxe in Maida Vale', *Daily Telegraph* (8 January 1936), p.12.
[79] Reginald Blomfield, 'Piecemeal Architecture', *Daily Telegraph* (11 January 1936), p.10.

wiser and larger outlook on these vital matters can be found'.[80] Sydney Tatchell went further: 'It appears to me that unless a building speculator recognises that as a neighbour he owes a duty to the community to preserve the amenities of the town and countryside in which he is operating, no legislation can be devised that can altogether circumvent his activities.'[81] Gilbert H Cotton went further still, arguing that existing legislation in the form of the Town and Country Planning Act (1932) made provision for local authorities to control the design of elevations under Section 12, but that these powers were being underused.[82] The fate of the Trotters' villa, therefore, spoke to widely shared concerns about public amenity and democratic mechanisms to control development.

After the destruction of the neighbouring property (Fig. 4.6), the Trotters rechristened their home 'the Mutilated House', and thereafter it became the nerve centre of their campaigning activities.[83] In February 1936, they

Fig. 4.6 The Mutilated House, 'Shutters up in Portland Place', *AR* (June 1938), p.292, image courtesy of the Museum of Domestic Design & Architecture, Middlesex University, http://www.moda.mdx.ac.uk

[80] 'Sentence on Old Villas: Amenities an Issue for the Public', *Daily Telegraph* (10 January 1936), p.12.
[81] Ibid.
[82] 'Maida-Vale Flat Proposal: Control of New Designs', *Daily Telegraph* (14 January 1936), p.9.
[83] Letter from Dorothy Warren, *Country Life* (25 January 1936), p.103.

Fig. 4.7 Local residents of Portland Town, photograph by Margaret Monck (c.1938), IN15002, Museum of London, © The Estate of Margaret Monck

founded 'The Londoners' League' intended, in their words, 'to defend and foster the beauties and virtues of London home-life, architectural, horticultural and sociological'.[84] By September their primary campaign was in support of the preservation of Portland Town on the periphery of St John's Wood in the Borough of St Marylebone. Developed in the 1820s on a belt of farmland leased from the Duke of Portland, it was a network of around twenty streets of cottage terraces and courts (Fig. 4.7), bounded by Avenue Road to the east, Prince Albert Road to the south, St John's Wood High Street to the west (formerly Portland Town Road), and St John's Wood Terrace to the north. In the early 1900s leases began to fall in, and the Howard De Walden Estate (as the Portland Estate eventually became by descent) extended leases for short periods. Portland Town had, however, retained its primarily working-class character, with generations of the same families still living there, often within close proximity to their work (Figs. 4.8 and 4.9).

St John's Wood had been the site of development for a number of luxury blocks of flats, as Trystan Edwards's letter to *The Times* had highlighted

[84] Gavin Stamp, 'How We Celebrated the Coronation', *Georgian Group Journal* (2012), pp.5–6.

234   DESIGNS ON DEMOCRACY

Fig. 4.8 Joseph Bunyan outside his fruit shop in Portland Town, photograph by Margaret Monck (c.1938), IN14985, Museum of London, © The Estate of Margaret Monck

Fig. 4.9 Rear of terraced housing in Portland Town, photograph by Margaret Monck (c.1938), IN14977, Museum of London, © The Estate of Margaret Monck

(Fig. 4.10). Robert Atkinson had designed Stockleigh Hall and Oslo Court (Fig. 4.11), both opened in 1938, and Marshall and Tweedy had designed Viceroy Court and Bentinck Close (Fig. 4.12) nearby.[85] The North Gate mansion-block, which had been one of the first tall apartment-block developments in London when it opened in 1904, was also extended in the 1930s. The original mansion-block was designed by EP Warren—an irony unnoticed at the time, given his daughter's subsequent involvement in the campaign to protect Portland Town and her claim to his credentials as 'old friend & associate of William Morris', who had played a role in the preservation of Abingdon Street, Old Palace Yard, and Victoria Tower Gardens, the first of which remained a contentious case in the 1930s.[86]

At some point in 1936 the Regents Park Development Company arrived on the scene, ready to develop the estate into more luxury apartment-blocks.

Fig. 4.10   Construction of Townshend Court, Portland Town, photograph by Margaret Monck (c.1938), IN14971, Museum of London, © The Estate of Margaret Monck

---

[85] 'Flats in London', *AR* (June 1938), pp.278–85. This article immediately preceded one on the destruction of Portland Town, acknowledged in an editorial note.
[86] SPAB Archives, GGGC, Dorothy Warren Trotter, 'Relations of the Londoners' League to the SPAB' (written late 1937); Robert Byron, *How We Celebrate the Coronation* (1937), p.7.

Fig. 4.11 Oslo Court, Prince Albert Road, Regent's Park, London: the entrance façade on Charlbert Street seen from the north, Robert Atkinson, photograph by Dell & Wainwright (1938), RIBA8253, Architectural Press Archive/RIBA Collections

In July, fifty tenants in Charbert, Culworth, and Newcourt Streets were asked to vacate their homes.[87] The AR would later note that the Communist Party intervened, helping the residents to form 'a well-disciplined Tenants' Defence League' which called for a protection of residents' interests, alternative accommodation within the borough, and the replacement of a certain number of working-class dwellings near workplaces, shops, and amenities.[88] At a fraught meeting in the De Walden Institute on Charlbert Street, it was noted that 300 families had been moved from the district in the previous three years. Local architect Frank Elgood proposed that the LCC and St Marylebone Borough Council seek assurances from the developers about their intentions to 'provide a site and erect dwellings, suitable for weekly wage-earners already living on the estate, and to be let at rents within their means'.[89]

---

[87] Ralph Parker, 'Shutters up in Portland Town', AR (June 1938), p.294.   [88] Ibid.
[89] 'Workers Evicted for Flats: A St John's Wood Problem', The Times (24 July 1936), p.11.

Fig. 4.12 Bentick Close, Prince Albert Road, Regent's Park, London: corner of the main elevation, Robert James Hugh Minty, photograph by Alfred Cracknell (1938), RIBA64754, Architectural Press Archive/RIBA Collections

By September, a petition organized by the Trotters had gained ground; residents were seeking reassurances from the Minister of Health, requesting that Portland Town 'be zoned and developed as a working-class area' on the basis that St John's Wood and South Hampstead had become 'over-flatted'.[90] In October, Julian Huxley, Edgar Bonham Carter, Lutyens, and many others had signed the petition, and it was submitted to the LCC Housing Committee; by November further signatories included Reginald Blomfield, Philip and Ottoline Morrell, AE Richardson, and, significantly, Douglas Goldring.[91] Nevertheless, by April 1937 evictions in Portland Town were proceeding apace. Criticism of the evictions and 'over-flatting' of St John's Wood persisted. At a meeting convened by the Londoners' League in

---

[90] 'Luxury Flats at Portland Town: Local Opposition to Re-Development', *The Times* (19 September 1936), p.10.
[91] 'Tenants of Portland Town', *The Times* (6 October 1936), p.11.

238 DESIGNS ON DEMOCRACY

September 1937, the petition had reached 3,000 signatures.[92] In the summer of 1938, as the *AR* noted, the shutters were up in Portland Town, and at a dolorous meeting of the St Marylebone Housing Association in March 1939 it was lamented by the Association president, Lord O'Neill, that despite a willingness to help, 'site values were prohibitive because of the development of luxury flats'.[93] There was some hope that a ninety-nine-year lease from the Eyre Estate (which owned large tracts of St John's Wood) might close a shortfall of flats. The need was manifestly great—a proposed development of fourteen flats on Allitsen Road by the Association received 140 applications. Henry House, designed by Louis de Soissons, opened in early 1940 and *The Times* noted that the tenants in what was eventually 12 two-, three- and four-bedroom flats were 'all families from the neighbourhood, whose old homes were pulled down and replaced by expensive flats'.[94]

The campaign to preserve Portland Town was, therefore, unsuccessful. The rate of rehousing the displaced working-class tenants was limited, and the complex of streets and buildings was demolished. Nevertheless, the campaign and the society it spawned, the Londoners' League, were significant because of the nuanced understanding of Georgian preservationism which they championed. However, the activism of organizations like the Londoners' League—which felt itself to give voice to the proprietary public— was frustratingly eclipsed by the Georgian Group, founded in May 1937 amidst the Portland Town controversy. This was despite the fact that some of those prominent in the Georgian Group had been attached to the Londoners' League and participated in the Portland Town campaign. Douglas Goldring later recalled that he had made contact with a couple 'whose Regency home in Maida Vale had been bi-sected by flat speculators'—the Trotters, though tellingly he does not name them—and that he had tried to publicize their efforts. He claimed to have 'put the project of forming a society to protect Georgian architecture before them', and that they had had 'frequent discussions, committee meetings and telephone conversations of inordinate length'.[95] By contrast, Dorothy Warren Trotter claimed to have given Goldring an opportunity, through her friend Christopher Hussey, to publish an article in *Country Life* on the demolition of Georgian buildings, and complained that he had betrayed this and other

---

[92] 'Protection of Community Life: Luxury Flats Criticised', *The Times* (20 September 1937), p.22.
[93] 'Workers Displaced by Luxury Flats', *The Times* (23 March 1939), p.12.
[94] 'New Block of Flats in St Marylebone', *The Times* (19 February 1940), p.3.
[95] Goldring, *Odd Man Out*, p.64.

VIGILANCE   239

favours by launching his own group and publicly denying the Trotters' and Londoners' League's role.[96]

The basic difference between the League and the newly formed Group was that the League was intended as the defender 'of good Georgian Domestic architecture in residential London areas, and of "Little Londons" and their village-like communities'.[97] Its primary criterion, unlike that of the 'Goldringites' and 'Groupists' as an exasperated Trotter described Georgian Group members, was to make a difference in 'sociological and housing controversies'.[98] This meant that the targets of their defence—exemplified by Portland Town—were not just prestige monuments and middle-class Georgian squares, but also the persistent threat to 'various residential areas when a few individual buildings of architectural merit may be harmoniously neighboured by buildings & open spaces of PLANNING, but not intrinsic architectural merit'.[99] The 'planning' merit of the everyday Georgian domestic architecture which included working-class communities like Portland Town distinguished its focus from that of the nascent Georgian Group.

Gavin Stamp rightly noted that Trotter was 'scandalised and disgusted' by the 'anti-clericism' of Robert Byron's influential pamphlet, How We Celebrated the Coronation, often championed as the clarion-call for the establishment of the Georgian Group.[100] In it Byron had been critical of the Church of England's disregard for Wren's imperilled City Churches, some of which they had tried to sell off. In truth, however, Trotter was even more exercised by the fact that Goldring and the 'Groupists' had appropriated Londoners' League victories as their own, and by the shift of sociological emphasis which thereby took place.[101]

If they differed on clericalism, Byron and the Trotters were united in their anti-socialism. Trotter made frequent public criticisms of the Labour-run LCC and its Town Planning Committee. Indeed, the politics of interwar preservationism made for a complex picture. As the AR noted, 'all the organising ability of the communists, the sentiment of the liberals, the patient committee work of the socialists, and the machinations of tories can do

---

[96] SPAB Archives, GGGC, Memorandum by Dorothy Warren Trotter entitled 'Relations of the Londoners' League to the SPAB'.

[97] Ibid., Dorothy Warren Trotter to Albert Richardson (7 November 1937).

[98] Ibid.   [99] Ibid., Trotter, 'Relations of the Londoners' League'.

[100] Gavin Stamp, 'How We Celebrated the Coronation', Georgian Group Journal (2012), p.6.

[101] In a letter to the Telegraph, Goldring made no mention of the League in relation to Portland Town; SPAB Archives, GGGC, Philip Trotter to Albert Richardson (7 November 1937). For the offending letter see 'LCC Town Planning', Daily Telegraph (5 October 1937).

240 DESIGNS ON DEMOCRACY

nothing to preserve Portland Town as it existed a few years ago'.[102] Douglas Goldring—an avowed Christian Socialist—was nevertheless highly critical of 'the Socialist authorities at County Hall [who] in regard to housing and town planning have contrived to exasperate all classes of Londoners from the humblest workers upwards'.[103] He alluded to one campaign poster from the local elections of 1937 in which there was a 'vast blue hand demolishing on one side of the picture, the remains of Georgian London, and on the other side substituting hideous blocks of flats, adorned with the detested "communal balconies"'.[104] Yet despite his own left-leaning beliefs, he ultimately disengaged from the Trotters' Londoners' League because of its progressive objectives: 'I was not prepared to be diverted from my original purpose by becoming involved in a politico-sociological movement, however admirable its object'.[105] Goldring's strange dismissal of a 'politico-sociological movement' in favour, by implication, of an 'aesthetic' movement, arguably clouded similar motivations of other early prominent members of the Georgian Group.

In March 1937 Trotter—who referred to 'Socialist town messing' rather than town planning—also commented on the forthcoming LCC elections, writing to *The Times* that the 'vast number of London's municipal electors, [were] horrified at "What Labour has done to London," determined that they will not set their hand to the furtherance of professional party politics at the expense of London's intimate and intricate needs'.[106] Despite 'propaganda deficiencies', she continued, the Municipal Reform Party boasted 'a handful of men who are really able and staunch defenders of existing amenities for existing residents'.[107] Although unnamed, these will have included figures like Dr S Monckton Copeman and the Reverend WR Hornby Steer, representatives for Hampstead on the LCC, and Basil Marsden-Smedley who represented Chelsea and was a founder-member of the Chelsea Society. Marsden-Smedley, who 'saw in Chelsea something of the character of a

---

[102] Ralph Parker, 'Shutters up in Portland Town', *AR* (June 1938), p.294.
[103] Douglas Goldring, 'Demolition "Massacre"', *Daily Telegraph* (18 February 1937), p.18.
[104] Ibid. The association of particular colours with political parties was not yet firmly established: the blue hand represented the Labour Party, not the Conservative Municipal Reform Party.
[105] Goldring, *Odd Man Out*, p.64.
[106] Dorothy Trotter, 'London Government', *The Times* (2 March 1937), p.12. For 'town messing', see SPAB Archives, GGGC, Philip Trotter to Albert Richardson (7 November 1937).
[107] Trotter, 'London Government', p.12.

village',[108] also wrote critically of the 'Socialists' in the LCC in relation to Portland Town, who in his view had failed to exercise powers to recondition (recommended by the Moyne Report of 1935 and enshrined in the subsequent Housing Act):

> ...the true position is that there are no slums in Portland Town. It is a village of small houses, for the most part in sound condition or capable of repair...Local communities such as Portland Town are characteristic of London and very worthy of protection. These precious collections of people should be treasured with the same reverence as its great monuments of stone and iron.[109]

These conservative voices in planning and preservationism, which spoke neither for traditionalism nor for defence of a particular style, but for a different built ideal of working-class community, have been written out of the narrative of progressive development.

The contribution of this unshowy movement, driven by those with a training in and sensibility for architecture and design, to a broader culture of self-conscious engagement with working-class life was important. Ideologically distinct and more seriously grounded in a coherent understanding of urbanism, it was overshadowed by the more famous and better-promoted Mass Observation (MO). This project to create an anthropological study of everyday life developed out of a meeting between the anthropologist Tom Harrison, a radical Liberal, and poet Charles Madge, a member of the Communist Party: 'As a political project, MO's aim was to enable the masses to speak for themselves, to make their voices heard above the din created by press and politicians speaking their name. In this way the organization—bridging the gulf between elite and popular culture—would help to place democracy on a firm and stable footing.'[110] Although the group's first major project was on 'Worktown', a study of Bolton initiated by Harrison in 1937, its first publication took the form of a 'Day-Survey', the first of which took place on 12 May, the day of George VI's

---

[108] 'Mr Basil Marsden-Smedley', *The Times* (8 September 1964), p.12.

[109] Basil Marsden-Smedley, 'Portland Town', *The Times* (22 October 1936), p.12.

[110] James Hinton, *The Mass Observers: A History, 1937–1949* (Oxford, 2013), p.3. The connection between 'Georgians and Mass Observers' is noted in Miles Glendinning, *The Conservation Movement: A History of Architectural Preservation, Antiquity to Modernity* (Abingdon, 2013), p.234.

242 DESIGNS ON DEMOCRACY

coronation, through the form of submitted diaries and testimony.[111] There was a deliberate echo of this in Byron's *How We Celebrate the Coronation* which, while rhetorically aimed to shock a visitor to London, contains in it the ideal of collective self-reflection and observation which lay at the heart of the MO project. Observations on 'how *we* celebrate' find their echo in the MO's diary project. There is a neat symmetry in the fact that the first meetings of the Mass Observation movement were held in a Georgian terraced house in Blackheath, 6 Grotes Buildings.[112]

MO was part of a wider political impulse, as Alexandre Campsie has shown, 'towards studying "everyday life", arguing that politics should be constructed around the insights gleaned from these critical inquiries'.[113] Left intellectuals and writers like Amabel Williams-Ellis wrote features in *Left Review*, in which a 'literary language of artisanal "craft"' was cultivated.[114] Closely linked manifestations of this fascination were apparent in the discussion of the material culture of 'everyday things' and 'everyday life' in progressive architectural and design reform circles in Chapters 1 and 3. As well as Williams-Ellis, there were further links to architectural culture through the documentary film movement and the newly appointed editor of the *Architectural Review*, JM Richards. In June 1938, the *AR* published a report on the St John's Wood campaign, 'Shutters up in Portland Town' (Fig. 4.13).[115] The article was written by Ralph Parker, later Moscow correspondent for *The Times*, who also wrote for the *Daily Worker* and who had, we can presume, Communist sympathies.[116] Photographic illustration was provided by Margaret Monck, married to the documentary film-maker John Monck (formerly Goldman), who herself was well known for her photographic studies of East London working-class life. Captions included 'The Tally Man comes once a week', 'Back Street life', 'Old faces', and the article provided not only a historical but also a sociological study of life in Portland Town, a way of life that was ultimately to be lost (Figs. 4.14 and 4.15, see also Figs. 4.8 and 4.9):

---

[111] Humphrey Jennings and Charles Madge (eds.), *May the Twelfth: Mass-Observation Day-Survey 1937 by Over Two Hundred Observers* (1987).

[112] The Blackheath Society was also founded in 1937 to protect against the threat to the area's Georgian heritage.

[113] Alexandre Campsie, 'Mass-Observation, Left Intellectuals and the Politics of Everyday Life', *English Historical Review* 131.548 (February 2016), pp.95–6.

[114] Ibid., pp.96–7.

[115] Parker, 'Shutters up in Portland Town', pp.286–94.

[116] 'Mr Ralph Parker', *The Times* (27 May 1964), p.14.

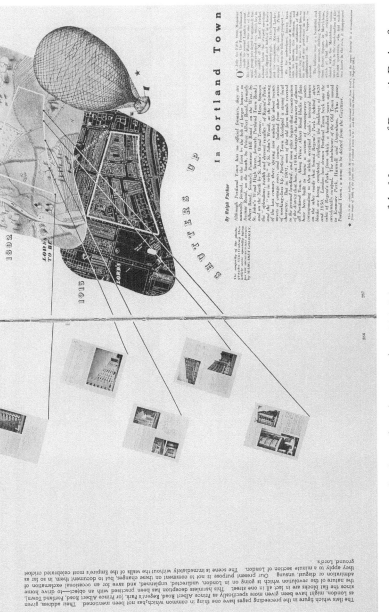

Fig. 4.13 'Shutters up in Portland Town', AR (June 1938), pp.286–7, image courtesy of the Museum of Domestic Design & Architecture, Middlesex University, www.moda.mdx.ac.uk

Fig. 4.14 'Shutters up in Portland Town', AR (June 1938), pp.290–1, image courtesy of the Museum of Domestic Design & Architecture, Middlesex University, www.moda.mdx.ac.uk

VIGILANCE 245

Fig. 4.15 'Shutters up in Portland Town', *AR* (June 1938), p.289, image courtesy of the Museum of Domestic Design & Architecture, Middlesex University, www.moda.mdx.ac.uk

> The busy broken life of the working class, with its succession of meetings, its chain of short conversations, its calls across the wall…is replaced by the secretive comings and goings of the middle class—the discreet curtains through which you can only see one way…[117]

[117] Parker, 'Shutters up in Portland Town', p.294.

246   DESIGNS ON DEMOCRACY

Parker's connections to the Communist movement led him to write with some confidence that the group of Portland Town tenants in 1936 had been organized by the Communist Party into a 'well-disciplined Tenants' Defence League'. Communist agitation had, of course, been prevalent in the rent strikes of East London between 1935 and 1937. The most famous of these, the Stepney Tenants' Defence League, a movement led by Jewish women in East London, seems to have been established a year after the Portland Town experiment. It may have been that the Trotters' anti-socialism and proprietary attitude to the campaign subsequently obscured this significant early engagement by the Communist Party.

The Portland Town campaign facilitated by the Londoners' League, although ultimately unsuccessful, matters for a number of reasons. First and foremost, it shows a different side to Georgian preservationism in the early 1930s. The Trotters, Goldring, Trystan Edwards, and many others were motivated by the preservation not only of street architecture and planning ensembles but also of the 'everyday life' which animated them. As Lord Crawford wrote in 1935, 'A much humbler and more numerous type of building is threatened—namely, the small dwelling-houses of the eighteenth century and earlier, which gave so much to so many country towns and villages in England and Scotland.'[118] In other words, Georgian preservationism was more tightly bound up in the growing debate about slum-reconditioning and giving voice to the 'slum dweller' than we have tended to think. This 'bread and butter' Georgianism has been obscured by the polemical focus on public buildings and monuments. For figures like Stanley Adshead, Albert Richardson, Trystan Edwards, and others, these more ordinary remnants of eighteenth-century architecture and planning were as important as monumental set-pieces. This Georgianism in many respects overlapped with the 'Georgianism' Mark Crinson has described in relation to early twentieth-century Dublin and its tenements, though the presence of eighteenth-century architecture in the imperial metropolis held a different significance to postcolonial Ireland.[119] This also prefigured post-war debates, in which, as Erika Hanna has shown in the case of 1960s housing campaigns in Dublin to preserve Georgian terraces, 'social conservation

---

[118] 'Old Buildings', *The Times* (19 December 1935), p.8.
[119] Mark Crinson, 'Georgianism and the Tenements, Dublin 1908–1926', *Art History* 29.4 (2006), pp.625–59.

elided in many aspects with ideas of architectural preservation, and there was considerable overlap in terms of their vision for the city'.[120] 'They could not be dismissed as irrelevant or elitist; they rested on the testimony of working-class people against the bureaucratic strength of state and machinery of the speculator.'[121] This underlying principle of preservation—'the broad-brush preservation of the older parts of a city', the 'character' of a place—was, Hanna contends, rejected in favour of monuments 'which have the permanent values of architectural order and real artistic quality' as defined by campaigners like John Summerson in his influential essay 'The Past in the Future'.[122] Summerson's essay was, as we shall see, a response to the development of early listing criteria, a result of conversations on the Maclagan Committee on which he sat as a representative of the Georgian Group.

Summerson's attitude to preservationism and conservation was only one of a number of competing strategies which grew out of interwar campaigns and controversies. The Trotters' defence of the 'sociological', of the 'village life' of 'Little Londons', as the basis for preservation was another powerful model. This was also part of a powerful and complex Georgian imaginary: Portland Town, inhabited by successive generations of the working classes, was a built embodiment of a valuable way of conceiving a social community. Their argument was that improvement should fundamentally be sensitive to this rationale.

Portland Town helps us to reconceptualize Georgian preservationism outside its institutionalization in the Georgian Group, particularly in light of the constitution of the listing process in post-war planning legislation. This wider context, I argue, in fact also informed the approaches of some of the early and active members of the Georgian Group, although this nuance has been subsequently written out. Belying what was to become the aristocratic and dilettantish reputation of the Group, Goldring argued that eighteenth-century architecture 'deserves careful preservation' because 'it is part of the artistic inheritance of the common people'.[123]

---

[120] Erika Hanna, *Modern Dublin: Urban Change and the Irish Past, 1957–1973* (Oxford, 2013), p.113.
[121] Ibid.   [122] Ibid., p.5.   [123] Goldring, *Odd Man Out*, p.90.

248   DESIGNS ON DEMOCRACY

The Georgian Group

Campaigns like the one to save Portland Town in the mid- to late 1930s place the Georgian Group in a wider context of vigilant preservationism, and in a broader debate about class and proprietorship. The foundation of the Georgian Group needs, therefore, to be retold in this light—to be examined not just in terms of the high-profile campaigns for prominent ensembles, such as Regent Street, but also at the fault lines exposed by the animosity with the Londoners' League in relation to Portland Town. It also needs to be examined in terms of the sorts of people the Group attracted and their motivations—not all were the aesthetes and dilettantes who became so closely associated with its activities then and since. The wider pool of those involved in the Group's early days, and some of the debates about the nature of preservationism and its relationship to development have been suppressed or forgotten. Furthermore, the work that active members of the Group did under its aegis to promote statutory listing, later enshrined in Section 28 of the Town and Country Planning Act (1947) which related to buildings of historic or special interest, still remains obscure. A huge amount of energy was generated by the volunteer activism of the Carlton House Defence League, the Londoners' League, and the early Georgian Group itself; the ad hoc protective measures like the Crown Lands Advisory Committee; the panel system; and the vigilance of associations and voluntary bodies often led by architects. Yet despite this, there was a decisive shift to greater powers for the state in the preservation of architecture and amenity, and a curtailment of public proprietorship as a result. Private interest and the powers of landowners in particular could only be effectively controlled by statute, perhaps implying some recognition of the limited efficacy even of highly actively voluntary associations like the Georgian Group.

The Georgian Group was established by the poet, biographer, and diplomat, Lord Derwent (1899–1949), and the writer Douglas Goldring, as a pressure group within the SPAB. It sought to correct a perceived bias against architecture built after 1714 in limited and often ineffectual conservation legislation, governmental initiatives, and existing amenity groups, namely the Ancient Monuments Act (1931), the Royal Commission on the Ancient and Historical Monuments and Constructions of England, and the SPAB itself. The SPAB in particular had been, in Goldring's view, 'far too busy dealing with the many cases brought to its notice to have time to indulge in press propaganda for the purpose of educating public opinion on the subject of Georgian architecture.[124] The new Group by contrast would agitate through vociferous publicity and public relations for its casework. Sometimes perceived as young, privileged, and bellicose— charges with more than a little justification—the founders and early members also exploited their connections to lobby for changes in legislation which culminated in the statutory listing of buildings in consultation with expert amenity groups.

Although strong complaint and powerful invective were often meted out when 'prestige' monuments were threatened, as we have seen, little was achieved by way of successful preservation, and less still in determining consistent principles of protection, repair or demolition of buildings built in the eighteenth and early nineteenth centuries.

In 1936, George Harcourt Johnstone, the third Baron Derwent (1899–1949) (who went by Peter and used the pseudonym George Vandon), was readying to introduce a motion to the House of Lords to have a list drawn up of Georgian buildings worthy of protection thereafter to be maintained by the Office of Works.[125] Derwent, young and pompous, had inherited the late-eighteenth-century Hackness Hall, Scarborough, along with his title, from his uncle in 1929.[126] A politician and diplomat often away from England, Derwent was also a biographer—an early study on Prosper Mérimée (1926) is worthy of particular note because the novelist and dramatist was also, from 1834, inspector-general of historical monuments in France.[127] During preparation for the motion, Derwent met Douglas Goldring who supplied him a wealth of background information. A further meeting in Paris in late 1936 spawned the idea of a new society.[128] Goldring had, as we have seen, been agitating for greater public involvement in the protection of buildings for some years. An exchange with the third Viscount Esher (1881–1963), chairman of the SPAB, in February 1937 brought forward the sensible suggestion that Derwent and Goldring's efforts were best channelled through an active group within the SPAB as parent body.[129] In April 1937, the Georgian Group came into existence at a meeting attended by Derwent and Goldring as sole members and chairman and honorary secretary respectively. A conversation in April 1937 between

[124] Ibid., p.61.   [125] Ibid., p.65.
[126] George Vandon (George Harcourt Johnstone), *Return Ticket* (1940), pp.196–8.
[127] George Harcourt Johnstone, *Prosper Mérimée: A Mask and a Face* (1926), pp.82–5.
[128] Goldring, *Odd Man Out*, p.65.
[129] Charles Hind, 'Sound and Fury: The Early Days of the Georgian Group', *The Georgian Group Report and Journal 1986*, p.46.

250 DESIGNS ON DEMOCRACY

Robert Byron, who had recently published *How We Celebrate the Coronation*, his editor JM Richards, Lord Derwent, and others led to the travel writer's early and prominent involvement in the initiative.[130]

The initial organization of the Group was determined at the inaugural committee meetings. The first was held at the beginning of June in 1937, at which Derwent and Goldring's offices were confirmed and other key posts established and filled. Albert Richardson, professor at the Bartlett School of Architecture, prolific historian of Georgian architecture and social life, as well as upholder of the Georgian tradition in modern design, proposed Byron as deputy chairman, seconded by the elderly Guy Dawber, prominent in the Council for the Preservation of Rural England, who had written publicly against the destruction of Waterloo Bridge and Carlton House Gardens in the national press. Richardson also proposed his former office assistant, Trystan Edwards, as vice chairman. Though Edwards stepped down from that position at the following meeting—succeeded, incidentally, by Richardson—he remained an active member of the Group until the 1940s. Edwards's book, *Good and Bad Manners in Architecture* (1924), was an influential invective against the destruction of Nash's Regent Street. Goldring acknowledged his debt to the book, 'which made a profound impression' on him, and without which 'there would probably have been no Georgian Group'.[131] Edwards's nomination was seconded by a young John Summerson, who had published his book on John Nash in 1935. Others present included James Lees-Milne, the driving force behind a reinvigorated National Trust as secretary to its Country Houses Committee from 1936, and two key figures from the SPAB, William Palmer, who had succeeded AR Powys (1881–1936) as secretary in 1936, and Henry Everett who was elected honorary treasurer of the new Group.[132]

The second meeting was hosted at the glamorously decorated and, according to the Earl of Rosse, 'exotically furnished' Piccadilly flat of society hostess Baroness Catherine D'Erlanger (1874–1959) in Stratton House (she owned the eighteenth-century Falconwood on Shooter's Hill, as a country house, had owned 139 Piccadilly, a refaced eighteenth-century townhouse,

---

[130] See James Knox, *Robert Byron* (2003), pp.376–89.

[131] Goldring, *Odd Man Out*, p.47.

[132] The early minutes and proceedings of the Georgian Group are found in the Georgian Group and SPAB's uncatalogued institutional archives. Cf. Huntington Library, Katharine A Esdaile Papers, Box 3, Folders 1, 3, and 9; Birr Castle Archives, Papers of the 6th Earl of Rosse, especially T/44/1 and T/44/8.

VIGILANCE   251

and in the 1920s restored Palladio's La Malcontenta with Oliver Messel).[133] Her flat became the primary meeting-place of the Group until July 1939 when her husband, Baron Emile D'Erlanger, died unexpectedly. Stratton House, neighbouring the new Devonshire House, included notable neo-Georgian interiors. Later meetings were held in the offices of Basil Ionides, another prominent neo-Georgian architect and interior designer. It was at this meeting that a young financier and barrister, Angus Acworth, was presented as assistant secretary (without Goldring's approval and much to his chagrin) and that it was agreed that all those who came to the first meeting would now form the Executive Committee, the primary decision-making body of the Group which was to comprise thirty people.[134] The wider Committee (later renamed the Council) was made up of other influential figures who had contributed to the efforts of the Group.

Though Goldring would later bitterly recall that this second meeting 'had more the atmosphere of a socialite sherry party than a gathering of experts and enthusiasts engaged in fostering a national movement', members of the Executive Committee present and proposed there showed a range of expertise and knowledge of the Georgian that was by no means myopically architectural or lightweight. Goldring himself conceded that 'the "Mayfair" element, if such it can be called, is subsidiary to the solid professional majority'.[135]

A great deal of wrangling followed throughout this period of infancy—as well as a clash of personality between the rather pious and easily offended Goldring and his brusque, snobbish chairman, tensions were exacerbated by a perceived censorious control by the SPAB of finance and communications. Derwent's long and frequent absences and Goldring's administrative ineptitude led to misunderstandings quickly perceived as slights. At first mediated by Byron, himself known for his 'habit of ungovernable rages' as recalled by Hugh Casson,[136] by December 1937, Goldring was manoeuvred

---

[133] 'The Earl of Rosse', *Georgian Group News* (December 1979), n.p. See also Hannah Marynissen, 'La Fiamma: Keeping the Flame of Baroness Catherine d'Erlanger Alive', National Portrait Gallery blog (10 October 2019), https://www.npg.org.uk/blog/la-fiamma-keeping-the-flame [accessed 2 April 2021].

[134] Simon Swynfen Jervis, *The Leche Trust, 1963–2013: A Commemoration of Fifty Years* (2013) and Jervis, 'Angus Whiteford Acworth (1898–1981), financier and conservationist', *ODNB* (May 2015), https://doi.org/10.1093/ref:odnb/106012 [accessed 27 May 2020].

[135] Goldring, *Odd Man Out*, p.90.

[136] British Library, National Life Stories Collection, C408/16/01–24, Transcript of interview with Hugh Casson, p.85, https://sounds.bl.uk/related-content/TRANSCRIPTS/021T-C0408X 0016XX-0000A0.pdf [accessed 27 May 2020].

252 DESIGNS ON DEMOCRACY

out of his position, despite support from Palmer, resigning in January of the following year.

This falling out within the first six months of the Group's activity has given rise to a suitably tumultuous origin story for a group happy to cast itself as the *enfant terrible* of a staid and placid preservationist establishment. It has been referred to rightly as 'sound and fury' by a later historian.[137] These were all literary men, quick to put pen to paper and record their arguments with voluminous correspondence. Byron himself resigned in 1939 and was killed by enemy action in 1941. Derwent, often absent as an attaché, was on active service first at Berne and then in the Royal Air Force. Although their networking and writing raised awareness of the Group, neither made any major contribution to its long-term organization. Thus, while these early conflagrations between the founding triumvirate 'signified nothing', they have come to obscure the collective efforts of other early members of the Georgian Group.

There was, undeniably, a high society element. As well as the Earl of Rosse (1906–79), later chairman of the Group, there was also the assistant editor of the *Architectural Review*, John Betjeman, who had known Lees-Mile from Oxford in the 'Acton Set', Christopher Hussey of *Country Life* and Lord Gerry Wellesley, later the seventh Duke of Wellington, a practising architect and at this time Keeper of the King's Pictures, who would occasionally chair meetings until his retirement in late 1944. He presumably introduced John Steegman (1899–1966), with whom he had collaborated on the *Iconography of the First Duke of Wellington* (1935), and who also authored *The Rule of Taste from George I to George IV* (1936).[138]

There were others in this circle of 'bright young things': John Dugdale (1905–63), another Oxford contemporary of Betjeman, whose father owned Samuel Pepys Cockerell's Sezincote, was one. The young assistant secretary of the Group (who succeeded Acworth after his loftier ambitions became apparent), Billa (Wilhemine) Cresswell, once briefly engaged to Betjeman, met her future husband Roy Harrod, the Oxford economist, at a party there. She resigned after one month. Byron, another Oxford contemporary, was also part of this social group (and indeed was in love with the Earl of Rosse's younger brother, Desmond Parsons). A number of young barristers including JH Holman Sutcliffe, Basil Marsden-Smedley, and Derric Stopford Adams were also enthusiastic early members of the Executive Committee.

---

[137] Hind, 'Sound and Fury', pp.45–54.
[138] 'John Steegman', *The Times* (16 April 1966), p.10.

VIGILANCE 253

Some, including Rick Stewart-Jones, a close friend of James Lees-Milne, were involved in the early days of the Chelsea Society, as was Marsden-Smedley as earlier noted.[139] Holman Sutcliffe had been a founder of the Boston Preservation Trust, established in 1935 to save Fydell House.[140] Activists in local amenity groups, in other words, and their experience in successful campaigning were brought into the Group early on.

But it was not only young men: a group of formidable and influential women scholars also attended these initial meetings and contributed to casework and publicity for over a decade. The literary critic and historian, Dame Una Pope-Hennessy (1867–1949), who had been involved in the SPAB, attended Executive Committee until 1946 and was particularly active in the Publicity Sub-Committee in later years. She had spent formative summers at Coole House, an eighteenth-century country house built for the Gregory family, and a centre of the Irish Literary Revival, often attended by WB Yeats, in the early twentieth century.[141] Margaret Jourdain, the historian of interiors, attended meetings occasionally, as more regularly did Katharine Ada Esdaile, who preferred to be known as Mrs Arundel Esdaile (her husband was secretary to the British Museum). A renowned expert in post-Reformation English sculpture, she had contributed numerous articles, reviews, and editorials on a variety of subjects in leading titles of the architectural press.

Esdaile and Pope-Hennessy were both active on the SPAB. Despite its perceived prejudice against Georgian architecture, many came from the parent body: as well as Guy Dawber, there was another Arts and Crafts architect, Thomas Gerard Davidson, who retired in June 1938 and was replaced by the painter Maresco Pearce (1874–1964), a student of Sickert and Orpen, whose paintings of architectural subjects were known for 'delighting in such details as the scrolled ironwork of Regency Balconies.'[142] This older contingent also included Harold Clifford Smith (1876–1960), curator and historian of English furniture of the period, who contributed yet another area of expertise. He had been keeper at the Victoria and Albert Museum, having retired in 1936, and was active on the Executive Committee into the 1940s.

---

[139] 'Mr R Stewart-Jones: Champion of Historic Buildings', *The Times* (28 September 1957), p.8.

[140] 'Mr J H Holman Sutcliffe', *The Times* (21 October 1982), p.10.

[141] John Pope-Hennessy, *Learning to Look* (1991), p.6; Crinson, 'Georgianism and the Tenements', p.636.

[142] 'Mr Maresco Pearce', *The Times* (10 December 1964), p.14.

254 DESIGNS ON DEMOCRACY

Meetings were dominated by casework, including a number of high-profile campaigns for the preservation of Norfolk House, Old Palace Yard and Abingdon Street, Brunswick Square, and neighbouring Mecklenburgh Square, in which a Georgian ball was held in the summer of 1938. The Group also campaigned against plans to remove the Euston Arch. Questions about publicity and tactics as well as organizational appointments and refinements continued, and in 1938–9 the administrative machinery of the Group was reinforced to put it on a much firmer footing to intervene in the growing debate about statutory listing.

As well as figures from the arts, a number of politicians were drafted in, putting the drive for legislative change on a par with casework and publicity. The Conservative MPs Sir Alfred Beit and Alfred Bossom had both spoken out about Georgian preservation in the Commons chamber in early 1937. Bossom was also secretary of the Amenities Group in the House of Commons. These two men, along with Edward Keeling (1888–1954), another Conservative MP, at first a peripheral figure but later deputy chairman of the Group from 1944, were part of a Legislation Sub-Committee formed in October 1938, which also included Marsden-Smedley, Dugdale, Acworth, and others.[143]

In early 1939, this Sub-Committee, in which Acworth was particularly active, drafted a memorandum on the deficiencies of existing conservation legislation and proposed an Architectural Amenities Bill which would make provision for an Architectural Amenities Board consisting of twenty members of named amenity bodies and a chair appointed by the Commissioners of Works. The proposal was shared and discussed amongst various groups, but did not reach Parliament.[144] It was, however, a key achievement for the founders and early members of the Georgian Group: the working through of these ideas made Acworth and his colleagues in the Group poised to contribute developed and sensible ideas in the debate around reconstruction.

The real, and still underrated, achievement of the Georgian Group was the establishment of the listing following the Town and Country Planning Act (1944), and the resulting Maclagan Committee, chaired by Eric Maclagan and including Summerson as the Group's representative, to advise

---

[143] Georgian Group, *First Annual Report* (1939), p.29.
[144] 'Conscription of Amenities: Georgian Group's Bold Policy', *Sunday Times* (14 May 1939), p.30.

VIGILANCE 255

on listing criteria, implemented from 1946.[145] The Group's continued cultivation of political figures placed it in a unique position to influence this new legislation. Indeed, these crucial provisions are still widely thought to have been the initiative of private individuals when in fact there was a strong element of coordination by the Group's Executive Committee.

Particularly crucial in this endeavour was Harry Strauss, parliamentary secretary to the sceptical Minister for Town and Country Planning, WS Morrison. Strauss, who had been a member of the Executive Committee since 1939 but attended meetings rarely, paved the way for an amendment by a private member carried on a free vote in the Commons. Keeling, by now deputy chairman of the Group, was the natural ally and duly tabled amendments having corresponded with Acworth and others on the Group. These were eventually withdrawn, but Strauss used them as leverage to implement the clause enabling the minister to draw up lists with the requirement of consultation of (in this Act) unnamed specialist bodies. In the 1947 Town and Country Planning Act these provisions were strengthened so that ministers were now obliged to compile such lists. This was tabled by the fifth Marquess of Salisbury, who as Viscount Cranborne (until 1947) had also been on the Committee (the precursor of the Council) since 1939. He was to become the Group's first president in 1948.

Under Angus Acworth as secretary, the clarified objectives of the Group were to awaken public interest and appreciation in Georgian architecture, and crucially, the Georgian tradition in architecture (this latter clause was contested and later removed); provide advice to owners and local authorities on conservation and repair; save buildings and ensembles from wholesale destruction and encourage retention of heritage assets when areas were being replanned; and encourage the Georgian tradition of civics and town planning. This final objective was also amended to endorse harmonizing (though permissibly contrasting) buildings with the old. Attitudes to the definition of Georgian tradition amongst the Group were often divided.

Georgian taste, as Alexandra Harris has characterized it, had a powerful effect on the 'Romantic Moderns' of the interwar years. It captured a tone of frippery and aristocratic exuberance. It attracted a particular kind of dilettantism expressed through fancy dress, masques, and balls.[146] The notorious

---

[145] Andrew Saint, 'How Listing Happened' in Michael Hunter (ed.), *Preserving the Past: The Rise of Heritage in Modern Britain* (Stroud, 1996), pp.125–7.
[146] Alexandra Harris, *Romantic Moderns: English Writers, Artists and the Imagination from Virginia Woolf to John Piper* (2010), pp.59–85.

256 DESIGNS ON DEMOCRACY

histrionics of the early Georgian Group cemented this reputation. But the Georgian could have a serious purpose too; for architects like Grey Wornum and critics like Gloag its perceived praxis informed design principles. The Georgian, therefore, was inextricably bound up with debates about the neo-Georgian, and no account of the interwar years can escape the prevalence of Georgian stylistic motifs in architectural design. The ambivalence towards the preponderance of the neo-Georgian is a tension explored in the present and following chapters; where did the Georgian end and the neo-Georgian begin? And how did imagined ideals of Georgian design, society, and culture inform contemporary architectural and planning discourse?

In a letter to Godfrey Samuel, a young architect and member of Lubetkin's Tecton, John Summerson, still then a member of MARS with a growing interest in 'Georgian London', reflected on the dynamics of the early Georgian Group. It was, he outlined,

> ...a heterogeneous mixture of opinion. There are die-hard reactionaries like Byron, wistful antiquaries like Lovell & Clifford Smith, bright boys like Betjeman & O. Messel, cranks like A E Richardson & Tri Edwards [sic] and level-headed journalists like Chris Hussey [sic] and, if I may say so, myself.[147]
>
> As soon as discussion at one of the Wednesday meetings gets on to planning & architectural design the committee is at 6's and 7's. But its terms of reference are strict and its function is simply and solely to interest people in the Georgian and to make the hell of a row when something indisputably worth keeping is threatened. For myself, I have always pressed the view that preservation can only be satisfactorily considered as part of large-scale town planning. But I cannot say truthfully that the ctee [sic] considers that point of view relevant.[148]

These ambivalences are important, and yet have been largely written out of the architectural history of the period. As Gavin Stamp noted in his history of the foundation of the Group, JM Richards, in sympathy with Summerson, would later recall the fear that the Group's 'aims might be confused with

---

[147] The allusions are to Percy Lovell (secretary of the London Society), Oliver Messel (the artist and interior designer who was the brother-in-law of the Earl of Rosse, one of the founding members), Arthur Trystan Edwards, and Christopher Hussey (architectural editor of *Country Life* and significant figure in the promotion of Modernism in the 1920s).

[148] RIBA, Godfrey Samuel Papers, SaG\89\5, Correspondence on literary works, 1937–1939, John Summerson to Godfrey Samuel (8 April 1938).

those of the neo-Georgian architects'. Richards recalled, 'It is difficult to appreciate now how deadening their influence was.'[149] The Group's Second Annual Report, however, was careful to explain that, though it did not 'advocate a return' to the Georgian, it 'hoped that means may be found to promote the beginnings of a manner of building freed from whimsicality and fashion', one that would spark 'the renaissance of English architecture'.[150] Even in 1944, Angus Acworth, the increasingly omniscient secretary, wrote to Albert Richardson outlining his reform agenda, stressing that it would be 'fatal' if the Group came to be regarded as merely antiquarian in concern. He even went so far as to propose that the 'Group stands not only for the preservation of Georgian buildings of beauty and importance but also for the principles of the Georgian tradition in the architecture of town and countryside'.[151] The Third Annual Report, issued in 1945, more ambivalently stressed that there was an 'eclectic attitude' of the Group towards preservation. There was a clause that the Group's objectives were for new buildings to 'harmonise (though may contrast) with old', but it also encouraged 'town-planning as orderly and as dignified as prevailed in the Georgian period'.[152] In reality, therefore, the place of the neo-Georgian was a moot point, and remained so even into the 1960s.[153]

Nevertheless, an impression of 'camps' has endured—Georgian preservationists of a Modernist bent on the one hand and neo-Georgian architects and sympathizers on the other. And because the orthodoxy of preservationism then and since has fixed on monuments and ensembles under threat, some of the broader imaginative hold of the Georgian response to planning has been lost. Significantly, the Georgian imaginary that architects and campaigners promoted itself contained ideals of a proprietary public, of a well-ordered social hierarchy, and in turn of the performance of public propriety, the subject of the next chapter. In Portland Town and for the Londoners' League it was the 'sociological' as much as the

[149] Quoted in Gavin Stamp, 'How We Celebrated the Coronation', p.19. See also fn.67, p.21. NB a much later reminiscence in private correspondence with Stamp.

[150] Georgian Group, *Second Annual Report* (1940), p.49.

[151] SPAB Archives, GGGC, Angus Acworth to Albert Richardson (18 February 1944). See also the resulting reports: ibid., 'Georgian Group Policy Sub-Committee—First Report: Clarification of the Objectives of the Group' (14 April 1944), and 'Georgian Group Policy Sub-Committee—Second Report' (19 May 1944).

[152] Richardson had been championing this source: 'Foreword', *Third Annual Report* (1943), pp.53–5.

[153] Birr Castle Archive, Papers of the 6th Earl of Rosse, T/44/8, Anthony Wagner to Lord Rosse (5 February 1968); Cf. Acworth's letter to Rosse on the same issue in the same file (8 February 1968).

258   DESIGNS ON DEMOCRACY

'architectural' which was at stake, and an understanding of the historic environment as intrinsic to town planning.

The arc of this chapter has shown how public proprietorship of built heritage reflected a shifting consensus about the role of the state in preservationism, and changing ideals from the supremacy of the rights of private ownership to collective community custodianship and thence to augmented state intervention. In regulatory terms, these changing values informed the development of the listing system enshrined in the Town and Country Planning Act (1947). The Georgian Group was particularly influential in framing this part of the legislation in the late 1930s.

Conclusion

This chapter has shown how architects and heritage campaigners mobilized notions of public proprietorship to make their claim for the integration of the historic built environment into new development in the 1920s and 1930s, particularly Georgian monuments and ensembles. Building on the legacy of pioneer preservationists in the late nineteenth century, most notably the founders of the SPAB, architects defined their role as defenders of public amenity. In the new age of mass democracy, the appeal for Georgian preservationism was often directly addressed to the public. The Georgian Group, established in 1937, talked explicitly about forming and directing public opinion, of lobbying public authorities and Parliament through public relations, and of using novel methods of publicity to draw attention to their cause.

In 1938, Henry Stuart Goodhart-Rendel made a controversial inaugural speech as president of the RIBA. He suggested that architectural culture was overly concerned with the preservation of the historic environment, and not enough concerned with exerting control on new building. There should be 'modern enthusiasts equivalent to the Georgian Group to see that what is built in its place is as good of its kind'.[154] He advocated the establishment of architectural 'vigilance committees', 'made up of competent persons outside the profession' who 'could do an enormous amount of good by securing the early publications of designs for prominent buildings and their exposure to public criticism'.[155] He continued:

[154] 'Notes and Topics', *AJ* (17 November 1938), p.787.
[155] 'The President's Address', *AJ* (10 November 1938), p.751.

VIGILANCE   259

Against my proposal it can be urged that we already have a Fine Arts Commission [Royal Fine Art Commission] and in some places voluntary architectural panels. I say in reply that the fine Arts Commission hardly ever speaks until it has been spoken to, and that architectural panels deal by their nature with such smaller matters than those I have in mind. My idea of a vigilance committee is one that would speak quite loudly when nobody had spoken to it at all, often, I hope, in praise as well as in blame. Architecture is not created for architects only, but for the public; and the public ought to stir itself into some more useful activity than that of grumbling when it is too late for anything to be done.[156]

Goodhart-Rendel's speech brings this chapter full-circle, returning to the theme of 'vigilance' with which it began. Despite the various institutions, committees, and campaigns that had been organized, there was a persistent sense that meaningful, democratic public proprietorship had not been fully achieved. The targets of Goodhart-Rendel's proposed vigilance committee would be speculative housing and sprawl, as well as the tendency towards flat-living in tall apartment-blocks.

This refrain was picked up by the *Architects' Journal* and became a particular focus in the 'News and Topics' column authored by Astragal.[157] On the question of membership he proposed the Georgian Group 'as public-spirited citizens of taste who already have the habit, as it were, of going about with their eyes open', and who might be convinced to 'extend their activities in this more positive direction'.[158]

Lord Derwent—roving around the Continent on diplomatic missions—responded to the challenge, underscoring the Group's interest in contemporary architecture, singling out for praise the Air Ministry's aerodromes, Battersea Power Station, Broadcasting House, 55 Broadway, the Imperial Airways terminus at Victoria, and Radio City in New York—'a hotch-potch' of modern buildings. Derwent echoed Goodhart-Rendel's argument for advisory panels monitoring 'the question of *elevation*'.[159]

---

[156] Ibid.

[157] The exchange can be followed in sequence in the *AJ* using the following references: 'Notes and Topics' (17 November 1938), pp.786–7; (1 December 1938), pp.894–5; (8 December 1938), pp.932–3; (15 December 1938), pp.970–1; (22 December 1938), pp.1008–9; (5 January 1939), pp.4–5; see 'Letters from Readers: Modern Buildings' (12 January 1939), p.46; 'Notes and Topics' (2 February 1939), pp.194–5; 'Lord Derwent' (9 February 1939), p.233; 'Notes and Topics' (9 February 1939), pp.234–5; (23 February 1939), pp.312–13; (2 March 1939), pp.358–9; (9 March 1939), pp.398–9; (4 May 1939), pp.718–19; (25 May 1939), pp.846–7.

[158] Ibid.

[159] 'Letters from Readers: Modern Buildings', *AJ* (8 December 1938), p.936.

260   DESIGNS ON DEMOCRACY

There ensued, as Derwent described it in a private exchange with Lord Rosse, 'a grotesque & to me very droll correspondence' about modern architecture in London.[160] Astragal's agitation for a hypothetically representative 'vigilance committee' persisted; it would require 'men of culture and education' interested in modern buildings.[161] When Derwent responded proposing a 'plebiscite', Astragal proposed a laymen vigilance committee, putting forward the names of Frank Pick, Lord Horder, JM Keynes, Lord Beaverbrook, and Herbert Morrison, and encouraging readers to propose further names to settle 'whether the intelligent layman is really capable of discrimination about architecture—or at least whether the *prominent* layman is also the intelligent one'.[162] Further names duly came: the Mayor of Bexhill, Earl de la Warr, the proprietor of John Lewis, Spedan Lewis, Lord Harewood, Edward James, Anthony Bertram, McKnight Kauffer, John Betjeman, Clive Bell, Bernard Ashmole, James Bone, and James Lees-Milne among them.

The exchange of letters culminated in the formation of a 'Vigilance Committee' of lay experts who would vote on the best modern buildings of the previous twenty years—Osbert Lancaster, Henry Moore, and Charles Marriot also eventually participated in the list of sixty-three men and women who were asked to nominate the best buildings of the decade. It was this poll which famously returned the Peter Jones Store on Sloane Square as the best modern building, with Battersea Power Station as a close second, followed by 55 Broadway, the De la Warr Pavilion, Tecton's Penguin Pond at London Zoo, Arnos Grove Tube Station, and Finsbury Health Centre. Lower down the list came 66 Portland Place, Kensal House, Shell-Mex, and Simpson's of Piccadilly, as well as a host of more obscure buildings (a fire station at Epsom, Parliament Hill Lido, Bishop Andrew's Church, Morden, Scarborough Hospital). Tecton emerged as the most popular practice, with twenty-six votes, followed by Adams, Holden and Pearson with seventeen and Serge Chermayeff with sixteen.[163]

Astragal's intention 'to ask Lord Derwent which ten people from those nominated' could 'form a *real* vigilance committee' came to nought; by the end of the summer international relations had deteriorated and Derwent's diplomatic mission took precedence. Nevertheless, Goodhart-Rendel's call

---

[160] Birr Castle Archives, Papers of the 6th Earl of Rosse, T/44/1, Lord Derwent to Lord Rosse (5 February 1939).

[161] 'Notes and Topics', *AJ* (5 January 1939), pp.4–5.

[162] 'Notes and Topics', *AJ* (2 February 1939), pp.194–5.

[163] For the poll, its results and analysis, see *AJ* (25 May 1939), pp.850–62.

VIGILANCE 261

for a vigilance committee and the subsequent exchange between Derwent and Astragal draws us back to a number of cognate themes running through the chapter.

Despite the growing successes of the preservationist lobby and developing techniques of campaigning in asserting public proprietorship and participation in architecture and planning, Goodhart-Rendel's speech expressed an unresolved anxiety. As a leader in the *AJ* picked up during Derwent and Astragal's correspondence, Goodhart-Rendel's public declamation presented a particular problem because by '1938 the profession had almost got it into the heads of laymen that only an architect is fit to judge what kind of a building half a million people should look at almost daily for a hundred years; and then the President gave the game away. He asked for a vigilance committee of *laymen* ...'[164] The reference was of course to the recently passed Architects Registration Act, which had restricted the title 'architect' to those listed by the Architects Registration Council of the United Kingdom. Public proprietorship—lay vigilance—ironically could be seen to undermine architects' claims to expertise. There was a real scepticism about how useful 'laymen' could actually be, particularly in the propagation of contemporary (Modernist) architecture. Astragal regretted that 'the high-ups in the Georgian Group, who represented the kind of distinguished laymen who might be expected to become members of the vigilance committees...did not show more signs of wanting a contemporary style of architecture, quite apart from admitting one might already exist.'[165] The *AJ's* Vigilance Committee was, therefore, intended to expose the fact that those who spoke of 'lay vigilance' were conservative preservationists; while, in fact, this chapter has shown that this was a deliberately misleading picture.

Astragal's comment reflected another significant shift, however; whereas earlier in the century architects had seized upon championing and participating in vigilance committees, emphasizing the language of public proprietorship particularly in preservationist campaigns, there was an emerging consensus that this was both an untested idea and one which in fact sat in opposition to architects' self-interest. What was particularly revealing about Astragal's Vigilance Committee was that, much like the reams and reams of 'public opinion' it gave light to during the Carlton House Terrace controversy, these laymen were drawn largely from 'Society', far away from the working-class communities of Portland Town. That case

---

[164] 'Lord Derwent', *AJ* (9 February 1939), p.233.   [165] Ibid.

262 DESIGNS ON DEMOCRACY

showed that there was another approach, one which wrestled with how to give meaningful expression to working-class communities and which considered the historic environment holistically. To think more about specific characterizations of the enfranchised public, we need to look more closely at the housing debates of the interwar years, and at the writings of one particular activist: Arthur Trystan Edwards.

5

Manners

Public Propriety and Civic Design

Introduction

If the debate about the fate of old Regent Street brought to the fore the claims of a proprietary public, the new street opened up questions about public propriety. In the summer of 1926, Arthur Trystan Edwards wrote a final series of articles on the closing phases of the rebuilding of Regent Street, a subject on which he had written extensively in the early 1920s. His vociferous protest against the destruction of Nash's street—encapsulated by an earlier series of 'obituaries' penned for the *Architects' Journal*[1]—had earned him the sobriquet of Regent Street's 'chief mourner'.[2] Edwards was one of a number of critics melodramatically standing at the grave and weeping, some of whom were attached to the Liverpool School, such as Charles Herbert Reilly, SD Adshead, and Edwards himself, and others like Beresford Chancellor, chronicler of a disappearing London, and Steen Eiler Rasmussen who famously set down the 'True and Sad Story of Regent Street' in his book *London: The Unique City*.[3]

The distinction between preservationism and development has already been problematized by the preceding analysis of the Georgian Group. Critics and journalists were particularly interested in negotiating change: 'What the Building Said' was a series of ten articles on the changing face of London written by Edwards between 1926 and 1927. The first three were devoted to Regent Street, and the others covered the Strand, the riverside

---

[1] These included some special sketch-illustrations by Max Fry. See Arthur Trystan Edwards, 'Regent Street: An Obituary.—I', *AJ* (23 January 1924), pp.177–83; Edwards, 'Regent Street: An Obituary.—II', *AJ* (30 January 1924), pp.213–17; and Edwards, 'Regent Street: An Obituary.—III', *AJ* (6 February 1924), pp.252–7.

[2] Geoffrey Scott, 'Humanism, Good Manners and Civic Values', *Architecture*, 3:26 (December 1924), p.80.

[3] McKellar, 'Georgian London before *Georgian London*', pp.38–51.

Designs on Democracy: Architecture and the Public in Interwar London. Neal Shasore, Oxford University Press.
© Neal Shasore 2022. DOI: 10.1093/oso/9780192849724.003.0006

264   DESIGNS ON DEMOCRACY

around Westminster, and Hyde Park.[4] These were short, provocative pieces published in the *Architectural Review* in which a perambulating narrator conversed with buildings, and witnessed buildings arguing and fighting with each other. The use of Socratic dialogue made for an eccentric form of writing with which Edwards experimented sporadically over the course of his journalistic career. An early essay was a fictional exchange under the same title with Adelaide House in 1925 published in the periodical *Architecture*, and he refined the technique in a series for *Architectural Design and Construction* (later *Architectural Design*) entitled 'A Dialogue of Bead and Reel', two fictional office assistants, in the early 1930s.[5]

In the Regent Street articles Edwards reflected on the final phases of rebuilding. The dialogic form allowed him to express ambivalence towards the blocks of the new street. In the first article (Fig. 5.1), the narrator came across Swan and Edgar's Department Store on Piccadilly Circus, which terminated and bridged the Quadrant and Piccadilly (Fig. 5.2). He heard a 'distressing groaning behind me', the result of an 'unequal fight' between the old building and Reginald Blomfield's replacement, 'destined in a few weeks to attain a complete victory'.[6] Meekly reasoning with some defects of its successor's design, the old stucco building received a 'powerful punch below the belt, which caused it to gasp for breath, and for several minutes there was silence'.[7]

Later, the new building for Ingersoll's Watch Company, neighbouring Vigo House, protested at the arrogant censure of 'these wretched little stucco buildings' (Fig. 5.3):

[4] See the first three 'What the Building Said' articles: Arthur Trystan Edwards, 'What the Building Said—I. Overheard in Regent Street', *AR* (June 1926), pp.294–6; Edwards, 'What the Building Said—II. Overheard in Regent Street', *AR* (July 1926), pp.34–5; Edwards, 'What the Building Said—III. Overheard in Regent Street: The Quick and the Dead', *AR* (August 1926), pp.80–1. Neal Shasore, 'Conversations with Buildings', *AR* (April 2014), pp.120–1.

[5] Edwards, 'What the Building Said I: Adelaide House', *Architecture* 3.28 (February 1925); Edwards, 'What the Building Said II: The Bush Building', *Architecture* 3.30 (April 1925), pp.309–13. The same form is used in: Arthur Trystan Edwards, 'High Words in Piccadilly or What Barclays Bank said to The Westminster Bank', *AR* (March 1928), pp.88–92; Edwards, 'The Clash of Colour or The Moor of Argyll Street', *AR* (June 1929), pp.289–99; Edwards, 'The Royal Academy: Overheard in the Architectural Room', *AR* (June 1930), pp.314–18. For the anonymous fictional dialogues by 'Messrs Bead and Reel' in *Architectural Design*, see 'The Dialogue of Bead and Reel I—Garden Suburbs', *Architectural Design and Construction* (December 1930), pp.69–71; 'The Dialogue of Bead and Reel II—The RIBA Competition', *Architectural Design and Construction* (May 1931), pp.299–300; 'The Dialogue of Bead and Reel III—Flood Lighting', *Architectural Design and Construction* (October 1931), pp.531–2; 'The Dialogue of Bead and Reel IV—Democratic Architecture', *Architectural Design and Construction* (January 1932) pp.116–19; 'The Dialogue of Bead and Reel V—Waterloo Bridge' (March 1932), pp.231–3.

[6] Edwards, 'What the Building Said—I. Overheard in Regent Street', p.294.   [7] Ibid.

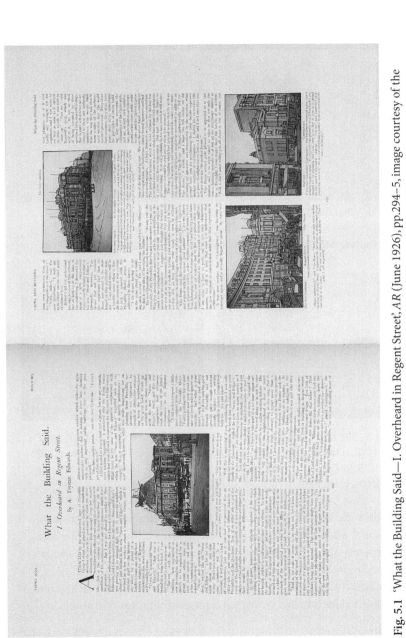

Fig. 5.1 'What the Building Said—I. Overheard in Regent Street', *AR* (June 1926), pp.294–5, image courtesy of the Museum of Domestic Design & Architecture, Middlesex University, www.moda.mdx.ac.uk

Fig. 5.2 'At Piccadilly Circus', showing the new Swan and Edgar's rising behind the old, 'What the Building Said—I. Overheard in Regent Street', *AR* (June 1926), pp.294–5, image courtesy of the Museum of Domestic Design & Architecture, Middlesex University, www.moda.mdx.ac.uk

Fig. 5.3 The new Quadrant, Vigo House, Ingersoll and Carrington's, Regent Street, 'What the Building Said—I. Overheard in Regent Street', *AR* (June 1926), pp.294–5, image courtesy of the Museum of Domestic Design & Architecture, Middlesex University, www.moda.mdx.ac.uk

> One would think from the way they talk that in them resides all the architectural wisdom that the world has ever possessed. They alone have manners, they alone have grace, they alone understand the principles of street building, *they* alone represent the culmination of the classic style, and are, in fact, civic architecture, metropolitan architecture, grand architecture, noble architecture, and the highest expression of the national genius.[8]

---

[8] Ibid., p.295.

MANNERS   267

And yet, over the following two articles, the narrator continued to encounter brusque, bad-mannered modern buildings along the new Regent Street. He came across a stretch with

> ...a dozen or more tall shops having about them a rather puzzled air. To my surprise they all began to speak at once; 'Why am I here?' 'What on earth do I mean?' 'Which is my main cornice?' 'Have I any cornice?' 'Where does my basement begin?' 'Have I a basement?' 'What have we done, that we are not allowed one minute's repose?' 'Why are we crowded together so that none of us has room to breathe?'[9]

The concave façade of East India House (Fig. 5.4)—Liberty's Department Store's facing Regent Street—was singled out for praise, but the neighbouring shop, Fullers, quickly intervened with criticism of 'quite inexcusable rudeness'.[10] It in turn was chastised by the narrator for talking as though 'we all lived in the good old times of a hundred years ago when it was customary for buildings to be neighbourly and to pay a courteous regard for each other's feelings'.[11] Tudor House, the newly built half-timbered building also for Liberty around the corner, elicited hysterical laughter from the narrator and its surrounding neighbours. In the end, the building itself, after a brief pretence of seriousness, also 'lifted up its voice in peals of merriment'.[12]

These fictional dialogues demonstrate the continuing emotional and imaginative pull of Regent Street. Edwards used dialogue to anthropomorphize buildings, and thereby to examine their social aspect. The failure of these interactions is expressed satirically and ironically; their awkwardness, their cacophony, even their physical violence were deployed by Edwards to convey viscerally the consequences of bad manners in architecture, of a collapse of social order, of impropriety. Edwards had earlier written that 'Architectural criticism should concern itself with the personalities of buildings rather than with the personalities of architects...until the independence and separate personalities of buildings are properly understood and accepted there will never be any real public recognition of the *vitality* of architecture'.[13] Buildings, he went on, 'are endowed with life and are or should be capable of taking cognisance of each other'.[14] The critic, significantly, should 'with the utmost freedom animadvert upon the social faults of a building', without assuming these 'are a reflection of corresponding

---

[9] 'What the Building Said—II. Overheard in Regent Street', pp.34–5.
[10] Ibid., p.35.   [11] Ibid.   [12] Ibid.
[13] Edwards, *Good and Bad Manners*, 1st edn., p.243.   [14] Ibid.

Fig. 5.4 'The Domed Shop. Liberty's, facing Regent Street' and 'Dickins and Jones. Liberty's in Great Marlborough Street', 'What the Building Said—II. Overheard in Regent Street', *AR* (July 1926), pp.34–5, image courtesy of the Museum of Domestic Design & Architecture Middlesex University, www.moda.mdx.ac.uk

faults in the mind of its architect'.[15] 'What the Building Said' literally enacted these aspirations. New Regent Street was typified by bad-mannered buildings.

Alongside a developing sense of a proprietary public in architectural culture was also a perceived need for public propriety, of decorum and manners in the public realm. For Trystan Edwards manners was a foundational principle of 'civic design', an expression synonymous with 'civic art' and 'Stadtbaukunst', practised by architect-planners in the early twentieth century. 'Manners', of course, had a long pedigree in Classical architectural thought deriving from rhetoric. Charles Cockerell's attitude to ornament had been underpinned by ideals of 'decorum' expressed in outward appearance and propriety. 'Manners' formed part of the Georgian imaginary. In the eighteenth century the performance of 'manners' had been akin to the language of politeness. The importance of 'manners' to the functioning of 'society' was popularized by Steele and Addison in *The Spectator* and *The Tatler*. Lord Shaftesbury wrote on 'Men, Manners, Opinions, Times', and Shaftesbury's influence on the 'Architect Earl' Lord Burlington, though problematized in recent scholarship, was widely accepted in the early twentieth century.[16]

'Manners' became intrinsic to a neo-Georgian, and neo-Regency, approach to urban design which aspired to be contextualist, restrained, and nationalistic. Manners related to contextualism in the sense that the phrase encapsulated the purpose of a growing number of systems for the control of elevations in building development through statutory instruments, by-laws, or local lobbying groups.[17] Manners also spoke to a preference for understatement among sections of the architectural community. We have seen the repeated critique of laissez-faire individualism in the political economy of the nineteenth century, and the ill effects this was felt to have had on urban and suburban development by contemporaries in the early twentieth century. Manners seemed a corrective to the resulting hypercommercialism, manifest architecturally in ever taller buildings and in exuberant façades for shops and factories. In so far as it was an expression of neo-Georgian design, manners related not only to the quotidian but also

---

[15] Ibid., p.244.

[16] John Summerson, *Georgian London* (Harmondsworth, 1962), p.95; Alexander Echlin and William Kelley, 'A "Shaftesburian Agenda"? Lord Burlington, Lord Shaftesbury and the Intellectual Origins of English Palladianism', *AH* 59 (2016), pp.221–52.

[17] Anthony Jackson, *The Politics of Architecture: A History of Modern Architecture in Britain* (Toronto, 2017).

270 DESIGNS ON DEMOCRACY

to the ideal of public service. And it was, therefore, nationalistic in that it was strongly associated with Englishness, and a particular vision of gentlemanliness, in some contexts parochially, but most ambitiously in its expression of a pervasive urbanity. Fundamentally, an invocation of architectural good manners was a rhetorical device to manage competing claims on the making of the built environment, by-products of mass democracy and mass culture, whereby it was felt the needs of the public had increasingly to be balanced with private interest. The concept of 'good manners' was further coloured by a New Liberal socio-political ideal which emphasized the importance of social or community obligations alongside social ordering and civilizing. Manners regulated social interaction through privileging courtesy and deference: the good-mannered citizen stood in contrast to the deviant and disorderly, manifested as the 'spiv' in post-war rhetorics of urban reconstruction.[18]

The first sections of this chapter look more closely at Trystan Edwards's writings, placing his ideas about 'manners' and public propriety in the broader context of his principles of civic design. In his socio-political vision of civic life—in which design and architecture were central—manners had a bearing not only on criticism but also on practice, through campaigning and voluntary activity. The remainder of the chapter turns to Edwards's campaigning vehicle, the Hundred New Towns Association (HNTA), established in 1933, which advocated a national programme of low-rise, high-density house-building and associated public amenity. It was a vision of a good-mannered and well-ordered society, in which urbanity was celebrated and fostered through a civic spirit. He so often worked against the grain of orthodox thought—he was described as 'a hostile witness to his own age'—that the HNTA provides an almost anti-history of mainstream planning and architectural approaches to the housing question. In addition to design, the chapter explores Edwards's surprising connections to movements in heterodox economics, liberal Anglicanism, and positive eugenics—discourses which were intrinsic to liberal intellectual culture, and posed fundamental questions about community need and benefit, as well as social control. For Edwards, they were a means of bolstering a well-mannered physical and social public realm.

---

[18] Richard Hornsey, *The Spiv and the Architect: Unruly Life in Postwar Britain* (Minneapolis, 2010), pp.16–25.

Good and Bad Manners

The idea of 'good manners' in architecture was re-popularized thanks to Trystan Edwards's (Fig. 5.5) spirited writing and campaigning.[19] Edwards was in his education and early career exposed to new forms of town-planning practice, and was surrounded by some of the most skilled architectural propagandists and campaigners of the early decades of the twentieth century. Having studied classics and philosophy at Hertford College, Oxford, Edwards served articled pupillage with the Edwardian grandee Reginald Blomfield. With a growing interest in town planning, and having failed to gain admission to the Royal Academy schools where Blomfield had recently and unsuccessfully attempted to establish an English *Ecole des Beaux-Arts*, Edwards went up to the Liverpool School of Architecture to study for a diploma in civic design in the new department which had been founded there by Reilly, led by Stanley Adshead as chair, and effectively deputized by Patrick Abercrombie. Here, Blomfield's

Fig. 5.5 Studio portrait of Arthur Trystan Edwards, Owen, Merthyr, photographer unknown (c.1918), DXQN/25/14, Cardiff, Glamorgan Archives

[19] Shasore, "'A stammering bundle of Welsh idealism'", pp.175–204.

272   DESIGNS ON DEMOCRACY

philosophy of the 'Grand Manner' held sway.[20] As the first dedicated department and chair in town planning, civic design at Liverpool was pioneering in advocating a new philosophy of urban design which privileged formality, monumentality, and urbanity, a reaction to the growing strength of the Garden City lobby in moulding housing and planning policy. In time Edwards became the most consistent, prolific, and articulate voice among this loose coalition of writers and practitioners, penning two precocious— and perspicacious—critiques of the Garden City movement in the department's journal, the *Town Planning Review*, in 1913 and 1914.[21]

After finishing at Liverpool, Edwards worked briefly for the young firm Richardson and Gill. Edwards therefore was immersed in modern classical design and in progressive neo-Georgian circles. Following naval service in the Great War, Edwards worked as a temporary assistant architect in the Local Government Board and then the Ministry of Health under Raymond Unwin on what became the 'Homes Fit for Heroes' state-subsidised housing scheme initiated by the Addison Act (1919).

Edwards has been seen as a conservative thinker, a quintessential example of English interwar architectural culture's insularism in the English context. As this book has argued, however, such a model for our understanding of the period is a gross over-simplification. Edwards and his ideal of manners have been all too easily corralled into a crude equivalence of anti-Modernism with anti-progressivism.[22] In fact, the picture was more complex. Edwards was a progressive, albeit of an idiosyncratic kind. As an undergraduate at Oxford he had joined the Fabians, combining this with a strong interest in Nietzsche.[23] This tension was later mirrored by Edwards's progressive programme for slum clearance and house-building on the one hand, and his 'great admiration for Herr Hitler's approach' to housing on the other.[24]

---

[20] Blomfield had written Adshead's letter of recommendation. Reilly praised Blomfield's works as 'textbooks' in the teaching of the Liverpool School. Mark Swenarton, 'The Role of History in Architectural Education', *AH* 30 (1987), p.205.

[21] Arthur Trystan Edwards, 'A Criticism of the Garden City Movement', *TPR* 4.2 (July 1913), pp.150–7; Edwards, 'A Further Criticism of the Garden City Movement', *TPR* 4.4 (January 1914), pp.312–18.

[22] Louise Durning, 'The Architecture of Humanism: An Historical and Critical Analysis of Geoffrey Scott's Architectural Theory', Ph.D. thesis, University of Essex, 1989, pp.1–9.

[23] A revealing record of Edwards's participation in Trinity term 1907 is thinly concealed by a strikethrough: 'In public business Mr AT Edwards of Hertford gave a paper on Nietzsche & Socialism. A discussion ~~for the most part hostile~~ followed & ~~the meeting concluded. House adjourned at 10–45~~ & the writer/author of the paper replied. Oxford, Bodleian Libraries, Oxford University Fabian Society Records, MSS Top Oxon d 465–467, Minutes, fo.111.

[24] Correspondence appended to a pamphlet in the Eugenics Society's papers: Wellcome Library, Eugenics Society Archive, SAEUG/D/101, 'The Hundred New Towns Association:

His education at Liverpool certainly had a progressive inflection, as Reilly—a self-professed socialist—himself later acknowledged, and Edwards described himself as a 'life-long adherent of the Labour Party'.[25] His fundamental interest in public service and tackling social questions forms the substance of this chapter.

Many of Edwards's eccentric and eclectic interests were expressed at length in his first book, *The Things Which Are Seen*, published in 1921 although largely composed during the war. The book was a manifesto for Edwards's integrated and holistic vision of post-war societal reconstruction. An aesthetic treatise on the surface, it contained capacious theses setting out an ethical vision and materialist understanding of the world, explored through a new hierarchy of the visual arts and a highly idiosyncratic grammar of design, derived from divine, natural, and artistic examples and precedents.

Significantly, it adumbrated a set of roles and responsibilities for the critic and the designer, who were also subject to codes of manners and conduct.[26] This was a theme to which he sporadically returned. In some 'Further Reflections upon Good and Bad Manners' in 1933, he argued that the critic had a responsibility to make design 'political': 'that is to say, they must confer about it and arrive at decisions which must be implemented by some form of governance. If the profession cannot do this of its own accord, the time will come when a code of architectural decency and order will be imposed by agents outside the profession.'[27] The 'concept of good manners in architecture has been a useful bridge between architects and the public because it has enabled them to discuss the essentials of civic design in a

---

Formation, Progress and Future Policy', Charles Paton Blacker, Hon Sec of Population Investigation Committee to Dr SS Fitzrandolph (3 July 1939). Edwards also wrote admiringly of National Socialist Labour Camps, see Arthur Trystan Edwards, 'Labour Camps in Germany', *The Listener* (21 November 1934), p.875. There is no evidence to suggest that Edwards had profound Nazi sympathies. Though deeply unpalatable, these views should be understood as unintended consequences of Appeasement and wider transnational intersecting policy interests, namely housing and eugenics. John Gloag published a series in the *AJ* in 1938–9 entitled 'Germany Builds', which was endorsed by Edwards in a letter published on 5 January 1939. Edwards's mother, Johanna Emilie Philipine Steinthal, was German (born in Frankfurt-am-Main), and possibly herself of Jewish extraction.

[25] Labour History Archive and Study Centre, LP/GS/PREM/105ii, extract of letter from Trystan Edwards to Anthony Greenwood, forwarded to Morgan Phillips (29 February 1956) about an accommodation scheme for Labour Members of Parliament on the South Bank. 'Mr A Trystan Edwards', *The Times* (3 February 1973), p.16.

[26] Shasore, '"A stammering bundle of Welsh idealism"', *AH* (2018), pp.183–7.

[27] 'Some New Reflections upon Good and Bad Manners in Architecture VI', *Architectural Design and Construction* (October 1933), p.467.

274   DESIGNS ON DEMOCRACY

proper phraseology and in terms of ideas with which the average man is very popular'.[28] The critic and the designer also had an obligation to behave impersonally in the public sphere, to envisage 'the self in its true perspective' in order to 'understand the needs of society'.[29] Manners encouraged a set of ethical praxes for the critic, campaigner, and designer, and Edwards himself deployed this as a critical and campaigning strategy. Architects were cast as arbiters and defenders of 'manners': a well-planned environment under-pinned the formation of orderly subjects. Manners framed architects' participation in governmentality.

Most salient for our immediate purposes is the new hierarchy which Edwards devised according to his understanding of the needs and wants of 'the average man', a social unit of an expanded and newly enfranchised 'public', analogous to the 'man in the street' or 'man on the Clapham omnibus'—a construct of working-class opinion as much as anything else. Providing a mouthpiece for the 'average man' in public discourse was a recurring theme in his criticism and campaigning. In the life of the average man, Edwards proposed, the first priority was the cultivation of human beauty; second came the art of manners; third, dress; fourth, architecture; painting and sculpture were relegated to fifth and sixth place. Adherence to good manners mattered because

> When a people despises the first of the visual arts [the cultivation of human beauty] there results a defective industrial and social organisation and the prevalence of personal vices of all kinds; when it despises the second [manners] we have mutual ill-will between the various sections of society, and a universal vulgarity which not only finds its expression in the demeanour of men and women but is most certainly reflected in the arts of dress, architecture, painting and sculpture.[30]

Adherence to manners could, in this formulation, provide a means of limiting dissidence not only socially but also in the realms of art, design, and architecture. The 'average man' therefore was subject to certain strictures of propriety in Edwards's vision of a highly coded and hierarchical social organization.

---

[28]   Ibid.
[29]   Arthur Trystan Edwards, *The Things Which Are Seen: A Reevaluation of the Visual Arts* (1921), 1st edn., p.337.
[30]   Ibid., p.46.

MANNERS 275

This level of prescription reflected Edwards's own wartime experiences as a 'British Bluejacket', a low-ranking seaman on the HMS *Nelson* as a Naval Volunteer Reservist.[31] Edwards closely observed his colleagues—some professional seamen, others civilians—later publishing *Three Rows of Tapes* which described 'the social life of the lower deck', its traditions, structures, and 'manner'.[32] This naval service, which he acknowledged as 'one of the principal cultural influences' in his life, informed his criticism and campaigning in two fundamental ways.[33] First, it emphasized the importance of social hierarchy, deference, and convention—in short, manners. But equally importantly, it showed how ideas of manners and propriety were linked in Edwards's mind to ideals of service and later veteranhood. The average man, in the post-war context, took on a greater significance, and deserved a greater enfranchisement. The 'Ex-Servicemen's Group' of the HNTA was devised by Edwards to give voice to a group that he had felt was voiceless in social questions which directly concerned them. Edwards still played the role of 'interpreter', echoing the middle-class observations of working-class life and culture discussed in the previous chapter.

The theme of manners and public propriety—and the parallel reintegration of morality into architecture—was developed in Edwards's second major publication, *Good and Bad Manners in Architecture* (1924).[34] The book devoted a lengthy chapter to an exegesis of the principles which had inspired John Nash and his contemporaries in the design and construction of Regent Street. It spawned, Edwards would later claim, a Regency revival in architecture in the 1920s, but it also inspired the movement towards Georgian preservationism which had thitherto privileged Wren and the vernacular Georgian over the formality and urbanity of the later eighteenth-century and Regency periods. 'Good manners' typified the architecture and town-planning devices of William Chambers at Somerset House (on which Edwards produced a short essay for Stanley Ramsey's series on 'modern architects'), John Wood the Younger at Bath; and Nash in Regent Street and on the Strand.[35]

---

[31] Arthur Trystan Edwards, *Three Rows of Tape: A Social Study of the Lower Deck* (1929), p.4, republished as: *British Bluejacket, 1915–1940: A Social Study of the Royal Navy* (1940).

[32] Edwards, *Three Rows of Tape*, p.2.   [33] Edwards, *British Blue Jacket*, p.7.

[34] Edwards, *Good and Bad Manners*, 1st edn. It was later republished as: *Good and Bad Manners in Architecture: An Essay on the Social Aspects of Civic Design* (1944), 2nd edn. Where possible I cite the second, more widely available, edition unless this undermines the chronology or particularity of my account and reference.

[35] Arthur Trystan Edwards, *Sir William Chambers* (1924); Edwards, 'John Wood and Bath', *ABN* (4 November 1927), pp.713–18.

276   DESIGNS ON DEMOCRACY

This chapter puts the Georgian and the 'neo-Georgian' styles in a broader socio-political context through an exploration of 'manners'. Style and debates about style were manifestations or phenotypes of a broader set of attitudes about the ethics of architectural design and development, about notions of public propriety—of public faces in public spaces—and the responsibility of citizens, architects, and developers to the wider community. 'Manners' also referred to taste. It was an almost vernacular interpretation of decorum, one which was deliberately English. Neo-Georgian architects often complained about the ubiquity of bad manners in contemporary architecture, trying to recover or recapture some sense of an imagined more mannerly past. Propriety—a visible display of good manners—was seen to be essential to the maintenance of social order, in particular after the destabilizing effects of the Great War.

In Edwards's writing, but also in the works of other contemporaries such as Geoffrey Scott, there were important moral and ethical imperatives in architectural practice and design which good manners encapsulated. Edwards owed a great debt to the writings of Scott in this regard, and the connections between the two men were immediate. Near contemporaries at Oxford, they were friends and closely intellectually aligned.[36] Edwards recalled Scott's 'singular personal charm' and the 'wit and vitality of his conversation'.[37] Edwards had reviewed Scott's book for the *Architectural Review* in 1914 as 'a very solid contribution to aesthetic philosophy'.[38] Scott in turn reviewed *Good and Bad Manners in Architecture* in 1924, the same year that the second edition of *The Architecture of Humanism* was published. In his review, he seized upon the theme of propriety. Appropriateness would not be determined by functionalist criteria, but by behavioural ones: 'Every projection and recess, every void and solid, every repetition or inflection is now contributing to a sense of consistent behaviour, and we have only to consider whether, in the circumstances, the behaviour is mannerly and appropriate'.[39]

Scott's *Architecture of Humanism* had an unparalleled influence on architectural thought in the interwar years.[40] The book was intended as the

---

[36] Arthur Trystan Edwards, 'The Architecture of Humanism', *AR* (September 1914), p.65; Edwards, 'Geoffrey Scott', *AR* (September 1929), p.152. For Scott on Edwards, see Geoffrey Scott, 'Humanism, Good Manners and Civic Values', *Architecture (Journal of the Society of Architects)*, 3.26 (December 1924), p.83.

[37] Edwards, 'Scott', p.152.   [38] Edwards, 'Architecture of Humanism', p.65.

[39] Scott, 'Humanism', p.81.

[40] Geoffrey Scott, *The Architecture of Humanism: A Study in the History of Taste*, 1st edn. (1914). Katherine Wheeler, *Victorian Perceptions of Renaissance Architecture* (Farnham, 2014),

first volume in a two-volume study which would dismantle the critical procedures of Victorian architectural theory and criticism, and secondly to provide a defence of Renaissance values in architecture which could never be fulfilled according to the fallacious precepts of the Gothic Revival. It was also intended as a special defence of the later Renaissance period, the Baroque. The famous Victorian 'fallacies' which Scott used to structure the argument of the book were false analogies of good architecture with Romantic literature, ethics and morality, evolutionary biology, and mechanical functionality. Louise Durning has described these 'reductive critical procedures' as in fact 'not strictly fallacies at all, even for Scott, but rather "half-truths"': 'as customarily applied they are fallacious yet, he suggests, each contained, and drew its strength from some valid perception embedded within it.'[41] Scott's project was to 'show that there is a true, not a false, analogy between ethical and aesthetic values.'[42] It has thus been a fundamental misinterpretation of the text to suggest, as David Watkin notably did in *Morality and Architecture*, that *The Architecture of Humanism* argues for a 'hedonistic', 'autonomous formal satisfaction.'[43] Edwards was similarly criticized by contemporaries, along with Howard Robertson—who borrowed much from him—for being 'more concerned with aesthetics applied to buildings than with buildings as a total experience.'[44] In fact, Scott's contention was that the link between architecture and morality (or ethics) was one established by ancient precedent.

Edwards took up the challenge to recalibrate their relationship. Scott's proposed connection between ethics and architecture derived from the subjective judgement of taste and from the projection of the self in terms of the architecture. This was *Einfühlung*, inadequately translated as 'empathy theory', propagated by the philosopher Theodor Lipps and others in the German art-historical tradition, such as August Schmarsow.[45] Edwards, in stark contrast, imposed moral or ethical standards onto *things*—the social effects, purposes, and roles of buildings—and furthermore challenged 'the artist' (the architect or even the critic) to subjugate their personal and subjective preferences in design, instead adopting an impersonal manner to

---

pp.125–54; John Macarthur, 'Geoffrey Scott, the Baroque and the Picturesque' in John Macarthur, Andrew Leach, and Maarten Delbeke (eds.), *The Baroque in Architectural Culture, 1880–1980* (2016), pp.61–71; Durning, 'Architecture of Humanism'.

[41] Durning, 'Architecture of Humanism', p.100.   [42] Ibid.   [43] Ibid., p.101.

[44] James M Richards, 'Architectural Criticism in the Nineteen-Thirties' in John Summerson (ed.), *Concerning Architecture: Essays Presented to Nikolaus Pevsner* (1968), p.255.

[45] Emilie Oléron Evans, 'Transposing the *Zeitgeist*? Nikolaus Pevsner between *Kunstgeschichte* and Art History', *Journal of Art Historiography* 11 (December 2014), pp.15–18.

278   DESIGNS ON DEMOCRACY

benefit society and conform to the needs and wants of the greater number of people.[46] Whereas, therefore, Scott relied on the concept of *Einfühlung* to instil architecture with morality, Edwards distinguished between what he called 'form', the designed outward appearance, and 'subject', the social and practical use or function of the building. Good manners in architecture would be achieved by the balancing of these critical criteria—architecture needed appropriate form to fulfil its function and to take its place in a social hierarchy, but just as essentially it needed the right subject. A good example of this is in the use of domes in Edwards's writings, compared with that of Scott and his intellectual progenitor, Bernard Berenson. Berenson had argued, in his essay 'A Word for Renaissance Churches'—which he would later accuse Scott of plagiarizing—that Italian Renaissance design sought after spatial composition more than a Gothic impression of awe. The centralized church was key to 'embodying this aesthetic ideal', in which Renaissance architects strove to resolve the horizontal vista along a nave with the vertical emphasis of the dome. In the empathy-theory reading of architecture, the dome imputes a feeling of soaring through the 'Renaissance tension between centralized dome or longitudinally designed spaces'.[47] Domes, curiously, also appear as a common motif in Edwards's writings. When discussing the importance of lay supervision in the setting out of cities, he contended that '"*How* to build a dome" is a question for the expert. But "*When* to build a dome" is a question for the public'.[48] In his analysis of William Chambers's work at Somerset House he singled out for praise the small dome in the central section of the river frontage as enhancing the longitudinal, horizontal urbane composition. In other words, the social aspect of the employment of the low dome trumped the formal impulse to have a high dome.[49] The importance of the social aspect of the dome was again emphasized in an episode of 'What the Building Said' in which the narrator on the Strand saw 'two noble domes—the one belonging to the Gaiety Theatre, and the other to the distinguished building occupied by the *Morning Post*', who respond in happy unison to Edwards's 'How-do-you-do, domes?'[50]

---

[46]   Edwards, *Things Which Are Seen*, 1st edn., pp.337–46.
[47]   Wheeler, *Victorian Perceptions of Renaissance Architecture*, p.136.
[48]   Edwards, *Good and Bad Manners*, p.22.
[49]   Edwards, *Chambers*, p.13. Edwards, 'Things I Like: X.—The Low Dome', *ABN* (31 December 1926), p.781.
[50]   Edwards, 'What the Building Said. X—In the Stand (III)', *AR* (March 1927), p.108.

MANNERS 279

'Manners' in Edwards's formulation described a quality of urbanity linked to a civic ideal. This civic ideal manifested itself in certain formal attributes in architectural and town planning, such as the domes just discussed. The Georgian imaginary in contemporary architecture had hitherto been largely dominated by the example of Wren and of the vernacular Georgian favoured by later Arts and Crafts architects and Garden City planners. In the early twentieth century, however, there was a growing preference for more formal, urbane, and 'academic' use of the Georgian and the Classical in domestic and public architecture.[51] Its champions were not only designers but also skilled propagandists in print and, through the schools of architecture, growing in strength and influence. Albert Richardson was among the most significant of these figures. Not only did he use a later Georgian vocabulary in his own design work, but he published extensively and taught, serving as professor of architecture at the Bartlett School of Architecture, University of London, from 1919. In 1914 he published *Monumental Classic Architecture*, a compendium of photographs, drawings, and plans with a scholarly commentary, charting monumental neo-Classical architecture in the 'academic style' from 1730 onwards. This was an explicit celebration of urbanity, monumentality, and the 'academic spirit', and a rebuttal of the late-nineteenth-century tendency to revive more 'provincial' styles of architecture characterized by 'haphazard individuality'.[52]

This academicism informed *Good and Bad Manners*: of old Regent Street, an exemplar of 'stucco-faced building', Edwards wrote that it was 'apt to express not only politeness but intellectuality. This is because a composition in stucco is a question of form rather than of craftsmanship'.[53] This fundamentally distinguished Edwards's approach from those later Arts and Crafts, Lethabian influences outlined in the earlier chapters of the book. Edwards was steeped in classicism. Stanley Adshead, whose offices neighboured Richardson's, was also at the forefront of this shift, though with less emphasis on monumentality;[54] with Stanley Ramsey he had produced the highly formal and carefully integrated Duchy of Cornwall Estate at Kennington, the first phase of which was completed in 1913. Adshead was

[51] For some, the aristocratic connotations of 'neo-Georgianism' were insurmountable. CR Ashbee, *Where the Great City Stands: A Study in the New Civics* (1917), pp.26–8.

[52] AE Richardson, *Monumental Classic Architecture in Great Britain and Ireland during the Eighteenth and Nineteenth Centuries* (1914), p.5.

[53] Edwards, *Good and Bad Manners*, p.63.

[54] Simon Houfe, Alan Powers, and John Wilton-Ely (eds.), *Sir Albert Richardson, 1880–1964* (1999). Edwards may have been recommended to Richardson by Adshead: see WA Downe, 'Some Memories', ibid., pp.23–5.

280 DESIGNS ON DEMOCRACY

strongly influenced by what Peter Richmond has described as the 'Liverpool Manner', exemplified by a collaboration between Charles Herbert Reilly, Patrick Abercrombie, and Adshead for Dormanstown.[55] This model village for the steel contractors Dorman Long included terraces of workers' housing showing the possibilities of more standardized elements and the company's own 'Dorlonco' construction system. Revived principles of Georgian architecture were felt to be particularly appropriate for this method. This was Trystan Edwards's world.

Despite its influence on the early members of the Georgian Group, of which Edwards was of course one, *Good and Bad Manners in Architecture* was not a preservationist text. It was more fundamentally concerned with good principles of design and development and with calibrating a role for the 'average man' through the fostering of a civic ideal and through instilling a 'proprietary feeling' among a vigilant public through systems of 'aesthetic' and democratic control. For this reason, one of the book's primary targets was contemporary commercial architecture, of which buildings like Bush House on the Aldwych were the worst examples in their disregard for their immediate context. Tall buildings in general were undesirable; the 'unsociable skyscraper' was singled out for particular censure. Regent Street, however, lent 'distinction to the very idea of commerce',[56] a 'classic example of commercial building worthy of the closest study'.[57]

Regent Street was a particular focus for a number of reasons. Firstly, it allowed Edwards to explore street architecture: 'It is important for architects and the public to unite in providing the conditions which are necessary to the creation of beautiful streets.'[58] As an example of good manners, it also provided a 'convenient form in which to comment upon some of the most important aspects of civic design.'[59] And though it involved an analysis of the 'political' elements of preservation, it also opened up questions about the limits of Georgian revivalism: 'Can the spirit of old Regent Street still live? This is only possible if there is a resuscitation of the *forms* of Regent Street.'[60] 'Form', however, meant neither straightforward revival or copyism but 'copies or variations of elements of ancient buildings.'[61]

---

[55] Peter Richmond, 'The Call to Order: Neo-Georgian and the Liverpool School of Architecture' in Holder and McKellar (eds.), *Neo-Georgian Architecture*, pp.25–37.
[56] Edwards, *Good and Bad Manners*, p.48.　　　[57] Ibid., p.52.
[58] Ibid., p.45.　　　[59] Ibid., p.46.
[60] Ibid., p.86.　　　[61] Ibid.

The Civic and the Domestic

The connection between the civic and the commercial, expressed through Nash's Regent Street, was a cogent theme in *Good and Bad Manners*, drawing on critical tropes about shop architecture and commercialism from the late Victorian period. More fundamentally, however, the themes of the book and even the example of Nash and Regent Street related to Edwards's thoughts about housing. This reflected the primary concern of architects in the early to mid-1920s, particularly figures like Edwards who served under Unwin in the Ministry of Health until 1925. *Good and Bad Manners*, compiled from a number of articles written from 1922 to 1924, should therefore be read in the context of the abandonment of the Addison Act's 'Homes Fit for Heroes' campaign, and the passing of the Chamberlain (1923) and Wheatley (1924) Housing Acts which superseded it. Edwards was, perhaps, trying to initiate a conversation about design which he felt had been lost in the context of an increasingly technocratic focus on economization and delivery, and one dominated by the Garden City lobby.

In 1924, presumably to publicize *Good and Bad Manners*, Edwards published two articles on 'Civic and Domestic Qualities in Architecture', the essential argument of which was that 'the two chief qualities proper to a house are the domestic and the civic.'[62] It was this idea of the civic to which Edwards repeatedly returned, a political aspiration as much as a formal one. The final two chapters of *Good and Bad Manners* were therefore explicitly concerned with design principles which would affect housing design. In 'The Bugbear of Monotony', Edwards showed how so-called monotonous terraces of standardized house units could be enlivened. This was an argument essentially against the semi-detached Tudoresque villa typical of speculative private development of the time. He took particular umbrage with 'the ubiquitous gable' in 'villadom': 'A complete lack of sociability seems characteristic of the gable because its effect is to accentuate a building or part of a building and to establish its formal differentiation from what lies either side of it.'[63] Edwards outlined how to achieve 'unity' and formality in domestic architecture at some length, arguing against what he termed the 'vice of prettiness' and *for* 'the essential modernity of the "Georgian" style':[64] 'The sedate and comely forms of the eighteenth century house are a perfect

---

[62] Arthur Trystan Edwards, 'Civic and Domestic Qualities in Architecture—II', *AJ* (2 July 1924), p.5.

[63] Edwards, *Good and Bad Manners*, p.99.   [64] Ibid., p.122.

MANNERS IN ARCHITECTURE.

terrace house, one front and one back they seem to have one front and three backs, and sometimes, when the tiny windows of lavatories and bathrooms obtrude themselves upon the façade abutting on the road, they may be said to have four backs and nothing at all which deserves to be designated as a front.

The question sometimes arises as to how far it is legitimate to *disguise* the windows of domestic offices

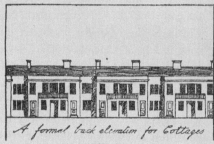

FIGURE 37

and make them balance windows of rooms of a quite different character, such as a library or dining room for instance. An architect of the school of Vanburgh would not scruple in a design of a country house to balance a great reception hall on one side of a court with a similar block sub-divided into kitchen offices on the other side, but such an arrangement is not really satisfactory, because here there is a deliberate deception which impairs the expressiveness of the composition. It is not necessary that such elements in a plan as are of little interest should pretend to be something other than what they are. It suffices if they acknowledge their subordinate status by assuming a polite unobtrusiveness. Of course, there are many occasions such as in large buildings on island sites where lavatory windows are totally concealed from public view by being put in a small interior court.

138

Fig. 5.6 AT Edwards, *Good and Bad Manners in Architecture* (London: Philip Allan & Co., 1924), 1st edn., pp.138–9

TRUTHFULNESS, URBANE AND OTHER.

Where, however, a residential building is so placed that it is exposed to public view on all sides, a special effort should be made to mitigate the crudities of design which tend to mar the façades when domestic offices must reveal their presence. Figures 38, 39 show arrangements of grouping such offices around a recess. In one case a small suite of rooms belonging to a communal house or block of service flats has its own kitchen and lavatory accommodation and in the other two bed sitting-rooms have bathrooms side by side. All the pipes are carried down on the inside surface of the slight projection of wall forming the recess, and thus would be invisible from the outside. Such recesses admit of great variation in design and the corresponding elevations can be adapted to many styles of building.

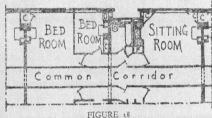

FIGURE 38

It may be conceded that in architecture we need above all things truth, but we must distinguish the truthfulness which is urbane from the truthfulness which is not urbane. It is only this latter kind of truthfulness which is being impugned in these pages. A peculiarity of the small truths is that they often obscure the big truths. The art of living very largely consists in the suppression of these small truths, for unfortunately many small truths do not necessarily make a big truth, and they may easily be added together to make a big lie. For instance, in architecture a façade may make a conspicuous

139

Fig. 5.6 *Continued*

284   DESIGNS ON DEMOCRACY

embodiment of the social spirit. They belong to the community. They are born of the discovery that in domestic architecture individuality is most securely established when houses defer to a common cultural standard.'[65]

Significantly, in a rhetorical about-turn, Edwards disavowed the term 'Georgian' and its stylistic and historicist connotations, instead championing its philosophical aspects: 'the devotion to reason and propriety' and its essentially 'urban' character.[66] In the final chapter—'Truthfulness, Urbane and Other'—Edwards argued for the 'virtues of concealment' in the upholding of a well-mannered social life. The 'fatal doctrine of the priority of the *plan*', he argued, inhibited not only the sociability of individual buildings but also blocks of buildings, and town plans too.[67] Concealment had its advantages, by contrast, in inspiring solutions for the untidy backs of houses with services and gutters on display. This bathetic application of a principle of 'truth' in concealment is characteristic of Edwards's obsessive holism: tidying up the rear elevations of houses was a particular bugbear of Edwards's and later in the decade he drew up detailed proposals for 'recesses' for concealing pipes and refuse storage near service doors (Fig. 5.6).

In the mid- to late 1920s, Edwards's focus on housing became sharper and sharper. The focus on the later Georgian and Regency also came fully into view—the book on Chambers presented Somerset House as a prototype of civic design and essays on John Wood at Bath provided a defence of the architect as the progenitor of the 'English movement' of town planning.[68] The contemporary work of Adshead and Ramsey was praised in this vein.[69] Edwards's very first published articles were criticisms of the Garden City movement which appeared in the *Town Planning Review* in 1913, and which outlined principles he would continue to refine after the war.[70] Among other criticisms, Edwards advanced the argument that workers 'quite unconsciously show their disapproval of the well-meant schemes of those who would reform them. If upon the edge of an industrial district a speculative builder erects workmen's cottages, it frequently occurs that they will go untenanted.'[71] By contrast, dilapidated terraced houses in city centres were in relatively high demand. The solution, therefore, was to improve the provision of housing at high density, and to avoid the confusion between ventilation and overcrowding. The Garden Suburb was singled out for

---

[65] Ibid.   [66] Ibid., p.124.   [67] Ibid., p.130.
[68] Edwards, 'John Wood and Bath', p.713.   [69] Ibid.
[70] Edwards, 'A Criticism of the Garden City Movement', pp.150–7; Edwards, 'A Further Criticism of the Garden City Movement', pp.312–18.
[71] Edwards, 'A Criticism of the Garden City Movement', p.154.

MANNERS 285

particular censure: 'It gives us the advantages neither of solitude nor of society.'[72]

Edwards, nevertheless, shared the fundamental belief with Howard, Unwin, and their followers that a policy of decentralization, a major national programme of building, and improvement for the poor was of pressing need. But he proposed its realization by different means. First, he was adamant that Ebenezer Howard's formulation—that the solution to the damage done to town and country was to create a hermaphroditic town-country—was mistaken. Secondly, Edwards's policy of de-centralization was to relieve congestion from overcrowded cities not to abandon urban centres. 'Our towns', he wrote in 1913, 'should be so beautiful that everybody would wish to stay inside them. If they are unhealthy we must make them healthy. If they are noisy we must take steps to make them less so. If they are too smoky, we must abolish smoke.'[73] Edwards advocated the creation of new urban centres with high densities, arguing that controlled crowding would generate urbanity of an appropriate density capable of forging civic bonds.

Edwards's ideas about housing design were not solely developed in opposition to the Garden City and 'Homes Fit for Heroes'. He was capable of measured innovation in planning and detailing, and this became a consistent theme in his journalistic output of the 1920s. In 1927, a series on 'The Twentieth Century House' appeared in the *Architect and Building News*,[74] and some ideas featured here were carried forward into later projects and the Hundred New Towns campaign. He fleshed out in detail questions of lighting and ventilation for houses with greater standards of hygiene, which he called 'The Aesthetics of Sanitation' or 'The Aesthetics of Hygiene'. The accompanying speculative designs incorporated ideas such as a 'recess' to contain pipes and other services concealed by the 'slight projection of wall at the opening of the recess'.[75] He also returned to earlier work on sunlight and ventilation (published in the *Town Planning Review* earlier in the decade), in which he attempted to demonstrate the lack of a sound evidence base for planning regulation.[76] The suggested space of 70 feet between the fronts of houses on a street and in the garden space back to back—intended to ensure sunlight in all rooms—reflected a particular

---

[72] Ibid., p.155. [73] Ibid., p.154.
[74] Arthur Trystan Edwards, 'The Twentieth Century House–I', *ABN* (7 January 1927).
[75] Edwards, 'II.—The Aesthetics of Sanitation', p.90.
[76] See Arthur Trystan Edwards, 'Sunlight in Streets', *TPR* 8.2 (1 April 1920), pp.93–8, and Edwards, 'Sunlight in Streets II', *TPR* 9.1 (1 March 1921), pp.26–36.

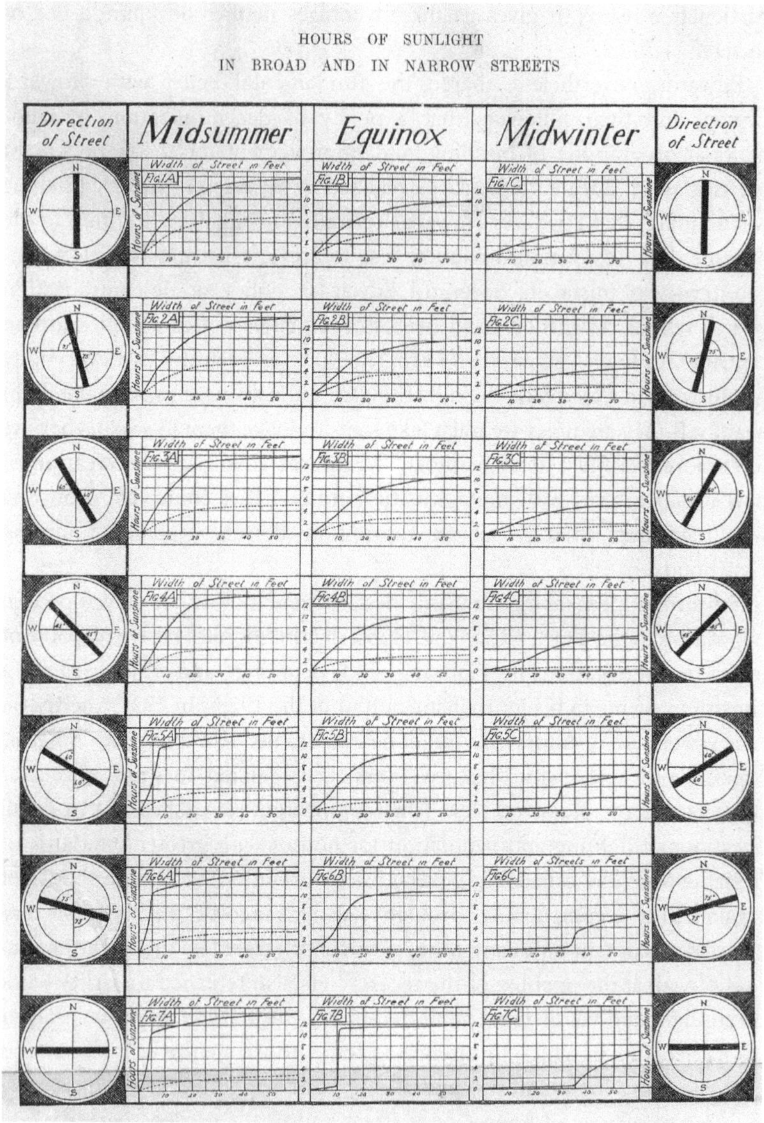

286 DESIGNS ON DEMOCRACY

Fig. 5.7 'Hours of Sunlight in Broad and in Narrow Streets', reproduced in Arthur Trystan Edwards, 'Sunlight in Streets', *TPR*, 8.2 (April 1920), pp.93–8 (Liverpool University Press)

frustration with existing regulation and Edwards devised a table of graphs showing hours of sunshine according to width of street, direction of street, and variations at different times of the year (Fig. 5.7). Edwards may well have been aware of Walter Gropius and Waler Schwagenscheididt's research on orientation and sunlight for application in Ernst May's Frankfurt housing schemes of the late 1920s (Frankfurt was his mother's birthplace).[77] Though never declared, Edwards must have been aware of continental developments; there is a faint rebuttal of canonical projects such as JJP Oud's Kiefhoeck in Rotterdam (1927), reflected in his coloured perspectives later reproduced in promotional literature for the Hundred New Towns Association.

Edwards also developed speculative plans for small houses which departed from Tudor Walters conventions. In one, the front of the house was placed almost on the road—the outer wall being separated from the pavement solely by the depth of a 4-feet porch. A broad frontage of 38 feet allowed for a shorter garden without compromising too much on overall surface area. An additional door on the street front for coal, goods, and tradesmen obviated the need for alleyways, and sanitary services could also be placed at the street front, tidied up with the use of recesses. These designs, along with further proposals for larger or semi-detached houses, amounted to sophisticated and sustained design research. They formed a personal pattern book on which Edwards would draw in his propaganda campaigns.

Another of Edwards's speculative designs for working-class housing was for a street that provided for 'The Exclusion of Dust and Noise' generated by increased motorcar ownership. The standard solution to this problem had been to put houses further away from main roads and highways, but this could also cause issues with sewage and untidy front gardens. For Edwards, the 'obvious solution' was 'to place the houses right on the pavement to act as a screen between the gardens and the public thoroughfare', and then place the main living rooms towards the rear garden.[78] The diagrams show the suggestion of a blind wall facing the street inspired by Soane's perimeter wall for the Bank of England (or even Dance's Newgate Prison), punctuated by blind windows and column screens, and recesses for two entrance doors as in the other small house plans. This concept evolved into the 'Silent House', exhibited at the Building Trades Exhibition at Olympia in 1930,

---

[77] May had also studied with Raymond Unwin, though before Edwards worked for him in the Ministry of Health.

[78] Arthur Trystan Edwards, 'The Twentieth Century House XI.—The Exclusion of Dust and Noise', *ABN* (8 April 1927), p.614.

288   DESIGNS ON DEMOCRACY

designed by Edwards and organized with HG Montgomery. Here, Edwards explored the possibility of sound insulation and dampening internally as well as externally, designing a suite of rooms exhibiting sound-resistant materials produced by British manufactures, providing opportunities for the public to test the effects on insulation.[79] The 'Hush-Hush House' shown the following year at the Ideal Homes Exhibition in 1931 took the idea further. Here the sound-insulated frontage was put into practice with a decorative front door and no windows on the front or side walls, though with 'ample scope...afforded for artistic treatment of the brickwork'. The house, featuring a roof garden and pergola, was enveloped with a 'sound-proof blanket of special material and lined with a wallboard [Treetext] which is a sound and heat insulator'.[80] The 'Silent House' and the 'Hush-Hush House' show Edwards's growing interest in publicity and action, but also his ability to prototype and his belief in the applicability of his solutions to real-life problems.

A Hundred New Towns for Britain!

Various housing and planning reforms in the early 1930s, and the growing critique of the Garden City lobby, heralded by the publication of *Town and Countryside* (1932) by Thomas Sharp, who admired Edwards's early writings, signalled a mood change in the housing and slum clearance debate.[81] The Moyne Report (a result of the Ministry of Health's Departmental Committee on Housing), published in March 1933, had a particularly powerful effect, despite its deficiencies and failures. Moyne called for a withdrawal of local authorities from housing activities except slum clearance, instead arguing for a greater role for public utility societies in building, renovating, and managing low-cost housing, bolstered by the formal creation of a Central Public Utility Council to coordinate activity.[82]

---

[79] *AJ* (17 September 1930), p.425.

[80] 'Real House of Peace', *Daily Mail* (10 March 1931), p.5, and '"Hush-Hush!" House: Secrets of Silence', *Daily Mail* (2 April 1931), p.4; Deborah Sugg Ryan, *Ideal Homes, 1918–1939: Domestic Design and Suburban Modernism* (Manchester, 2018).

[81] Thomas Sharp, *Town and Countryside: Some Aspects of Urban and Rural Development* (Oxford, 1932); John Pendlebury, 'The Urbanism of Thomas Sharp', *Planning Perspectives* 24.1 (January, 2009), pp.3–27.

[82] Patricia Garside, 'Central Government, Local Authorities and the Voluntary Housing Sector, 1919–1939', in Alan O'Day (ed.), *Government and Institutions in the Post-1832 United Kingdom*, Studies in British History 34 (Lampeter, 1995), pp.85–126, p.87; James Alfred Yelling,

MANNERS 289

Though ultimately rejected, as local authorities reasserted their primacy in house-building, Moyne had two important consequences which must have inspired Trystan Edwards.

First, as Elizabeth Darling has shown, despite the reassertion of local authority control, far from the public utility sector being emasculated and decimated, in the wake of the Moyne Report housing associations took on a more 'advisory' than 'provisory' role, developing powerful propaganda work which nonetheless had tangible effects on policy both before and after the Second World War. They used media, including radio and film, exhibitions, and other forms of campaigning to influence policy-makers and the public, and the institution of the Housing Centre was exemplary of this.[83] Secondly, through the proposal of a nationwide public utility society to coordinate municipal and private enterprise, Moyne had shown that associational culture could have national scope, and emphasized the need for imaginative and joined-up thinking at this scale to tackle the housing question.[84] Edwards's campaign built on both of these insights.

On Armistice Day in 1933, a group of ex-servicemen congregated at the Royal Mint, Tower Hill. They formed 'a procession heralded by a band and by men carrying banners with inscriptions'.[85] The inscriptions related to a scheme for a nationwide housing programme which the group championed, and they 'marched through some of the worst slums of London' to illustrate the problems they sought to alleviate. The ex-servicemen will have been promoting a scheme authored by one of their own—Ex-Serviceman J47485—who used the impersonality and anonymity of his service number 'to indicate that he regards himself not as an individual but as a type and a symbol'.[86] Having conferred with a group of ex-servicemen—'a new fraternity of Ex-Soldiers and Sailors'—they called for 'A Hundred New Towns for Britain! The project is both a memorial and a call for action.'[87]

The true author of the pamphlet was, of course, Trystan Edwards. While the service number was certainly real, the rest of this vignette may or may

Slums and Redevelopment: Policy and Practice in England, 1918–1945, with particular reference to London (1992), p.76.

[83] Elizabeth Darling, '"To induce humanitarian sentiments in prurient Londoners": The Propaganda Activities of London's Voluntary Housing Associations in the Inter-War Period', *London Journal* 27.1 (1 May 2002), pp.42–62, p.50.

[84] This in fact manifested itself as a much weaker National Federation of Housing Societies, established in 1935.

[85] Paul Thomas Radford-Rowe Kirk, *New Towns for Old: An Account of the Aims of the Hundred New Towns Association* (Westminster, 1942).

[86] Edwards, *Hundred New Towns*, p.1.

[87] Ibid., p.7.

290   DESIGNS ON DEMOCRACY

not be.[88] There are no corroborative records of this foundational moment yet discovered—no photographs, no newspaper reports; indeed, no mention of the event at all until five years later in a promotional pamphlet.[89] Moreover, there are no substantive records for the campaign in general—it is a patchy history to piece together—and yet the Hundred New Towns Association, of which this group of ex-servicemen apparently formed the kernel, was a significant campaigning body for low-rise, high-density housing development on a national scale, in new compact towns through a programme of decentralization, and through rebuilding former slums at comparable densities to the housing that they replaced. It was one of the only serious and coherent programmes which offered a third way in housing policy, deviating from what had become the normal formula of either peripheral village estates or increasingly higher-rise tenements or 'block dwellings' built over razed inner-city slums. Furthermore, it had at its core radical proposals for enfranchising the public in the housing question. It promoted a social vision, the culmination of Edwards's various strands of design and criticism, ones which above all retained a commitment to well-mannered urban development through civic design. It was also an ambitious social programme designed for public benefit.

Despite the scant detail, the origin myth of the HNTA gestures towards the ambitions of the campaign and its significance. The Royal Mint as the symbolic start of the procession, for instance—why there? We can assume that there was an appropriateness to Edwards in gathering in front of the building designed by Robert Smirke between 1807 and 1812. But there was a greater significance still—the Mint made money, and any scheme of mass house-building would need money. But why not the Treasury or the Bank of England? The Mint was chosen because it produced the 'little bits of paper' and the 'tokens of exchange' of currency—notes and coinage.[90] These references must be understood in the context of the Gold Standard, a contentious factor in interwar economic policy; as Glynne and Oxborrow argued, 'the forced departure from gold in 1931 [by the Bank of England] was a liberating influence which made new attitudes and policies possible in

---

[88] See TNA, ADM 188/741/4785 for Trystan Edwards's service record.
[89] Wellcome Library, Eugenics Society Archive, SAEUG/D/101, 'The Hundred New Towns Association: Formation, Progress and Future Policy', p.3. The first edition of the first pamphlet of the Association had been printed in October 1933.
[90] Edwards, *Hundred New Towns*, p.20.

MANNERS 291

the 1930s'.[91] By the time he came to launch the HNTA Edwards had aligned with a number of influential people in the monetary reform and Social Credit movements, both stimulated by the abandonment of the Gold Standard. Moreover, the Mint's geographical position allowed the group to process through East London slums—such performative acts were common, for instance Basil Jellicoe ceremonially throwing models of pestilential slum bugs on a fire at the Sidney Street estate in Somers Town.

Also significant in this vignette was the choice of Armistice. The meaning and significance of Armistice Day was changing in the early 1930s, particularly in East London where 'wider domestic problems of slump and unemployment found a greater role' in commemorations.[92] Indeed in East London in particular, at Poplar and Stepney, British Legion branches used the occasion 'to highlight the level of ex-service unemployment'.[93] The choice of 11 November—Armisticetide, as it was sometimes called at this time, connoting a new religiosity in the rituals which marked it—was, therefore, imbued with certain meanings for those ex-servicemen engaged in shifting forms of memorialization that honoured not just the dead and bereaved, as often emphasized, but living ex-soldiers and sailors too.

The HNTA and the Ex-Servicemen's Group thus constituted a project fashioning a new more active, participatory veteranhood. This was made explicit by Edwards's own self-fashioning: as well as the use of his war service number, he was also a member of the Navy League, the Fleet Street branch of the British Legion, and of TocH, the interdenominational Christian movement set up by the Reverend Tubby Clayton near Ypres in 1915.[94] How architects and other professionals in the built environment channelled their experiences of war service in the interwar years has been an understudied subject, save for memorials to the dead through the Imperial War Graves Commission, or more extreme forms of mental and physical disability. Edwards provides a rare and highly self-conscious example of a different form of veteranhood amid wider debates about design, practice, and professionalism.

[91] Sean Glynn and John Oxborrow, *Interwar Britain: A Social and Economic History* (1976), p.122.
[92] Mark Connelly, *The Great War, Memory and Ritual: Commemoration in the City and East London, 1916–1939* (London: Royal Historical Society, 2002), p.177.
[93] Ibid., p.178.
[94] King's College London, Liddell Hart Military Archives, GB0099 KCLMA Hamilton, Papers of General Sir Ian Standish Monteith Hamilton, letter from Trystan Edwards to Hamilton (4 March 1934). Edwards appended a brief 'Record of Ex-Service Man J47485' (himself).

292   DESIGNS ON DEMOCRACY

Significantly, though it was a 'political fraternity of ex-soldiers and sailors', no uniforms were required in the group.[95] The new fraternity, it was at pains to emphasize, was 'loyal to the Throne' and to the Imperial Commonwealth.[96] It sought to create a 'domestic policy', from which 'parliamentary government will receive a new lease of life'.[97] The group was also lay; it was 'not a group of technicians—town-planners, engineers or architects—who might be suspected of seeking to use the machinery of the State for the advancement of their professional interests'.[98]

A campaign run, therefore, 'not for ex-service men but by ex-service men', it would take the form of a memorial—but a vital memorial 'of their war experience' which would 'seek to accomplish something which would profit the nation as a whole'.[99] The programme was positioned as fundamentally different from the 'Homes Fit for Heroes' on which Edwards had indeed worked, and the Association sought to give voice to the public—the ex-servicemen and slum-dwellers who had been excluded from policy-making. The HNTA captured a moment of new, more productive constructions of veteranhood analogous to what Eleanor O'Keefe has described in Glasgow, where civic ceremony, pageantry and procession, which characterized the HNTA's foundation in London, and civic society were increasingly important in 'shaping representations of veteranhood; the affinity and intersections of military and civic culture made the 'urban sphere...a productive one for commemoration'.[100]

These were the mythical origins of the HNTA. What is fact is that the Association and campaign were spearheaded by Trystan Edwards. In letters to Thomas Sharp in 1933, Edwards had discussed the potential formation of a society to promote civic design.[101] The HNTA seems to have been its eventual manifestation. Aside from the Moyne Report, there were two other significant forces behind the emergence of the scheme. The first was the Cambridge academic Mansfield Forbes, Fellow of Clare College. Forbes had a longstanding interest in modern architecture and aesthetics.[102] He had commissioned the refitting of his home, Finella, by Raymond McGrath (1927–9), a dazzling modern interior in which he gathered together figures

---

[95] Edwards, *Hundred New Towns*, p.35.   [96] Ibid., p.30.   [97] Ibid., p.7.
[98] Ibid., p.35.   [99] Ibid., p.5.
[100] Eleanor O'Keefe, 'Civic Veterans: The Public Culture of Military Associations in Inter-War Glasgow', *Urban History* 44.2 (2017), p.302.
[101] Newcastle University Thomas Sharp Archive, THS 1.79, Letter from Edwards to Thomas Sharp on 13 January 1933.
[102] Harry Godwin, 'Obituary: "Manny"', *Cambridge Review* (7 February 1936), pp.226–7; Hugh Carey, *Mansfield Forbes and His Cambridge* (Cambridge, 1984), pp.82, 131, 119, 132; Alan Powers, '"Simple Intime": The Work of Raymond McGrath', *Thirties Society Journal* 3 (1982), p.5.

influential in art and architecture, among them leading Modernists like McGrath himself, Jack Pritchard, Wells Coates, and Serge Chermayeff, but crucially also Trystan Edwards whose work he consistently championed. Astragal recalled an early meeting with Forbes in his rooms in Clare, during which Forbes 'launched into an attack on the people who had pinched and plagiarized Trystan Edwards's ideas'.[103] Forbes had become increasingly interested in monetary reform, partly as a response to the economic turbulence of the early 1930s. He believed that 'the shortage of liquidity caused by the contraction of credit during the years of depression must be counteracted by an increase in the money supply'.[104] This led to agitation for the Social Credit movement. Forbes was an indefatigable supporter of Edwards's scheme, and his economic interests permeated the HNTA. Finella and his rooms at Clare became 'distributing agencies' for the early editions of the HNTA pamphlets.[105] In December 1934, he wrote to proselytize, noting the circulation to luminaries including the former Liberal chancellor Reginald McKenna, the Cambridge economist and statistician Colin Clark, JM Keynes, and Alfred Bossom: 'We must "grid" the Kingdom systematically', Forbes enthused, with 'zealous distributors and salesmen/women'.[106]

'Gridding' was an apt metaphor, because the other significant factor which unlocked Edwards's conception of a bold scheme on a national scale was the commencement of operations of the Central Electricity Board's (CEB) National Grid in 1934. The grid had a profound effect on the possibilities of decentralized industry and redistribution of the industrial population. In this regard in particular, it touched on 'the debate about the respective merits, and relative moral values, of town and country'.[107] As we have seen, Edwards was fervently against suburban sprawl. Sprawl was linked to industry, particularly in the peripheries of major metropoles. In London, formerly north-west Middlesex, sprawl was facilitated first by the carving out of arterial roads, like the Great West Road, and then by light industrial development— the so-called 'fancy factories'—which sprang up along them. Housing was needed for the industrial population, and private speculative 'ribbon' development of suburban housing followed to meet demand. The Restriction of Ribbon Development Act (1935) also will have encouraged the prospect

---

[103] 'Notes and Topics', *AJ* (30 January 1936), p.185; Elizabeth Darling, 'Finella, Mansfield Forbes, Raymond McGrath, and Modernist Architecture in Britain', *Journal of British Studies* 50.1 (2011), pp.125–55.

[104] Carey, *Forbes*, p.132.   [105] Ibid.

[106] Emanuel College Archives, University of Cambridge, COL.9.59(a).122, letter from Forbes to DW Harding (16 December 1934).

[107] Bill Luckin, *Questions of Power: Electricity and Environment in Inter-War Britain* (Manchester, 1990), p.1.

of a more considered national house-building campaign, and this was explicitly mentioned in the new Association's promotional material (Fig. 5.8). The Act reflected the growing need felt among professionals and voluntary associations for some regulation to stymie urban sprawl, statutory plans having proved ineffective instruments of development control.

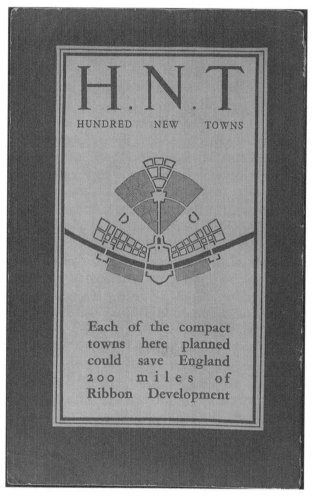

Fig. 5.8 Back cover of the original promotional pamphlet, showing one of Edwards's type plans, AT Edwards, *A Hundred New Towns for Britain: An Appeal to the electorate by Ex-Serviceman J47485* (London: Simpkin Marshall, 1934)

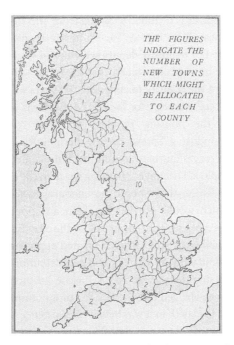

Fig. 5.9 A map of mainland Britain showing the disposition of the new towns, AT Edwards, *A Hundred New Towns for Britain: An Appeal to the electorate by Ex-Serviceman J47485* (London: Simpkin Marshall, 1934), p.36

Developments in the provision of energy supply therefore were profoundly related to town-planning issues, as Bill Lucin has argued. The spread of the grid—heralded by the march of the CEB's pylons (for which Reginald Blomfield had acted as design consultant)—represented electricity as a 'mass service' of social transformation, stimulating 'a second and cleaner industrial revolution, the decentralisation of mass production, and a rejuvenation of a deeply depressed agrarian society'.[108] Builders, landlords, and housing committees would need to think 'more electrically' than they had hitherto.[109]

Through his campaign for a Hundred New Towns for Britain, Trystan Edwards had indeed begun to think electrically. Forwarding his prospectus and credentials to General Sir Ian Hamilton, from whom he was trying

---

[108] Luckin, *Questions of Power*, p.11.   [109] Ibid., p.52.

296 DESIGNS ON DEMOCRACY

to elicit support, Edwards included a cutting from *The Times*. The article on 'Electricity in Town Planning: A Factor in Harmonious Development' described a talk by GA Sherrard, deputy secretary of the CEB, for the Town Planning Institute in which he argued 'that the factor which would fashion the development of the country for the next 100 years was electricity'.[110] In the early promotional literature for the HNTA, Edwards was explicit: key to the solution of the housing problem was the reorganization and redistribution of industry. Sprawl on the peripheries of existing towns created unsatisfactory suburban conditions, but 'As there are now large numbers of unemployed occupying housing space in the existing towns and have no industrial ties, they should be encouraged to migrate to new environments which would provide for them an opportunity for active citizenship'.[111] The campaign was facilitated by the electric grid, which made industry more mobile and in the process created opportunity for a national industrial and manufacturing strategy and redistribution of the industrial population. Endorsing the scheme in his Roscoe Lecture of 1934, Charles Herbert Reilly acknowledged that the HNTA's programme was 'a very much more feasible idea to-day than it was before the existence of the electric grid distributing power everywhere and almost inviting the moving of factories'.[112]

Edwards's interventions were timely, if not prescient: in 1934 Parliament had passed the Special Areas Act (formerly the Depressed Areas Bill, whose name was ultimately deemed too depressing itself), following an inquiry into areas suffering from intense industrial depression (namely Tyneside, West Cumbernauld, and parts of South Wales), which later resulted in a number of Trading Estates with the promise of associated housing. These lacked the civic ambition, however, of the Hundred New Towns campaign. The Commission on the Redistribution of the Industrial Population (which produced the Barlow Report) was appointed in 1937, to which Edwards and the HNTA gave evidence. Their plan was praised by Barlow as being the only scheme presented to the Commission which encompassed a truly national scale.[113]

---

[110] 'Electricity and Town Planning: A Factor in Harmonious Development', *The Times* (10 February 1934), p.9.
[111] Edwards, *Hundred New Towns*, p.12.
[112] Charles Herbert Reilly, *Scaffolding in the Sky: A Semi-Architectural Autobiography* (1938), p.329.
[113] 'A Trystan Edwards', *AR* (May 1973), p.240.

The Scheme

We have become accustomed to the idea that there was a general consensus around Garden City principles for the delivery of housing and wider urban development, associated with 'the science of Town Planning' in Edwards's eyes. Certainly this held true with regard to official policy. But Trystan Edwards's persistent criticism of *bona fide* low-density Garden City development, as well as the ribbon development of private speculation that bastardized its forms, demonstrates that these ideas could be contested. By the end of the interwar period, Edwards had developed a series of worked-out policies advocating a different approach derived from 'the art of Civic Design'.

As Simon Pepper has noted, there were fundamentally two aspects of the housing crises of the interwar period. One side concentrated on the delivery of new housing units, of which the state-sponsored 'Homes Fit for Heroes' campaign is the best-known example. It was wound down in the early 1920s after delivering well short of its aims amid fears aroused by growing economic turbulence, but perversely at the precise point that the cost of building materials was coming down.[114] Local authorities continued to deliver house-building at scale, through successive Housing Acts. The other aspect of the housing crisis was the scourge of the slums—slum clearance and the question of how to redevelop slum lands and rehouse the working classes become increasingly politically urgent in the 1930s.[115]

Pepper and Richmond have defined the two primary remedies to the housing problem: to rebuild upwards (increasingly higher-rise 'walk up' tenements), or outwards (large-scale cottage estates on the peripheries of towns). It was clearly economically untenable to redevelop slum lands at low, Garden City densities of twelve dwellings to an acre on valuable inner-city urban sites. At the same time, displacing communities from the inner cities to peripheral cottage estates, such as Becontree in Dagenham developed by the LCC in the 1920s and early 1930s, was also unworkable.

---

[114] Swenarton, *Homes Fit for Heroes.*

[115] Simon Pepper and Peter Richmond, 'Homes Unfit for Heroes: The Slum Problem in London and Neville Chamberlain's Unhealthy Areas Committee, 1919–1921', *TPR* 80.2 (March–April 2009), pp.143–71; and their 'Upward or Outward? Politics, Planning and Council Flats, 1919–1939', *Journal of Architecture* (February 2008), pp.53–90; 'Stepney and the Politics of High-Rise Housing: Limehouse Fields to John Scurr House, 1925–1937', *London Journal* 34.1 (March 2009), pp.33–54.

298   DESIGNS ON DEMOCRACY

These sorts of estates had been designed with the 'labour aristocracy'[116] in mind and did little to tackle the endemic housing problems of the lower working classes, many of whom did not necessarily aspire to the Garden Suburb ideal but instead simply wished for improvements to their original areas.

Despite initial resistance to 'walk up' tenement blocks of up to six storeys, Pepper and Richmond have charted the emergence of standard higher-rise tenement blocks by the LCC, and their promotion by an initially hostile Labour Party after their takeover of the Council in 1934. This policy was not universally popular, and Pepper and Richmond cite an instance of political radical Aubrey Westlake's protest against the Labour Party's housing policy in Bermondsey, in which he 'drew attention to Trystan Edwards's little-known proposals for high-density, low-rise housing as a viable alternative.'[117]

The premise of the proposal was that industry and the industrial population needed to be more effectively distributed around the country, but that decentralization would serve not to eradicate urban centres and urban life; instead it would make them more sustainable in the long term. Once the new towns had been created, existing cramped accommodation would be retrofitted and smaller cottages even combined to form larger dwellings. This was also in line with housing policy, in which the possibility of wide-scale 'reconditioning' was increasingly seen as part of a broader package of reforms.[118] The new towns would be distributed across the United Kingdom—76 in England, 15 in Scotland, and 9 in Wales. A higher proportion would be located in the seven northern counties to mitigate southerly migration, and no new towns would be built within a 25-mile radius of Charing Cross (Fig. 5.9). The plans of the new towns would have 'Compactness', in other words high density, 'Order', zoning, and 'Flexibility', mixed-use development and adaptability to different topographies and circumstances (Figs. 5.10–5.12). In the HNTA's proposals, Edwards returned to the bugbear of density, dismissing once again the 12-acre limit on open development and demonstrating that high-density terraces, even of a similar density to some slum areas, could be made amenable.

Edwards's proposals showed ideal new towns arranged on circular plans, but with predominantly sector-based zoning within the circular plan;

[116] Darling, '"To induce humanitarian sentiments"', p.43.
[117] Pepper and Richmond, 'Upward or Outward?', p.79.
[118] Simon Pepper and Peter Richmond, 'Cottages, Flats and Reconditioning: Renewal Strategies in London after World War One', *Construction History* 23 (2008), pp.99–117.

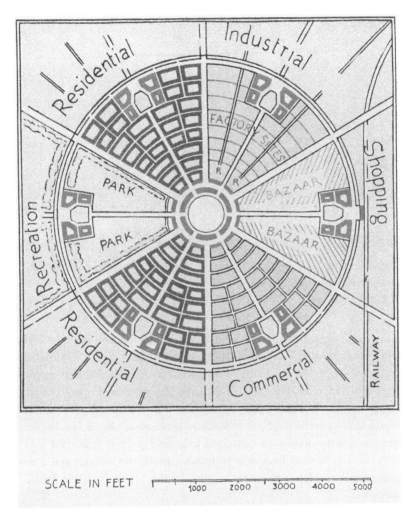

Fig. 5.10 The 'archetype' town plan, elsewhere referred to as 'A "Model" Town Designed for Traffic', reproduced in the *TPR* 14.1 (May 1939), p.35, this version reproduced in AT Edwards, *A Hundred New Towns for Britain: An Appeal to the electorate by Ex-Serviceman J47485* (London: Simpkin Marshall, 1934), p.40

concentric links and repeating features would provide an easily accessible full set of amenities mitigating the need for Garden City satellites connecting to a parent city. Green wedges would substitute green belts, particularly once major metropoles like London had been significantly decentralized. Sitte-esque informality was written out altogether—individual units would

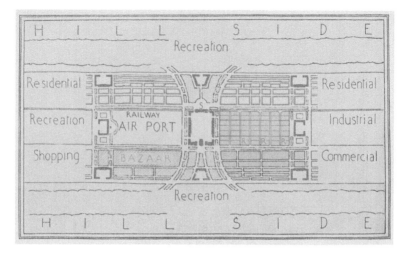

Fig. 5.11 'A Town in a Valley', AT Edwards, *A Hundred New Towns for Britain: An Appeal to the electorate by Ex-Serviceman J47485* (London: Simpkin Marshall, 1934), p.44

make more formal terraces set around squares of around twenty to thirty houses per acre at a lower end, and—in a clear nod to Georgian and Regency precedent—with the possibility of brick-facings or painted stucco on concrete or steel frames (Fig. 5.13). At the front of his typical proposed houses, facing inwards to open public space, glazed doors on the ground floor would offer convenient access to a shared quadrangle (Fig. 5.14). The rear elevations of the houses were designed to be neat and tidy to face the street with recesses hosting back-door entrances, waste and storage, and a low screen wall to keep 'passers-by a little distance away from the kitchen windows'.[119]

Forbidden Houses

Although the scheme received some limited support after its initial flurry of activity, the campaign failed to make a significant impact. In August 1935, however, a second push was made in part through enlisting more

[119] Edwards, *Hundred New Towns*, p.56.

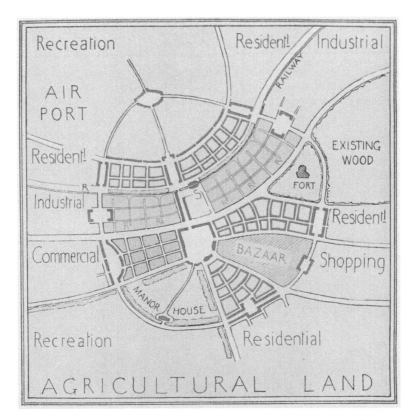

Fig. 5.12 'A Town on Special Site', AT Edwards, *A Hundred New Towns for Britain: An Appeal to the electorate by Ex-Serviceman J47485* (London: Simpkin Marshall, 1934), p.45

high-profile support for a letter to *The Times*.[120] Viscount Esher, inveterate chair of numerous committees, was a signatory, along with Frederick Gowland Hopkins, the biochemist and then-president of the Royal Society, who had signed the first public letter, but there were new backers too: Sir Richard Paget, a barrister later described as a 'brilliant amateur scientist' and pioneer in sign-language,[121] and Dean Hewlett Johnson, the Red Dean of

---

[120] 'Rebuilding Britain', *The Times* (5 August 1935), p.6.
[121] 'Sir Richard Paget', *The Times* (28 October 1955), p.11.

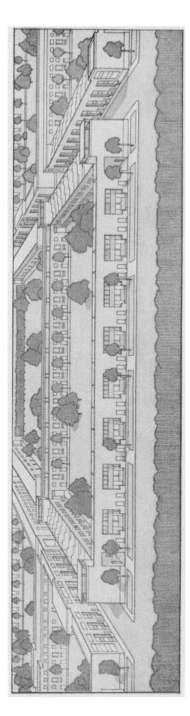

Fig. 5.13 Perspective view of terraced housing in quadrangular formation, AT Edwards, *A Hundred New Towns for Britain: An Appeal to the electorate by Ex-Serviceman J47485* (London: Simpkin Marshall, 1934), p.48

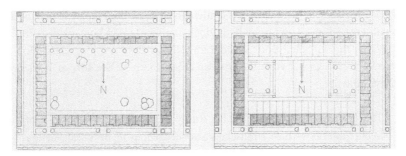

Fig. 5.14 AT Edwards, *A Hundred New Towns for Britain: An Appeal to the electorate by Ex-Serviceman J47485* (London: Simpkin Marshall, 1934), p.50

Canterbury, socialist and leading advocate of the Social Credit movement.[122] Johnson had come on board earlier that year, presumably introduced by Mansfield Forbes, corresponding with Edwards on the prospect of a book on housing to be published by Stanley Unwin.[123] Around the same time Edwards made contact with Commissioner David C Lamb, a senior figure in the Salvation Army who served as director of the organization's Emigration Department and later as its first International Secretary for Social Work.[124] The HNTA actively encouraged intra-imperial migration and Lamb accepted the invitation to become vice-president, 'heart and soul' in sympathy with the organization's aims.[125] The letter to *The Times*—a small intervention—caught the organization at a difficult period. Neither Lamb nor Forbes would sign it, but Edwards used it as an 'indirect means of increasing the number of HNT Vice-Presidents', and thus extending its network.[126]

The Association lost momentum between its initial launch and 1936, a situation worsened by the sudden death of Mansfield Forbes in January of that year at the age of forty-six. In February 1936, however, Edwards published an article in *The Nineteenth Century and After* in which he introduced a new campaigning slogan, 'Gentlemen of the Slums' and in which he called for slum-dwellers to 'exercise a formative influence upon

---

[122] John Butler, *The Red Dean of Canterbury: The Public and Private Faces of Hewlett Johnson* (2011).
[123] University of Kent, Hewlett Johnson Papers, UKC-JOH-COR, 232–245, Edwards to Johnson (24 May 1935) [259].
[124] Ibid., Commissioner David C Lamb to Edwards (22 May 35) [260].   [125] Ibid.
[126] Ibid., Edwards to Johnson (23 May 1935).

304 DESIGNS ON DEMOCRACY

housing policy.[127] The epithet 'Gentlemen' echoed the emphasis on good manners and social hierarchy, betraying a familiar bias in housing discourse towards the so-called poor aristocracy. Nonetheless, working-class slum-dwellers were in his view the best qualified to know the sort of housing they wanted:

> The vast majority of these folk are sturdy English types who, in spite of living conditions which, it must be acknowledged, are highly unsatisfactory in many ways, yet succeed in maintaining a high standard of cleanliness in upholding the sanctities of family life. Such people may very properly be described as "Gentlemen of the Slums", and if they have certain objections to the new dwellings now being provided for them, their point of view should require careful consideration by the Government and local authorities.[128]

The article repeated Edwards's consistent complaints against low-density 'open development' and walk-up tenements, inimical to the needs and wants of slum-dwellers. There was, however, the beginnings of a shift in tone away from the design of new towns to an emphasis on the replacement of tenements on slum clearance sites.

Building on this theme, Edwards and the HNTA mounted an exhibition at the Housing Centre on 13 Suffolk Street in autumn 1936 entitled 'Forbidden Houses: Designed for the Gentlemen of the Slums.'[129] The title was chosen to explain 'that the types of dwelling illustrated, although they met with approval of the slum dwellers themselves, are forbidden at present by the law of the land.'[130] Exhibits included a number of type plans and Edwards's scheme for model compact towns. The Housing Centre had been founded two years earlier as an 'umbrella group for experts in housing who operated outside government.'[131] It was also a centre for housing activists of a Modernist bent, many of whom were involved in organizing the influential 'New Homes for Old' exhibitions, including one in 1936. These were events which aimed to set the agenda in the wider housing debate and the Centre's

---

[127] Arthur Trystan Edwards, 'Gentlemen of the Slums', *Nineteenth Century and After* (February 1936), p.150.

[128] Ibid., p.151.

[129] 'Houses for Slum Dwellers', *The Times* (23 October 1936), p.11; Wellcome Library, Eugenics Society Archive, SAEUG/D/101, 'The Hundred New Towns Association: Formation, Progress and Future Policy', p.10.

[130] '"Forbidden Houses"', *The Times* (19 November 1936), p.4.

[131] Darling, '"To induce humanitarian sentiments"', p.54.

honorary technical consultants in the late 1930s included Patrick Abercrombie, Wells Coates, Elizabeth Denby, Walter Gropius, Maxwell Fry, Lancelot Keay, Barry Parker, and Louis de Soissons. Edwards was a listed supporter.[132] The Centre was chaired by Reginald Rowe, a significant figure in housing and economic reform who had founded the Improved Tenements Association with Octavia Hill in 1900. Rowe was a supporter of the HNTA and it was perhaps through him that Edwards was able to rent out the Centre's exhibition spaces for 'Forbidden Houses'. The exhibition was opened in late October by Major-General Sir Frederick Maurice, president of British Legion, and Patrick Abercrombie presided over the occasion in his capacity as chair of the Centre.[133]

In 1936, therefore, the Hundred New Towns was campaigning for two different but connected proposals which reflected the two sides of interwar housing policy. On the one hand, Edwards and the HNTA advocated a programme of decentralization to new compact towns distributed around the United Kingdom. On the other, Edwards's rhetoric increasingly focused on the slum-dweller's needs and wants. This brought with it the realization that the question of how to rebuild former slum areas, or even recondition them, needed consideration not least as means to maintain the networks of kinship and community that had existed there, as well as ease of access and supervision for women and young families.[134] This chimed with other voices in housing reform, such as Elizabeth Denby, the self-styled housing consultant and leading figure at the Housing Centre. Her ground-breaking paper, 'Rehousing from the Slum-Dweller's Point of View' was the first sessional paper in the RIBA's history to be given by a woman, and in it she argued forcefully for inner urban development, echoing Edwards's diagnosis that 'the choice for a town dweller between a flat at fifty and a cottage at twelve to the acre is a choice between two impractical and unnecessary extremes'.[135] She praised instead Regency terraces with densities of thirty-five to forty to

[132] Lambeth Council Archives, Housing Centre Trust Records, IV/III/1/17, Fourth Annual Report of the Housing Centre, p.13.

[133] 'Houses for Slum Dwellers', p.11.

[134] Mark Clapson, *Working Class Suburbs: Social Change on an English Council Estate, 1930–2010* (Manchester, 2012); Clapson, 'Working-Class Women's Experiences of Moving to New Housing Estates in England since 1919', *Twentieth-Century British History* 10.3 (1999), pp.345–65.

[135] Elizabeth Denby, 'Rehousing from the Slum Dweller's Point of View', *JRIBA* (November 1936), p.66; 'Correspondence: The Hundred New Towns Association', *JRIBA* (5 December 1936), p.150; 'Correspondence', *JRIBA* (19 December 1936), p.192; 'Correspondence', *JRIBA* (9 January 1937), p.243. I am grateful to Elizabeth Darling for drawing my attention to this correspondence; Elizabeth Darling, 'Elizabeth Denby, Housing Consultant: Social Reform and

306 DESIGNS ON DEMOCRACY

the acre. The paper coincided with Edwards's exhibition, and he used the opportunity to point out the similarities between his proposals and Denby's argument, noting provocatively that Denby had visited the exhibition on a number of occasions: 'It is all the more gratifying to us, therefore, that the housing policy which she describes as her own, in essentials so closely resembles the one which has been consistently advocated by the Hundred New Towns Association since its formation in 1933.'[136] Edwards argued, however, that Denby's recommendation of around thirty-five dwellings to the acre was too low and that higher densities and urban decentralization were not mutually exclusive. Denby was swift to retaliate and unequivocal in her response: 'in essentials,' she wrote, 'my policy is *entirely* opposite to theirs and has been since the formation of the association.'[137] She was certainly firmly against decentralization on the basis of common assumptions about imminent and drastic population decline. Denby favoured instead 'urban replanning', emphasizing reconditioning and improvement to existing urban areas rather than the HNTA's new centres.[138]

An Alternative to Tenements

'Forbidden Houses' failed to make a major impact on the architectural and planning worlds save for a few formal press notices. Edwards's brusque exchange with Denby was also characteristic of his inability to forge alliances with the sorts of skilled propagandists who might help gain the scheme more attention. In the non-specialist press too, though the exhibition gained some favourable comment, the response was limited, though Edwards noted that some of the models and drawings displayed and commissioned subsequently reached a wider audience at the Merchant Navy Week Exhibition at Southampton in July 1937.[139]

The exhibition was a significant milestone for the HNTA, nevertheless, bringing the programme to a wider audience under the auspices of an influential institution, the Housing Centre. Though little evidence of its displays remain, Edwards used his 'Forbidden Houses' to illustrate the

Cultural Politics in the Inter-War decades', Ph.D. thesis, UCL, 1999. Cf. *The Builder* (25 March 1938); (1 April 1938), p.637; and (15 April 1938), p.735.

[136] 'Correspondence: The Hundred New Towns Association', *JRIBA* (5 December 1936), p.150.

[137] 'Correspondence', *JRIBA* (19 December 1936), p.192. [138] Ibid.

[139] Wellcome Library, Eugenics Society Archive, SAEUG/D/101, 'The Hundred New Towns Association: Formation, Progress and Future Policy', p.10.

Fig. 5.15 'Houses at 40 to the Acre with blocks of Flats at Corners', AT Edwards, *Modern Terrace Houses: Researches on High Density Development* (London: John Tiranti Ltd, 1946), p.xiv

campaign's next major intervention, 'An Alternative to Tenements', which marked a decisive shift in the HNTA's policy.[140] Recognizing it was not politically expedient to carry out a national campaign of reconstruction, Edwards refocused the HNTA in line with a wider shift in housing policy toward slum clearance and reconstruction. To the 'third way' of tackling the housing problem (besides the prevalent 'upward' or 'outward' approach, Edwards had of course proposed compact new towns), Edwards now added a fourth: rehousing 'in self-contained cottages at the same densities as are the tenements as a more immediate and popular remedy'.[141]

Edwards presented type plans of individual units of three types—those that could be set out at 30–40 dwellings per acre (Figs. 5.15 and 5.16), 40–50, and 50–60 of two, three and four storeys respectively. Particular motifs pertaining to well-mannered design persisted as Edwards continued

---

[140] Arthur Trystan Edwards, *An Alternative to Tenements* (1938). This pamphlet reproduced articles originally published in *The Builder* in February 1938.
[141] Ibid., p.2.

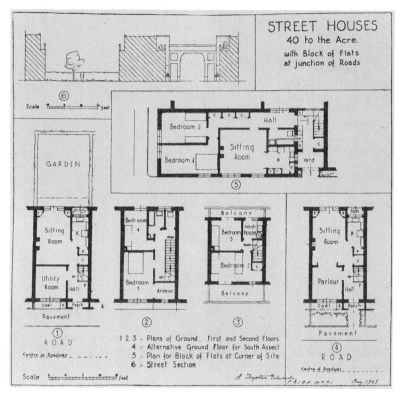

Fig. 5.16   Plans and a section showing 'Street houses at 40 to the acre with Blocks of Flats at junction of Roads', AT Edwards, *Modern Terrace Houses: Researches on High Density Development* (London: John Tiranti Ltd, 1946), p.xv

to play within his own design controls of number, punctuation, and inflection, and address his concerns about dust, noise, sanitation, and hygiene—recesses for services and refuse were assiduously incorporated so that 'both the front and back elevations are equally decorous'.[142]

Essentially, Edwards argued for a holistic revision of building and planning regulations through new minimum housing standards emancipated by what he called a 'Charter of Freedom', which would give designers greater scope for an imaginative response to the challenge of mass housing, based on sound principles properly evidenced.[143] Here too Edwards adumbrated for the first time coherently his plans for a 'pyramidal' street section, a

[142] Ibid., p.5.   [143] Ibid., p.11.

MANNERS 309

development of his earlier research into 'Sunlight in Streets' and Edwards's proposals also featured roof terraces prominently.[144]

The pyramidal street section was a significant innovation, and one carried through to Edwards's later research, published as *Modern Terrace Houses* in 1946.[145] This was funded by the Chadwick Trust from a benefaction by Alfred Bossom, after an open call for research into reasonable density 'for small houses with gardens, suitable especially for the intermediate and outer zones of large towns'.[146] The 'pyramidal' street section provided a solution to the basic problem of obtaining the highest cubical content of accommodation, on a site that was consistent with maintenance of the angle of sunlight. With stepped-back terraces, more sunlight could penetrate rooms of houses, though up to the limit at which the 'centre part of the base of the pyramid would be in darkness' (i.e. the total depth of the section could not be more than twice the depth of the room on each side, though the centre part could receive extra light from a dome or roof light at the top of a staircase well), Edwards concluded that the pyramidal street section would allow for no more than two floors above the ground floor. The higher densities this would facilitate would be compensated by easy access to communal public open space (terraces would largely be in quadrangular formation) and to private roof gardens, conceived in particular for families where children could play under convenient supervision of their mothers.[147]

The pyramidal street section in terrace formation was influential on later debates about low-rise, high-density social housing in the post-war years.[148] In a housing scheme for St Pancras by Leslie Martin and Colin St John Wilson published in *Architectural Design* in July 1959, for instance, reference was made to higher densities achieved not solely by higher tower blocks but also

> ...equally by two-storey houses arranged in terraces, three- or four-storey houses, four-storey maisonettes, low blocks of flats, tall blocks of flats or by a combination of these, as well as by many other forms and relationships

[144] Ibid., p.12.
[145] Arthur Trystan Edwards, *Modern Terrace Houses: Researches on High Density Development* (1946).
[146] 'Notes', *JRIBA* (August 1944), p.270.   [147] Ibid.
[148] Edwards had perhaps known of the stepped terraces of Henri Sauvage in mid-1920s Paris. The Bethnal Green and East London Housing Association had also built a number of flats at Lennox House, Cresset Road, designed by JEM MacGregor (1936–7), a much bolder use of the pyramidal street section than Edwards proposed, with an intended covered market in the building's central section.

310 DESIGNS ON DEMOCRACY

of dwelling that we have yet to explore. Mr Trystan Edwards demonstrated this very clearly in his essay on 'Modern Terrace Houses' in 1946 using several forms of narrow-fronted dwellings.[149]

It is notable that three years later the same partnership, which included Patrick Hodgkinson in both instances, produced Harvey Court for Gonville and Caius College, Cambridge, characterized by stepped terraces in quadrangular formation. As Mark Swenarton has shown in his comprehensive survey of low-rise, high-density housing in post-war Camden, pyramidal street sections were also used by Neave Brown, most notably at the Alexandra Road Estate, under the influence of Hodgkinson who had used the same device for the Brunswick Centre.[150] There are essential differences between the ziggurat forms of medium-rise blocks of flats in the 1950s and 1960s and Edwards's street sections, but this pedigree of unorthodox social housing owed a debt to Trystan Edwards which has not been properly acknowledged.

The story of the HNTA during the reconstruction debates and into the post-war years is beyond the scope of this present analysis. Edwards participated in the important Barlow Commission on the distribution of the industrial population. He appeared with the agricultural reformer Lord Northbourne and MCM Athorpe, members of the Executive Committee of the Association. Recapitulating the main proposals of the group, they were met with scepticism by Abercrombie, although the chairman praised them as 'the boldest we have had to consider'.[151] Edwards was also proactive in drawing up alternative reconstruction plans for London. His plan for 'Greater London' was predicated on mass migration out of London to the new towns, bringing the population down from 8.5 million (population estimate of 1937) to 6.5 million. The plan sought a balance between 'the *conservative* element and the *radical* element'.[152] The 'conservative' element would prevail where preservation of 'the relics of former London' could be ensured and in concentrations of architectural quality, Hampstead,

---

[149] 'Housing Development, St Pancras London NW', *Architectural Design* 29.7 (July 1959), p.279. *Modern Terrace Houses* was also cited by Chamberlain, Powell, and Bon in their report for the Barbican development. See Elain Harwood, *Space, Hope and Brutalism* (New Haven, 2015), pp.69, 90, 634–5.

[150] Mark Swenarton, *Cook's Camden: The Making of Modern London* (2017).

[151] *Minutes of Evidence Taken Before the Royal Commission on the Geographical Distribution of the Industrial Population* 19 (1938), pp.596–617, p.617.

[152] 'A Plan for "Greater London"', *The Builder* (5 February 1943), pp.128–9; 'Shelters into Houses', *The Builder* (10 July 1942), pp.28–9.

MANNERS   311

Richmond, Blackheath, Greenwich, and so on, and the rest of the built-up areas would be 'an appropriate field for the operation of the radical instincts of the town-planner, that is to say, we need not scruple here to undertake a very large programme of demolition and of replacement'.[153] Edwards advocated the use of 'green wedges' instead of the green belt, which had by that time become orthodox.[154] These slices of 'open country or park' would separate distinct 'townships' associated with the central metropolitan area and give London's urban development a cruciform pattern. This system of clearance would preserve 'only certain historical villages and a number of new buildings which might be used for recreational purposes'. Wimbledon, Willesden, Lewisham, and Willesden would all be swept away. This was a long-term plan, stretched over fifty or a hundred years.

The post-war period also allowed Edwards to put into practice some of his ideas as consultant planner to Hastings Corporation—a period he later referred to as 'The Second Battle of Hastings'—and then in his native Merthyr Tydfil until 1950, later publishing *Merthyr, Rhondda and 'The Valleys'*.[155]

Heteredox Economics, Liberal Anglicanism, Public Health, and Eugenics

In early pamphlets of the HNTA, Edwards wrote:

We have everything which is needed for the building of the Hundred New Towns, except the requisite amount of money, little bits of paper, the tokens of exchange, are not present in sufficient quantities. Who is it that

---

[153] 'A Plan for "Greater London"', p.129.

[154] Paul Thomas Radford-Rowe Kirk, *New Towns for Old: An Account of the Aims of the Hundred New Towns Association* (Westminster, 1942), p.9. See also 'A Type Plan for New Towns', *Building* (July 1942), p.140.

[155] For Hastings see RIBA, EdA/1/1, Box 1, Folder 1, 'Some Reflections on Possible Post-War Developments in the Borough of Hastings submitted to the consideration of The Plans and Town Planning Committee of the Council of the County Borough of Hastings'. A book publication—never completed, along with a number of others including his autobiography, *Second Best Boy*—is listed in his *Who's Who* entry. See '(Arthur) Trystan Edwards', *Who's Who and Who Was Who* https://www-ukwhoswho-com.liverpool.idm.oclc.org/view/10.1093/ww/9780199540891.001.0001/ww-9780199540884-e-154155 [accessed 1 June 2020]. See also Arthur Trystan Edwards, *Merthyr, Rhondda and 'The Valleys'* (1958).

312 DESIGNS ON DEMOCRACY

makes the money? The answer to this question is that it is the money power that makes money.[156]

The Hundred New Towns campaign presented a financial scheme in which it was proposed that the Treasury would assume the right to use banknotes without corresponding gold reserve or any other security 'than that of the real wealth to be created by its use'.[157] An administrative authority would be created to build the new towns—new money created and not loaned, but used for paying contractors subject to competitive tender so that the state would have 'benefit of private initiative and competition'.[158] Having created new money, the state would 'receive' the buildings, which would be state-owned. Occupiers would pay rent—the householder, local authority, administrative officials, commercial companies, whoever 'chooses to take advantage of the State offer to finance the erection of its business premises'.[159]

The underlying assumption, as Edwards later wrote, was that, though the HNTA was uncommitted to one financial technique, a new economy was coming: 'the old financial orthodoxies are now passing away', it declared, and a new financial technique evolving 'which will enable the nation to take full advantage of the productive capacity of its citizens'.[160]

Recalling the launch of the ex-servicemen's group which championed the HNT campaign at the Royal Mint, his references to 'little bits of paper' was not a sign of financial illiteracy or naivety. Instead, Edwards was promoting ideas derived from a coherent financial scheme. And despite declamations that the campaign was not wedded to any particular financial technique, this belied a deep involvement with discourses of monetary reform, deriving in particular from the Social Credit movement.

Indeed, there were many prominent monetary reformers and adherents of the Social Credit movement who attached themselves to what became the HNTA. Mansfield Forbes, as we have seen, himself was a monetary reformer and probably introduced Edwards to these ideas and this milieu. As his obituary noted, Forbes's 'charity led to every vital interest in social affairs, legislation and reform, and of recent years he gave an immense amount of time to the furtherance of the Hundred New Towns and the Douglas Social

---

[156] Edwards, *A Hundred New Towns*, p.20.
[157] Ibid., p.20.   [158] Ibid., p.21.
[159] Ibid., p.23.
[160] Wellcome Library, Eugenics Society Archive, SAEUG/D/101, 'The Hundred New Towns Association: Formation, Progress and Future Policy', p.12.

MANNERS   313

Credit Schemes'.[161] Forbes had begun 'to study the economics of the creation of new money, believing that the shortage of liquidity caused by the contraction of credit during the years of depression must be counteracted by an increase in the money supply'.[162]

Social Credit grew out of the Guild Socialist movement which had had some prominence in late-nineteenth- and early twentieth-century architectural and building discourse, not least through AJ Penty, a former assistant to Raymond Unwin. Its progenitor CH Douglas had been much influenced by Alfred Orage, the proprietor of the Guild Socialist newspaper, *New Age*, who had close links to Penty.[163] There were strong philosophical affinities with the Ruskinian tradition in architectural thought, which constituted a compelling and forcible critique of political economy and which continued to influence generations in the opening decades of the twentieth century.[164] Edwards, who had a complex attitude towards Unwin and Ruskinian precepts, was not consciously locating himself in this intellectual tradition—if anything, he tried to position himself against it— but clearly his support for progressive politics, and the involvement of intellectuals and economists of socialist and progressive persuasions in the HNTA brought him into close contact with these ideas.

The Social Credit 'movement' comprised an economic theory predicated on social justice and ecological sustainability. It essentially argued that money had no intrinsic purpose. The 'use of gold...as a global monetary standard, replacing other forms of token money, blurred the distinction between the function of money as a medium of exchange and its secondary function as a store of wealth':[165] Douglas and *New Age* emphasized 'real capital', the potential to make the commodities required by the community, 'over' financial capital, the potential to make a financial return.[166]

Douglas's interpretation rested on the 'A + B Theorem' which problematized the prevalence of credit: 'money is constantly created and destroyed by the financial system for the specific purpose of making money in the future'.[167] Not all monetary reformers subscribed dogmatically to Social Credit, even if they were influenced by it. Edward Holloway, the

---

[161] 'Obituary: Manny', *Cambridge Review* (7 February 1936), p.277.
[162] Carey, *Forbes*, p.132.
[163] Frances Hutchinson and Brian Burkitt, *The Political Economy of Social Credit and Guild Socialism* (1997); David Thistlewood, 'AJ Penty (1875–1937) and the Legacy of 19th-Century English Domestic Architecture', *JSAH* 46.4 (1987), pp.327–41.
[164] Swenarton, *Artisans and Architects*, pp.163–90.
[165] Ibid., p.36.   [166] Ibid., p.42.   [167] Ibid., p.48.

314　DESIGNS ON DEMOCRACY

businessman and economist, having come into contact with Douglas and Social Credit, was dismayed 'that the movement supporting him was unprepared to associate with anybody who did not accept the Douglas analysis in its entirety'.[168]

Holloway, a great friend of Edwards, had in 1936 founded the Economic Reform Club (ERC), acting as its directing secretary for many years.[169] He had been profoundly affected by the unemployment crisis brought on by the Slump. Inspired by the Irish writer Eimar O'Duffy's book *Life and Money*, based on Social Credit ideas, Holloway was particularly exercised by the failure of the promise of a 'Land Fit for Heroes'.[170] Holloway's support for the HNTA shows how profoundly associated the campaign was with a considered heterodox economic critique. Such was its penetration that when Ramsay MacDonald challenged Lloyd George to develop a coherent programme for his Keynesian 'New Deal' for public scrutiny in early 1935 Edwards and Holloway were given an interview, and found Lloyd George 'desperately seeking every idea he could conjure up to make good his undertaking to provide a detailed plan for recovery'.[171]

The ERC, known briefly as the 'Petition Club', became increasingly important in garnering support for the HNTA. Established in 1936, its aim was to focus on fundamental and potentially workable theories of monetary reform which emphasized the centrality of community need and advantage in reformulating the economy. It also argued for land reform—recognizing 'the land as the primary source of all wealth' and insisting 'that its resources shall be utilised for the full benefit of the community'.[172] So ideologically close were Edwards and Holloway and their respective organizations that they shared a number of vice-presidents and public supporters: Vernon Bartlett, Lord Horder, David Lamb, and Lord Sempill were all involved, as were Lord Northbourne and Reginald Rowe, both particularly effective advocates for the HNTA.[173]

Walter James, the fourth Baron Northbourne, was a prominent agriculturalist and champion of the rural economy who presented the Hundred New Towns scheme to the Barlow Commission with Edwards. His presence was connected to the campaign's stated aim to 'save the countryside', not only through the clear separation of town and country

---

[168] Edward Holloway, *Modern Matters: A Modern Pilgrim's Economic Progress* (1986), p.11.
[169] Holloway, *Modern Matters*, ch. 3.　　[170] Ibid., p.11.　　[171] Ibid., pp.18–19.
[172] Edward Holloway, *The Economic Reform Club and Institute: What It Is—and What It Does* (October 1944), p.4.
[173] Ibid., pp.8–12.

MANNERS 315

which Edwards had espoused but also through stimulation of the rural economy. Reginald Rowe, an active supporter of the HNTA not least through the Housing Centre, was also involved in the ERC, assuming its presidency in 1939. During wartime debates about reconstruction Edwards was given a platform to promote the HNTA in a special collaboration between the ERC (by now the Economic Reform Club and Institute) and the journal *Calvacade* on their 'Towards the Future Series'. 'Democracy's Other War', as the volume was entitled, included a paper by Rowe himself on 'Land, Power and Money' in which he openly endorsed the HNTA.[174]

Theology lay at the core of Trystan Edward's world-view and infused his idea of manners and public service. He was a member of TocH, the soldiers club founded by the Reverend Tubby Clayton with a progressive emphasis on public service influenced by the Settlement Movement. The title of Edwards's first book, *The Things Which Are Seen*, had derived from a sermon he had heard at Hope Chapel, a Welsh Calvinistic Methodist chapel, in his hometown of Merthyr Tydfil.[175] Edwards's own denominational progression is obscure—he clearly retained links with Welsh nonconformity but was participant in the Anglican Communion. It was through his local rector Canon Pugh, for instance, that he gained his interview with David Lloyd George.[176]

Through the HNTA, Edwards forged foundational links with Liberal Anglicans—indeed, the HNTA's campaigns were fundamentally informed by Liberal Anglican ideals and critiques of political economy, themselves part of a wider progressive New Liberal politics and British Idealist philosophy with which Edwards had interacted first at university in Oxford and then at Liverpool.

Liberal Anglicans, especially leading figures like William Temple, were profoundly interested in the idea of 'community', a social category more capacious than 'Society'.[177] The theory and rhetoric of 'community', as Matthew Grimley has shown, was a response to the democratizing impulses

---

[174] *Democracy's Other War. By famous contributors on vital subjects* (Calvacade's Towards the Future Series) (1942).

[175] TG Davies, 'Arthur Trystan Edwards', *Year Book: Society of Architects in Wales* 4 (Macclesfield, 1982), pp.38–42.

[176] Presumably John Richards Pugh, later Archdeacon of Carmarthen. This connection to Lloyd George is mentioned in: University of Kent, Hewlett Johnson Papers, UKC-JOH-COR, 8315–8500 (1931–1966), letter from Edwards to Johnson (3 August 1935). In 1947, Edwards was married by Hewlett Johnson: University of Kent, Hewlett Johnson Papers, UKC-JOH-COR, 168–231, letter from Edwards to Johnson (2 November 1962).

[177] Matthew Grimley, *Citizenship, Community, and the Church of England: Liberal Anglican Theories of the State between the Wars* (Oxford, 2004), pp.2–3.

316   DESIGNS ON DEMOCRACY

catalysed by the Great War and its aftermath. The 'national moral community' Liberal Anglicans propagated would create a 'moral consensus, appeal to universal ideals of citizenship which were not exclusively Christian, even though they had a Christian inflection'.[178] Associational culture and volunteerism were core to this conception of community and citizenship. The Conference on Christian Politics, Economics, and Citizenship, held at Birmingham in 1924, had notably asserted the right for the Church to intervene in social questions of import.[179]

Housing and Town Planning were central concerns—indeed, the rhetoric of 'community' grew out of town-planning discourse and the Community Centre movement. The year 1933—the foundational year of the HNTA— was significant. Marking the centenary of the Oxford Movement—the first *Tract for the Times* was published in 1833—the Archbishops of Canterbury and York called on members of the Church of England to bolster support for public utility societies (building on earlier exemplars, such as that of Basil Jellicoe at St Pancras), and to promote slum clearance through a National Housing Corporation to coordinate large-scale house-building, as Moyne had recommended.[180]

It is therefore unsurprising that prominent Anglicans lent support to Edwards's scheme right from the start. David Lamb was one such figure, and before Hewlett Johnson's involvement from 1935 his predecessor as Dean of Canterbury, HRL 'Dick' Sheppard, had been a signatory to the campaign. Later, Albert Mansbridge, a proponent of Church reform, joined as a vice-president; Mansbridge was a founder of the Workers' Educational Association, of which William Temple was inaugural president.[181] Marshall Lang, brother of the Archbishop of Canterbury, Cosmo Lang, himself a prominent figure in the Church of Scotland, was also a vice-president of the HNTA from 1938.[182]

These links were strengthened during wartime. In 1942 Edwards contributed an essay on 'Town and Country Planning' to a volume, *Towards a Christian Order*, edited by the Bishop of Chelmsford, based on papers presented at the Malvern Conference of the previous year convened by William

---

[178] Ibid., p.12.   [179] Ibid., p.32.
[180] See 'The Church and the Slums', *The Times* (16 May 1933), p.15.
[181] Grimley, *Citizenship*, pp.5, 42.
[182] Lambeth Palace Library, MD7333.E3 [P]. The copy of *A Hundred New Towns for Britain* is annotated. Lambeth Palace's catalogue notes its provenance in Archbishop Lang's papers. A handwritten note contained in it shows the connection was Forbes.

Temple, then Archbishop of York.[183] Edwards cast the core principles of the HNTA programme as essentially Christian: 'a plan, which is the more Christian because it is practical, the Christian being of all men most inclined to realism and least attracted by mere head-in-air sentimentality'.[184]

Edwards's presence at Malvern was particularly significant because 'in the course of discussion it became apparent that the representative of the Industrial Christian Fellowship was profoundly dissatisfied with recent tendencies in housing policy'.[185] They were seeking a programme in which the built environment 'ministers to the spiritual and physical well-being of men, women and children'.[186] Indeed, the Industrial Christian Fellowship (ICF) had convened an Economic and Town Planning Conference in 1941 which considered Edwards's scheme favourably. The Reverend PTR Kirk, general director of the ICF, was unequivocal about prevailing housing policy, later writing that '"Homes For Heroes" became a phrase to stink in the nostrils of everyone who knew how little was done and how badly that was done which was done'.[187] 'The Church,' he continued, 'which should have been foremost in urging action, was mainly silent'.[188] The call for renewed social activism in the Church was focused on housing policy and a commitment to effective reconstruction.

In 1942 the ICF published a pamphlet by Kirk, 'New Towns for Old', adumbrating the HNTA scheme, praising it for placing 'the principal House of God in an enclosed space by itself, within reach of all who would come'.[189] In a subsequent joint pamphlet, Edwards made the links between his design philosophy and religious praxis explicit: 'architecture', he wrote, 'is an historic meeting group of the Christian and the aesthetic ideals' in that it could 'promote his Christian virtues of friendship and sociability':[190] 'Town and

---

[183] Arthur Trystan Edwards, 'Town and Country Planning' in *Towards a Christian Order: Essays Suggested by the Findings of the Malvern Conference* (1942), p.48.

[184] Ibid.

[185] Economic Reform Club and Institute, *'The World We Want': A Conference held in London on May 7th, 8th and 9th, 1943, under the joint auspices of the Industrial Christian Fellowship and the Economic Reform Club & Institute* (1943), p.9. Edwards presented a paper at the conference and this was his recollection.

[186] Ibid.

[187] Arthur Trystan Edwards, *A Hundred New Towns for Britain: A National Scheme of Building...With an Introductory Essay on the Place of Architecture in a Christian Community* (Westminster, 1942), p.1.

[188] Ibid.

[189] Paul Thomas Radford-Rowe Kirk, *New Towns for Old: An Account of the Aims of the Hundred New Towns Association* (Westminster, 1942), p.9.

[190] Edwards, *A Hundred New Towns for Britain...With an Introductory Essay on the Place of Architecture in a Christian Community*, p.3.

318 DESIGNS ON DEMOCRACY

Country Planning can be the Expression of Christian Sociology.[191] This Christian and Anglican inflection permeated heterodox economic thought—in 1943 the ECR organized a joint conference with the ICF chaired by Reginald Rowe, which included not only Trystan Edwards but also Albert Mansbridge.

One of the primary stated aims of the HNTA was to 'Make an A1 population.[192] What did this mean in practice? Certainly, Edwards and the HNTA engaged with public health issues. The support of Squire Sprigge, editor of *The Lancet* shows this, as does the engagement of Jane Walker, a physician and specialist in the open-air treatment of tuberculosis, who at the opening of 'Forbidden Houses' had spoken about nursery schools and child welfare.[193] Frederick Gowland Hopkins had been awarded the Nobel Prize in 1929 for his part in discovering 'accessory food factors', or vitamins.[194] These were typical of the profound connections between working-class housing and health reform stretching back to the nineteenth century, which reached a peak in the interwar decades. As Darling has argued, this was a 'preoccupation which, above any other, can be said to have under-pinned the reformist agenda in inter-war Britain', and had manifest-ations in the architecture of healthcare first at the Pioneer Health Centre in Peckham, opened by Lord Horder in 1935, and later at Tecton's Finsbury Health Centre.[195]

There were, however, further dimensions to Edwards's engagement with question of public health, physical fitness, and the problem of housing which evolved over the 1920s and 1930s. Edwards, in common with many social reformers, was certainly by the 1930s in profound sympathy with positive eugenics—and eugenics sat at the heart of question of public health and social reform for many, including housing. Concerns about national 'efficiency' often thinly veiled the eugenicist paradigm.

In *The Things Which Are Seen*, Edwards had posited the 'cultivation of human beauty' as the first in his new hierarchy of the visual arts.[196] This was a call 'to cease to tolerate ugliness, and especially preventable ugliness, in

---

[191] Ibid. [192] Edwards, *Hundred New Towns*, p.20.

[193] Sprigge was a vice-president. A review of the scheme was published in *The Lancet*: 'A Hundred New Towns for Britain', *The Lancet* (10 March 1934), pp.537–8. See also '"Forbidden Houses"', *The Times* (19 November 1936), p.4.

[194] 'Obituary: Sir F Gowland Hopkins', *The Times* (17 May 1947), p.7.

[195] Darling, *Re-forming Britain*, pp.51, 61.

[196] Arthur Trystan Edwards, *The Things Which Are Seen: A Philosophy of Beauty* (1946), 2nd edn., pp.23–35.

human beings', as Edwards's put it explicitly.[197] Though on the face of it eugenicist, in fact Edwards at this stage was drawing more on the language of health and fitness, disavowing an overly scientific approach: 'The science of hygiene needs to be related to an aesthetic ideal.'[198] 'It is especially necessary', he continued 'to resist the presumption of those who would breed men as if they were cattle.'[199] He advocated, at this stage, a more evolutionist argument—if conditions were apposite 'then the race will progress naturally and spontaneously, without the assistance of scientific busy-bodies who take it upon themselves to improve human beings although ignorant of humanity.'[200] As the historian of health reform, Ina Zweiniger-Bargielowska, has argued, techniques of what she has termed 'body management' fell broadly into two categories, 'biological rhetoric and hereditarian principles.'[201] The cultivation of human beauty drew heavily on the former, which instead of 'emphasis on hereditary differences between individuals or social groups' argued that 'a healthier, fitter and more beautiful body was within reach of anybody who observed a hygienic regimen.'[202] A 'social revolution' would take place

> ...if, in very truth, men were determined to remove those causes which obviously contribute to the uglification of their species. The abolition of poverty, as we now know it, healthy conditions of housing and employment; the spread of opportunities of athleticism, a wonderful development of the dance both for men and women—all these things would follow if only people could be induced to value the human body at its proper worth.[203]

In championing the cultivation of human beauty, Edwards was part of a much wider cult of health and fitness. These factors had a great impact on European and American Modernist architecture. Terraces, sun-roofs, and 'outdoor rooms' are emblematic of Modernism's fixation with 'light, air and openness', as Paul Overy has shown.[204] In Edwards's work, his fixation on sufficient sunlight in streets, his own deployment of terraces and easy access to open space, as well as his sustained interest in sanitation and hygiene all suggest Edwards was aware both of continental developments and of

---

[197] Ibid., pp.23–4.   [198] Ibid., p.34.   [199] Ibid., p.33.   [200] Ibid.

[201] Ina Zweiniger-Bargielowska, *Managing the Body: Beauty, Health, and Fitness in Britain 1880–1939* (Oxford, 2010), p.2.

[202] Ibid.   [203] Edwards, *The Things Which Are Seen*, 2nd edn., p.33.

[204] Paul Overy, *Light, Air and Openness: Modern Architecture between the Wars* (2007).

320 DESIGNS ON DEMOCRACY

innovative healthcare provision such as that offered at the Pioneer Centre. What perhaps distinguishes the HNTA's proposals is the extent to which they had normally been associated with apartment-blocks and open development, whereas Edwards showed how they could be integrated into low-rise, high-density development too.

By the mid- to late 1930s, however, although the HNTA continued to advocate housing design which promoted positive body management spurred on by the National Fitness Campaign and the Physical Training and Recreation Act (1937), more explicitly eugenicist rhetoric began to appear in Edwards's writings. Edwards's interest in eugenicist themes was longstanding and involved. He had a precocious interest in the philosophy of Nietzsche while at Oxford. Nietzsche's writings came to exert a significant influence on the British eugenics movement primarily through his image of the Übermensch,[205] which Edwards conceived as a breed of working-class superman.

Eugenicist themes permeated political discourse—in 1918 David Lloyd George spoke of the impossibility of running an 'A1 empire with a C3 population'.[206] These categories were used by the army 'to label the physical qualities of recruits',[207] and it was this language that Edwards deliberately echoed in the HNTA's slogan. A key organization in the propagation and lobbying for the eugenicist position was the Eugenics Society, of which Charles Paton Blacker became secretary in 1931.[208] The Society distinguished between positive eugenics (methods of promoting the fertility of 'superior, healthy and useful stocks'), and negative eugenics (predicated on restricting and diminishing the fertility of 'below average' persons through the prohibition of marriage, forced sterilization, and abortion).[209] Blacker and Julian Huxley were central figures in the pro-sterilization lobby. Blacker had been taken on to turn the Society 'into a more modern, scientific and socially acceptable organisation'.[210] Furthermore, once the move towards promoting sterilization through legislation was abandoned in 1934, the Society began to look for more positive campaigning strategies. This ambition was aided by the fact that in 1934 many commentators were talking openly of a population crisis and the looming possibility of human extinction. This reached the pages of *The Times* by 1936, leading the Eugenics

---

[205] Dan Stone, *Breeding Superman: Nietzsche, Race and Eugenics in Edwardian and Interwar Britain* (Liverpool, 2002).
[206] Richard Overy, *The Morbid Age: Britain between the Wars* (2009), p.98.
[207] Ibid.   [208] Ibid., pp.120–6.
[209] Ibid., p.108.   [210] Ibid., p.122.

MANNERS 321

Society to establish a Population Investigation Committee (PIC) at the London School of Economics for which Blacker also acted as secretary.[211] The PIC, incidentally, was chaired by Lord Horder, also president of the Eugenics Society and a vice-president of the HNTA. Also involved was Colin Clark. Another link to Trystan Edwards was the barrister Cecil Binney, who would later serve as best man for his wedding in 1947 (over which Hewlett Johnson officiated).[212] Binney had provided a statement on legal issues for the Eugenics Society's Committee for Legalising Eugenic Sterilisation and contributed a number of articles to the Society's journal, *Eugenics Review.*[213]

It was through these links, and with these intellectual interests established, therefore, that Edwards published an article entitled 'Birth-Control Barracks', in the *Fortnightly Review* of June 1938.[214] Here, he rehearsed current arguments relating to the wider depopulation panic, and underscored the need to remove the causes of sterility. One major cause of decline, he argued, was the paucity of homes designed for supporting and enhancing family life, and inadequate space standards for homes that were being built, particularly by the LCC in East London.[215] Replacing slums with self-contained cottages at comparable densities would stimulate population growth. It was this article that Edwards sent to CP Blacker, 'a new piece of research' as he described it, which need further development from housing experts and policy formation.[216] The PIC, from whom Edwards was seeking medical data, was itself planning a survey on the fertility of flat-dwellers compared to those who lived in cottages and houses.[217]

---

[211] Ibid., pp.131–2. See also CM Langford, *The Population Investigation Committee: A Concise History to Mark its Fiftieth Anniversary* (1988) for more information.

[212] Merthyr Tydfil Library, Trystan Edwards Biographical File, Press Clipping, 'Mr Trystan Edwards and Miss M Meredyth Smith Wed', *Merthyr Express* (22 March 1947).

[213] He later collaborated with Blacker on a further campaign for positive sterilization. See Wellcome Library, Carlos Paton Blacker Papers, PPCPB/B/22, 'Memoirs and Obituaries for Eugenics Review: Cecil Binney, Sir A Carr-Saunders, Lord Horder and Margaret Sanger' https://wellcomelibrary.org/item/b1822877x#?c=0&m=0&s=0&cv=32&z=-0.7875 per cent2C-0.1359 per cent2C3.5749 per cent2C1.6669 [accessed 2 June 2020].

[214] Arthur Trystan Edwards, 'Birth-Control Barracks', *Fortnightly Review* (June 1938), pp.706–13.

[215] Ibid., pp.709–10.

[216] Wellcome Library, Eugenics Society Archive, SAEUG/D/101, 'The Hundred New Towns Association: Formation, Progress and Future Policy', letter from Arthur Trystan Edwards to CP Blacker (3 August 1938).

[217] Ibid., letter from CP Blacker to Arthur Trystan Edwards (5 August 1938).

322   DESIGNS ON DEMOCRACY

Conclusion

Monetary reform, Liberal Anglicanism, eugenics, and public health—though these may all seem at first glance remote from the normal presentation of architectural culture in interwar Britain, and remoter still from 'manners' and public propriety, they were in fact inextricably linked.

Body management and eugenics were related to 'disciplinary techniques' for the body.[218] Self-discipline and the effects of a good physical environment would make for better citizens. Edwards and the HNTA can be read productively in terms of Foucauldian biopolitics, and this shows too an engagement with governmentality in the discourse of manners and the corralling of 'average men', 'ex-servicemen', and 'slum-dwellers'. Heterodox economics, particularly monetary reform, in its emphasis on community obligations over individualistic capitalism also related to mannerly development. The economic metaphor laissez-faire was frequently invoked to describe the urban condition bequeathed by the nineteenth century. Edwards was particularly attuned to this, beginning *Good and Bad Manners* with reflections on the relationship between architecture and commerce. Liberal Anglican rhetorics echoed this emphasis on community—indeed, they shared a serious and fundamental critique of contemporary political economy. In creating 'a moral consensus' among a national community, Liberal Anglicans appealed 'to universal ideals of citizenship and fellowship which were not exclusively Christian, even though they had a Christian provenance'.[219] Manners—gentlemanliness and neighbourliness—was precisely such an ideal.

Despite the rich and varied links he forged, Edwards's constant efforts and financial support over a decade amounted nonetheless to no new towns or urban development along the principles advocated by the HNTA being realized. The veteran editor of the *Architectural Review*, JM Richards, was unambiguous in his assessment of the HNTA, whose proposals were 'not regarded as realistic in the urban-planning and architectural professions and had no impact on official policies'.[220] Nevertheless, Lord Greenwood bemoaned that Trystan Edwards was 'appallingly under-recognized', and that there was 'no doubt that he greatly influenced the Barlow Committee,

---

[218] Zweiniger-Bargielowska, *Managing the Body*, p.7.

[219] Grimley, *Citizenship, Community, and the Church of England*, p.12.

[220] JM Richards, '(Arthur) Trystan Edwards', *Grove Art Online* (Oxford: Oxford University Press, 2003), https://www.oxfordartonline.com/groveart/view/10.1093/gao/9781884446054.001. 0001/oao-9781884446054-e-7000024973 [accessed 2 June 2020].

the Scott Committee and the Reith Committee', to which the HNTA provided interviews and statements in the late 1930s and early 1940s.[221] One obituarist described the first HNTA pamphlet as a 'prophetic document'.[222] Revisionist work in the history of early twentieth-century housing has emphasized the advisory rather than provisory role associational culture played in these debates, and a reassessment of the HNTA in that light suggests that in fact its reach and influence may have been much greater than hitherto assumed. Edwards's stammer and eccentricities limited his persuasive abilities, and it is in part for this reason that the value of his work was underestimated by the architectural profession at the time and since. It is important to remember, though, that Stanley Adshead and Edwin Lutyens were vice-presidents of the HNTA. Through Lionel Brett, Philip Powell, and Patrick Hodgkinson, Edwards's work and the work of the Association had a key place in mid-century discourses.

Edwards would boast that at least 'a dozen architecture writers and popular lecturers upon architecture' had adopted 'good manners' as 'their principal canon of architectural criticism'.[223] He went so far as to claim in one instance that 'the phrase may even be heard on the lips of Cabinet Ministers and of speakers engaged to give discourses by the British Broadcasting Corporation'.[224] These are, perhaps, overestimates but they do reflect the fact that 'manners' and the need for 'good manners' in particular chimed with an interwar sensibility. It is a word which captures many elusive but recurring ideas in interwar architectural discourse. In the previous chapter, we considered vigilance at length as a tool of public participation. Manners was a corollary of this, in some respects a more positively framed means of defending public taste and decorum.

The concept of 'manners' helps to explain the institution of the Royal Fine Art Commission (an idea descended from the early nineteenth-century 'Committee of Taste'), which advised on *inter alia* Giles Gilbert Scott's designs for the General Post Office's Telephone Kiosk. The K2 phone box, with its understated nods to the neo-Regency and its inoffensive ubiquity, encapsulated good manners. Scott's involvement in the design of Battersea Power Station was analogously to provide its elevations with good manners, through Expressionist brickwork and fluted concrete columns.

---

[221] 'Mr A Trystan Edwards', *The Times* (3 February 1973), p.16.

[222] 'A Trystan Edwards', *AR* (May 1973), p.240.

[223] Arthur Trystan Edwards, 'Some New Reflections upon Good and Bad Manners in Architecture—VI.' *Architectural Design and Construction* (October 1933), p.467.

[224] Edwards, *The Things Which Are Seen*, 2nd edn., p.314.

324   DESIGNS ON DEMOCRACY

Other architects' panel systems controlled elevations in this period. The famous 'Bath Clause' was derived from the Bath Corporation Act (1925) which established a panel to scrutinize elevations submitted to it.[225] Though not the first such clause or by-law devised by a local authority (the first was Clause 66 of the Ruislip-Northwood Town Planning Scheme, which provided 'for control of the artistic appearance of buildings'), it became a useful expression for the aspiration to promote professional standards under the aegis of public concern.[226] The joint panels of the Council for the Preservation of Rural England the Royal Institute of British Architects (RIBA) in the 1930s, known as the Longden Scheme, were typical of this. In his report on 'The Preservation of the Countryside' for the RIBA, Longden accepted that development was inevitable, but argued that too often it was being conducted by the wrong people in the wrong way.[227] Only public opinion would correct this, along with the institution of architects' panels which could provide expertise to the speculative builder at low cost to prevent offensive design. Control of elevations had become a cliché by 1924 when Edwards published *Good and Bad Manners*, even if it was inconsistent. It was remarked, when the Royal Fine Art Commission was established in the same year, that its institution 'will gradually tend to establish a higher standard of public taste. The mere fact of its creation shows that the public are willing to be guided further along the path of aesthetic perception upon which their feet are already, although perhaps falteringly, placed.'[228] Good manners constituted the unspoken criterion for this 'aesthetic perception' and for good principles of development.

What was particularly innovative about Edwards's invocation of manners, however, was the way in which he sought to open up the perception of good manners to the 'average man', to working-class as much as middle-class opinion. Although this could still be seen as a rather patrician conception of working-class needs and wants, it did demonstrate a real concern to recalibrate architects' relationship with the public. For Edwards this was not just discursive; it fundamentally informed his campaigning too and informed the connections he sought to make for the HNTA.

---

[225] See Robin Lambert, 'The Bath Corporation Act of 1925', *Transactions of the Ancient Monuments Society* 44 (2000), pp.51–62.

[226] RIBA, Town Planning, Housing and Slum Clearance Committee Minutes (1) (5 August 1921–4 January 1934), 19 December 1926, fo.99.

[227] RT Longden, 'Some Proposals in Reference to the Panel System as Applied to the Architectural Amenities of the Country' (October 1930), n.p.

[228] AJ Youngson, *Urban Development and the Royal Fine Art Commissions* (Edinburgh, 1990), p.30.

Furthermore, Edwards's flexible 'hierarchy' meant that buildings had to have good manners. There is a surprisingly close correspondence between some of Edwards's ideas about manners and public propriety and those of Richard Sennett half a century later in his study of urbanism and urban life, *The Fall of Public Man*. Building on Habermas's ideas of the public sphere, Sennett took aim at what he called 'The Tyranny of Intimacy', which led, in Sennett's formulation, to the fall of public man from the apogee of the eighteenth century in the major metropoles of the Western world (in particular, Paris and London) to the nadir of the industrial nineteenth century.[229] In the urban eighteenth century, Sennett argued, public life in the city flourished because playacting with strangers in the city was seen not as deceptive, but rather as necessarily impersonal: 'social encounters [were made] meaningful...through codes of belief'.[230] Man was understood as actor, and street was understood as stage. The *theatrum mundi* of the eighteenth-century social world meant that appearances or semblances were conducive to a thriving public life:

> Playacting in the form of manners, conventions, and ritual gestures is the very stuff out of which public relations are formed, and from which public relations derive their emotional meaning. The more social conditions erode the public forum, the more are people routinely inhibited from exercising the capacity to playact. The members of an intimate society become artists deprived of an art.[231]

It is tempting to understand the exchanges in Edwards's 'What the Building Said' in these terms. In setting down these highly dramatic scenes—with ghosts, violence, posturing, and shouting—Edwards conjured up the street as a kind of stage, the *theatrum mundi* in which buildings themselves become actors. What the performance perhaps shows, however, is that the new buildings of Regent Street are not able to be impersonal. Rather they kicked and ridiculed and dismissed the architecture of the Regency in a way that threatened the safety of the public realm of the street. Tellingly, the only precedent for this form of writing is from eighteenth-century Parisian architectural culture. From the 1730s a series of texts appeared 'in which architectural writers represented buildings as speaking a lot', in some instances appearing 'in the guise of characters speaking as though on a

---

[229] Richard Sennett, *The Fall of Public Man* (2003), p.64.   [230] Ibid.
[231] Ibid., pp.28–9.

326 DESIGNS ON DEMOCRACY

stage'.[232] For Richard Wittman, these texts were designed to translate the experience of architecture and their public meanings into the public sphere, a way of communicating, or actualizing in Wittman's words, public 'presence' 'for a dispersed atomized public'.[233] Likewise, Trystan Edwards's 'What the Building Said' series can be read as an attempt to permit 'far-flung isolated readers to relate to a remote building collectively with something like the directness and immediacy of phenomenal experience'.[234]

---

[232] Richard Wittman, 'Architecture, Space and Abstraction in the Eighteenth-Century French Public Sphere', *Representations*, no.102 (Spring 2008), p.2.
[233] Ibid.   [234] Ibid., p.3.

6
The Architectural Mind
Topographical Projections on the Public Realm

Introduction

'The Architectural Mind' was the title given by the editors of *The Times* to their publication of a letter written by Sir Giles Gilbert Scott in May 1930 in response to ongoing controversy over the proposal for a new river crossing at Charing Cross.[1] Scott's concern was to emphasize that architects' training provided them with skills to 'achieve a proficiency in solving complex problems possessed by no other profession'.[2] This was a claim of intellectual breadth as well as technical skill. The prospect of a new bridge at Charing Cross related to three overarching developmental challenges in central London much discussed from the 1910s to the 1940s: firstly, traffic and cross-river communication, incorporating, as well as Charing Cross, proposed new bridge crossings at Waterloo and St Paul's; secondly, the development of the riverside, particularly the area now known as the South Bank; and thirdly, the wider development of the so-called 'Surrey side' of London to the south of the river. These questions were practical in relation to the functionality of the city but also symbolic in terms of understandings of the historic urban environment and of the ideological procedures of civic design. This topography became a site of projection for concepts of both the 'architectural mind' and an architecturally minded public. Whilst there was clearly no singular architectural mind, there was a strong concern to shape an architectural mentality which would speak to wider socio-political concerns—an architecturally literate public enabled thus to be more critically engaged citizens within a mass democracy. The core themes of the book are pulled together in this concluding chapter, which interrogates what was at stake in debates about the interrelationship between professional claims,

---

[1] 'The Architectural Mind', *The Times* (13 May 1930), p.17. [2] Ibid.

Designs on Democracy: Architecture and the Public in Interwar London. Neal Shasore, Oxford University Press.
© Neal Shasore 2022. DOI: 10.1093/oso/9780192849724.003.0007

328   DESIGNS ON DEMOCRACY

design imperatives, and appeals to the public. What was the significance of the 'mind'? What were its designs on democracy?

In 1936 John Summerson was awarded the Royal Institute of British Architects (RIBA) Silver Medal for an essay entitled the 'Tyranny of Intellect: A Study of the Mind of Sir Christopher Wren', subsequently published in the *Journal of the Royal Institute of British Architects* in February 1937.[3] Summerson argued that the embeddedness of Wren's architecture in broader intellectual and social debate in natural philosophy had limited his purely architectural imagination. An interpretation which drew selectively on elements of both seventeenth-century and early twentieth-century critical polemic, in particular from literary criticism, it embodied Summerson's view of what was wrong with approaches to architecture in his own day. Perversely, on the one hand, Summerson's project of critically embedding a wider socio-cultural and philosophical context helped to understand the architect better, while on the other, such an embeddedness was somehow felt to limit the architecture; an intense formalism—pursuit of 'pure architectural values'—was posited as the only redemptive course.[4] Consequently, in the end Summerson's critique was essentially formalist. Summerson derived this from what Eliot had called the dissociation of sensibility in the mid-seventeenth century.[5]

Summerson had worked briefly in Giles Gilbert Scott's office in the late 1920s and had been 'disappointed', he later recalled, 'that the creator of so passionate a piece of architecture as Liverpool Cathedral could be so unpassioned in his person'.[6] Scott's 'main interest seemed to be golf'.[7] Scott perhaps seemed typical of the overly intellectual, 'anti-poetical', even fastidious, approach among contemporary architects which Summerson disliked. The alienation may, however, have been more a matter of personality and presentation. Moreover, Scott was known for ceding little control to his staff in the design process: 'Sir Giles designed everything. It was our business to make it work, and nothing ever left the office for the job unless it had been thoroughly detailed to half-inch and full-size. Once we had the small-scale

---

[3] John Summerson, 'The Tyranny of Intellect: A Study of the Mind of Sir Christopher Wren in Relation to the Thought of His Time', *JRIBA* (20 February 1937), pp.373–90; republished as 'The Mind of Wren' in John Summerson, *Heavenly Mansions and Other Essays on Architecture* (1949), pp.51–86.

[4] Anthony Geraghty, 'The "Dissociation of Sensibility" and the "Tyranny of Intellect": TS Eliot, John Summerson and Christopher Wren', in Frank Salmon (ed.), *The Persistence of the Classical: Essays on Architecture Presented to David Watkin* (2008), p.37.

[5] Ibid., pp.26–33.

[6] John Summerson, unpublished autobiography, private collection, p.23.   [7] Ibid.

THE ARCHITECTURAL MIND   329

sketches we knew that the design was safely in Sir Giles' head.'[8] In Scott's letter to *The Times* he dismissed the idea that architects were 'dreaming artists only, with no value in practical matters of planning'[9]—this binary opposition was in itself an oversimplification of the complex interconnectedness of professional practice and design. As a designer, he demonstrated as much engagement with representationalism and romanticism as he did with pragmatism and practicality.

An architecturally minded public was often exercised by development questions in the 1920s and 1930s. The socio-political context of the interwar period made this a distinctively self-conscious process, as the articulation of professional values was projected in terms of new conceptions of the public: public relations and public opinion, public institutions, public propriety and proprietorship, and indeed the physical public realm. Certainly, the idea that architecture and planning represented a new sort of mental exercise was a recurring motif in contemporary commentary and one which centred on cross-river traffic, the riverside, and Surrey-side development. Responding to an exhibition held by the London Society in 1929 on new schemes for Charing Cross, Clough Williams-Ellis mused on the 'Riddle of Charing Cross': 'a bridge is roadway, a building, and a slice of town-planning all in one, which is why those who care about such things feel so fiercely about these particular structures, and are moved to defend or attack them or proposals concerning them in speeches and letters to the Press that are refreshingly vigorous and outspoken'.[10] He saw an analogy with

> …what the civilized citizens of Renaissance Italy used to do—that is, taking an intelligent and eager interest in our city. Perhaps this great bridge controversy may mark the end of an age of blind indifference and the dawn of a new era of magnanimity and civic pride! Such pride, however, is neither easy nor justified unless supported by noble works of our own time, and though there are ample practical and economic reasons for constructing this bridge there are psychological reasons just as good for its being done imaginatively, graciously—even magnificently.[11]

[8] Leslie K Watson, 'Obituary: Sir Giles Gilbert Scott', *AAJ* (May 1960), p.230. Summerson corroborates this view: 'Scott was too fastidious to allow his staff any designing scope.' Summerson worked on drawings for the William Booth Memorial College, Denmark Hill and All Hallows, Gospel Oak. Summerson, unpublished autobiography, p.23.

[9] 'The Architectural Mind', p.17.

[10] Clough Williams-Ellis, 'The Riddle of Charing Cross Bridge', *The Listener* (18 December 1929), p.813.

[11] Ibid., p.814.

330   DESIGNS ON DEMOCRACY

Reflecting in 1933 on the imminent demolition of the Adam brothers' Adelphi terraces, Herbert Baker argued that 'It would be wise…that the façade of the new Adelphi Terrace should be designed on a unified scheme with the whole front, including Somerset House, from the Waterloo Bridge head even to a Charing-Cross bridge-head.'[12] Principles of grand design needed to be reinvigorated in a modern political culture: 'How we are under democratic institutions to find active, potent and encouraging patronage such as a James gave for the drama, or a Medici for art? Can the Fine Art or other Commissions, constituted as they must be, give our designs more than chilling criticism?'[13] The Liberal politician and London County Council (LCC) stalwart, Percy Harris, thought more optimistically in 1934 of the significance of broad public engagement:

> A few years ago you could not get even a flicker of interest in London problems. Now London Planning is providing a new game for its intelligent citizens. Everyone has his own little pet scheme, and people move streets and construct bridges as a substitute for working out crossword puzzles or selecting players for the Test Match.[14]

This aspiration for public debate—for controversy marking the end of blind indifference, in Williams-Ellis's terms—was keenly promoted and defended. The siting of the LCC's new County Hall, built between 1912 and 1922, on the river front adjacent to Westminster Bridge, catalysed and canalized public discussion of this kind towards the development of the south side of the river, the river front itself, and cross-river communication.

The architectural mind was an imaginative one that produced topographical projects which mapped onto a wider visual and material culture. The text on the cover of the first 'A–Z' *Street Atlas and Guide to London and Suburbs* in 1936, for instance, was framed by a line-drawing of Tower Bridge with its central section raised—the same iconic emblem of the openness of the city imaged in the centrality (and recognizability) of the Thames and one of its most famous bridges—as was to be devised by the Anglo-Italian 'Two Cities' film company founded in 1937. Both projects represented new perspectives on the city, celebrating and glamourizing it at the same time as domesticating it in the public imagination. In his 1925 book, *The London Perambulator*, James Bone, the London editor of the

---

[12] Herbert Baker, 'The Thames Front', *The Times* (28 July 1933), p.15.   [13] Ibid.
[14] 'The Planning of London', *The Times* (18 July 1934), p.10.

THE ARCHITECTURAL MIND 331

Manchester Guardian, had already emphasized the significance for the twentieth-century Londoner of elaborations of 'The Road View and the Air View'.[15] Bone's book, illustrated by his brother, the draughtsman and etcher Sir Muirhead Bone, was a paean to London drawn from a long association with the city and a deep sensitivity to the built environment, to different ways of representing it, and to its generative cultural resonances. To Bone the car and the aeroplane compressed space in ways which seemed—paradoxically—to renew the city's intelligibility. As well as having means of quicker entrance and egress from the city along new arterial roads, the public were again 'learning the districts like the old stage-coachman'.[16] The 'road view' created 'carscapes',[17] as well as attending to the ongoing perspectives of the urban 'perambulator'. The 'air view', publicized through the growth of aerial photography and film, encompassed the panoptic perspective of the planner, as well as the novelty of seeing the whole pattern of the city in miniature. Aerial views had 'significant effects on the representation of London's built environment'[18] and were 'absorbed into two domains that were deeply concerned with the image of the modern metropolis—tourism and urbanism'.[19] The aerial perspective clarified the transitions between city, suburb, and country. Whilst this could be pathologized by preservationist opponents of ribbon development, it was not a unitary perspective. Kitty Hauser's distinction between the 'archaeological imagination' and the 'preservationist sensibility' gestures towards a complex relationship to modernity in the interwar period: just as aerial photography exposed traces of deep time in the ancient field-patterns which were only revealed in certain lights from above, it also revealed patterns of urban connection which were impossibly cluttered at ground level, and acted as a reminder of historical perspective.[20] Bone's first sight of London had been from a plane during the war; he had been struck in particular by the bright and shining river, snaking across his view—'the traitorous Thames which has signalled London to the enemy by day and night'.[21] Reflecting on the river in a time of peace, he underlined its continued centrality, as image and artery. The Thames

---

[15] James Bone, *The London Perambulator* (1931), pp.197–202.   [16] Ibid., p.198.

[17] Kathryn Morrison and John Minnis, *Carscapes: The Motor Car, Architecture and Landscape in England* (New Haven, 2012).

[18] Davide Deriu, 'Capital Views: Interwar London in the Photographs of Aerofilms Ltd', *London Journal* 35.3 (November 2010), pp.255–76.

[19] Ibid., p.255.

[20] Kitty Hauser, *Shadow Sites: Photography, Archaeology, and the British Landscape, 1927–1955* (Oxford, 2007), pp.1–29.

[21] Bone, *London Perambulator*, pp.200–1.

332   DESIGNS ON DEMOCRACY

was older than England, as was the Portland stone of which so much of London—old and new—was built. Fossil shells emblematizing a sea-borne empire long before it existed could be seen in the new Bush Building as in the south parapet of St Paul's—in the contemporary imagination as well as that of Wren's.[22] The city—a palimpsest of its long history—was open to new challenges of representation and urban propriety, and to new forms of public engagement, which were themselves inflected by an awareness of the dynamics of historical process. The river and the riverside lay at the heart of this process. Discussion of three projects focused on the Thames will illuminate conversations between architects and the public, and the creative interrelationship between the 'architectural mind' and architecturally minded 'intelligent citizens'.

Waterloo Bridge—Relics, Romance, and Representationalism

In October 1923, the editor of the *Architects' Journal*, GJ Howling, crossed John Rennie's Waterloo Bridge and 'noticed something unusual about the bridge parapet' (Fig. 6.1): 'No one of any sensitiveness', he wrote in his paper,

> ...can cross Waterloo Bridge on foot nowadays without feeling something of that sinking sensation associated in youthful memory with the downward rush of the switchback railway car. The pavement and roadway are distinctly, even alarmingly, undulating throughout the length of the bridge—the rises corresponding with the piers and the falls with the centres of the arches. The parapets add to the sense of insecurity by not only going up and down, but by leaning over—now inwards, now outwards.[23]

He published an accompanying photograph and because of his intervention—so he claimed—'people suddenly realised that there was something wrong with Waterloo Bridge'.[24] The Lambeth-side piers of the bridge were subsiding, and at the time part of the cause was thought to be increased motor vehicle traffic (Fig. 6.2). In any case, the bridge was too narrow for modern

---

[22] Ibid., pp.37–56. The book was dedicated 'To the Isle of Portland: The Matrix of London's Grandeur'.

[23] Astragal, 'Notes and Topics', *AJ* (27 August 1942), p.132. Astragal was quoting Christian Barman who had described the incident on the radio the previous week.

[24] Ibid.

Fig. 6.1 Waterloo Bridge: sightseers inspecting cracks in the parapet, photographer unknown (1924), 236070, image © London Metropolitan Archives (City of London)

usage.[25] A temporary iron bridge was constructed alongside Rennie's and opened to traffic in August 1925. The subsequent decade saw near-constant debate about what to do with the ailing fabric—whether to preserve it as it was, rebuild it with some minor modification, or replace it entirely. In the end the decision fell to, or at least was claimed by, Herbert Morrison, the former Labour Transport Minister, who in 1934 had become the leader of the LCC as a result of Labour's unexpected local election victory.[26] After what he described as the dithering of the Municipal Reform Party (the name for the Conservative-allied group in the Council) for nearly ten years—'The Tory Council had consistently wobbled in its policy about the bridge. The bridge had wobbled too'—Morrison sought decisive action to demonstrate Labour's commitment to modernization and public amenity.[27]

---

[25] *London County Council: Waterloo Bridge. Reports by the Chief Engineer to the Improvements Committee and letters received from the Society for the Protection of Ancient Buildings and other bodies and persons on the subject of the reconstruction of the bridge* (July 1924).
[26] Herbert Morrison, *Herbert Morrison: An Autobiography* (1960), p.144.
[27] Ibid., p.149.

THE WATERLOO BRIDGE CONTROVERSY: CAUSES OF THE SUBSIDENCE.

DRAWN SPECIALLY FOR "THE ILLUSTRATED LONDON NEWS" BY G. H. DAVIS. (COPYRIGHTED.)

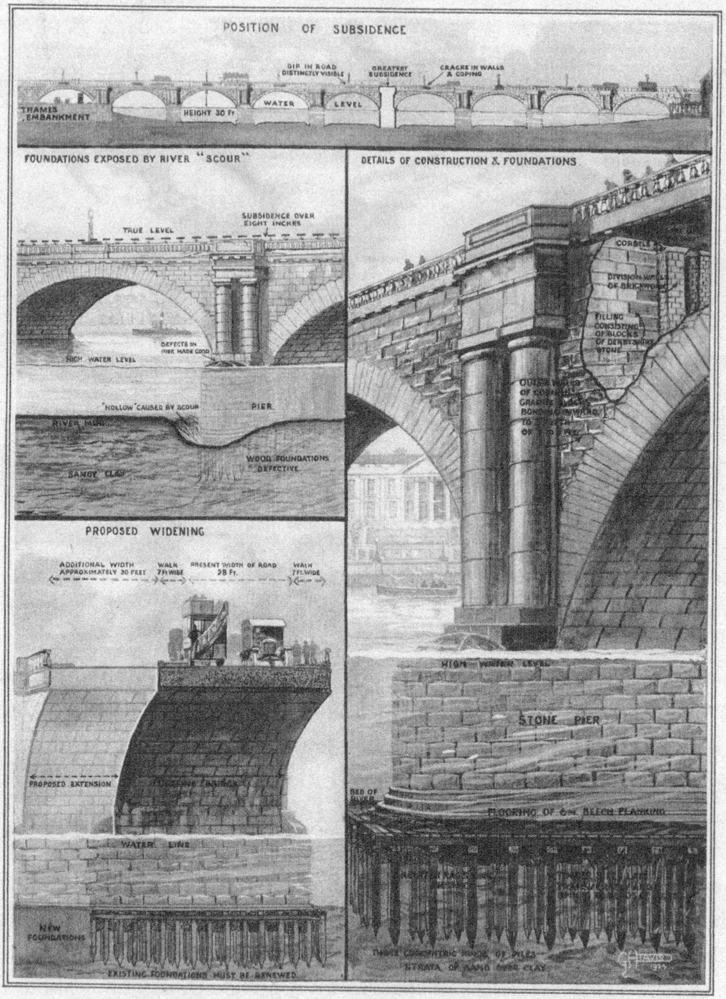

THE FATE OF "THE FINEST BRIDGE EVER BUILT" NOW IN THE BALANCE: DIAGRAMS SHOWING DETAILS OF THE STRUCTURE OF WATERLOO BRIDGE, WHICH HAS DEVELOPED AN OMINOUS SUBSIDENCE, AND OF THE PROPOSED WIDENING.

The scheme for the reconstruction and widening of Waterloo Bridge (owing to the recent subsidence), at a cost of about £1,000,000, now before the London County Council, has caused acute controversy, in which not only architects and engineers have participated, but men of eminence in art and literature, including Sir Squire Bancroft, Mr. Arnold Bennett, Mr. Frank Brangwyn, Sir Martin Conway, Sir Sidney Lee, and Mr. Bernard Shaw. The bridge was designed by John Rennie, and was opened on the second anniversary of the Battle of Waterloo, June 18, 1817, and has been described by Sir Reginald Blomfield, the well-known architect, as, "from the æsthetic point of view, the finest bridge ever built." The Improvements Committee of the L.C.C. said in a statement accompanying their report to the Council: "The bed of the river in and towards the centre is composed of gravel, but underlying the gravel is the London clay. . . . The thickness of the gravel bed is relatively small. Under the masonry of the third and fourth piers from the Lambeth side the gravel is only about 9 ft. to 10 ft.; consequently, piles of the length shown on Rennie's drawings would pass right through the gravel and be standing in the London clay. . . . In 1882-84 the late Metropolitan Board of Works expended about £62,000 in laying concrete slabs around the timber platforms with the object of protecting them from erosion or scour."

Fig. 6.2 'The Waterloo Bridge Subsidence: Causes of the Controversy', *ILN* (12 April 1924), p.11, © Illustrated London News Ltd/Mary Evans

THE ARCHITECTURAL MIND   335

In June 1934, therefore, in an act of defiance against the House of Commons, which had voted to preserve the old bridge, the now Labour-dominated LCC voted to demolish it and build a new one, paying the cost out of the rates. The following day, photographs of Morrison, George Strauss (then chairman of the LCC Highways Committee), and Reginald Pott (vice-chairman of the Highways Committee) appeared in the press showing Morrison prising off one of the bridge's masonry blocks, initiating its destruction. It was, as Morrison would later recall, an 'unofficial ceremony'—'unauthorised and irregular', but an effective piece of public relations.[28] At the end of the month, the *Illustrated London News* ran a story charting the progress of demolition (Fig. 6.3).[29] Three images were arranged vertically, much like frames on a short strip of film, with the first showing Morrison defiantly posed, cigarette in mouth, using a hammer and chisel to remove the first block off the bridge. The symbolism of the socialist leader posed with an angled hammer—albeit *sans* sickle—must have been particularly chilling for more conservative-minded preservationists, and Robert Byron, surveying the 'mountain of debris' of the remains of the bridge in 1937, would use a similar vignette of Morrison hoisting the loosened masonry before a gathered crowd in *How We Celebrate the Coronation*.[30]

The dismantling of Waterloo Bridge was described as an event itself, though one 'with no spectacle or thrill'.[31] Rather it was 'One of the most intricate engineering feats of the century'.[32] Quick demolition by explosives was not possible for practical and safety reasons—the bridge was neighboured by its temporary replacement, sited in a densely built-up riverside, and over-arched the Victoria Embankment, an essential west–east traffic artery.[33] It was instead unbuilt (Figs. 6.4–6.8). First the balustrades were taken off, shown in the second and third images of the *ILS* article, followed by the road and footways, and then the 'next thing was to break down the masonry and brickwork'.[34] This was a simple exercise—the removal, merely, of the

[28] Ibid., p.151.   [29] 'The End of Waterloo Bridge', *ILN* (30 June 1934), p.1047.

[30] The image bears the caption: 'Mr. Herbert Morrison performs a ceremony: lifting the first stone to inaugurate the work of destroying Waterloo Bridge.' In Byron, *How We Celebrate the Coronation*, p.29.

[31] LSA, Scrapbook 28, 'Dismantling Waterloo Bridge', newspaper-clipping (15 August 1932), fo.7.

[32] Ibid.

[33] Christine Wall, 'William Arrol and Peter Lind: Demolition, Construction and Workmanship on London's Waterloo Bridge (1934–46)', in *Building Knowledge, Constructing Histories* (Brussels: 6th International Congress on Construction History, 2018), pp.1347–54.

[34] LSA, Scrapbook 28, clipping of Alfred Best, 'The Un-Building of Waterloo Bridge', *The Listener* (2 September 1936), p.413, fo.9.

Fig. 6.3 'The End of Waterloo Bridge', *ILN* (30 June 1934), p.1047, © Illustrated London News Ltd/Mary Evans

Fig. 6.4 A view of men working on the demolition of the old Waterloo Bridge with buildings on the north side of the river in the background, photograph by Charles William Prickett (1936), CXP01/01/102, Source: Historic England Archive

'top hamper' as the *Telegraph* described it.[35] The more complex operation was the dismantling of the arch structures, which happened 'simultaneously and uniformly at each arch'.[36] Piers were bridged with temporary steel trusses fixed with suspension bars drilled through each arch. These protruding bars were used to hold steel centring in place. These steel centrings—akin to supporting formwork—were floated into position before being secured, effectively 'suspended from the overhead steel gantries'.[37] This allowed the arches to be safely 'nibbled' away, stone by stone, 'until there only remained a strip of each arch about twelve feet wide'.[38] The stones of Rennie's old arches were transported to Harmondsworth by barges.[39] All that

---

[35] 'Waterloo Bridge Souvenirs', *Daily Telegraph* (4 July 1934), p.11.   [36] Ibid.
[37] LSA, Scrapbook 28, Alfred Best, 'The Un-Building of Waterloo Bridge', *The Listener* (2 September 1936), p.416, f.9.
[38] Ibid.
[39] The reason for the decision to relocate the stones to Harmondsworth is unclear. Diane K Bolton, HPF King, G Wyld, and DC Yaxley, 'Harmondsworth: Economic and Social History' in TFT Baker, JS Cockburn, and RB Pugh (eds.), *A History of the County of Middlesex: Volume 4*,

Fig. 6.5 A view across the River Thames showing the demolition of the old Waterloo Bridge, photograph by Charles William Prickett (1936), CXP01/01/097, Source: Historic England Archive

remained in 1935 were what the *Evening News* named 'The Last Seven Sentinels', the last of the granite piers, standing in the water 'stripped and barren of their purpose'.[40] They were demolished within steel sheet-pile cofferdams, and then themselves loaded onto barges using derrick cranes. Thus John Rennie's Waterloo Bridge—'The Bridge of Memories'[41]—much eulogized and lamented, was removed stone by stone from London's cityscape.

Parts of the bridge, particularly lamp standards, balusters, and granite slabs, took on the status of architectural relics—indeed *The Times* described

Harmondsworth, Hayes, Norwood With Southall, Hillingdon With Uxbridge, Ickenham, Northolt, Perivale, Ruislip, Edgware, Harrow With Pinner (Victoria County History) (London: Victoria County History, 1971), pp.10–15, http://www.british-history.ac.uk/vch/middx/vol4/pp10-15, [accessed 16 June 2015]; LMA, ACC/3499/EH/02/01/367, John Rennie Memorial, Waterloo Bridge, fo.14.

[40] LSA, Scrapbook 28, 'The Last Seven Sentinels. Waterloo Bridge Nearing End. All that Will Greet 1936' (26 July 1935), fo.150.

[41] 'The Bridge of Memories Waterloo Stones Go Overseas', *Daily Telegraph* (21 August 1934), p.12.

THE ARCHITECTURAL MIND 339

Fig. 6.6 A view of the old Waterloo Bridge during its demolition with people working on a boat beneath the bridge, Charles William Prickett (1936), CXP01/01/100, Source: Historic England Archive

them so in August 1935.[42] Some went to institutions with vested interests in the bridge and its preservation. The RIBA, leaders of the preservation lobby defending the bridge, was gifted a baluster by one of its fellows, Ewart Gladstone Culpin, a senior Labour figure in the LCC and chairman of the Greater London Regional Planning Committee. The old bridge is pointedly commemorated on the bronze doors of its new building at Portland Place, despite the initiation of its demolition in the year it was opened. The Institute of Civil Engineers took a panel of twelve balusters.[43]

The LCC also enabled the public to buy mementoes of the old bridge—Strauss arranged for contractors to sell granite balusters at 20s per baluster.[44] At Seeley & Paget's Eltham Palace for Samuel and Virginia Courtauld, a

---

[42] 'Relics of Waterloo Bridge', *The Times* (17 August 1935), p.10.
[43] LMA, LCC Council Minutes (26 March 1935) reproduced a Report of the LCC Highways Committee (14 March 1935), 'Waterloo Bridge—Souvenirs'.
[44] 'Waterloo Bridge Mementos', *Daily Telegraph* (27 June 1934), p.10. A limit was set on the number any individual could buy.

Fig. 6.7 A view across the River Thames showing the demolition of the old Waterloo Bridge, with the shot tower at the Lambeth Lead Works on the right of the background, photograph by Charles William Prickett (1936), CXP01/01/099, Source: Historic England Archive

baluster from the bridge was incorporated into the garden.[45] Applications, however, exceeded the number of balusters available and by July 1934 £742 worth of stone from the old bridge had been sold by the LCC.[46] The unofficial price of the stone steadily increased—some pieces, the *Telegraph* reported in August 1934, were fetching as much as £10, blackened granite balusters being peddled unofficially in salvage yards. An employee of Sam Nicholl of Kentish Town remarked that it was 'all a matter of supply and demand'.[47] The Royal Hospital at Chelsea took six sandstone slabs.[48] The LCC also offered the London Museum some stonework for preservation, and the trustees took on two balusters, coping, and a portion of the plinth in March

[45] Gilbert Ledward, 'Eltham Palace', *The Times* (4 August 1936), p.15. Ledward also incorporated columns from the old Bank of England.
[46] 'Waterloo Bridge Souvenirs', *Daily Telegraph* (4 July 1934), p.11.
[47] 'The Bridge of Memories', *Daily Telegraph* (21 August 1934), p.12.
[48] LMA, LCC Council Minutes (26 March 1935) reproduced a Report of the LCC Highways Committee (14 March 1935), 'Waterloo Bridge—Souvenirs'.

THE ARCHITECTURAL MIND   341

Fig. 6.8 Waterloo Bridge: demolition work in progress, photographer unknown (1935), 236187, image © London Metropolitan Archives (City of London)

1935.[49] A memorial designed by JA Paterson of the Office of Works—a baluster converted into a sundial surrounded by seating—was set up at Rennie's birthplace, Phantassie, East Linton, and included a bronze portrait medallion by the sculptor Alexander Carrick.[50]

[49] Ibid.   [50] 'Old Waterloo Bridge', *The Times* (9 June 1936), p.16.

342 DESIGNS ON DEMOCRACY

Orders came from the United States, South Africa, and New Zealand; 'in many a garden at home and in Dominions fragments of it will be treasured for years to come—little bridges of sentiment linking the Empire just as the big old bridge used to link the banks of the Thames.'[51] A 2.5-tonne block of granite from the Surrey side of the bridge was shipped to New Zealand, having been offered by the LCC to the prime minister of New Zealand, GW Forbes, on a trip to London in 1935.[52] It was intended for the new Parliament Buildings in Wellington (presumably the second half of Parliament House, which was never built). The Commonwealth of Australia also acquired several blocks for its new Parliament buildings in Canberra, and four of these were used on the Commonwealth Avenue Bridge.[53] The government of Western Australia took two slabs for a new bridge over the River Swan in Perth.[54] Several requests came from colonial municipalities in Southern Rhodesia, including Bulawayo, Salisbury, Umtalia, Gwelo, and Gatooma, for slabs of granite and lamp standards.[55] Requests for balusters came from Limbe Town Council, Nyasaland.[56]

Even the timber piling was held to have particular value, having been discovered in surprisingly good condition. Beech, elm, and scotch pine had all been used, both in cylindrical boles of around 19 feet, as well as in crooked stems of 16 feet.[57] *The Times* itself incorporated some of the wood into the veneer of the panelled Composition Room at its new premises on St Andrew's Hill, London.[58] Some of the furniture in a flat on the SS *Orcades*, a passenger steam ship to Australia, was made out of elm used in the old bridge's foundations.[59] Weathered elm was also used for the entrance to the bridge-deck of the Union-Castle motor liner, the *Durbar Castle*, on its maiden voyage to south and east Africa in 1938.[60] Giles Gilbert Scott, around 1940, planned to use bits of wood from the old bridge to form the stem of a processional cross to give to Ampleforth Abbey.[61]

---

[51] 'The Bridge of Memories', *Daily Telegraph* (21 August 1934), p.12.
[52] 'Waterloo Bridge Relic Shipped', *Daily Telegraph* (23 August 1935), p.13.
[53] 'Relics of Waterloo Bridge', *The Times* (17 August 1935), p.10.
[54] Ibid. See also 'From Thames to Swan', *Daily Telegraph* (18 March 1935), p.12.
[55] Ibid. The Publicity Association of Umtala had requested relics to place in the Turner Memorial Library: 'The specific purposes for which the relics are required are not mentioned in all the letters.'
[56] Ibid.
[57] 'Waterloo Bridge Built on Wood', *Daily Telegraph* (23 March 1936), p.7. See also 'Timber Foundations of Waterloo Bridge', *The Times* (23 March 1936), p.9.
[58] 'Design of the New Building', *The Times* (2 December 1937), p.31.
[59] 'British Empire Woods', *The Times* (24 November 1937), p.19.
[60] 'New Liner's Maiden Voyage', *Daily Telegraph* (19 December 1938), p.10.
[61] See RIBA, Scott Papers, ScGG/91/2.

THE ARCHITECTURAL MIND   343

The scattering and scavenging of relics, the claims on a part of the body of the imperial metropolis, are significant. The incorporation of bits of Rennie's bridge into the fabric of parliament buildings made material an emotive connection. The claim by colonial *municipalities* as well as 'national' Dominion administrations demonstrates the important transnational interlinking of towns and cities across the Empire by ruling elites.

The process of demolition was charted by contemporary artists; the topographical painter Charles Cundall captured the scene in two paintings of 1935. There were more romantic and evocative descriptions: Muirhead Bone produced engravings of the demolition, for instance, showing a cross-section of one of the bridge piers and material being hoisted down to waiting boats, the gantry looming threateningly overhead. Not just the fact of the old bridge's condemnation, but the slow and intricate process of demolition itself and the distribution of architectural relics, drew on a romantic sensibility in visual and architectural culture of the time. Giles Gilbert Scott would channel this in the bridge he designed to replace Rennie's.

The story of Waterloo Bridge thus pulls together many of the themes of this book. Romance, heritage, and history as well as a particular approach to modernization all played their part both in the preservation battle for the old bridge and indeed in the conception of a new one. As John Rennie's original bridge transmuted from river-crossing to relic—the 'King Charles's head of municipal politics,' as the *Telegraph* once wryly described it[62]—it also accrued a whole set of powerful apocrypha about its design and indeed status within the city and among the other famous river crossings in London.

This was evident in the two-act play, *Waterloo Bridge*, by the American playwright and screenwriter, Robert E Sherwood, which premiered on Broadway in 1930, and was subsequently made into two films in 1931 and 1940. The play—in which both the opening and closing scenes are set on the bridge itself—was a romantic story of an American soldier, Roy, serving in the Canadian expeditionary force in France during the Great War, who, entering London on leave via Waterloo, encounters a chorus girl, Myra—'An American with cockney mannerisms'—by a bench set into the bridge's parapet wall.[63]

The clamour around the fate of the sinking bridge doubtless recommended it as a locus for Sherwood's dramatization; this was the bridge that Monet had painted in the first decade of the twentieth century in evocative

---

[62] 'Waterloo Bridge Again', *Daily Telegraph* (26 March 1934), p.10.
[63] Robert E Sherwood, *Waterloo Bridge: A Plan in Two Acts* (1930).

344 DESIGNS ON DEMOCRACY

depictions of London's atmosphere from his hotel room in the Savoy. Additionally, the area around Waterloo had been a known site of assignation and solicitation. The association of women with the bridge, in particular with prostitution, destitution, and suicide, was unsurprisingly absent from the preservationist account of the bridge. Only the *Telegraph* noted in passing, as Rennie's masterful access staircases were pulled down in late 1934, that they had 'figured in many novels and dramas dealing with poverty in London and London life generally'.[64] It did, however, later call the demolition of Rennie's bridge 'the passing of a romantic link with history and romance'.[65]

Sherwood's story came from his own experiences of London as an American before the war and subsequently (serving in a Canadian regiment) during war-time. He had in fact met a young woman who propositioned him at Peace Day celebrations in Trafalgar Square in 1918, but he forgot her address and never saw her again.[66] In 1912, on his first visit, the city had seemed smug, stolid, and permanent: 'London was eternal'.[67] In 1917 he returned as a private solider on leave, arriving at Waterloo Station—'all Canadian solders always seemed to arrive at Waterloo, no matter where they might be coming from'—and crossed Waterloo Bridge to the Strand.[68] The 'all-conquering pride' and 'insular complacency' of the British Empire which London had expressed had gone.[69] Sherwood described the darkness of the city—streetlights were painted black and car headlights were switched off as soon as the air-raid alarms sounded.[70] That American impression of decline and loss of confidence encapsulated the modernizing argument for renewed amenity in the post-war years.

Waterloo Bridge was not, therefore, merely an empty stage onto which Sherwood's story was projected. It opened up metaphorical and literal perspectives on the city. Indeed, the vantage-point it provided and the visual relationship between St Paul's Cathedral and Somerset House were felt to be as valuable as the bridge itself. The second film production of 1940 exploited the ongoing transformation of the bridge and recognized the impact of the return of war. In an early sequence, an older Roy, serving in the Second World War, crosses the silhouette of the temporary steel girders, which had been in place since the 1920s and were to remain when the new bridge was

---

[64] 'Famous Stairs to Go', *Daily Telegraph* (25 August 1934), p.8.
[65] 'London's Lost Bridge', *Daily Telegraph* (23 June 1934), p.14.
[66] Sherwood, *Waterloo Bridge*, pp.xix, xxi.   [67] Ibid., p.x.
[68] Ibid., pp.x–xi.   [69] Ibid., p.xi.   [70] Ibid., p.xv.

THE ARCHITECTURAL MIND   345

partially opened in 1942. The image signalled the modernization of the famous landmark. An extended flashback to the First World War follows, starting with the celebrated view of St Paul's seen from behind the balustrade of Rennie's elegant early nineteenth-century granite bridge. The end of the film returns to the temporary structure of 1940, as the hero sets off for France once more, for a very different war. A complex set of associations was suggested: affection for the old bridge; awareness of its global status as a key gateway in and out of London; the part it played in chance encounters which might have momentous effects; even its historical and artistic resonances of suicide—all stood for a dialogue between past and present in which layers of history and modernity co-constituted a sense of place.

It was the weight of these associations that made the demolition of John Rennie's Waterloo Bridge so traumatic, at least rhetorically. In the bridge's 'unbuilding', romance and sentiment played a significant role in its representation to the public. Sentiment, representationalism, atmosphere, and even aura had resonances in Scott's design for the new bridge completed in 1942 and opened fully in 1945.

The challenge in designing the new bridge was to produce a new amenity for London on the one hand, but to reconcile its modernity with the historic city on the other, both its immediate physical context and the sentimental associations it had accrued. Historicism and sentimentalism were the traditional enemies of Modernist historiography—Henry Russell-Hitchcock notably dismissed 'the sentimental comfort of representation'[71]—and it is for these reasons that architects like Scott were for so long excluded from critical analysis. Waterloo Bridge offers an opportunity to see how British architectural culture in this period engaged with functionalism, historicism, and representationalism, combining the intellectual, the imaginative, and the practical in its aspiration to higher levels of professionalism and public engagement. This tells us something fundamental about how contemporaries thought about architectural design and its communicative capacity, especially pertinent in a public monument which also served as public infrastructure. There was an ambition in Scott's work, even in so deceptively simple a design as Waterloo Bridge, which rose above questions of style and stylistic compromise.

Scott's attitude to 'functionalism' and Modernism was typical of the machine-craft view. In 1926, he had won an important competition for the

---

[71] Quoted in Neil Levine, *Modern Architecture: Representation and Reality* (New Haven, 2009), p.7.

346 DESIGNS ON DEMOCRACY

General Post Office (GPO) Telephone Kiosk, the ubiquitous red telephone boxes (K2 and the smaller and simplified K3) in a neo-Regency design inspired by the tomb of the wife of Sir John Soane in St Pancras Old Churchyard.[72] Inspiration from sepulchral and monumental form was significant. In the field of industrial architecture he had served as consulting architect to the London Power Company (LPC) for Battersea Power Station and Guinness for its first brewery outside Ireland on the Park Royal Estate in north-west London.[73] For Guinness, he took principles of representation very seriously, melding cultivation of image with the projection of a particular sense of public responsibility—in a context experienced very differently by the workforce and the viewing public, who saw it either from above as part of an abstract pattern or at speed from the major arterial roads. The commissions for semi-public clients in the form of the GPO and LPC equally constituted significant contributions to the new social infrastructure of public services for citizen-consumers.[74]

In the mid-1930s, Scott regularly espoused a stylistic 'middle line' between the 'extremes' of Modernism and Traditionalism. The 'middle line' would temper what, tongue in cheek, he referred to as 'the tyranny of the machine'.[75] Knowingly—surely—parodying Marinetti's *Futurist Manifesto* he wrote of a future where:

> ...I see the advocates of machinery puzzled and anxious and the masses restive and querulous; gradually the wave of discontent swells into a vast tidal wave, which breaks up at last in a wild fury of destruction. I see crowds marching on the factories, breaking up the machines, many being electrocuted or scalded to death in the wild orgy of destruction...Then, as an epilogue, we see the people back to a simpler and more human ideal, living hard working, simple but contented lives. I make a present of this idea to some film producer![76]

The latter image, of restored 'simple but contented lives', draws on a vision derived from Morris's *News from Nowhere* and the genre of utopian fiction with which it was connected, implying an affinity with the idealism of the

---

[72] Stamp, *Telephone Boxes*.
[73] Gavin Stamp, 'Battersea Power Station', *Thirties Society Journal* 1 (1982), pp.3–9.
[74] William A Robson (ed.), *Public Enterprise: Developments in Social Ownership and Control in Great Britain* (1937).
[75] Giles Gilbert Scott, 'The Inaugural Address', *JRIBA* 41 (November 1933), p.7.
[76] Ibid., p.8.

THE ARCHITECTURAL MIND 347

Arts and Crafts. The 'more human ideal' gestures to the humanism of Geoffrey Scott. In practice Scott's ambition was a balance between these positions. Giles Scott was not an anti-Modern, however convenient that label may have been in Modernist historiography's exclusion of the architectural culture which produced him. He sought to aim for 'quality rather than novelty, so that we may produce buildings that are not only efficient, practical and functional, but also refined and beautiful.'[77] These qualities were, perhaps lazily, summed up by Scott's use of the word 'traditional'.

There are two salient points to which Scott's words draw attention: firstly, the use of parody and the exaggerated language of the 'battle of the styles', which some historians have treated too much at face value. Architects of Scott's bent were too pragmatic to take up firm ideological stances of the kind their fathers and grandfathers had supposedly done in the nineteenth century. The interwar 'battle of the styles' was more a struggle to escape the confines of naïve historicist stylism, while being restrained by the descriptive and architectural languages of style. Secondly, and consequentially, the balance Scott was driving at was in fact less about style—the particular outward dressing of an elevation—and more about the underlying method or approach to the problem. Dismissive of the 'craving for a striking effect' of the expression of construction (leading, as he put it, 'the extreme modernist to tell the same constructional lies that he condemns so heartily in the work of the extreme traditionalist'), Scott's design for Waterloo Bridge subtly exposes its tensions quite deliberately while deploying humanizing details where possible.[78] On the face of it, Waterloo Bridge is very simply designed, but this belies, and in some cases deliberately conceals, the careful thinking that lay behind its engineering and form. The resulting architectural concept has to be understood as a response informed by the social debate about the nature of amenity and urban improvement often cast in intensely aesthetic terms.

Scott's association with a new Waterloo Bridge dated in fact from 1932.[79] He had initially proposed a monumental twin-arch bridge characterized by two pairs of pylons at each bridge head (Figs. 6.9 and 6.10).[80] These were

[77] Ibid., p.11. Scott ended: 'Gentlemen, with that platitudinous finale, I make my bow.'
[78] Ibid., p.10.
[79] LMA, LCC/CL/HIG/02/058 Highways Committee Papers—Waterloo Bridges, quotation from 'Improvement Committee Minutes (16 February 1932)'.
[80] RIBA, Scott Papers, ScGG/90/1, Waterloo Bridge Correspondence 1932–50 with Rendel, Palmer and Tritton, Memorandum intended for LCC Highways Committee entitled 'Waterloo Bridge: Architectural Notes' (5 February 1937), fo.324a.

Fig. 6.9 Unexecuted designs for Waterloo Bridge, London, for the London County Council: part plan and elevation, Giles Gilbert Scott (1932), RIBA97454, RIBA Collections

deeply unpopular and rejected by the Royal Fine Arts Commission (RFAC).[81] Nevertheless, the Labour-led LCC maintained its engagement with Scott and the engineers Rendel, Palmer, and Tritton after 1934 and Morrison's initiation of the demolition of Rennie's bridge. In his second proposal Scott aimed for a sleeker architectural effect, 'modern in character without being "modernistic"', the twin arches affording interesting plays of light and shade (Fig. 6.11).[82] The scheme was designed to bridge from the old upper bank of the Strand, rather than 'shore to shore' at Embankment level as his earlier design had proposed.[83] Adopting the higher level as the 'main abutment or

---

[81] LMA, LMA/4625/C/01/008 Royal Fine Art Commission—Project case files seeking consultation and approval from the RFAC for various London-wide architectural proposals and developments dating from 1924–1999, 'Royal Fine Art Commission Report on Waterloo Bridge, (21 May 1932)'. See also *The Crawford Papers: The Journals of David Lindsay, twenty-seventh Earl of Crawford and tenth Earl of Balcarres 1871–1940, during the years 1892 to 1940* (Manchester, 1984), ed. J Vincent, p.597. Crawford grandly recalled that the Commission had saved Scott's reputation by blocking them.
[82] RIBA, Scott Papers, ScGG/90/1, Waterloo Bridge Correspondence 1932–50 with Rendel, Palmer and Tritton, letter from Scott to Rendel, Palmer and Tritton (31 January 1936), fo.285.
[83] RIBA, Papers, ScGG/90/1, Waterloo Bridge Correspondence 1932–50 with Rendel, Palmer and Tritton, 'Demolition and Reconstruction of Waterloo Bridge: Joint Report by the Appointed Engineers and the Chief Engineer' (5 October 1934), fo.215b.

Fig. 6.10 Unexecuted designs for Waterloo Bridge, London, for the London County Council: perspective, Giles Gilbert Scott (1932), RIBA97455, RIBA Collections

'springing point' would allow a more streamlined design and open up 'the wonderful view of the curving Thames'.[84]

Although Scott was concerned with an overall effect of sleekness, the absence of opportunity for extensive ornamental detail in the bridge as built only reinforced the sculptural qualities noted by *The Times* architecture critic, Charles Marriot, as characteristic of a pervasive mind-set. Marriot, like many contemporaries, conceived of architectural design as 'a sort of higher form of sculpture—to the basic requirement of meeting functional needs was added the requirement of creating three-dimensional art on a monumental scale'.[85] Scott's fundamental approach to Waterloo Bridge reflected this, initially in the monumental sculptural qualities of the pylon

---

[84] Ibid., letter from EJ Buckton to Scott (22 June 1934), fo.211b.
[85] David Frazer Lewis, 'The Ideal of Architecture as Sculpted Mass During the Interwar Period', *Sculpture Journal* 25.3 (2016), p.344.

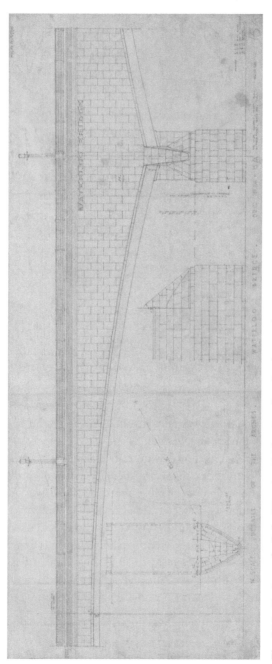

Fig. 6.11 Design as built for Waterloo Bridge, London, for the London County Council: 1/4" details of the arches, Giles Gilbert Scott (1937, with revisions dated 1938–40), RIBA97456, RIBA Collections

Fig. 6.12 Waterloo Bridge, London: the steps leading down to the Embankment with Somerset House, Strand, in the background on the right, Giles Gilbert Scott (1945), photograph by Dell & Wainwright (1946), RIBA25307, RIBA Collections

design, but also in the twin-arch structure common to both schemes. The cutwaters, though unadorned with sculpture or ornament, similarly were intended as 'prow-like' projections. The ribbed mouldings on the bridge parapet were borrowed from his earlier ecclesiastical designs, and intended to animate planar surfaces. At the four corners of the bridgeheads were plinths intended, initially, to have sculptures of lions on them (Fig. 6.12). No decision was ever made because Scott preferred them to lie empty than to have work which did not conform to the overall visual effect he had sought to create.[86]

His particular care in the treatment of structural and facing materials is also noteworthy. In early 1937 he made a number of enquiries into facing

---

[86] The proposed incorporation of sculpture on the four plinths at the bridgeheads shows this too. See AR Graves, 'Barbara Hepworth's Designs for Sculpture on Waterloo Bridge', *Burlington Magazine* 141.1161 (1 December 1999), pp.753–6.

352 DESIGNS ON DEMOCRACY

materials, writing to Adams, Holden, and Pearson about the composition of the mortar for the Portland Stone masonry of the London University buildings (he wanted as light a mortar as possible).[87] He also wrote to Maxwell Ayrton about types of exposed concrete used on his design at Twickenham. Scott was keen for a brush hammer or chiselled surface to show the aggregate and to a get a good colour effect.[88] Ayrton himself only ever used Portland Cement, the achieved colour effect depending on the aggregate and colour of the sand. At Twickenham, Ayrton used Thames Ballast, leaving parts of certain faces rough or fatty in order to achieve varying light effects.[89]

Despite the self-conscious 'functionalism' Scott adopted, the final design for Waterloo Bridge was nevertheless deliberately representational in some of its aspects. Scott explored this tension using materials. The bridge is essentially a reinforced concrete structure with a Portland Stone facing. At the time of submitting the design, Scott himself was at pains to explain that it was 'not intended to give the bridge the appearance of a stone bridge, but to employ stone for facing for the practical reason that it suits the London atmosphere as a weathering surface.'[90] This was reflected in the engineering too: the 'bearing wall [of the piers]…surrounded by, but completely separated from, a granite and Portland stone-faced reinforced-concrete shell', and yet 'The design of the stone facing is such that it is clearly an applied surface finish. It has been arranged by the architect in vertical strips so that the joins in no way imply heavy stones functioning as an arch or wall.'[91] There is a tension here, however, for despite Scott's claim to want the bridge not to look as though it was made up of stones and masonry, he was still keen to make sure it looked like an arched bridge (Fig. 6.13), 'reinforced concrete box girders, cantilevering, not arching'.[92] Moreover, though the spandrels of the 'arches', the piers, and abutments are all faced with Portland Stone, the chamfered rim of the arch soffit is teasingly formed of rough reinforced concrete to show the structural material beneath (Fig. 6.14).

Through a number of subtle conceits Scott was thus deliberately articulating an architectural tension. Although familiar in the rhetorics of the

---

[87] RIBA, Scott Papers, ScGG/89/2 London—Westminster—Waterloo Bridge 1930–1950—Correspondence, letter from Scott to Maxwell Ayrton (25 January 1937), fo.7.

[88] Ibid. [89] Ibid., letter from Maxwell Ayrton to Scott (28 January 1937), fo.9.

[90] RIBA, Scott Papers, ScGG/90/1 London—Westminster—Waterloo Bridge—Correspondence 1932–1950 with Rendel, Palmer and Tritton, 'Waterloo Bridge: Draft to Questions' (23 October 1934), fo.217a.

[91] EJ Buckton and J Cuerel, 'The New Waterloo Bridge', Journal of the Institute of Civil Engineers 7 (June 1943), p.164.

[92] Nikolaus Pevsner and Simon Bradley, London. 2, South (London, 1999), p.713.

Fig. 6.13 Waterloo Bridge under construction, River Thames, London, Giles Gilbert Scott, photograph by Dell & Wainwright (1945), RIBA25308, RIBA Collections

nineteenth-century Gothic Revival and early twentieth-century Modernism, this self-awareness by a non-Modernist architect is noteworthy. The conceits were intentional humanist critiques of functionalist Modernist discourse. They were modulated by different needs: the twin-arch structure provided 'the best facilities for river traffic as regards both space and view for navigation';[93] the reinforced concrete shell 'protects the main supporting member from damage by shipping', forming a permanent cofferdam whilst preventing 'excess movements of the superstructure';[94] and the Portland Stone facing offered resistance to weathering, giving rise to the popular myth that Waterloo is a self-cleaning bridge. Scott was conscious of the representational and visual possibilities of architecture, and his design plays with or tests these limits to create a bridge that not only felt contemporary but showed propriety in relation to its surroundings.

[93] Buckton and Cuerel, 'The New Waterloo Bridge', p.147.
[94] Ibid., p.153.

Fig. 6.14 Waterloo Bridge, London: structural detail of an arch span, Giles Gilbert Scott, photograph by Sam Lambert (1968), RIBA25215, Architectural Press Archive/RIBA Collections

Scott also had a romantic sensibility. He was alert to the emotional appeal of space, to its affective psychological potential. The sculptural three-dimensionality, romanticism, and representationalism in Scott's design were intensely focused in one seemingly incidental detail (notably featuring in both the 1932 and 1934 designs): Scott's memorial to John Rennie's bridge (Fig. 6.15). The Rennie Memorial, incorporated into the bridge itself, comprised a section of balustrade from the demolished structure, bracketed by two of its monumental Doric columns on the abutment wall of the south side of the river, closing the vista of the 'striking view' from the north to south bank, as Scott put it. The dropped granite balustrade, flanked by sentry-like granite Doric columns, themselves hugged by the twin concrete arches of Scott's new bridge will have created an almost elegiac atmosphere, the

THE ARCHITECTURAL MIND 355

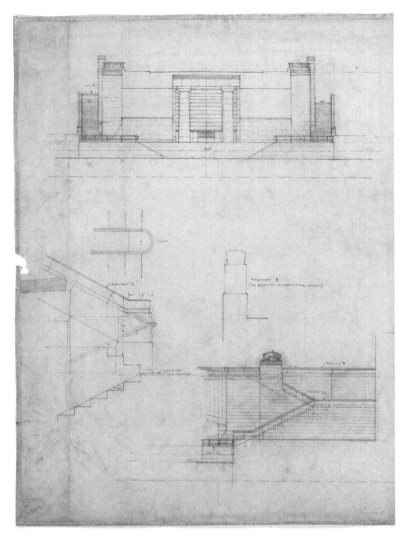

Fig. 6.15 Designs for Waterloo Bridge, London, for the London County Council: details of south abutment (with amendments), Giles Gilbert Scott (1935, amended between 1937 and 1938), RIBA97457, RIBA Collections

composition giving the effect of a kind of stele in bas-relief.[95] The arrangement was also a deliberate and playful abstraction of notable and familiar elements of the old bridge—the coupled Doric columns prised apart, the parapet's balustrade placed at the bottom. The composition had a powerfully sculptural quality. Yet it remained absent from an extensive photographic record of the new bridge and was barely mentioned in the contemporary press reports (Fig. 6.16).[96] Its significance has thus gone unremarked.

Fig. 6.16 Waterloo: detail of parapets and arches of Waterloo Bridge from South Bank Exhibition Site, photographer unknown (1948), 236093, image © London Metropolitan Archives (City of London)

---

[95] It evokes the Greek Revival in its stolidity. The arrangements resemble the niches in Archibald Elliot's screen-walls for Old Calton Cemetery in Edinburgh, a motif developed from the triumphal arch on his Regent Bridge leading to Waterloo Place—an obscure reference, if it was indeed deliberate, but a tempting one nonetheless.

[96] There may be purely practical reasons for this: it was underneath the arches and would have been difficult to photograph because of lighting conditions. Furthermore, there was no embankment on the south side of the river until the early 1950s, so it would have been even

The memorial would have been noticeable not only to those walking and driving along the Victoria Embankment, but also to tram passengers. Passengers on the trams emerging from the tunnel on the opposite abutment, and those walking along the footpath closest to the river or riding on a boat through the arches, would have spotted this elegy through a winter mist or summer haze. At the opposite abutment, Scott positioned the entrance to the Kingsway tramway subway between the twin arches (in the old bridge, the tramway tunnel was entered by the western staircase of the Victoria Embankment), in other words creating a void to answer the solidity of the southern abutment. This play of solid and void, exploiting the transparency of the twin-arch structure, was a characteristic feature of Scott's design.

Construction of the new Waterloo Bridge, undertaken by Peter Lind, began in October 1937. The bridge was opened to traffic in August 1942 (Fig. 6.17). Inaugurated with no ceremony, the new bridge was formally

Fig. 6.17 The south-west side of the newly built Waterloo Bridge viewed from the south bank of the River Thames, with a hut occupied by Peter Lind and Co., the company responsible for the bridge's construction, under one of the arches, photograph by JJ Samuels Ltd (1942–7), SAM01/03/0564, Source: Historic England Archive

harder to find a steady shot of the memorial. The Thames-side restaurant for the Festival of Britain by Fry and Drew would also have obscured it.

358 DESIGNS ON DEMOCRACY

opened by Herbert Morrison in December 1945. Because it was wartime and both the remnants of construction and the ungainly temporary bridge remained, the new bridge had received little critical attention in the architectural press in 1942, and it was difficult to photograph it effectively. It was then all too easily subsumed into the critical tastes of the contemporary architectural press in the mid-1940s, in ways which occluded the ambition of Scott's design. Its thoughtfulness, the tensions with which it played, went, it seems, unnoticed. Because of its apparently straightforward 'functionalism'—intensified, for instance, by the temporary handrails and lamp standards, in place of the ones Scott had designed—the bridge was unproblematically absorbed by the creation of the South Bank and the Festival of Britain.[97] The Rennie Memorial received no attention at all and although a memorial plaque was placed above the balustrade during the Festival of Britain at the suggestion of Hugh Casson, Festival Director of Architecture, the memorial was quickly forgotten.[98] It was demolished in 1956 to make way for the National Film Theatre, and only nearly twenty years later was another, very different memorial created on the Embankment side. The collapsing of these discrete elements into the post-war architectural project is a synecdoche of the wider scholarly neglect of the dynamic affinity of history and modernity, and the harnessing of public engagement through multiple media in the interwar period with which this book has been concerned. The interwar debates and architectural programmes which have been discussed were neither backward-looking nor merely anticipatory of a more developed modernity. They constituted a commitment to a professional integrity which enacted an ideal of public service. The goal was an approach to architecture and to urbanism which would in turn inspire and sustain a modern civic consciousness—a design for democracy.

Charing Cross—the Planner's Panoptic

The controversy about a new bridge at Charing Cross to replace Hungerford Railway Bridge had been an acute concern of architects from 1916. It was at this moment that concerted agitation by members of the profession and

[97] 'Waterloo Bridge, 1946', *AR* (August 1946), p.47.
[98] LMA GLC/AR/HB/01/0978 Historic Buildings Department Case Files, letter from Hugh Casson to Robert H Matthew, Architect to the LCC (19 September 1950).

the London Society in particular began. The London Society had been established in 1912 through the efforts of the editor of the *British Architect*, Thomas Raffles Davison, and had attracted significant architectural support, notably from Raymond Unwin, Reginald Blomfield, Stanley Adshead, and Edwin Lutyens. Aston Webb served as chairman.[99] Right from the start it made serious interventions into questions of infrastructure and design in the capital; as well as early agitation relating to the placement of arterial roads, a Planning Committee was formed to draw up a 'Development Plan', which was published and exhibited in various municipalities during the 1920s.[100] Two other early *causes célèbres* were the development of the riverside and 'Surrey side' of the Thames, as well as the replacement of the Hungerford Railway Bridge.[101]

Fig. 6.18   Hungerford Bridge by Herbert George Hampton (c.1920), 32367, image © London Metropolitan Archives (City of London)

---

[99] Helena Beaufoy, '"Order out of chaos": The London Society and the Planning of London 1912–1920', *Planning Perspectives* 12.2 (April 1997), pp.135–64; Aston Webb (ed.), *London of the Future* (1921).

[100] Lucy Hewitt, 'The London Society and Their Development Plan for Greater London', *London Topographical Record* 30 (2010), pp.115–31; Hewitt, 'The Civic Survey of Greater London: Social Mapping, Planners and Urban Space in the Early Twentieth Century', *Journal of Historical Geography* 30.3 (July 2012), pp.247–62.

[101] David Gilbert, 'A Short History of London in Wrought Iron: Empire, Art and Social Division on the Hungerford Bridge', *London Society Journal* 461 (2011), http://www.londonsocietyjournal.org.uk/461/davidgilbert.php [accessed 14 August 2014].

360 DESIGNS ON DEMOCRACY

John Hawkshaw's Hungerford Railway Bridge (1864) attracted special opprobrium on two grounds: firstly, for aesthetic reasons—the bridge was thought to be ugly (Fig. 6.18). It was described as a 'Blot on the Thames' in a letter to the *Manchester Guardian* from Aston Webb, who recalled the radical socialist politician John Burn's description of the bridge as 'that ugly red oxide Behemoth which sprawls from north to south'.[102] Webb, in collaboration with Burns and Blomfield, had produced an alternative scheme for the bridge with associated planning improvements. The aesthetic was, however, only part of the picture—the railway bridge, after all, had signalled to a generation earlier the modernity and romance of London, propagated by Monet's sequence of views of this bridge as well as Waterloo. More significant was that the presence of the railway bridge and the siting of Charing Cross Station represented the strength of private interest in determining the shape and future of urban development. The incursion of surface-level railways into the central areas of London was symptomatic of the worst excesses of Victorian capitalism, laissez-faire individualism, and their consequences for the city. Architects, in particular of the kind attracted to the London Society, were influenced by the idealism and the politics of the New Liberalism in which the needs of the community and the public, and the need for new instruments of planning and development, were being tested. Campaigners were therefore particularly exercised by the continuing presence not only of the bridge but also of the station on the north side of the river. This tapped into widespread concerns about land use and land reform, especially in the urban context. As Raffles Davison summarized:

> If the finest imaginable schemes were displayed to-day for the improvement of London, it would not follow that we should be a whit nearer great improvements, for the machinery for turning them into possibilities is lacking. Our only real hope lies in the creation of a responsible controlling and directing power which shall be urged into action by the determined desire and enlightened opinion of the public.[103]

The events of 1916 became a flashpoint because the South Eastern Railway Company (precursor to Southern Railway) was unsurprisingly

---

[102] LSA, BF/28/d, Aston Webb, 'The Blot on the Thames' (1916), pp.1–8. For the original article, see: 'The Blot on the Thames: Charing Cross Railway Bridge', *The Observer* (11 June 1916), p.9.

[103] Thomas Raffles Davison, 'The Opportunities of London' in Aston Webb (ed.), *London of the Future* (London: T Fisher Unwin Ltd, 1921), p.45.

THE ARCHITECTURAL MIND   361

firmly against the removal of the bridge and the station, in fact repeatedly lobbying for bridge-strengthening powers through private bills in the Commons.[104] Parliament did indeed confer these powers on the railway company in 1916 but subject to clear restrictions, specifically around limiting compensation for the company if any public improvement scheme required compulsory purchase of the site. These stipulations reflected the changing attitude of the state to the railways, characterized by a growing recognition of the need to replan the network in the public interest.[105] This of course pitted the interests of the railway company against removal or alteration of the bridge until the early 1930s, which frustrated progress time and time again.

In response to this, however, a cascade of schemes and a torrent of debate led by architects appeared in the technical and non-technical press, adumbrating proposals of almost every conceivable type: one commentator recalled that 'thousands of leading articles, letters and paragraphs have appeared in the Press, putting forward various suggestions for improving Charing Cross, and hundreds of plans have been drawn and published to the world'.[106] This was in part stimulated by the attempt of the City of London's bridge authority, the Bridge Houses Estate, to build a new bridge at St Paul's, another scheme that was vehemently contested for many years.[107] Around 1911 many were calling for a memorial bridge to the late king, and by 1916 others thought a new bridge and approaches would be fitting for an Imperial Memorial to the war dead. Herbert Baker, who suggested that the memorial should take the form of proposals put together by Webb, Blomfield, and Burns at Charing Cross, appealed in a letter to *The Times* that future schemes be 'publicly discussed, so that they could simmer in the mind of the public and be thought out by those qualified to give expert opinions'— an economically expressed appeal to the alignment of the professional and the public.[108]

The issue arose again in the early to mid-1920s. This was in part due to further agitation about the proposed new river crossing at St Paul's. In 1923,

[104] RIBA, RIBA/Env Waterloo Bridge Memorial Papers, 'Exhibition of Designs for a New Bridge at Charing Cross: Catalogue of Drawings, Models etc' (March 1923); George Swinton, *London: Her Traffic—Her Improvement and Charing Cross Bridge* (1924).

[105] Russell Haywood, 'Railways, Urban Form and Town Planning in London: 1900–1947', *Planning Perspectives* 12 (1997), pp.37–69.

[106] Swinton, *London*, p.41.

[107] The debate surrounding proposals for a bridge at St Paul's has been little commented on, and deserves a much fuller study and analysis than is possible here.

[108] 'The New London: A Great Imperial Memorial', *The Times* (17 November 1916), p.11.

362   DESIGNS ON DEMOCRACY

coinciding with the bicentenary of Christopher Wren's death, there was particular anxiety about the state of the building fabric of St Paul's, and the architectural community strongly resisted the placing of a new bridge on axis with the Cathedral. This culminated in the first report of the newly established RFAC which asserted that reverberations from a traffic bridge at this point would undermine the building's foundations. Coincidentally, in 1923 the provisions of the Railways Act (1921) came into effect, forming the 'Big Four' railway companies, among them Southern Railway, and architectural campaigners spotted a convenient lobbying opportunity. It was partly for these reasons that in March 1923 the London Society promoted an exhibition of schemes by its members relating to Charing Cross Station and the Hungerford Railway Bridge at the old London County Hall on Spring Gardens. These displays were, in the words of Captain George Swinton, a former leading member of the Municipal Reform Party in the LCC and later of the New Delhi Town Planning Committee, evidence of 'how fine our modern architecture can be', and he encouraged the public to examine 'various carefully worked-out projects for dealing with what is acknowledged to be our most desirable London improvement'.[109] Additionally in the autumn of 1923 Waterloo Bridge began to show signs of serious subsidence, and this amplified the attention drawn to the prospect of a new road bridge at Charing Cross.

Continuing agitation about the wider question of river crossings and cross-river traffic culminated in the Prime Minister's appointment in 1926 of a Royal Commission on Cross River Traffic chaired by Arthur Lee, Viscount Lee of Fareham, and including Lawrence Weaver. In consultation with the engineer, Owen Williams, the Commission recommendations for Charing Cross comprised a double-deck bridge with railway tracks below and a roadway above, crossing at a high level (Fig. 6.19). It further suggested that during the period of construction there should be no interference with the workings of the existing station and railway bridge. The government accepted the basic recommendations (Fig. 6.20) and the scheme was further developed first by a Committee of Engineers in 1928 (Fig. 6.21), and then further still into 1929 in consultation with Edwin Lutyens (Figs. 6.22 and 6.23), appointed directly by Wilfred Ashley, the Minister of Transport, after repeated and vociferous complaint by the architectural community

---

[109] George Swinton, 'Charing Cross Bridge', *The Times* (21 March 1923), p.10.

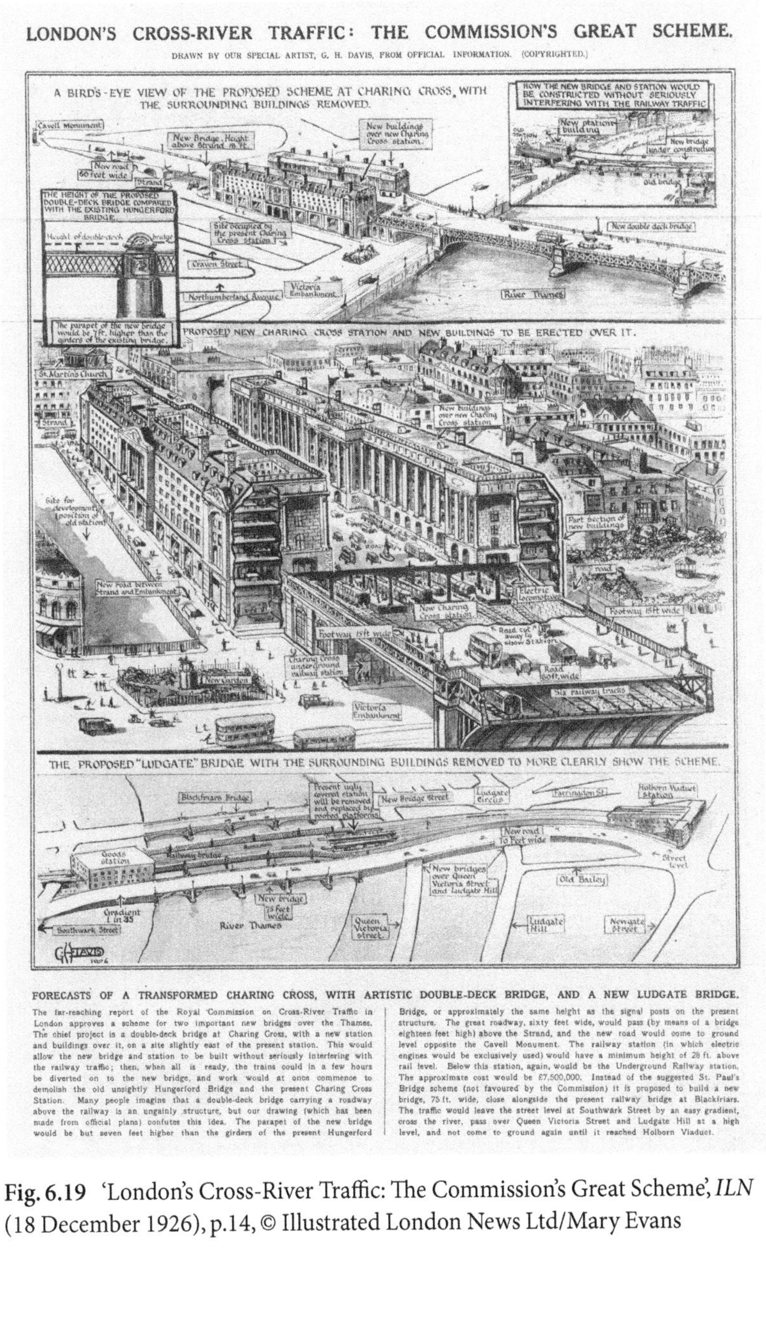

THE ARCHITECTURAL MIND   363

Fig. 6.19 'London's Cross-River Traffic: The Commission's Great Scheme', *ILN* (18 December 1926), p.14, © Illustrated London News Ltd/Mary Evans

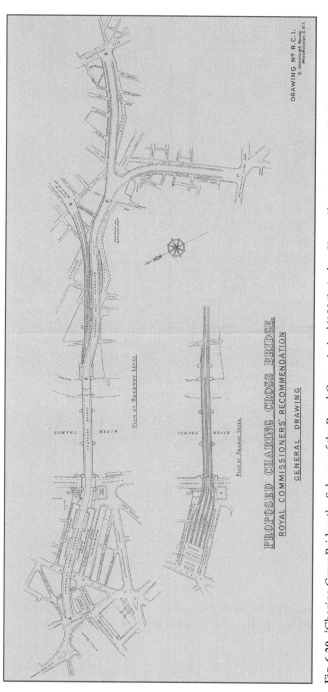

Fig. 6.20 'Charing Cross Bridge: the Scheme of the Royal Commission' (1926), Arthur Keen, *Charing Cross Bridge* (1930), p.54

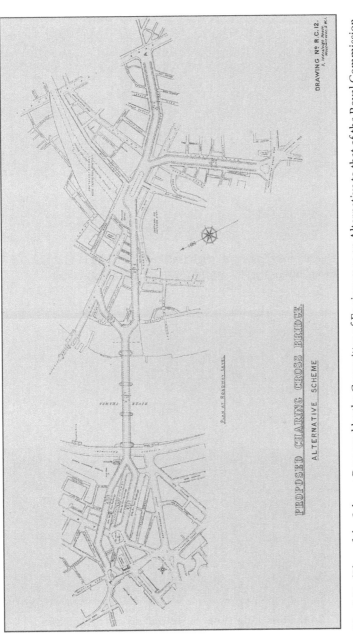

Fig. 6.21 'Plan of the Scheme Proposed by the Committee of Engineers as an Alternative to that of the Royal Commission on Cross-River Traffic London' (1928), Arthur Keen, *Charing Cross Bridge* (1930), p.56

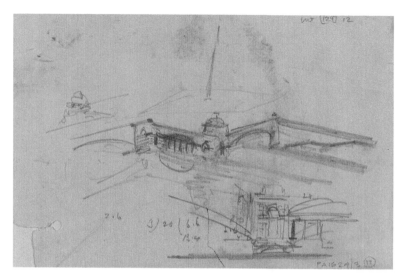

Fig. 6.22 One of several sheets of rough sketches for a bridge head at Charing Cross by Edwin Lutyens (c.1929–30), PA1624/3/12, RIBA Collections

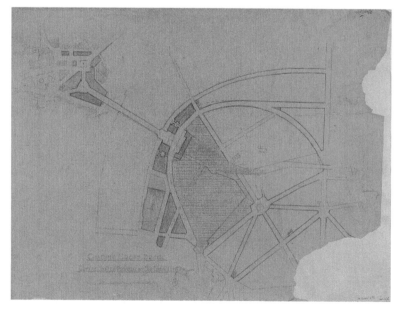

Fig. 6.23 'Charing Cross Bridge: Copy of Sketch Proposals by Sir Edwin Lutyens': sent with a letter from Mott, Hay & Anderson (4 June 1929), PA1624/3(2), RIBA Collections

that their professional expertise was being ignored.[110] The LCC was co-sponsor of this official, government-endorsed scheme.[111]

Lutyens's presence failed to provide much reassurance, indeed it stoked further professional controversy: 'Charing Cross raised important questions about the powers of local authorities to embark on major schemes of redevelopment without consulting architectural opinion, and Lutyens seemed to be conniving.'[112] Architectural opinion thus began to turn against the scheme. In February 1930 *Country Life* published 'The Case for Reconsideration', stressing the importance of town-planning considerations and the opportunity for the development of the south bank which would be seriously hampered by adoption of the official scheme.[113] The railway company remained reluctant to move across the river, arguing that it would be an inconvenience for the travelling public, and criticism was mounting in the press from learned and architectural societies.

Nevertheless, the new Labour government continued to champion it. On 19 February 1930, Herbert Morrison, now Minister of Transport, commended the LCC (Charing Cross) Bill to the House, threatening that the LCC would demolish Waterloo Bridge if it were rejected.[114] During the debate, the RIBA came in for special censure when Herbert Morrison produced a letter, handed over to him by Lutyens, which had been sent by Arthur Keen, vice-president of the RIBA and chairman of the Thames Bridges Conference, a lobbying group which brought together a number of architectural and amenity societies. The private note—unfortunately sent on Institute-headed paper—asked Lutyens to 'publish a letter denying responsibility for the Charing Cross layout'.[115] Morrison took this as an underhand gesture, 'quoting it as typical of RIBA dirty tricks'.[116] Lutyens subsequently resigned from the Institute, irritated not only by this episode but also by an earlier one where his professional conduct had been called into question regarding a housing development on the Grosvenor Estate. Though seemingly a minor incident, it was an unwelcome stain on the Institute's reputation among

[110] Hansard, HC vol.235, col.1510 (19 February 1930). Early sketches of Lutyens's plans are held by the RIBA, see *Edwin Lutyens: Catalogue of the Drawings Collection of the Royal Institute of British Architects* (Farnborough: Gregg International, 1973), p.27.

[111] Arthur Keen, *Charing Cross Bridge* (1930), p.64. There are three plates of photographs of the model interleaved here.

[112] Jane Ridley, *Edwin Lutyens: His Life, His Wife, His Work* (2003), pp.366–7.

[113] 'The Official Scheme for Charing Cross Bridge: The Case for Reconsideration', *Country Life* (1 February 1930), p.156.

[114] Bernard Donoughue and George William Jones, *Herbert Morrison: Portrait of a Politician* (2001), 2nd edn., p.152.

[115] Ridley, *Lutyens*, p.369.   [116] Ibid.

368   DESIGNS ON DEMOCRACY

parliamentarians, as it was actively seeking statutory recognition to control standards of entry into the architectural profession. Lutyens was a persistent thorn in the Institute's side for much of the 1930s as a result of this dispute. His individualism sat uneasily with the corporate demands of the profession, and in particular the heavy hand of the RIBA. After his resignation, he took on the presidency of the Institute of Registered Architects and vocally questioned the RIBA's legitimacy as the voice of the profession. Professional politics was never far away from architectural controversy at this time.

Although the bill passed the Commons vote, it faltered under the scrutiny of the Private Bill Select Committee. The Committee concluded that, although it approved the proposals for the Westminster side with certain minor amendments, the proposed 'tunnels', created by railway tracks bridging over roads, and the large and complex circus on the Lambeth side were unacceptable.[117] The inflexibility of Southern Railway—against public interest, sticking firmly to the valuable Lion Brewery site if they were to be moved to the south side—was another insurmountable barrier to the scheme's progress.

In response to the collapse of the government-backed official scheme, Frank Pick wrote to *The Times* in May 1930. Pick suggested that the proliferation of schemes might have been counter-productive:

> During the proceedings upon the Bill, and in fact on the very day the Bill was rejected, schemes were being constantly put forward by architects, engineers and others. Even the members of the committee had their schemes for consideration. Every one [sic], indeed, who turned his attention to this subject produced a fresh scheme. Every one was an expert, and, amid a welter of conflicting schemes, none has survived. A large public improvement cannot be approached in this individualistic fashion. It can only be possible where there is cooperation towards making one scheme representative of the combined skill and pains of all.[118]

Architects, in particular, needed to accept their rightful place: 'He [the architect] is servant and not master. He may suggest and modify, he may

---

[117] The proceedings of the Committee including Lutyens's appearance are chronicled in 'Charing Cross Bridge', *The Times* (4 April 1930), p.21. See also '"Arcades" in New Bridge Scheme', *Daily Mail* (4 April 1930), p.6.

[118] Frank Pick, 'Charing Cross Bridge', *The Times* (9 May 1930), p.17.

not dictate and define.'[119] It was to this sentiment that Scott responded in a letter published four days later as 'The Architectural Mind'. Scott set out a public case for the early and full consultation of architects in urban improvement projects: 'Architects are essentially planners...It may be confidently asserted that the finest planners in the country are found in the architectural profession, and by fine planners I mean men who provide the best working plans; in this respect they excel the engineers, who are primarily constructors.'[120]

The wider context is vital: Scott was defending 'the architectural mind' at a time when the Registration Bill was being debated within the RIBA and in Parliament. Only in October 1929 had the Institute begun to pull together effective parliamentary support for the bill. Resistance from the Incorporated Association of Architects and Surveyors had been stepped up early in 1930, leading to renewed questions about the Institute as registrar, and it was only in late spring of 1931 that the bill began to make serious advances through the parliamentary machine. At the same time—indeed in June 1930—the RIBA was calling for a public inquiry into the growth of the architecture department of the Office of Works, complaining that private practice was being robbed of rightful opportunities to design nationally important and state or governmental buildings. Scott had been chairing the Official Architecture Committee where much of this debate and dissension was located. It was, in other words, a politically sensitive time, and one at which Scott and the RIBA were at pains to explain what sort of public contribution—and public privileges—the profession should enjoy.

In June 1930, the LCC appointed a body of experts to try to resolve Parliament's objections and to build consensus. The Charing Cross Bridge Advisory Committee was chaired by Leslie Scott, a former Tory MP for Liverpool Exchange, a land reformer and active member of the Council for the Preservation of Rural England (CPRE). The vice-chair was Frank Pick, at this point managing director of the London Underground. The Committee of sixteen included political representation from affected local authorities; the railways, including Southern Railway; professional bodies, including the Town Planning Institute and RIBA represented by Longstreth Thompson and Raymond Unwin; as well as amenity and artistic societies, namely the RFAC and the Royal Academy (RA) represented by Giles Gilbert Scott and Reginald Blomfield respectively.

---

[119] Ibid.   [120] 'The Architectural Mind', *The Times* (13 May 1930), p.17.

370 DESIGNS ON DEMOCRACY

Leslie Scott had overenthusiastically told the press that 'he would be prepared to consider any proposal'.[121] In part in response to the London Society's repeated agitations and the Parliamentary Committee's rejection, many schemes were again circulating publicly with much comment. As a result, the first work of the Committee was to consider as many ideas and proposals as it could—seventy schemes were ultimately laid before the Committee with 128 sketch plans and diagrams examined and commented upon.[122] This audit provided a useful summary of the myriad proposals in play, some of which had their origins in schemes devised in the 1910s. HV Lanchester submitted extensive plans extending from Elephant and Castle to St Giles. Another submission named 'City Modernisation (London Trans-City Re-Planning Scheme)' proposed a twin bridge, the erection of an aeroplane station and Empire Food markets, among other features. John Murray, the Crown Architect and Surveyor, revived a much earlier plan from 1916 for an 'Empire Bridge', dressed in the 'English Renaissance' style.[123] It was designed 'to show how the amenities of Crown property in the Strand neighbourhood might be protected and improved in connection with the proposed new Bridge' (Fig. 6.24).[124] The gamut of suggestions by the architecturally minded public were surveyed, and the Committee analysed each for their essential proposal and possible contribution to an effective solution.

The Committee then deliberated over six proposals in detail, championed by different factions and interests on the Committee.[125] Of these, three are of particular interest (Figs. 6.25–6.28). The first was a scheme submitted by a multi-disciplinary team comprising WD Caröe, DB Niven, and Maxwell Fry, the planner Thomas Adams, and the engineers Murdoch MacDonald and William Muirhead (Fig. 6.29). These proposals were an amalgam of ideas developed over a number of years. Caröe and Niven had, of course, been active in the London's Society's agitations on the Charing Cross issue from the 1910s. In his role as architect to the Ecclesiastical Commissioners—

---

[121] 'Charing Cross Bridge', *The Times* (4 June 1931), p.11.
[122] *LCC Charing Cross Advisory Committee Report*, p.5.
[123] LMA, LCC/MIN/12/588, Special Committee on Charing Cross Bridge Scheme, July 1930 to July 1931, Minutes and Papers.
[124] LMA, LCC/MIN/12/588, Special Committee on Charing Cross Bridge Scheme, July 1930 to July 1931, Minutes and Papers, 'Charing Cross Bridge: Design suggested by Mr John Murray, FSA, FRIBA, FSI, MIStructE', and the two additional reports, 'Brief Description of The "Empire Bridge" at Charing Cross', and 'The "Empire Bridge" at Charing Cross', presented to the Committee on 9 October 1930.
[125] *LCC Charing Cross Advisory Committee Report*; LMA, LCC/MIN/12605, Charing Cross Bridge Advisory Committee: Schemes.

THE ARCHITECTURAL MIND 371

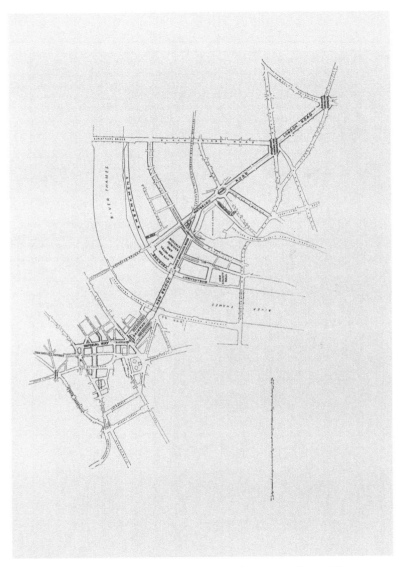

Fig. 6.24 'Scheme for Charing Cross Bridge and its approaches. With or without an elevated roadway across the new Charing Cross Square and a sub-way under York Road: John Murray, FSA, FRIBA, September, 1929', Arthur Keen, *Charing Cross Bridge* (1930), p.49

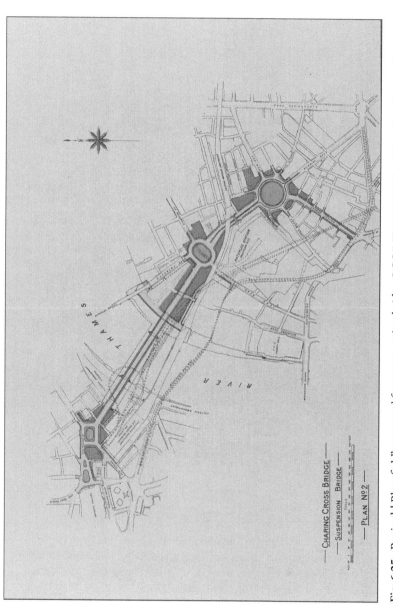

Fig. 6.25 Reginald Blomfield's proposal for a suspension bridge, LCC/MIN/12506, Plan 2, London Metropolitan Archives (City of London)

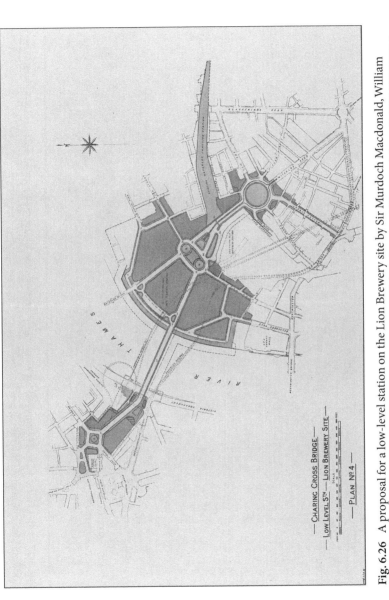

Fig. 6.26 A proposal for a low-level station on the Lion Brewery site by Sir Murdoch Macdonald, William Muirhead, David Barclay Niven, WD Caröe, Edwin Maxwell (Max) Fry and Thomas Adams, LCC/MIN/12506, Plan 4, London Metropolitan Archives (City of London)

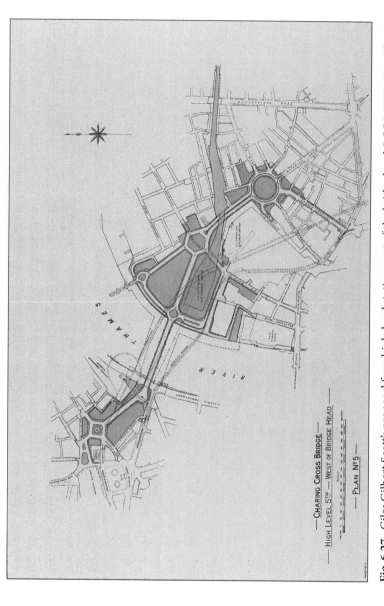

Fig. 6.27 Giles Gilbert Scott's proposal for a high-level station west of the bridge head, LCC/MIN/12506, Plan 5, London Metropolitan Archives (City of London)

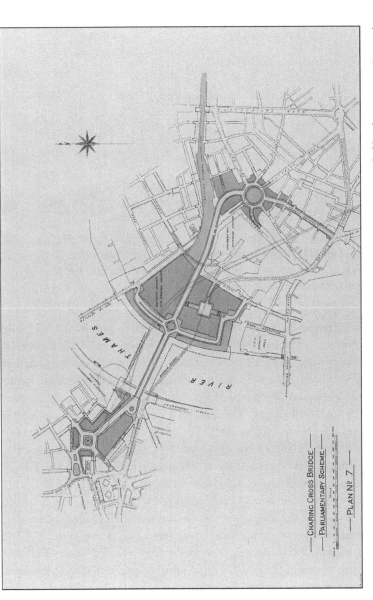

Fig. 6.28 Variation on the Parliamentary Scheme by the LCC Engineers (recommended by the Majority Report), LCC/MIN/12506, Plan 7, London Metropolitan Archives (City of London)

Fig. 6.29 'Charing Cross Bridge Scheme' prepared by Sir Murdoch Macdonald, William Muirhead, David Barclay Niven, WD Caröe, E Maxwell (Max) Fry and Thomas Adams, drawing by Max Fry (c.1930), LCC/MIN/12506. Plan 23, London Metropolitan Archives (City of London)

significant landowners on the south side of the river—as early as 1917 Caröe had proposed a low-level bridge, re-siting Charing Cross Station south of the river, opposite Waterloo Station, and renaming it 'Wipers,' anglicized in commemoration of the dead of Ypres (Fig. 6.30). A great colonnade would bring St John's Church into the group. The new joint-authored scheme proposed a 'low level' railway station on the Lion Brewery site, an idea which had originated with MacDonald.[126] The proposal was noteworthy not only because of the effectiveness of an interdisciplinary team of engineers, town planners, and architects but also because it shows the profound interconnectedness of architectural culture at this time, bringing together architects like Caröe and Niven, significantly older and conservative in their tastes, with Thomas Adams, by then an internationally active pioneering urban planner, and a young Modernist architect like Maxwell Fry.

The second and third schemes of interest were by Giles Gilbert Scott and Reginald Blomfield. Although representing corporate bodies, both were particularly keen to promote their own schemes and technical expertise, not least to demonstrate how a holistic architectural approach would secure a

---

[126] Thomas Adams was unambiguous in attributing it thus. 'Charing Cross', *The Times* (6 July 1931), p.8.

THE ARCHITECTURAL MIND 377

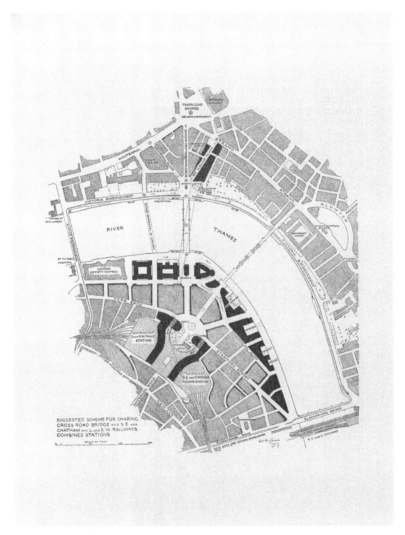

Fig. 6.30 The 'Wipers' scheme, 'Scheme for Charing Cross Bridge: W.D. Caröe, 1917', Arthur Keen, *Charing Cross Bridge* (1930), p.41

solution. Blomfield was particularly vocal in the Advisory Committee meetings, repeatedly lobbying for his own plan—a single-span suspension bridge neighbouring the Hungerford Railway Bridge to the east. Blomfield was at this time involved in the design of Lambeth Bridge for the LCC in collaboration with Council architect George Topham Forrest, a decorative mix of steel and stone punctuated by steel-lattice pylons (perhaps it was these that

Fig. 6.31 'A Sketch for a Suspension Bridge, Near Charing Cross, 800 feet span,' by Reginald Blomfield (1930), LCC/MIN/12506, Plan 18, London Metropolitan Archives (City of London)

THE ARCHITECTURAL MIND   379

recommended Blomfield to the Central Electricity Board for the electricity pylons linking its National Grid). His proposal for Charing Cross retained the station to the north; Blomfield was adamant that a southerly station would 'sterilize' the development of Lambeth. One of his particular concerns was architectural effect and its relationship to the urban landscape: 'One of the worst faults of the rejected [parliamentary] scheme was that it afforded no vista and involved some very unsatisfactory building sites from the point of view of Architecture. The scheme now suggested will provide a splendid vista.'[127] Blomfield provided striking perspective views of his suspension bridge design (Fig. 6.31). The masonry towers hosting the steel tables owed much to his design for the Menin Gate, completed four years before. Revealing something of Blomfield's intentions and ambitions, the monumental inscription in the plaque at the top of the tower structure included the RIBA motto: 'Usui Civium, Decori Urbium.' The inscription was merely impressionistic of both the opportunities for the tower's ornamentation, but it should be read in terms of the vigour of Blomfield's Grand Manner elevations and his City Beautiful aspirations. It is notable that in a memorial paper to the RIBA following the death of WR Lethaby, Blomfield wrote, encouraging the protection of Waterloo Bridge: 'I would urge all members of the Institute to do all in their power to save the bridge, and so to justify the proud claim of the Institute that it exists "usui civium, decori urbium".'[128]

Scott's approach was arguably more pragmatic and closely aligned to the rejected scheme. He could not, however, find a solution which got rid of the viaducts in Lambeth (the cause of the 'tunnel' effect) or which did not necessitate the removal of the railway station. He suggested instead 'a 3-span bridge, the central span being equal to three of the existing Hungerford Bridge spans and the two piers being in alignment with the existing piers of that bridge. This arrangement gives good visibility for craft navigating the bend in the river.'[129] From the north, Scott proposed that the bridge approach lead directly from the circus at the Strand to the bridge itself with 'a slight curve, similar in character to the Regent Street Quadrant', with a

[127] LMA, LCC/MIN/12588, Charing Cross Advisory Committee Signed Minutes and Presented Plans, R. Blomfield, 'Charing Cross Bridge' (7 October 1930), p.7.
[128] See 'WR Lethaby: An Impression and a Tribute', *JRIBA* (20 February 1932), pp.293–302, p.297.
[129] LMA, LCC/MIN/12/588, Special Committee on Charing Cross Bridge Scheme, July 1930 to July 1931, Minutes and Papers, letter from Giles Gilbert Scott (21 November 1930) forwarding scheme for a piered bridge with a new railway station between County Hall and the bridge approach, appended to Committee Meeting Minutes (15 January 1931), fo.56.

380   DESIGNS ON DEMOCRACY

bridgehead flanked by buildings on either side. On the Lambeth side the bridge would come to ground at a circus formed at the junction of Waterloo and York Roads.[130] As the plans developed, Scott proposed to move the Metropolitan District Railway Station (the Underground station) 'within the bridge structure, access from the bridge above being provided by escalators leading to and from booking halls on each side of the approach', in an arrangement loosely prefiguring the incorporation of the tram tunnel between the abutments of Waterloo Bridge.[131] At the Strand Circus, Scott proposed a circulating subterranean subway in the spirit of Piccadilly Circus. Scott's fundamental innovation on the Lambeth side was to move the new station west from the Lion Brewery site, towards County Hall, and then run a 'high level terrace road, parallel to the river', running east to a circus at the bridgehead of Waterloo.[132] The site between the two bridges would be carefully controlled, ideally in Scott's mind by the Council itself.[133] Though the scheme had the disadvantage of bringing the new railway tracks just 40 feet away from the front of Waterloo Station, this would free the large new circus formed from 'overbridging' by the railway lines (a significant criticism of the official scheme) and significantly reduce the amount of tunnelling. This was imperative because, as Scott urged the Committee to remember, 'Parliament rejected this scheme on account of the large areas of covered roads, or "tunnels" as they were termed' because they were deemed barriers to good further development of the area.[134]

None of these schemes garnered unanimous support. Indeed, although the majority recommended a plan quite closely resembling the rejected official scheme, there were a number of dissenting minority reports.[135] Nevertheless, in July 1931 the LCC resolved to promote legislation to authorize construction of a new Charing Cross Bridge along these lines. Although no new river crossing eventuated at Charing Cross, the various contributions by architects and the public hold some significance. In the case of Giles Gilbert Scott, the Charing Cross debacle shows how seriously he took the requirements of technical planning. At Waterloo, planning requirements were eventually superseded by traffic management and

---

[130] Ibid.   [131] *LCC Charing Cross Advisory Committee Report*, p.30.
[132] Ibid.
[133] RIBA, Scott Papers, ScGG/89/1 (2 of 2 folders), letter from Scott to Raymond Unwin (12 February 1931), fo.70.
[134] LMA, LCC/MIN/12/588, Special Committee on Charing Cross Bridge Scheme, July 1930 to July 1931, Minutes and Papers, Memorandum by Sir Giles Gilbert Scott, 'A Comparison Between Schemes CP4A and CP5' (5 February 1931), appended to Minutes of Committee Meeting (10 February 1931), fo.81.
[135] *LCC Charing Cross Advisory Committee Report*.

THE ARCHITECTURAL MIND   381

street-widening schemes; Scott's contribution was concentrated in the provision of amenity. At Charing Cross, he demonstrated sophisticated engagement with the technical requirements of planning. Indeed, as his public pronouncement to *The Times* declared, he believed that architects should position themselves as planners in order to claim greater stake in matters of public debate. The old 'sibling rivalry' with engineers was increasingly displaced by another. Architects, therefore, were by no means disengaged from developing conceptions of planning, as has been implied. We saw one manifestation of this in the campaigning and criticism of Trystan Edwards, but the ramifications were in fact much broader.

The 'idea of planning' provided the framework for the inaugural exhibition at the RIBA's new premises at 66 Portland Place on 'International Architecture, 1924–1934'. Intended as a comprehensive retrospective of the preceding ten years of architecture, it encompassed a range of examples from the Arts and Crafts to the International Style. Indeed, it is significant that to the organizers this may have represented a continuity and commonality of ethos. The exhibition, largely organized by Maxwell Fry, was divided into a number of sections: 'The Architecture of Pleasure', 'The Architecture of Public Buildings', 'Building for Worship', and 'The Architecture of Transport'. A number of the themed exhibition sections used 'planning' as their organizing principle: 'Planning the Dwelling', 'Planning for Industry and Commerce', and 'Planning for Health'. The climax of the exhibition was two displays at opposing ends of the Florence Hall: 'The Work of the Architect', which included 'documentary evidence' of the architect's activities (namely sets of drawings, specifications, bills of quantities, and relevant legislation and regulation relating to various projects), and in front of the Dominion screen, 'The Idea of Planning', including a large model of Charles Holden's 55 Broadway, with a photographic display behind showing the various stages of site selection, design, and construction.[136]

Fry pondered in the exhibition catalogue: 'By what quality shall an architect be known to the public? How can his sphere of usefulness be clearly recognised and valued?' To this, the answer was simple: 'The architect is a planner. He is a planner of space.'[137] This description of 'The Idea of Planning' was intended to capture the essence of architectural practice, a very definite shift from the image of the architect as 'artist' as well as beyond a mere professional. Drawing on a Corbusian theme, he described 'the architect

---

[136] ML Anderson (ed.), *International Architecture, 1924–1934: Catalogue to the Centenary Exhibition of the Royal Institute of British Architects* (1934).

[137] Ibid., p.74.

382 DESIGNS ON DEMOCRACY

coming to a new work as an ORGANISER, faced with the problem of making a machine which we *call* a building, but which is none the less a working machine.[138]

'Planning' in the early 1930s was increasingly seen as the solution to a wide range of societal, economic, and industrial problems across the political spectrum, a nail in the coffin for the laissez-faire which contemporaries had felt characterized the nineteenth century.[139] The word 'planning' therefore inevitably took on new resonances in architectural discourse at this time, and attached itself to a coalescing set of attitudes in British Modernism in particular, some in relation to the planning of individual buildings, others at a wider urban or regional scale.

Although increasingly seen as a 'panacea', planning was a contested idea despite the seemingly optimistic consensus of the early 1930s. By the late 1930s and early 1940s it was being claimed by different agendas. 'Physical planning'—to distinguish itself from but align itself with sociological and economic planning discourse—was vocally championed in particular by the *Architects' Journal*, and within the realm of the physical was the new idea of 'visual planning' propagated by the *AJ*'s sister title, the *Architectural Review*. 'Visual planning' was the basis of the Townscape movement in the post-war years of reconstruction and beyond.[140] Although a tactic of Modernist reconstruction in its earliest manifestations, the Townscape and 'visual planning' of Gibberd, Sharp, and Cullen was in fact influenced by civic design's emphasis on the visual, the integration of the historic environment, and the idea of urbanity: on his death in 1973 the *AR*'s obituary noted that Trystan Edwards's early writings had been 'primers for Thomas Sharp, Gordon Cullen and others…it is in the top echelon of national physical planning that the achievements of this remarkable man should most deservedly be remembered'.[141]

Giles Scott, president of the RIBA when it mounted 'International Architecture', echoed Fry in the foreword to the exhibition catalogue: 'The purpose is to demonstrate the architect as PLANNER': '"Planning,"' he went on, 'is the key-word to a form of development peculiar to our own time.'

---

[138] Ibid., p.75.

[139] Daniel Ritschel, *The Politics of Planning: The Debate on Economic Planning in Britain in the 1930s* (Oxford, 1997).

[140] 'Physical planning' as a phrase and a concept has attracted significantly less attention than 'visual planning', though to contemporaries the two techniques and critiques were fundamentally linked. See IRM McCallum (ed.), *Physical Planning: The Ground Work of a New Technique* (1945).

[141] 'Arthur Trystan Edwards', *AR* (May 1973), p.344.

THE ARCHITECTURAL MIND 383

It stood for the 'co-ordination of every part and aspect of a building, its site, its structure, its equipment and the order of its apartments, and through all these the life of its occupants.'[142] Gavin Stamp later dismissed this 'worship of Planning' as an example of Scott's 'unthinking acceptance of many of the orthodoxies and tendencies of his day'.[143] Such a characterization of this attitude as 'unthinking', however, is more revealing of Stamp's attitude in the late 1970s toward the post-war architect-planners' perceived assaults on the historic city. It is an anachronistic perspective on the quotation's original context.[144]

If we take Scott's emphasis seriously in his own terms, we will understand better how contemporaries felt about their practice and professional role in the 1920s and 1930s. The architect-as-planner argument was a substantial one made by Scott in greater detail during the RIBA's centenary celebrations which accompanied the 'International Architecture' exhibition. In a speech to the Centenary Conference, he stressed that 'the great need of the moment is for planning and tidiness. If we, as a nation, could get some kind of planning into our efforts, then I feel that art will be found to have arrived naturally and without conscious effort.' Through planning, 'the architect, if he is permitted, can make a great and valuable contribution to public service'.[145] London, Scott continued, was 'rich in opportunities for planning; rapid transport by road and rail has so altered conditions that new problems have to be faced'.[146] The Thames riverside, in particular the south side of its central portion around Charing Cross and Waterloo, and including the south bank of the Surrey side of the river, was ripe for development: 'A great change is going to take place here, and although the river front will be the first to change, it should not be considered as a detached unit, complete in itself, but as part of a general scheme of which it will eventually form only a portion.'[147] Scott's framing of his speech underlined the political dimension of the architectural mind. As Lucy Hewitt has observed, planning history has tended to avoid 'all but the most cursory engagement with questions of power or theorizations of government', thereby ignoring a much wider field of activity outside chronicles of the rise of the profession, its

---

[142] Giles Gilbert Scott, 'Foreword' in ML Anderson (ed.), *International Architecture*, p.9.

[143] Gavin Stamp, 'Giles Gilbert Scott: The Problem of "Modernism"' in Gavin Stamp (ed.), *AD Profiles: Britain in the Thirties* vol.49 no.10–11 (1979), p.72.

[144] A period ambitiously revised by Otto Saumarez Smith in *Boom Cities: Architect-Planners and the Politics of Radical Urban Renewal in 1960s Britain* (Oxford, 2019).

[145] 'The President's Inaugural Address', *JRIBA* (8 December 1934), p.156.

[146] Ibid., p.157.   [147] Ibid.

384   DESIGNS ON DEMOCRACY

institutionalization, and its early achievements.[148] The implications of democratization—on political institutions, architectural institutions, and on architectural practice and professionalism in relation to the wider polity— were nevertheless, as we have seen, actively, even frenetically, discussed by architects in the 1920s and 1930s, and these conversations encompassed planning. Histories of town planning have tended to overstress professional boundaries which were being contested at the time.[149] There remained in spite of the formal professionalization of town planning, however, a strong architectural conception of civic design and planning, indeed predicated on the public role that the architectural profession was seeking to define. The different rhetorics at play were important in terms of self-understanding and political status, but their boundaries were shifting. Many contemporaries attempted to articulate a difference, especially by the 1930s, between civic design and professional town planning in the Garden City idiom, despite their common intellectual and practical origins, and overlapping agendas: the 'art' of civic design, as Trystan Edwards declared, was distinct from the 'science' of town planning, and this was a delineation also drawn by Thomas Sharp. The assertiveness of this distinction was often projected back onto the more fluid debates of the 1910s and 1920s.

Civic design was an articulation of a New Liberal theorization of government. To explain how, we must look beyond the confines of London's architectural culture and discourse to the centre of New Liberalism in the north-west of England, particularly Lancashire. Here, despite the city's own politically conservative traditions, Liverpool University and specifically the School of Architecture under Charles Herbert Reilly's management and Lord Leverhulme's patronage was an epicentre of this progressivism. CP Scott's *Manchester Guardian* also promoted a New Liberal agenda, and was supportive of urban improvement ideas in particular.[150] Scott—uncle to Geoffrey Scott—as Percy Worthington would later recall, had done 'a great deal for Architecture in

---

[148] Lucy Hewitt, 'The History of Planning and the Politics of History', http://socialhistoryblog. com/the-history-of-planning-and-the-politics-of-history-by-lucy-hewitt/ [accessed 3 June 2020]; Hewitt, 'Ordering the Urban Body: Professional Planning in Early Twentieth-Century Britain', *Social History* 41.3 (2016), pp.304–18.

[149] *Transactions of the Royal Institute of British Architects Town Planning Conference* 1910, facsimile edn. 2011, with introduction by William Whyte, n.p; Whyte, 'The 1910 Royal Institute of British Architects' Conference: A Focus for International Town Planning?', *Urban History* 39.1 (2012), pp.149–65.

[150] 'Mr Carnegie's "City Beautiful"', *Manchester Guardian* (9 December 1903), p.12; 'The City Beautiful: New Islington Hall Address', *Manchester Guardian* (5 February 1906), p.5; or 'The City Beautiful', *Manchester Guardian* (30 November 1906), p.3, a lecture by Patrick Geddes on 'Civics and Arts' at Manchester Art Gallery.

his paper'.[151] In Lancashire, and in London, the early Progressive Era of the United States in the 1890s was influential among reformers. A key ambition of this Progressive effort was the creation of the 'City Beautiful'—an idea derived from Arts and Crafts discourse—a sustained campaign of urban improvement, a central tenet of which was the creation in turn of 'Civic Centres', deliberately planned and grouped municipal buildings and public amenity, typically in a Beaux-Arts-inspired classical language, archetypical examples being Daniel Burnham's 'White City' for the World's Columbia Exhibition, 1893, his subsequent plan for Chicago fifteen years later, Walter Burley Griffin's proposals for Canberra in 1912, and Lutyens's plans for Imperial New Delhi for the British Raj.[152]

The network of progressives in Lancashire extended to the capital, and London was another focus of the 'City Beautiful' movement. It embarked on reconstructing itself as a capital worthy of Empire.[153] The 'New London' was heralded by substantial central improvement projects—the laying out of the Mall from Admiralty Arch by Aston Webb being a well-known example, but more significantly through municipal enterprise too—the LCC's development of the Strand and its northern precinct into the Kingsway/Aldwych being the pioneering project of the Holborn-to-Strand Improvement Scheme instigated by the Liberal and socialist coalition of 'Progressives' who dominated the nascent Council between 1899 and 1907. Indeed, as Chanin argues, the LCC was forged as part of this aspiration of 'bettering' London: 'It represented the first real determination to make London something better than an agglomeration of local vestries...'[154]

The Kingsway development, despite its ambition, was felt to have been of only limited success. The LCC continued to foster building projects throughout the interwar years in pursuit of making the 'New London'.[155] We must understand the anxieties around the Crown's rebuilding of Regent Street in this context too, which was refashioned as the 'first street of the Empire'.[156] It is notable that the leaders of the Liverpool School, Adshead and

---

[151] RIBA, Librarian's Papers, 6.4, Box 1, letter from Percy Worthington to EJ 'Bobby' Carter, 16 January 1932.

[152] For an early application of the civic centre in a British context, see NE Shasore, 'Southampton Civic Centre: Patronage and Place in the Interwar Architecture of Public Service' in Elain Harwood and Alan Powers (eds.), *Twentieth Century Architecture: The Architecture of Public Service* 13 (2018), pp.41–62.

[153] Eileen Chanin, *Capital Designs: Australia House and Visions of an Imperial London* (Melbourne, 2018).

[154] Ibid., p.17.

[155] Ibid. Also see Eileen Chanin, 'Regulation: The New London' in Jessica Kelly and Neal Shasore (eds.), *Reconstruction: Architecture, Society and the aftermath of the First World War* (Bloomsbury: London, 2022), forthcoming.

[156] Rappaport, 'Art, Commerce, or Empire?', p.96.

386 DESIGNS ON DEMOCRACY

Reilly in particular, took a great interest in the project. There were other focuses for these debates too—the work of the New Delhi Planning Committee, out of which Lutyens's Delhi grew, being a notable example which had implications for the aspirations of the imperial metropolis. Certainly it established Lutyens's credentials as an urban designer, and contextualizes his appointment as consulting architect for a number of improvement plans, including for both Waterloo and Charing Cross in the 1920s and 1930s.[157]

The picture of early planning, civic design, and urban improvement was complex and overlapping within the wider architectural culture discussed here. Significant lacunae in detailed historical analysis even of relatively well-known and extant projects 'have resulted in some misconceptions about the early planning movement'.[158] Simple equations between civic design and traditionalism, or Garden City planning and progressivism, are reductive—Trystan Edwards serving as a case in point. The evidence suggests that, as in Lancashire, civic design—despite its associations with Empire and autocracy—also contained a New Liberal critique, allied to other 'progressive' attitudes which percolated through interwar debates about planning and urban development, even if they grew more and more distant from explicit party politics. They inflected the discourse more widely, depositing another 'strange survival' of English Liberalism in interwar architectural culture.[159]

A common set of attitudes and assumptions about urban planning and development in relation to rural development and land use were brought to the fore by the debate about cross-river traffic and the development of the south side of the river. Liberals were deeply engaged with the land question, although, as Paul Readman has argued, the novelty of New Liberalism's collectivist ideals in respect of the land question has been overstated; this had been part of Liberal thought in the nineteenth century too.[160] Nevertheless, there was a growing consensus about the need to reform systems of land ownership.[161] The policy of land valuation in David Lloyd George's People's Budget (1909) is now infamous, along with the land campaign of 1913 which promoted smallholdings, an idea—as discussed in Chapter 1—which attracted socially progressive design reformers like Lawrence Weaver who carried them forward into post-war policy enactments.

---

[157] Robert Grant Irving, *Indian Summer: Lutyens, Baker, and Imperial Delhi* (New Haven, 1981).
[158] Beaufoy, ' "Order out of chaos", p.138.
[159] EHH Green and Duncan Tanner (eds.), *The Strange Survival of Liberal England: Political Leaders, Moral Values and the Reception of Economic Debate* (Cambridge, 2007).
[160] Paul Readman, 'The Edwardian Land Question' in Matthew Cragoe and Paul Readman (eds.), *The Land Question in Britain* (Basingstoke, 2010), p.194.
[161] Timothy Brittain-Catlin, *The Edwardians and Their Houses* (2020).

THE ARCHITECTURAL MIND   387

There was, however, also an urban dimension to the land question, relating primarily to compensation and compulsory purchase for public amenity. Ideals of concentrated land ownership vested in public authorities for public purposes became a recurring theme in the interwar years—underpinned by the ideal of public proprietorship and the aspiration for improved amenity—which were to manifest themselves in post-Second World War planning legislation.[162]

Crucially, then, bound up in the progressivism of the City Beautiful, civic design projects for urban improvement often had a New Liberal inflection. Architectural commentary on improvements was couched in its language; critiques of *laissez-faire* and vested interests, anxieties about hyper-commercialism and its effects on the city, the centrality of the public, the need for better amenity—all permeate the architectural press and the comment columns. Moreover, the aesthetic dimension, among its more sophisticated adherents, was not hedonistic but imbued with ethical imperatives, such as Geoffrey Scott and Trystan Edwards had tested. The political iconography of civic art, therefore, was complex. The Beaux-Arts city which civic designers sought to make was 'often associated with democracy, peace and social justice'.[163] This often led in turn to profoundly racist 'civilizing' and imperialist exclusionary rhetorics and practices—in the United States, of African American populations; in New Delhi, of the Indian population.

Leslie Scott, incidentally a former Conservative MP for Liverpool Exchange and an influential jurist, was another central figure in this debate. In the 1910s, Scott was vocal in the Tory land reform movement, later chairing a Reconstruction Committee on the Acquisition and Valuation of Land for Public Purposes in 1917.[164] This committee pressed for easing the methods of compulsory purchase (and clarifying a system of fair compensation) when land was required for the public interest. In the 1920s, Scott was a founding member of the CPRE, and an active proponent of the Town and Country Planning Act (1932), writing an essay in support of the bill entitled 'Planning the Whole Country: The Economic Case' in which he

---

[162] This counteracts a view that the 'urban land reform campaign was a failure before the First World War and during the interwar period it died as a major political movement' as Roland Quinnalt has argued. See Roland Quinnalt, 'London and the Land Question, c.1890–1914', in Cragoe and Readman (eds.), *The Land Question*, pp.168–181, p.177.

[163] Wolfgang Sonne, *Representing the State: Capital City Planning in the Early Twentieth Century* (Munich, 2003), p.288.

[164] Leslie Scott, *First Report of the Committee Dealing with the Law and Practice Relating to the Acquisition and Valuation of Land for Public Purposes* (1918). He had been active in these debates from at least the 1910s.

388 DESIGNS ON DEMOCRACY

advocated for regional planning and proactive development schemes.[165] It was these credentials which will have recommended Scott as the chair of the LCC's Charing Cross Bridge Advisory Committee issue in 1930 (the Council at this time was still under the control of the Municipal Reform Party). The Scott Committee—whose debates of course proved inconclusive— has been taken as demonstrative of 'the highly conservative nature of town planning at the time', but this underplays the serious intellectual engagement with the substantial issues raised by its chair and other protagonists, including Giles Gilbert Scott.[166] Leslie Scott's work in urban policy and land use fits into a much longer narrative of twentieth-century town planning, also obscured by an overemphasis on 'progressivism' allied to professionalization; in the 1940s, Scott chaired a commission on Land Utilisation in Rural Areas, resulting in one of the three seminal reports (along with Barlow and Uthwatt) which helped to frame the revolutionary legislation of the Town and Country Planning Acts (1944, 1947). Contiguous with and analogous to the Liberal William Beveridge, though on a more modest scale, Scott's trajectory is instructive for an architectural and planning history of the first half of the twentieth century as interested in continuity as it is in rupture.

Road, Rail, and River

Herbert Morrison, from his earliest days in office at the LCC, was 'exceedingly anxious for a great clean-up on the South side', envisaging a 'river terrace for pedestrians right along and a worthy development all along the riverside which would enormously improve the view from the north side of the river'.[167] The underlying idea was that the land adjacent to County Hall and between the two bridges, which had generated such controversy in early twentieth-century local and national politics, should be a showcase for public amenity and good municipal development. For these reasons, the south bank became a testbed for progressive developmental control—for the

---

[165] PA Landon (rev. Marc Brodie), 'Sir Leslie Scott', *ODNB* (January 2008), https://www.oxforddnb.com/view/10.1093/ref:odnb/9780198614128.001.0001/odnb-9780198614128-e-35992 [accessed 3 June 2020]. See 'Planning the Whole Country', *The Times* (25 May 1932), p.11.

[166] Iain Jackson and Jessica Holland, *The Architecture of Edwin Maxwell Fry and Jane Drew: Twentieth Century Architecture, Pioneer Modernism and the Tropics* (2016), p.36.

[167] 'Mr Morrison's Vision of Thames Improvements', *Daily Telegraph* (13 April 1934), p.15.

THE ARCHITECTURAL MIND 389

ability of major local authorities like the LCC to guide development in urban central areas without the need to seek authority from national government. It was, after all, intergovernmental politics that had dogged not only the resolution of the Charing Cross Bridge issue but also Waterloo Bridge in parallel. More widely, therefore, questions about riverside development on the south bank were cast as, and represented, the maturation of the institution of the LCC under Labour, reforming and expanding the machinery of London government through the physical extension of County Hall. Plans to expand County Hall had been developed under the Municipal Reform Party in 1931 but abandoned in light of the curtailment of public works prompted by the Slump. The scheme was picked up in 1934 and at this point Giles Gilbert Scott was brought in, having 'already advised the LCC on architectural and town planning matters', acting strictly as a consultant.[168] Though the bulk of the work fell to the LCC architect, Frederick Robert Hiorns, Scott proposed a number of traffic improvements to go with the extension project: he proposed 'turning Belvedere Road into a private road where it passed between County Hall and the new buildings, and by making a "traffic circus" at the junction of Westminster Bridge and York Roads'.[169] These suggestions were in the end adopted in the post-war period.[170]

The significance of Herbert Morrison and the LCC's decision to develop the south bank lies in the precedent it would set for compulsory acquisition of land. Although the principle of compulsory acquisition of land by local authorities was well established, it was in many regards unresolved. In July 1934, the Highways Committee of the LCC, chaired by Richard Coppock, presented the Council with plans for the acquisition of land neighbouring County Hall between Westminster and Waterloo Bridges. It required, in Morrison's view, control 'vested in a single owner': 'The Council as owners would behave as good public-spirited ground landlords, and stimulate a worthy development of a unique part of London', the most significant improvement since the development of Kingsway at the start of the century.[171] Though many local authorities outside London had obtained powers to acquire land in anticipation of future needs without specifying any particular purpose, this had not really happened in London (though the

---

[168] 'The New County Offices: North and South Blocks' in Hermione Hobhouse (ed.), *Survey of London Monograph 17, County Hall*, (London, 1991), pp.103–9. *British History Online*, http://www.british-history.ac.uk/survey-london/bk17/pp103-109 [accessed 4 June 2020].
[169] Ibid.   [170] Ibid.
[171] 'Improvement of London: River Promenade and Gardens', *The Times* (16 July 1934), p.9.

390   DESIGNS ON DEMOCRACY

Council could and had acquired powers for specified purposes). Morrison therefore resisted opposition calls to develop and publish a scheme in advance of permission: 'it would a great mistake to produce a scheme of development before Parliament had granted powers to acquire the land. There would inevitably arise great controversy between different schools of thought, which invariably take place on any question of aesthetics.'[172] Parliament would take fright and kill the scheme, as it had done with Charing Cross and for many years with Waterloo. 'If', Morrison continued, 'the Council became the owners of the property, a proper scheme of development must be evolved in relation to the realities of the situation.'[173] This is significant in light of the later land nationalization programme in which development by private individuals was forbidden until expressly permitted by the planning authority, and in which powers of compulsory purchase were strengthened.

From the perspective of a land reformer and in light of his recent experience with the Charing Cross Bridge Advisory Committee, Leslie Scott publicly urged the Council to produce detailed plans:

> it will be a great thing to make a start which will permit of a demonstration: for seeing is so much the essence of believing in the architectural planning of a city. If we are to create a public opinion in support of the wider scheme there is no better means building a first instalment of it, for people to look at it.[174]

Scott had previously advocated more joined-up thinking on these issues—in an interview with the *Manchester Guardian* in April 1934 he had stressed 'that an inquiry should be opened at once before any expenditure is made in re-building sites which may have to be developed in an entirely different way for making the new Charing Cross Bridge and for re-planning the south side of the river.'[175]

Morrison's approach won out, and the LCC eventually acquired significant holdings along the south shore. Proposals were developed and eventually published in November 1938 with a recommendation to acquire further land. Projected works included the embankment of the Thames, the widening and alignment of the Waterloo Bridge approach, the widening of York Road, and the riverside promenade, 100 feet deep with a footway, which

---

[172] 'The South Bank Scheme', *The Times* (23 July 1934), p.19.   [173] Ibid.
[174] 'South Side of the Thames', *The Times* (16 July 1934), p.8.   [175] Ibid.

Morrison had earlier suggested. These proposals would cost £1.629 million, and the Ministry of Transport agreed to contribute 60 per cent of the £500,000 road improvements.[176] Though the LCC would, it was proposed, be the sole landlord, sites would be developed by individual lessees: 'Apart from office and other commercial buildings it is expected that public buildings will be erected and a number of inquiries have already been made.'[177] As the *AJ* reported, the Council's proposals had been designed not to preclude the construction of a new bridge at Charing Cross, and had been 'very conscious of the need for obtaining well-proportioned blocks of buildings, arranged in such a manner as to take advantage of the opportunity presented by the rebuilding of Waterloo Bridge and the recent building development adjacent to the area'.[178]

Morrison's plans for the south bank, however, were curtailed by the onset of war in 1939. In January 1940, while president of the RA, Edwin Lutyens convened a Planning Committee of architect academicians alongside other invited experts to consider the question of post-war reconstruction. The Committee was chaired by Lutyens himself, and Charles Bressey, former chief engineer to the Ministry of Transport, assumed the position of vice-chair. Bressey and Lutyens had, between 1935 and 1937, collaborated on a Highways Development Report commissioned by the Ministry of Transport in 1934.[179] As Christopher Hussey, in his role as Lutyens's biographer, later recalled, 'an incident of this assignment was a flight over London—Lutyens's first and only adventure into the air. He did not enjoy it, mistrusted committing his 14 stone of weight to the heavens. But the aerial view of architecture fascinated him.'[180] Published in 1938 the Bressey–Lutyens Report, as it was commonly known, was a comprehensive survey of London's road system's needs, intended to bring forward recommendations that would serve Greater London for thirty years. It took in analysis of 250 existing schemes for metropolitan traffic improvements by over 150 local authority and regional committees that had been recently published. It was also asked to take into consideration cross-river communication and new riverside embankments.[181]

---

[176] 'Embankment on South Side: Scheme Approved by LCC', *The Times* (16 November 1938), p.16.

[177] 'New Embankment Scheme', *The Times* (21 March 1939), p.49.

[178] 'South Bank Improvement Scheme', *AJ* (17 November 1938), p.788.

[179] Charles Bressey, *Highway Development Survey 1937 (Greater London)* (1938).

[180] Hussey, *Lutyens*, p.549.

[181] 'The Bressey Report', *The Times* (17 May 1938), pp.33–5.

392   DESIGNS ON DEMOCRACY

With the disruption caused by the war, some of its key recommendations—including ring roads, roundabouts, and better links between centre and periphery—had not been fully explored. It was in part for this reason, therefore, that the RA Planning Committee took as its starting point the 1938 report. The Committee included some of the leading architects of the day: Giles Gilbert Scott, Albert Richardson, and Vincent Harris all served alongside younger progressives like Louis de Soissons, PD Hepworth, and Charles Holloway James. Curtis Green, Maufe, and Austen Hall—part of Lawrence Weaver's network of patronage—also participated, Hall acting as secretary to the Committee for its duration.

In August 1942, the Committee published an Interim Report alongside a display of plans and drawings at the Academy to publicize its work, expedited by the growing number of reconstruction plans emerging and competing for public attention, including the Modern Architectural Research Group (MARS) Plan and the LCC Plan for Greater London by Forshaw and Abercrombie, both of whom it should be said, were also nominal participants in the RA Committee.[182] The Committee had not, as Lutyens unambiguously declared in the report's foreword, 'attempted a town-planning scheme in the technical sense'.[183] It was instead a series of proposals developed 'from the architectural stand-point', a statement of 'the case for an architectural approach to a great opportunity'.[184]

The 'architectural approach' was, it was explicitly stated, derived from 'clear and harmonious civic design',[185] less concerned with the design of individual buildings themselves. The aim was to encourage London to profit from

> ...notable examples of good planning and building which already exist, and so give clearer expression to the leading motives of its vast and various activities. They [the Committee] feel sure of the support of enlightened public 'opinion' for foregrounding the 'aesthetic aspect'.[186]

---

[182] Junichi Hasegawa, 'Radical Reconstruction in 1940s Britain', *Twentieth-Century British History* 10.2 (1999), pp.137–61; John Pendlebury, 'Planning the Historic City: Reconstruction Plans in the United Kingdom in the 1940s', *Town Planning Review* 74.4 (October 2003), pp.371–93; John R Gold, 'The MARS Plans for London, 1933–1942: Plurality and Experimentation in the City Plans of the Early British Modern Movement', *Town Planning Review* 66.3 (July 1995), pp.243–67. Emmanuel Marmaras and Anthony Sutcliffe, 'Planning for Post-war London: The Three Independent Plans, 1942–3', *Planning Perspectives* 9.4 (1994), pp.431–53. Frank Mort, 'Fantasies of Metropolitan Life: Planning London in the 1940s', *Journal of British Studies* 43.1 (2004), pp.120–51.
[183] Edwin Lutyens, 'Foreword' in Royal Academy Planning Committee, *London Replanned* (London: Country Life, 1942), p.2.
[184] Ibid.
[185] 'A Nobler City' in Royal Academy Planning Committee, *London Replanned*, p.15.
[186] Ibid., p.27.

THE ARCHITECTURAL MIND   393

A new public authority, free from political caprice, would 'encourage architectural quality and establish purity and propriety in the design of buildings' to revive the 'spirit of English civic architecture';[187] this was a recurring motif in architectural discourse of the 1920s and 1930s, and indeed underlay the establishment of the RFAC in the mould of a 'committee of taste'. We saw this too in Raffles Davison's desire for a 'responsible controlling and directing power' for the urban development when establishing the London Society in 1912.[188] And the 'aesthetic' dimension, as we saw in the writings of Trystan Edwards, was far from hedonistic; the 'City Beautiful' was connected to New Liberal approaches to urban development.

The RA Committee had developed *inter alia* plans for a rationalized and expanded Piccadilly Circus, an arts centre at Covent Garden, and a new plaza connecting the British Museum to St George's Bloomsbury. These were proposals, in other words, for dramatic set-pieces in London, nodal points in an enhanced network of communication, predicated on major infrastructural development of ring roads, railways, and river communications. Among the various proposals was a new road bridge at Charing Cross—on which Lutyens had of course advised for the ill-fated LCC (Charing Cross Bridge) Bill in 1930—and an extended Trafalgar Square, a new roundabout on the Strand where it met Waterloo Bridge, as well as broader recommendations about the development of the southern side of the river in its central portion: 'embankments and gardens should be carried along both sides of the river; then, the shabbiness and confusion which degrade the south side could give place to a worthy architectural scheme which would immensely enhance the beauty of the capital, and would in time repay its cost by increasing site values'.[189]

The critical commentary on the RA's first offering was equivocal: the *Architect and Building News* could not decide whether 'the architectural treatment provides a basis of inspiration, or is on the contrary unsatisfying'.[190] John Summerson described the plans as 'bold, exciting, well worth seeing', despite a discomfort with the emphasis on symmetry and axiality.[191] There was, he wrote, 'no mistaking the seriousness of the general intention to carve symmetry into the irregular face of London, to give a patch here and a patch

---

[187] Ibid.
[188] Thomas Raffles Davison, 'The Opportunities of London' in Aston Webb (ed.), *London of the Future* (London: T Fisher Unwin Ltd, 1921), p.45.
[189] Royal Academy Planning Committee, *London Replanned*, p.18.
[190] 'Plan for London', *ABN* (16 October 1942), p.39.
[191] John Summerson, 'The Royal Academy Committee's Plan for London', *ABN* (30 October 1942), p.77.

394   DESIGNS ON DEMOCRACY

there a sense of nobility and Imperial affirmation', but he feared the sacrifice of what he called 'local symmetry'.[192]

Unambiguous in his condemnation, whilst in a sense elaborating on Summerson's theme, was Lionel Brett. In an excoriating assessment entitled 'The New Haussmann' published in the *AR*, he dismissed the 'boring axes and banal symmetries of the *Beaux-Arts*', the plan a 'reactionary absurdity', 'contemptuous' of meaningful precedent, luddite in its eschewal of technical analysis.[193] Brett's position was uncompromising, not least because he had begun to explore more radical Modernist approaches which would create constructive contrasts with historic fabric, representative of shifting preservationist attitudes.[194] It conformed too to the techniques of visual planning and townscape which characterized progressive architectural discourse in the 1940s, spearheaded by the Architectural Press's proprietor de Cronin Hastings, Nikolaus Pevsner, Gordon Cullen, and others. Townscape and 'visual planning', a subset of 'physical planning', was interested in the picturesque and in a form of critical regionalism in embryonic form. Brett lucidly articulated that, for a growing number of younger commentators and practitioners, the RA's approach was misguided and outmoded. However seductive this argument, and however much it may align with enduring tastes and prejudices, Brett's critical response ignored the context which this chapter has recovered. Neither Scott nor Lutyens, let alone others on the Committee, came to the question of reconstruction and planning without years of serious and critical engagement not only with the 'aesthetic' aspect, as Lutyens unhelpfully put it, but also with the 'technical' side, which Scott declaimed. Furthermore, as we saw not only in the case of Waterloo Bridge and in the RA's proposals but also in the manifestations of the Georgian imaginary, there was a different attitude to history and representationalism, one in which preservationism and development were elided, rather than strikingly contrasted. The merits or demerits of this approach, and the historian's preference for them, has obscured a more balanced historical analysis.

For Lutyens, at any rate, the Hausmannian badge was one worn with pride. And it was Hussey, the progenitor of the picturesque revival, who counteracted criticisms of Lutyens's plans with a line from Christopher Tunnard that to appreciate the picturesque 'we need the contrast of regularity'.[195] Nevertheless the RA's interim proposals mark a changing of the guard, a moment in

---

[192] Ibid.   [193] Lionel Brett, 'The New Haussmann', *AR* (January 1943), p.23.
[194] Saumarez Smith, *Boom Cities*, pp.124–58.   [195] Hussey, *Lutyens*, p.568.

THE ARCHITECTURAL MIND 395

which the constellation of the architectural establishment—Lutyens, Scott, Richardson—suddenly found themselves out of step, even derided. 'Civic design'—the architectural approach to planning—seemed obsolete, and even hedonistic in its emphasis on the aesthetic, summed up in Hall's exclamation that 'The sense of beauty must obliterate every other consideration', paraphrasing John Keats.[196] By the 1940s, more fluid and dynamic positions had begun to ossify.

After Lutyens's death at the start of 1944, Scott succeeded him in the chair and set about completing the Committee's final report and accompanying exhibition, *Road, River and Rail*. After Lutyens's 'aesthetic' approach, Scott proclaimed a greater focus on 'practical details'—on communications, by road, river, and rail, holistically considered with greater rhetorical clarity than before.[197] Yet in reality, Scott's approach deviated little from the basic lines that Lutyens had laid down. He was particularly interested in the inner Ring Road, first adumbrated in the Lutyens–Bressey Report, developed in the interim report and subsequently taken up by the LCC County of London Plan. The Ring Road would be punctuated by a series of junctions marked by 'circus' roundabouts which would give access to precincts and local areas.[198]

The roundabout or circus—this key feature of the new inner-city urban carscape—and the wider question of the integration of the motor vehicle with pedestrian needs were sources of contention, in particular to architect-motorists like Scott. Even Lutyens had insisted that they were controlled by a 'single mind'.[199] The idea of the 'circus' for the architectural and planning professions had a number of resonances which help to focus the argument of an at times unwieldy body of material. First and foremost, the circus was a tool of the civic designer and planner. The circus had a pedigree in the architecture of the Georgian period which had a particularly intense grip on the imaginations of architects and planners during this period: the residential circuses of the Woods in eighteenth-century Bath, of Dance the Younger in the City of London, and of Nash's junctions in Westminster at the intersections of Regent Street with Piccadilly and Oxford Street respectively. These were the formal exemplars for civic design. In the nascent

[196] RIBA, Scott Papers, ScGG/276/2, Royal Academy Planning Committee (1 of 2 folders), Austen Hall, 'A note on the work on the RA Planning Committee' (17 November 1942), appended to a letter from Austen Hall to Giles Gilbert Scott (18 November 1942), fo.121.

[197] Giles Gilbert Scott, 'Foreword' in Royal Academy Planning Committee, *Road, Rail and River in London* (1944), p.3.

[198] Ibid., pp.4–20.

[199] Charles Bressey, *Highway Development Survey 1937 (Greater London)* (1938), p.34. Lutyens provided examples of roundabout treatment in Appendix III of the report.

396   DESIGNS ON DEMOCRACY

town-planning profession 'circuses' were also synonymous with round-abouts. Raymond Unwin's Sollershot Circus at Letchworth Garden City, often claimed as the first roundabout, was in fact 'an intermediate stage between the traditional circus-with-central-feature, designed as an aesthetic device or pedestrian refuge, and the modern roundabout', more a tool of traffic management.[200] In the 1920s 'round-about' came to describe a method of clockwise traffic circulation in service of more seemly comport at busy junctions, distinct from the 'gyratory' nature prevailing in which motorists and pedestrians criss-crossed the circus junction to whichever opening they sought. Now the 'flow' of the stream of motorcars would be 'unimpeded' by keeping to the left.[201] Such traffic management systems were pioneered at Parliament Square, Hyde Park Corner, Trafalgar Square, and Piccadilly Circus.[202] These were interventions into the dense historic city; but they would also help to open up and guide development of the south side of the river, which at least in planners' minds was considerably less developed. The bridges of Lambeth and Westminster were keys to unlocking this potential. The superimposition of a circus on city plans and maps served as a shorthand for the sanitizing, often uncompromising rhetorics of the civic designers' improvements, but they were also understood from the perspective of the 'road view.'

For the RA Planning Committee's work, Scott envisaged multi-level circuses, suggesting some knowledge of American and European modernist discourses on the separation of the motor vehicle from the pedestrian (Fig. 6.32). In Scott's circuses (Fig. 6.33), shops would be placed on the 'ground' floor, with the ring round running beneath; above would be a higher level for pedestrians 'to cross the circus in any direction without any ramps or subways. Direct access is obtained from the surrounding precincts and from the converging roads without any crossing of traffic.'[203] Crucially, therefore, the order and rationalization that the ring round would bring would not unduly disrupt existing localities. The circuses would serve as 'strategic points of great value to the district around them', points of contact between 'the various areas of precincts that lie between the converging main roads', developed as 'main centres of communal activity'—'in fact, the old market place idea, developed and improved to fit modern life and

---

[200] Morrison and Minnis, *Carscapes*, p.327.
[201] 'The "Round-Abouts"', *The Times* (28 April 1926), p.17.
[202] Morrison and Minnis, *Carscapes*, p.335.
[203] Royal Academy Planning Committee, *Road, Rail and River in London* (1944), p.13.

Fig. 6.32 'A section of the sunk ring road round inner London, showing the banks of the cutting turfed and planted with trees, ramps connecting with a three-level roundabout', drawing by AC Webb, Royal Academy Planning Committee, *Road, Rail and River in London* (1944), p.5, image courtesy of Penn State University Libraries

conditions', whose use would be varied 'according to the locality'.[204] This conception of the precinct, whilst not articulated in great detail, clearly owed something to Abercrombie's innovation of the 'neighbourhood unit'. Indeed, a caption to a perspective of the south bank from Lambeth to Blackfriars—with a series of connecting circuses and junctions at 'sub-arterial' roads set back from the river front—noted that 'the unplanned areas bounded by new and improved roads are to be developed later as community and neighbourhood units'.[205]

---

[204] RIBA, Scott Papers, ScGG/276/2, Royal Academy Planning Committee (2 of 2 folders), memorandum by Giles Gilbert Scott entitled 'Traffic Circuses and Garages' (18 October 1943), fo.137 iv. Text from this and others of Scott's memoranda was incorporated into the final report, *Road, Rail and River in London*.
[205] Royal Academy Planning Committee, *Road, Rail and River in London*, p.10.

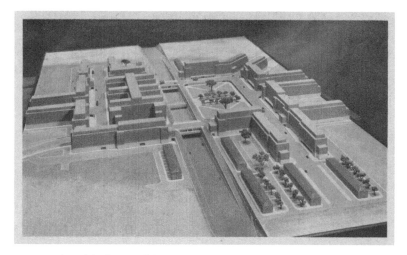

Fig. 6.33 'Model of a roundabout at a junction with the ring road', maker and photographer unknown, Royal Academy Planning Committee, *Road, Rail and River in London* (1944), p.15, image courtesy of Penn State University Libraries

The south bank (Fig. 6.34) would accommodate a new railway terminus (it was proposed once again that Charing Cross Station would be removed and replaced with a large circus, an 'architectural feature with underground garages entered through archways').[206] Respecting Morrison's intentions for a garden promenade on the river front, it was nonetheless felt 'advisable to avoid continuous garden treatment from the County Hall to London Bridge, which the Committee feel would be monotonous' (Fig. 6.35).[207] There would be room for some commercial building—'Buildings that front directly on the water have a peculiar charm'[208]—and Scott envisaged 'an important building...between the two bridges [Charing Cross and Waterloo] with part of the riverside gardens in front of it'.[209] In the accompanying perspectives, it is clear Scott imagined a building which would prefigure his last major riverside intervention, the Bankside Power Station (1947) (Fig. 6.36). Though beyond the geographical and narrative scope here, it emphasizes the importance attached to the question of riverside development by architects in this period. Scott much admired George Dance the Younger's plans for a 'Double Bridge' and a system of commercial quays and wharves

---

[206] Ibid., *London Replanned*, p.8.   [207] Ibid., *Road, Rail and River*, p.10.
[208] Ibid.   [209] Ibid., p.11.

Fig. 6.34 'Plan for the south bank of the Thames from Lambeth to Blackfriars', Royal Academy Planning Committee, *Road, Rail and River in London* (1944), p.8, image courtesy of Penn State University Libraries

running along the river front in the City.[210] There are perhaps echoes of this in his ambitions for Waterloo and Charing Cross.

---

[210] RIBA, Scott Papers, ScGG/276/1, Royal Academy Planning Committee, Typescript of a lecture given by Scott at the Royal Academy, 'The City and the River' (16 October 1941), fo.35 ii. The perspective view of this proposal is in the British Library, see: British Library, Maps K. Top.21.31.4.11 TAB, 'View of London, with the Improvements of its Port'.

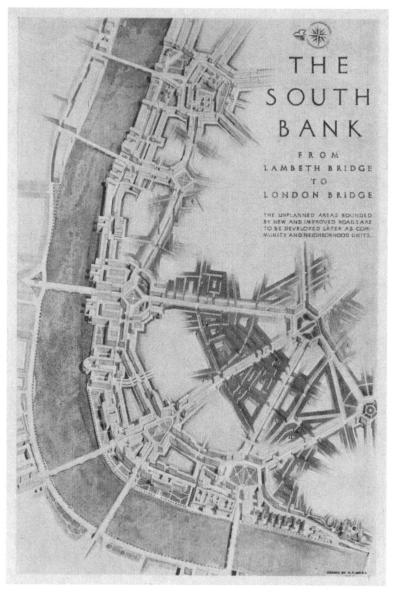

Fig. 6.35 'Isometric view of the south bank of the Thames between Lambeth and London Bridge', drawing AC Webb, Royal Academy Planning Committee, *Road, Rail and River in London* (1944), p.10, image courtesy of Penn State University Libraries

Fig. 6.36 'Waterloo Bridge, looking south, with Charing Cross Road Bridge on the right', drawing by AC Webb, Royal Academy Planning Committee, *Road, Rail and River in London* (1944), p.11, image courtesy of Penn State University Libraries

Although Lutyens had disavowed the 'technical' demands of town planning, Scott did engage with the legislative and financial implications of their sketch proposals. He assumed, for instance, 'powers of requisition of and complete unity of control over properties required for these great building operations'.[211] And the scheme—which would require a programme of public works financed through 'wealth-producing capital expenditure, and the temporary creation of credits for this purpose'—chimes with the economic assumptions shared by many in the construction industry.[212] Crucially, Scott also acknowledged the limitations of the architectural perspective—'we architects are tending to get too much involved in the sociological, and even political aspects that would well be left to sociologists and others'—returning to his repeated refrain that architects 'alone are trained to plan, and practice planning throughout their professional lives, and they alone have the imaginative qualification essential for good

[211] Ibid.   [212] Ibid.

402 DESIGNS ON DEMOCRACY

planning.[213] But this still implied a broad intellectual framework in terms which Summerson's rhetoric denied.

Road, Rail and River should have been the summative achievement of a particular paradigm of architecture and planning, and of a particular set of debates and proposals for central improvements in London, but—in part because of its timing—it was subsumed into a new dominating architectural and planning culture. The distinctive and creative work of the Committee and its embodiment of a changing relationship with the public were at the time and have subsequently been far too easily dismissed. This has had a distorting impact in turn on understandings of the 'architectural mind' as a whole.

Conclusion

The first chapter began with the British Empire Exhibition at Wembley; the final one ends just before the Festival of Britain a quarter of a century later, an event which is generally seen as 'both model and project for a future built by the emergent "Welfare State" after the ravages of the Second World War'.[214] The idea for an exhibition was publicly proposed by John Gloag in a letter to *The Times*—the exhibition would mark the centenary of 'the first occasion when the British Empire displayed to the world the results of its industrial enterprise'—and was also proposed by Gerald Barry in the form of an open letter to Stafford Cripps, then President of the Board of Trade, published in the *News Chronicle*.[215] Gloag and Cripps were both closely associated with Lawrence Weaver who had played such a central role in the organization and promotion of the Wembley Exhibition.

The narrative arc of this chapter has taken us from debates about the creation of 'The New London' as a grand late-nineteenth- and early twentieth-century imperial capital to the heralding of another kind of 'new London' in the post-1945 years, made manifest in the development of the South Bank, exemplified by Festival of Britain and the identification of this area as part

---

[213] RIBA, Scott Papers, ScGG/276/1, Royal Academy Planning Committee, letter from Scott to the Editor, *Architectural Design & Construction* (23 May 1944), fo.4.

[214] Nick Beech, '"Et Tu Peter?" Some Kinds of *Real*- (or not so) *Politik* at the Festival of Britain', *Journal of Architecture* 17.5 (2012), p.747.

[215] 'An Exhibition in 1951', *The Times* (11 September 1945), p.5. Gloag wrote, 'The next six years afford a great opportunity for our designers and manufacturers to be inventive, and for our statesmen to be far-sighted.'

THE ARCHITECTURAL MIND   403

of a pioneering Comprehensive Development Area by the LCC. These interventions were representative of at least two shifts: the securing of a Modernist hegemony on post-war design, and—as a corollary—the maturation of the discipline of town planning and the rise of the architect-planner. In reality, however, the prevailing paradigm of the interwar years did not dissipate; it remained a viable vision of 'alternative reconstruction' along civic design principles, and it indeed informed even the most representative 'Welfare State' plans. These were not distinct or discrete architectural cultures; they were enmeshed, overlapped, in dialogue with one another, especially when understood in a wider cultural field. Simplistic oppositions are unhelpful; for although Abercrombie might be praised for the foresight of the London Plan, his work in Plymouth (1943) was distinctly Beaux-Arts, as was his collaboration with Lutyens in the new plan for Hull (1945).[216]

There were continuities and contiguities from the early twentieth century which revisionist histories of mid-century British Modernism have struggled to see. They need to be drawn out. Britain's relationship with its Empire and the burgeoning Commonwealth is just one example. Although the Festival of Britain outwardly eschewed grand imperialist rhetorics, deliberately deploying narratives of 'national parochialism', inevitably Empire and the Commonwealth figured in the framing of the exhibition's significance and indeed its architecture.[217] The colonizing rhetorics of 'discovery' in the Dome of Discovery, the militarism of Games's 'Britannia' emblem; these had their immediate antecedents in Weaver's Palace of Industry and Herrick's lion.[218] These were intrinsic to the design reform movement right from its inception.

These spatial lexicons and visual languages could, of course, be strikingly different. The Empire Exhibition at Wembley, with monumental concrete palaces in a classical vocabulary, long axes and boulevards, borrowing much from the American City Beautiful, was a model itself for civic design principles. The Festival of Britain's South Bank site, by contrast, was an experiment in new techniques of urban landscaping and exhibition infrastructure. In a description of 'The South Bank Style', Lionel Brett

---

[216] Philip N Jones, ' "…a fairer and nobler City": Lutyens and Abercrombie's Plan for the City of Hull 1945', *Planning Perspectives* 13.3 (1998), pp.301–16.

[217] Jo Littler, ' "Festering Britain": The 1951 Festival of Britain, National Identity and the Representation of the Commonwealth' in Anandi Ramamurthy and Simon Faulkner (eds.), *Visual Culture and Decolonisation in Britain* (London: Routledge, 2006), pp.21–42 https://openaccess.city.ac.uk/id/eprint/6031/1/Jo%20Littler%20FOB.pdf [accessed 4 June 2020].

[218] Ibid.

404   DESIGNS ON DEMOCRACY

conjured an image of the festival site as one 'closed by no grandiose Palace of this or that', but instead characterized by the 'interplay between past and present, the solid and the evanescent, large spaces and little ones', creating a vintage architectural experience, indebted to Scandinavian 'New Empiricism', but rooted in the 'English tradition of landscaping', the picturesque of Townscape.[219] Moreover, the pseudo-monumentality of Wembley (as Siegfried Giedion would have characterized it) was mirrored by a 'New Monumentality' on the South Bank, later codified by Giedion and the Congrès Internationaux d'Architecture Moderne as a project for Modernism to find a representationalist architectural vocabulary that could articulate 'a building's moral and emotional functions in addition to its material functions'.[220]

The South Bank and its surrounding area, therefore, are productive sites for an analysis of how the architectural culture discussed in this book did not give way to, but rather was bound up in, a set of coalescing ideas about architecture and planning taken forward post-1945. The intense analysis of the loose site in central London between Westminster and Southwark, including the bridges at Waterloo and Charing Cross, exposes a number of tensions—tensions between the architectural aesthetics of civic design and the new picturesque theory of townscape and 'visual planning'; between the critique of laissez-faire and a burgeoning welfarist progressivism; between competing conceptions and imaginaries of the public; and between the representational possibilities and political iconographies of the city, nation, and Empire. All these critical positions had been articulated and creatively debated for decades.

This portion of the riverside was a cauldron of ideas and visions of the city. Sites and projects there were contested because they provided opportunities for visibility in the public sphere and demonstration of the architect's contribution to public amenity.

To the post-war historian of architecture and planning, the episodes described in this chapter and indeed the book as a whole should, taken together, serve as a reminder of longer trajectories in the twentieth century, ones which are not incidental or anecdotal but which can help both to unpack

---

[219] Lionel Esher, *A Broken Wave: The Rebuilding of England 1940–1980* (1981), p.303.
[220] 'In Search of a New Monumentality', *AR* (September 1948); Alan Powers, 'The Expression of Levity' in Elain Harwood and Alan Powers (eds.), *Twentieth Century Architecture: Festival of Britain* 5 (2001), p.54. The *AR* had published two articles on New Monumentality in 1948 and 1949: 'In Search of a New Monumentality', *AR* (September 1948), pp.117–28; Lewis Mumford, 'Monumentality, Symbolism, and Style', *AR* (April 1949), pp.173–80.

the emergence of Modernism and to problematize notions of its hegemony. The 1920s and 1930s, so easily reified as 'the interwar period', are not marooned on an inconsequential island but saw an intense period of serious intellectual engagement as architects reflected on the distinctive contours of their professional and public role. They identified and confronted ethical and social questions and contradictions, and offered holistic understandings of historical process.

The 1920s and the 1930s witnessed the formation of the modern architectural profession, a development shaped by the perceived and constructed needs and wants of the public—a particular expression of a mass democracy. The fostering and guiding of public debate about architecture were fundamental to the status of the architect. Whilst this could often be polarized stylistically for rhetorical effect, the crucial interplay between the architectural mind and an architecturally minded public was much more sophisticated and broad ranging. It touched on industrial design and imperial trade, the wider economy of the construction industry, the delivery of social housing, and significant interventions into urban improvement predicated explicitly on community interest. Above all, its dynamic came from a sense of the city as a rich historical palimpsest of global ideological resonance—as a context for the embedding of civic values. These concerns drove the architectural profession's designs on democracy.

Bibliography

Primary Sources

Archival Sources

Architectural Association Archives (AA Archives)
Birr Castle Archives, Papers of the 6th Earl of Rosse
British Library, National Life Stories Collection
Emmanuel College Archives, University of Cambridge
Georgian Group Archives
Hansard
History of Advertising Trust, Advertising Association Archive
The Huntington Library, Katharine A Esdaile Papers
King's College London, Liddell Hart Military Archives
Labour History Archive and Study Centre
Lambeth Council Archives, Housing Centre Trust Records
Lambeth Palace Library
London Metropolitan Archives (LMA)
London Society Archives (LSA)
Merthyr Tydfil Library
The National Archives (TNA)
National Library of Australia
Newcastle University Thomas Sharp Archive
Oxford, Bodleian Libraries
RIBA Drawings and Archive Collection (RIBA)
Society for the Protection of Ancient Buildings Archives
University of Glasgow, Archives & Special Collections
University of Kent, Hewlett Johnson Papers
University of Liverpool Archives
Wellcome Library
Wornum Family Private Collection

Databases/Reference Works
Oxford Dictionary of National Biography
Grove Art Online
Oxford Dictionary of Modern Design

Newspapers and Periodicals
Advertiser's Weekly
Architect and Builder's Journal (*ABJ*)
Architect and Building News (*ABN*)

408 BIBLIOGRAPHY

Architects' Journal (AJ)
Architectural Association Journal (AAJ)
Architectural Design and Construction (later *Architectural Design*)
Architectural History (AH)
Architectural Review (AR)
Architecture
The Builder
Building
Building Industries Survey
Cambridge Review
Commercial Art: A magazine devoted to art as a selling force
Country Life
Design for To-Day
DIA Quarterly Journal
Estates Review
Financial Times
Fortnightly Review
Horizon
Journal of the Ministry of Agriculture
Journal of the Royal Institute of British Architects (JRIBA)
Journal of the Royal Society of Arts
Journal of the Society of Architectural Historians (JSAH)
Kalendar of the Royal Institute of British Architects
The Keystone
Library Association Record
The Listener
The Nineteenth Century and After
Parthenon
Portico
Partisan Review
Thirties Society Journal
The Times Trade and Engineering Supplement: British Empire Exhibition Section
Town Planning Review (TPR)
Transactions of the Royal Institute of British Architects (TRIBA)

Websites/Blogs

'Modern British Studies at Birmingham: Working Paper No.1' (February 2014) www. birmingham.ac.uk/Documents/college-artslaw/history/mbs/MBS-Birmingham-Working-Paper-1.pdf [accessed 30 July 2015]

Barker, Stephen, 'The Oxford Vigilance Committee Report of November 1916 and fears over declining moral values in the city', http://ww1centenary.oucs.ox.ac. uk/?p=3614 [accessed 25 May 2020]

Hewitt, Lucy, 'The History of Planning and the Politics of History', http://socialhistoryblog.com/the-history-of-planning-and-the-politics-of-history-by-lucy-hewitt/ [accessed 3 June 2020]

BIBLIOGRAPHY   409

Hobhouse, Hermione (ed.), *Survey of London Monograph 17, County Hall* (London, 1991), pp.103–9. *British History Online*, http://www.british-history.ac.uk/survey-london/bk17/pp.103–9 [accessed 4 June 2020]
https://darkmatterlabs.org/ [accessed 6 June 2020]
https://edgedebate.com/ [accessed 6 June 2020]
'The Rebuilding of Piccadilly Circus and the Regent Street Quadrant', in FHW Sheppard (ed.), *Survey of London: Volumes 31 and 32, St James Westminster, Part 2* (London, 1963), pp. 85–100; *British History Online*, http://www.british-history.ac.uk/survey-london/vols31-2/pt2/pp.85-100 [accessed 10 June 2020]

Grey Literature

Bressey, Charles, *Highway Development Survey 1937 (Greater London)* (London, 1938)
Building Industries National Council, *The Case Against 'Economy' (revised edition) Building Industry Council of Review: Interim Report* (London, 1930)
'Findings of the RIBA Ethics and Sustainable Development Commission' (2018), https://www.architecture.com/knowledge-and-resources/resources-landing-page/ribas-ethics-and-sustainable-development-commission-final-report [accessed 6 June 2020]
'Forty-eighth annual report of the Local Government Board, 1918–1919' (HMSO, 1919), comd.413, p.150
Frank, H, 'Interim and Final Reports of the Committee on Crown Lands and Public Lands' (1922), p.7, *House of Commons Parliamentary Papers Online*, http://gateway.aa1.proquest.com/openurl?url_ver=Z39.88-2004&res_dat=xri:hcpp&rft_dat=xri:hcpp:rec:1922-025497 [Cmd. 1689] VII.225, [accessed 8 July 2015]
Georgian Group, *First Annual Report* (London: Georgian Group, 1939)
Georgian Group, *Second Annual Report* (London: Georgian Group, 1940)
London County Council Proposed Road Bridge at Charing Cross: Report by the Chairman of the Charing Cross Bridge Scheme Advisory Committee (March 1931)
Minutes of Evidence Taken Before the Royal Commission on the Geographical Distribution of the Industrial Population 19 (London: HMSO, 1938), pp.596–617
Report of the Royal Commission on Cross-River Traffic in London (London: HMSO, 1926)
Royal Academy Planning Committee, *London Replanned* (London: Country Life, 1942)
Royal Academy Planning Committee, *Road, Rail and River* (London: Country Life, 1944)
Scott, Leslie, *First Report of the Committee Dealing with the Law and Practice Relating to the Acquisition and Valuation of Land for Public Purposes* (London: HMSO, 1918)
Warne, EJD, *Review of the Architects (Registration) Acts 1931–1969* (London: HMSO, 1993)

Books

Anderson, ML (ed.), *'Everyday Things' 1936: Catalogue to the Exhibition Arranged by the Royal Institute of British Architects* (London: Royal Institute of British Architects, 1936)

410 BIBLIOGRAPHY

Ashbee, CR, *Where the Great City Stands: A Study in the New Civics* (London: Essex House Press, 1917)

Blomfield, Reginald, *Memoirs of an Architect* (London: Macmillan, 1932)

Bossom, Alfred, *Building to the Skies: The Romance of the Skyscraper* (London: Studio Publications, 1934)

The Building Industries National Council Year Book 1935 (London: 1936)

The Building Industries National Council Year Book 1938 (London: 1939)

The Business Features of Wembley (Compiled by the Investors' Chronicle) (London, 1924)

Byron, Robert, *How We Celebrate the Coronation* (London: Architectural Press, 1937)

Carr-Saunders, Alexander Morris, and Wilson, Paul Alexander, *The Professions* (Oxford: Clarendon, 1933)

Copnall, Edward Bainbridge, *A Sculptors' Manual* (Oxford: Pergamon, 1971)

de Cronin Hastings, Hubert, *Caricatures* (London: Architectural Press, 1925)

Democracy's Other War. By famous contributors on vital subjects (Calvacade's Towards the Future Series) (London: Argus Press, 1942)

Design in Modern Life and Industry: The Year Book of the Design and Industries Association 1924–25 (London: Benn, 1925)

The Development of the Civil Service: Lectures Delivered Before the Society of Civil Servants, 1920–21 (London: PS King & Sons, 1922)

Donald, Robert, *The Imperial Press Conference in Canada* (London: Hodder & Stoughton, 1921)

Economic Reform Club and Institute, *'The World We Want': A Conference held in London on May 7th, 8th and 9th, 1943, under the joint auspices of the Industrial Christian Fellowship and the Economic Reform Club & Institute* (London: Economic Reform Club and Institute, 1943)

Edwards, Arthur Trystan, *The Things Which Are Seen: A Revaluation of the Visual Arts* (London: Philip Allan & Co., 1921), 1st edn.

Edwards, Arthur Trystan, *Good and Bad Manners in Architecture* (London: Philip Allan & Co., 1924) 1st edn.

Edwards Arthur Trystan, *Sir William Chambers* (London: E Benn, 1924)

Edwards, Arthur Trystan, *Three Rows of Tape: A Social Study of the Lower Deck* (London: W Heinemann, 1929)

Edwards, Arthur Trystan, *A Hundred New Towns for Britain: An Appeal to the Electorate by Ex-Serviceman J47485* (London: Simpkin Marshall, 1934)

Edwards, Arthur Trystan, *An Alternative to Tenements* (London: Hundred New Towns Association, 1938)

Edwards, Arthur Trystan, *British Bluejacket, 1915–1940: A Social Study of the Royal Navy* (London: Simpkin Marshall, 1940)

Edwards, Arthur Trystan, 'Town and Country Planning' in *Towards a Christian Order: Essays Suggested by the Findings of the Malvern Conference* (London: Eyre & Spottiswoode, 1942)

Edwards, Arthur Trystan, *A Hundred New Towns for Britain: A National Scheme of Building... With an Introductory Essay on the Place of Architecture in a Christian Community* (Westminster: Industrial Christian Fellowship, 1942)

Edwards, Arthur Trystan, *Good and Bad Manners in Architecture: An Essay on the Social Aspects of Civic Design* (London: John Tiranti, 1944), 2nd edn.

BIBLIOGRAPHY 411

Edwards, Arthur Trystan, *Modern Terrace Houses: Researches on High Density Development* (London: John Tiranti Ltd, 1946)

Edwards, Arthur Trystan, *The Things Which Are Seen: A Philosophy of Beauty* (London: John Tiranti, 1946), 2nd edn.

Edwards, Arthur Trystan, *Merthyr, Rhondda and 'The Valleys'* (London: Hale, 1958)

Gloag, John, *Artifex; or, The Future of Craftsmanship* (London: Kegan Paul & Co., 1926)

Gloag, John, *Industrial Art Explained* (London: G Allen & Unwin, 1934)

Gloag, John (ed.), *Design in Modern Life* (London: Allen & Unwin, 1934)

Gloag, John, and Wornum, George Grey, *House out of Factory* (London: George Allen & Unwin, 1946)

Goldring, Douglas, *Odd Man Out: The Autobiography of a 'Propaganda Novelist'* (London: Chapman & Hall, 1936)

Gotch, John Alfred (ed.), *The Growth and Work of the Royal Institute of British Architects, 1834–1934* (London: Royal Institute of British Architects, 1934)

A Handbook of Empire Timbers (London: Empire Marketing Board, 1932)

'History of Architects': A Few Notes, addressed to Architects in salaried employment, and to students on English architectural politics of the period 1919–1935 (London: Association of Building Technicians, 1935)

Holloway, Edward, *The Economic Reform Club and Institute: What It Is—and What It Does* (October 1944)

Howarth, Patrick, *Squire: Most Generous of Men* (London: Hutchinson, 1963)

Hussey, Christopher, *The Picturesque: Studies in a Point of View* (London: GP Putnam's Sons, 1927)

Hussey, Christopher, *The Life of Sir Edwin Lutyens* (London: Country Life, 1950)

Jennings, Humphrey, and Madge, Charles (eds.), *May the Twelfth: Mass-Observation Day-Survey 1937 by Over Two Hundred Observers* (London: Faber, 1987)

Johnstone, George Harcourt, *Prosper Mérimée: A Mask and a Face* (London: Routledge, 1926)

Keen, Arthur, *Charing Cross Bridge* (London: Ernest Benn, 1930)

Kirk, Paul Thomas Radford-Rowe, *New Towns for Old: An Account of the Aims of the Hundred New Towns Association* (Westminster: Industrial Christian Fellowship, 1942)

Lancaster, Osbert, *From Pillar to Post: The Pocket Lamp of Architecture* (London: John Murray, 1938)

Longden, RT, *Some Proposals in Reference to the Panel System as Applied to the Architectural Amenities of the Country* (October 1930), n.p.

Mawson, Thomas, *Civic Art: Studies in Town Planning, Parks, Boulevards and Open Spaces* (London: BT Batsford, 1911)

Mawson, Thomas, *The Life and Work of an English Landscape Architect: An Autobiography* (London: Richards Press, 1927)

McCallum, IRM (ed.), *Physical Planning: The Ground Work of a New Technique* (London, 1945)

Metro-Land: 1924 Edition (London: Southbank Publishing, 2004), facsimile with introduction by Lawrence Green

Newton, William Godfrey, *Prelude to Architecture* (London: Architectural Press, 1925)

412   BIBLIOGRAPHY

Peach, Harry Hardy, *Craftsmen All: An Anthology* (Leicester: Dryad Press, 1926)

Phillips, Randal, *The House Improved* (London: Country Life, 1931)

Plant, Arnold, *Some Modern Business Problems* (London 1937)

Reilly, Charles Herbert, *Scaffolding in the Sky: A Semi-Architectural Autobiography* (London: G Routledge & Sons, 1938)

Richardson, AE, *Monumental Classic Architecture in Great Britain and Ireland during the Eighteenth and Nineteenth Centuries* (London: BT Batsford, 1914)

Robertson, Manning, *Laymen and the New Architecture* (London: John Murray, 1925)

Robertston, Manning, *Everyday Architecture: A Sequence of Essays Addressed to the Public* (London: T Fisher Unwin, 1924)

Scott, Geoffrey, *The Architecture of Humanism: A Study in the History of Taste* (London: Constable & Co., 1914), 1st edn.

Sharp, Thomas, *Town and Countryside: Some Aspects of Urban and Rural Development* (Oxford: Oxford University Press, 1932)

Sitwell, Osbert, *Those Were the Days: Panorama with Figures* (London: Macmillan, 1938)

Swinton, George, *London: Her Traffic—Her Improvement and Charing Cross Bridge* (London: John Murray, 1924)

Towndrow, Frederick, *Architecture in the Balance: An Approach to the Art of Scientific Humanism* (London: Chatto & Windus, 1933)

Vandon, George (Johnstone, George Harcourt), *Return Ticket* (London: William Heinemann, 1940)

Weaver, Lawrence, 'The State as Trader: Practical Difficulties' in *The Development of the Civil Service: Lectures Delivered Before the Society of Civil Servants, 1920–21* (London: PS King & Sons, 1922), pp.60–82

Weaver, Lawrence, *Sir Christopher Wren: Scientist, Scholar and Architect* (London: Country Life, 1923)

Weaver, Lawrence, *Exhibitions and the Arts of Display* (London: Country Life, 1925)

Weaver, Lawrence, *Tradition and Modernity in Plasterwork* (London: G Jackson & Sons, 1928)

Weaver, Lawrence, *Gas Fires and Their Settings* (London: Fanfare Press, 1929)

Webb, Aston (ed.), *London of the Future* (London: T Fisher Unwin Ltd, 1921)

Williams-Ellis, Clough, *England and the Octopus* (London: G Bles, 1928)

Williams-Ellis, Clough, *Lawrence Weaver* (London: G Bles, 1933)

Williams-Ellis, Clough, and Williams-Ellis, Amabel, *The Pleasures of Architecture* (London: Jonathan Cape, 1930)

Secondary Sources

Articles

Beaufoy, Helena, '"Order out of chaos": The London Society and the Planning of London 1912–1920', *Planning Perspectives* 12.2 (April 1997), pp.135–64

Beech, Nick, '"Et Tu Peter?" Some Kinds of *Real-* (or not so) *Politik* at the Festival of Britain', *Journal of Architecture* 17.5 (2012), pp.747–62

Campsie, Alexandre, 'Mass-Observation, Left Intellectuals and the Politics of Everyday Life', *English Historical Review* 131.548 (February 2016), pp.92–121

BIBLIOGRAPHY 413

Capie, Forrest, and Collins, Michael, 'The Extent of British Economic Recovery in the 1930s', *Economy and History* 13.1 (1980), pp.40–60

Carmona, Matthew, and Renninger, Andrew, 'The Royal Fine Art Commission and 75 Years of English Design Review: The First 60 Years, 1924–1984', *Planning Perspectives* 33.1 (2017), pp.577–99

Carullo, Valeria, 'Image Makers of British Modernism: Dell & Wainwright at the *Architectural Review*', *Journal of Architecture* 21.7 (November 2016), pp.1012–32

Clapson, Mark, 'Working-Class Women's Experiences of Moving to New Housing Estates in England since 1919', *Twentieth Century British History* 10.3 (1999), pp.345–65

Clarke, Peter, 'The Progressive Movement in England', *Transactions of the Royal Historical Society* 24 (1 January 1974), pp.159–81

Constantine, Stephen, 'The Buy British Campaign of 1931', *European Journal of Marketing* 21.4 (1987), pp.44–59

Crinson, Mark, 'Imperial Story-Lands: Architecture and Display at the Imperial and Commonwealth Institutes', *Art History* 22.1 (1999), pp.99–123

Crinson, Mark, 'The Powers that Be: Architectural Potency and Spatialized Power', *Architecture Beyond Europe* 4 (2013), http://journals.openedition.org/abe/3389 [accessed 6 June 2020]

Dark Matter Laboratories, 'Practice', *AA Files* 76 (2019), pp.134–8

Darling, Elizabeth, ' "To induce humanitarian sentiments in prurient Londoners": The Propaganda Activities of London's Voluntary Housing Associations in the Inter-War Period', *London Journal* 27.1 (1 May 2002), pp.42–62

Darling, Elizabeth, '*Focus*: A Little Magazine and Architectural Modernism in 1930s Britain', *Journal of Modern Periodical Studies* 3.1 (2012), pp.39–63

Darling, Elizabeth, 'Institutionalising English Modernism 1924–33: From the Vers Group to MARS', *Architectural History* 55 (2012), pp.299–320

Davies, TG, 'Arthur Trystan Edwards', *Year Book: Society of Architects in Wales* 4 (Macclesfield, 1982), pp.38–42

Echlin, Alexander, and Kelley, William, 'A "Shaftesburian Agenda"? Lord Burlington, Lord Shaftesbury and the Intellectual Origins of English Palladianism', *Architectural History* 59 (2016), pp.221–52

Gilbert, David, '*London of the Future*: The Metropolis Reimagined after the Great War', *Journal of British Studies* 4.1 (January 2004), pp.91–119

Gilbert, David, 'A Short History of London in Wrought Iron: Empire, Art and Social Division on the Hungerford Bridge', *London Society Journal* 461 (2011), http://www.londonsocietyjournal.org.uk/461/davidgilbert.php [accessed 14 August 2014]

Gold, John R, 'The MARS Plans for London, 1933–1942: Plurality and Experimentation in the City Plans of the Early British Modern Movement', *Town Planning Review* 66.3 (July 1995), pp.243–67

Harrison, Ewan, ' "Money Spinners": R Seifert & Partners, Sir Frank Price and Public-Sector Speculative Development in the 1970s', *Architectural History* 61 (2018), pp.259–80

Hasegawa, Junichi, 'Radical Reconstruction in 1940s Britain', *Twentieth Century British History* 10.2 (1999), pp.137–61

414 BIBLIOGRAPHY

Haywood, Russell, 'Railways, Urban Food and Town Planning in London 1900–1947', *Planning Perspectives* 12 (1997), pp.37–69

Hewitt, Lucy, 'The London Society and Their Development Plan for Greater London', *London Topographical Record* 30 (2010), pp. 115–31

Hewitt, Lucy, 'The Civic Survey of Greater London: Social Mapping, Planners and Urban Space in the Early Twentieth Century', *Journal of Historical Geography* 30.3 (July 2012), pp.247–62

Hewitt, Lucy, 'Ordering the Urban Body: Professional Planning in Early Twentieth-Century Britain', *Social History* 41.3 (2016), pp.304–18

Hind, Charles, 'Sound and Fury: The Early Days of the Georgian Group', *Georgian Group Report and Journal 1986*, pp.45–54

Hommelen, Ruth, 'Building with Artificial Light: Architectural Night Photography in the Inter-War Period', *Journal of Architecture* 21.7 (November, 2016), pp.1062–99

Hooper, Glenn, 'English Modern: John Gloag and the Challenge of Design', *Journal of Design History* 28.4 (November 2015), pp.368–84

Hornsey, Richard, '"The Penguins Are Coming": Brand Mascots and Utopian Mass Consumption in Interwar Britain', *Journal of British Studies* 57.4 (October 2018), pp.812–30

James, Kathleen, 'Expressionism, Relativity and the Einstein Tower', *Journal of the Society of Architectural Historians* 53.4 (December 1994), pp.392–413

Jones, Philip N, '"...a fairer and nobler City": Lutyens and Abercrombie's Plan for the City of Hull 1945', *Planning Perspectives* 13.3 (1998), pp.301–16

L'Etang, Jacqui, 'State Propaganda and Bureaucratic Intelligence: The Creation of Public Relations in 20th Century Britain', *Public Relations Review* 24.4 (1998), pp.413–41

Lambert, Robin, 'The Bath Corporation Act of 1925', *Transactions of the Ancient Monuments Society* 44 (2000), pp.51–62

Marmaras, Emmanuel, and Sutcliffe, Anthony, 'Planning for Post-War London: The Three Independent Plans, 1942–3', *Planning Perspectives* 9.4 (1994), pp.431–53

McKibbin, Ross, 'The Economic Policy of the Second Labour Government 1929–31', *Past and Present* 68 (August 1975), pp.95–123

Mort, Frank, 'Fantasies of Metropolitan Life: Planning London in the 1940s', *Journal of British Studies* 43.1 (2004), pp.120–51

Nott, James, 'Dance Halls: Towards an Architectural and Spatial History, c.1918–65', *Architectural History* 61 (2018), pp.205–33

O'Keefe, Eleanor, 'Civic Veterans: The Public Culture of Military Associations in Inter-War Glasgow', *Urban History* 44.2 (May 2017), pp.293–316

Oléron Evans, Emilie, 'Transposing the *Zeitgeist?* Nikolaus Pevsner between *Kunstgeschichte* and Art History', *Journal of Art Historiography* 11 (December 2014), n.p.

Pendlebury, John, 'Planning the Historic City: Reconstruction Plans in the United Kingdom in the 1940s', *Town Planning Review* 74.4 (October 2003), pp.371–93

Pendlebury, John, 'The Urbanism of Thomas Sharp', *Planning Perspectives* 24.1 (January, 2009), pp.3–27

BIBLIOGRAPHY 415

Pepper, Simon, and Richmond, Peter, 'Cottages, Flats and Reconditioning: Renewal Strategies in London after World War One', *Construction History* 23 (2008), pp.99–117

Pepper, Simon, and Richmond, Peter, 'Upward or Outward? Politics, Planning and Council Flats, 1919–1939', *Journal of Architecture* 13.1 (February 2008), pp.53–90

Pepper, Simon, and Richmond, Peter, 'Homes Unfit for Heroes: The Slum Problem in London and Neville Chamberlain's Unhealthy Areas Committee, 1919–1921', *Town Planning Review* 80.2 (March–April 2009), pp.143–71

Pepper, Simon, and Richmond, Peter, 'Stepney and the Politics of High-Rise Housing: Limehouse Fields to John Scurr House, 1925–1937', *London Journal* 34.1 (March 2009), pp.33–54

Pevsner, Nikolaus, 'The Modern Movement in Britain' in *Twentieth Century Architecture: British Modern (Journal of the Twentieth Century Society)* 8 (2008), pp.17–38

Powers, Alan, ' "Architects I have Known": The Architectural Career of SD Adshead', *Architectural History* 24 (1981), pp.100–23, 160–4

Powers, Alan, 'CH Reilly: Regency, Englishness and Modernism', *Journal of Architecture* 5.1 (2000), pp.47–64

Powers, Alan, 'The Expression of Levity' in Elain Harwood and Alan Powers (eds.), *Twentieth Century Architecture: Festival of Britain* 5 (2001), pp.48–56

Punter, John, 'A History of Aesthetic Control: Part 1, 1909–1953: The Control of the External Appearance of Development in England and Wales', *Town Planning Review* 57.4 (October 1986), pp.351–81

Rappaport, Erika, 'Art, Commerce, or Empire? The Rebuilding of Regent Street, 1880–1927', *History Workshop Journal* 53.1 (April 2002), pp.94–117

Ryu, Jiyi, 'The Queen's Dolls' House within the British Empire Exhibition: Encapsulating the British Imperial World', *Contemporary British History* 33.4 (19 October 2019), pp.1–19

Saint, Andrew, 'Americans in London: Raymond Hood and the National Radiator Building; Architects: Stanley Gordon Jeeves, in association with Raymond Hood', *AA Files* 7 (September 1984), pp.30–43

Scalzo, Julia, 'All a Matter of Taste: The Problem of Victorian and Edwardian Shop Fronts', *Journal of the Society of Architectural Historians* 68.1 (March 2009), pp.52–72

Shasore, Neal, 'Southampton Civic Centre: Patronage and Place in the Interwar Architecture of Public Service' in Elain Harwood and Alan Powers (eds.), *Twentieth Century Architecture: The Architecture of Public Service* 13 (2018), pp.41–62

Shasore, Neal, ' "A Stammering Bundle of Welsh Idealism": Arthur Trystan Edwards and Principles of Civic Design in Interwar Britain', *Architectural History* 61 (2018), pp.175–204

Sloman, Peter, 'Can We Conquer Unemployment? The Liberal Party, Public Works and the 1931 Political Crisis', *Historical Research* 88.239 (February 2015), pp.161–84

Stamp, Gavin, 'Neo-Tudor and Its Enemies', *Architectural History* 49 (January, 2006), pp.1–33

Stamp, Gavin, 'How We Celebrated the Coronation', *Georgian Group Journal* 20 (2012), pp.1–22

416 BIBLIOGRAPHY

Suga, Yasoku, ' "Purgatory of taste" or Projector of Industrial Britain? The British Institute of Industrial Art', *Journal of Design History* 16.2 (2003), pp.167–85

Swenarton, Mark, 'The Role of History in Architectural Education', *Architectural History* 30 (1987)

Swenarton, Mark, 'Rammed Earth Revival: Technological Innovation and Government Policy in Britain, 1905–1925', *Construction History* 19 (2003), pp.107–26

Swenarton, Mark, 'Breeze Blocks and Bolshevism: Housing Policy and the Origins of the Building Research Station 1917–1921', *Construction History* 21 (2005–6), pp.69–80

Taylor, James, ' "A Fascinating Show for John Citizen and his Wife": Advertising Exhibitions in Early Twentieth-Century London', *Journal of Social History* 51.4 (2018), pp.899–927

Waters, Suzanne, 'In Search of Gerald Barry: The Man Behind the Festival of Britain' in Alan Powers and Elain Harwood (eds.), *Twentieth Century Architecture* 5 (2001), pp.37–46

Whiteley, Nigel, 'Modern Architecture, Heritage and Englishness', *Architectural History* 38 (1995), pp.220–36

Whyte, William, 'The Englishness of English Architecture: Modernism and the Making of an International Style, 1927–1957', *Journal of British Studies* 48.2 (April 2009), pp.441–65

Whyte, William, 'The 1910 Royal Institute of British Architects' Conference: A Focus for International Town Planning?', *Urban History* 39.1 (February 2012), pp.149–65

Wittman, Richard, 'Architecture, Space and Abstraction in the Eighteenth-Century French Public Sphere', *Representations* 102 (Spring 2008), pp.1–26

Zamarian, Patrick, 'The Origins of the Oxford Conference within the Networks of 1930s Student Activism', *Journal of Architecture* 24.4 (2019), pp.571–92

Ph.D. Theses

Darling, Elizabeth, 'Elizabeth Denby, Housing Consultant: Social Reform and Cultural Politics in the Inter-war Decades', Ph.D. thesis, UCL, 1999

Durning, Louise, 'The Architecture of Humanism: An Historical and Critical Analysis of Geoffrey Scott's Architectural Theory', Ph.D. thesis, University of Essex, 1989

Haggith, Toby, ' "Castles in the Air": British Film and Reconstruction of the Built Environment, 1931–1951', Ph.D. thesis, University of Warwick, 1998

Lewis, David Frazer, 'Modernising Tradition: The Architectural Thought of Giles Gilbert Scott', D.Phil. thesis, University of Oxford, 2014

Powers, Alan, 'Architectural Education in Britain 1880–1914', PhD thesis, University of Cambridge, 1982

Ryu, Jiyi, 'Visualising and Experiencing the British Imperial World: The British Empire Exhibition at Wembley (1924/25)', Ph.D. thesis, University of York, 2018

Schwarzkopf, Stefan, 'Respectable Persuaders: The Advertising Industry and British Society, 1900–1939', Ph.D. thesis, Birkbeck, University of London, 2008

Books

Addis, Bill, 'The Contribution Made by the Journal *Construction History* towards Establishing the History of Construction as an Academic Discipline' in *Proceedings of the First Construction History Society Conference* (Cambridge, 2014), pp.iii–x

BIBLIOGRAPHY 417

Anthony, Scott, *Public Relations and the Making of Modern Britain: Stephen Tallents and the Birth of a Progressive Media Profession* (Manchester: Manchester University Press, 2012)

Ashby, Charlotte, *Modernism in Scandinavia: Art, Architecture and Design* (London: Bloomsbury, 2017)

Banham, Reyner, *Theory and Design in the First Machine Age* (London: Architectural Press, 1960)

Benton, Tim, Benton, Charlotte, and Woods, Ghislaine (eds.), *Art Deco 1910–1930* (London: V&A, 2003)

Bowley, Marion, *The British Building Industry: Four Studies in Response and Resistance to Change* (Cambridge: Cambridge University Press, 1966)

Bremner, GA (ed.), *Architecture and Urbanism in the British Empire* (Oxford: Oxford University Press, 2016)

Brittain-Catlin, Timothy, *The Edwardians and Their Houses* (London: Lund Humphries, 2020)

Bullock, Nicholas, 'Imagining the Post-War World: Architecture, Reconstruction and the British Documentary Film Movement', in Penz, François, and Thomas, Maureen (eds.), *Cinema and Architecture: Méliès, Mallet-Stevens, Multimedia* (London: British Film Institute, 1997), pp.52–61

Butler, John, *The Red Dean of Canterbury: The Public and Private Faces of Hewlett Johnson* (London: Scala, 2011)

Byron, Robert, *The Appreciation of Architecture* (London: Wishart & Co., 1932)

Carey, Hugh, *Mansfield Forbes and His Cambridge* (Cambridge: Cambridge University Press, 1984)

Carey, John, *The Intellectuals and the Masses: Pride and Prejudice among the Literary Intelligentsia* (London: Faber & Faber, 1992)

Carrington, Noel, *Industrial Design in Britain* (London: George Allen & Unwin, 1976)

Chanin, Eileen, *Capital Designs: Australia House and Visions of an Imperial London* (Melbourne: Australian Scholarly Publishing, 2018)

Clapson, Mark, *Working Class Suburbs: Social Change on an English Council Estate, 1930–2010* (Manchester: Manchester University Press, 2012)

Clark, Alan (ed.), *A Good Innings: The Private Papers of Viscount Lee of Fareham* (London: J Murray, 1974)

Clarke, Jonathan, *Early Structural Steel in London Buildings: A Discreet Revolution* (Swindon: English Heritage, 2014)

Clarke, Linda, *Building Capitalism: Historical Change and the Labour Process in the Production of the Built Environment* (London: Routledge, 1992)

Clarke, Peter, *Lancashire and the New Liberalism* (Cambridge: Cambridge University Press, 1971)

Clendinning, Ann, *Demons of Domesticity: Women and the English Gas Industry, 1889–1939* (Aldershot: Ashgate, 2004)

Colpus, Eve, *Female Philanthropy in the Interwar World: Between Self and Other* (London: Bloomsbury Academic, 2018)

Connelly, Mark, *The Great War, Memory and Ritual: Commemoration in the City and East London, 1916–1939* (London: Royal Historical Society, 2002)

418 BIBLIOGRAPHY

Cooper, Peter, *Building Relationships: The History of Bovis 1885–2000* (London: Cassell & Co., 2000)

Cornforth, John, *The Search for a Style: Country Life and Architecture 1897–1935* (London: Deutsch, 1988)

Creagh, Lucy, Kåberg, Helena, and Lane, Barbara Miller (eds.), *Modern Swedish Design: Three Founding Texts* (New York: MOMA, 2008)

Crinson, Mark, *Modern Architecture and the End of Empire* (Aldershot: Ashgate, 2003)

Crinson, Mark, and Lubbock, Jules, *Architecture, Art or Profession? Three Hundred Years of Architectural Education in Britain* (Manchester: Manchester University Press, 1994)

Crouch, Christopher, *Design Culture in Liverpool, 1880–1914: The Origins of the Liverpool School of Architecture* (Liverpool: Liverpool University Press, 2002)

Crow, Thomas, *Modern Art in the Common Culture* (New Haven: Yale University Press, 1996)

Dannatt, Trevor, *Modern Architecture in Britain: Selected Examples of Recent Britain* (London: Batsford, 1959)

Darling, Elizabeth, *Re-forming Britain: Narratives of Modernity before Reconstruction* (London: Routledge, 2007)

Donoughue, Bernard, and William Jones, George, *Herbert Morrison: Portrait of a Politician* (London: Phoenix, 2001), 2nd edn.

Dyos, Harold James, and Aldcroft, Derek Howard, *British Transport: An Economic Survey from the Seventeenth Century to the Twentieth* (Leicester: Leicester University Press, 1969)

Elwall, Robert, *Photography Takes Command: The Camera and British Architecture 1890–1939* (London: RIBA Heinz, 1994)

Esher, Lionel, *A Broken Wave: The Rebuilding of England 1940–1980* (London: Allen Lane, 1981)

Fellows, Richard, *Sir Reginald Blomfield: An Edwardian Architect* (London: Zwemmer, 1985)

Foxell, Simon, *Professionalism in the Built Environment* (London: Routledge, 2018)

Freeden, Michael (ed.), *Minutes of the Rainbow Circle, 1894–1924* (London: Royal Historical Society, 1989)

Frichot, Hélène, Gabrielsson, Catharina, and Runting, Helen, *Architecture and Feminisms: Ecologies, Economies and Technologies* (London: Routledge, 2017)

Garside, Patricia, 'Central Government, Local Authorities and the Voluntary Housing Sector, 1919–1939' in O'Day, Alan (ed.), *Government and Institutions in the Post-1832 United Kingdom*, Studies in British History 34 (Lampeter: Edwin Mellen Press, 1995), pp.85–126

Geppert, Alexander CT, *Fleeting Cities: Imperial Expositions in Fin-de-Siècle Europe* (Basingstoke: Palgrave Macmillan, 2010)

Glendinning, Miles, *The Conservation Movement: A History of Architectural Preservation, Antiquity to Modernity* (Abingdon: Routledge, 2013)

Glynn, Sean, and Oxborrow, John, *Interwar Britain: A Social and Economic History* (London: Allen & Unwin, 1976)

BIBLIOGRAPHY 419

Gold, J. R., and Ward, S. V., 'Of Plans and Planners: Documentary Film and the Urban Future, 1935–1952', in Clarke, David B (ed.), *The Cinematic City* (London: Routledge, 1997), pp.59–82

Green, EHH, and Tanner, Duncan (eds.), *The Strange Survival of Liberal England: Political Leaders, Moral Values and the Reception of Economic Debate* (Cambridge: Cambridge University Press, 2007)

Greenhalgh, Paul, (ed.), *Modernism in Design* (London: Reaktion, 1990)

Grimley, Matthew, *Citizenship, Community, and the Church of England: Liberal Anglican Theories of the State between the Wars* (Oxford: Oxford University Press, 2004)

Gunn, Simon, 'The Public Sphere, Modernity and Consumption: New Perspectives on the History of the English Middle Class' in Kidd, Alan J, and Nicholls, David, *Gender, Civic Culture and Consumerism: Middle-Class Identity in Britain, 1800–1940* (Manchester: Manchester University Press, 1999), pp.12–29

Hanna, Erika, *Modern Dublin: Urban Change and the Irish Past, 1957–1973* (Oxford: Oxford University Press, 2013)

Hanson, Brian, *Architects and the 'Building World' from Chambers to Ruskin: Constructing Authority* (Cambridge: Cambridge University Press, 2003)

Harris, Alexandra, *Romantic Moderns: English Writers, Artists and the Imagination from Virginia Woolf to John Piper* (London: Thames & Hudson, 2010)

Harwood, Elain, *Space, Hope and Brutalism* (New Haven: Yale University Press, 2015)

Hicks, Ursula K, *British Public Finances: Their Structure and Development, 1880–952* (Oxford: Oxford University Press, 1954)

Hinton, James, *The Mass Observers: A History, 1937–1949* (Oxford: Oxford University Press, 2013)

Hitchcock, Henry-Russell, *Architecture: Nineteenth and Twentieth Centuries* (New Haven: Yale University Press, 1987), 4th edn.

Hobhouse, Hermione, *A History of Regent Street* (London: Macdonald and Jane's in association with Queen Anne Press, 1975)

Hobhouse, Hermione, *Regent Street: A Mile of Style* (Chichester: Phillimore, 2008)

Holder, Julian, and McKellar, Elizabeth (eds.), *Neo-Georgian Architecture 1880–1970: A Reappraisal* (Swindon: Historic England, 2016)

Holloway, Edward, *Modern Matters: A Modern Pilgrim's Economic Progress* (London: Sherwood Press, 1986)

Hornsey, Richard, *The Spiv and the Architect: Unruly Life in Postwar Britain* (Minneapolis: University of Minnesota Press, 2010)

Houfe, Simon, Powers, Alan, and Wilton-Ely, John (eds.), *Sir Albert Richardson, 1880–1964* (London: RIBA Heinz, 1999)

Hunter, Michael (ed.), *Preserving the Past: The Rise of Heritage in Modern Britain* (Stroud: Alan Sutton, 1996)

Hussey, Christopher, *The Life of Sir Edwin Lutyens* (London: Country Life, 1950)

Hutchinson, Frances, and Burkitt, Brian, *The Political Economy of Social Credit and Guild Socialism* (London: Routledge, 1997)

Irving, Robert Grant, *Indian Summer: Lutyens, Baker, and Imperial Delhi* (New Haven: Yale University Press, 1981)

420 BIBLIOGRAPHY

Jackson, Anthony, *The Politics of Architecture: A History of Modern Architecture in Britain* (Toronto: University of Toronto Press, 2017)

Jackson, Frank, *Sir Raymond Unwin, Architect, Planner and Visionary* (London: Zwemmer, 1985)

Jackson, Iain, and Holland, Jessica, *The Architecture of Edwin Maxwell Fry and Jane Drew: Twentieth Century Architecture, Pioneer Modernism and the Tropics* (London: Routledge, 2016)

Jervis, Simon Swynfen, *The Leche Trust, 1963–2013: A Commemoration of Fifty Years* (London: Leche Trust, 2013)

Johnson, Paul Barton, *London Fit for Heroes: The Planning of British Reconstruction, 1916–1919* (Chicago: University of Chicago Press, 1968)

Joly, William Percy, *Lord Leverhulme: A Biography* (London: Constable, 1976)

Joyce, Patrick, *The Rule of Freedom: Liberalism and the Modern City* (London: Verso, 2003)

Karol, Eitan, *Charles Holden, Architect* (Donington: Shaun Tyas, 2007)

Kaye, Barrington, *The Development of the Architectural Profession in Britain: A Sociological Study* (London: G Allen & Unwin, 1960)

Kelly, Jessica, and Shasore, Neal (eds.), *Reconstruction: Architecture, the Built Environment and the Aftermath of the First World War* (London: Bloomsbury Academic, forthcoming)

Knox, James, *Robert Byron* (London: John Murray, 2003)

L'Etang, Jacqui, *Public Relations in Britain: A History of Professional Practice in the Twentieth Century* (Mahwah: Lawrence Erlbaum, 2004)

Langford, CM, *The Population Investigation Committee: A Concise History to Mark its Fiftieth Anniversary* (London: Population Investigation Committee, 1988)

Lea, FM, *Science and Building: A History of the Building Research Station* (London: Building Research Station, 1971)

Leslie, Ian M, '40 Years On: The Building Centre Success Story 1932–1971', *Building Centre Intelligence Report* no.5 (London: 1971)

Light, Alison, *Forever England: Femininity, Literature and Conservatism between the Wars* (London: Routledge, 1991)

Lingard, Jane, and Lingard, Timothy, *Bradshaw Gass & Hope: The Story of an Architectural Practice—The First One Hundred Years 1862–1962* (London: Gallery Lingard, 2007)

Littler, Jo, ' "Festering Britain": The 1951 Festival of Britain, National Identity and the Representation of the Commonwealth' in Ramamurthy, Anandi, and Faulkner, Simon (eds.), *Visual Culture and Decolonisation in Britain* (London: Routledge, 2006), pp.21–42, https://openaccess.city.ac.uk/id/eprint/6031/1/Jo%20Littler%20 FOB.pdf [accessed 4 June 2020]

Lloyd Thomas, Katie, Amhoff, Tilo, and Beech, Nick (eds.), *Industries of Architecture* (London: Routledge, 2015)

Lubbock, Jules, *The Tyranny of Taste: The Politics of Architecture and Design in Britain 1550–1960* (New Haven: Yale University Press, 1995)

Luckin, Bill, *Questions of Power: Electricity and Environment in Inter-War Britain* (Manchester: Manchester University Press, 1990)

BIBLIOGRAPHY 421

Lutyens, Edwin, *Catalogue of the Drawings Collection of the Royal Institute of British Architects* (Farnborough: Gregg International, 1973)

Lutyens, Mary, *Edwin Lutyens* (London: John Murray, 1981)

Macarthur, John, 'Geoffrey Scott, the Baroque and the Picturesque' in Macarthur, John, Leach, Andrew, and Delbeke, Maarten (eds.), *The Baroque in Architectural Culture, 1880–1980* (London: Routledge, 2016), pp.61–71

Mace, Angela, *The Royal Institute of British Architects: A Guide to its Archive and History* (London: Mansell, 1986)

Mandler, Peter, 'Rethinking the "Powers of Darkness": An Anti-history of the Preservation Movement', in Hall, Melanie (ed.), *Towards Worlds Heritage: International Origins of the Preservation Movement, 1870–1930* (Farnham: Ashgate, 2011), pp.221–40

Marchal, Jules, *Lord Leverhulme's Ghosts: Colonial Exploitation in the Congo* (London: Verso, 2008)

Marples, Joseph, Powers, Alan, and Shippabottom, Michael, *Charles Reilly and the Liverpool School of Architecture, 1904–1933* (Liverpool: Liverpool University Press, 1996)

Matless, David, *Landscape and Englishness* (London: Reaktion, 1996)

McKibbin, Ross, *Classes and Cultures: England 1918–1951* (Oxford: Oxford University Press, 1998)

Morrison, Kathryn, and Minnis, John, *Carscapes: The Motor Car, Architecture and Landscape in England* (New Haven: Yale University Press, 2012)

Nehls, Edward (ed.), *DH Lawrence: A Composite Biography* (Madison: University of Wisconsin Press, 1958) vol.2, p.695

Overy, Paul, *Light, Air and Openness: Modern Architecture between the Wars* (London: Thames & Hudson, 2007)

Overy, Richard, *The Morbid Age: Britain between the Wars* (London: Allen Lane, 2009)

Payne, Alina, *From Ornament to Object: Genealogies of Architectural Modernism* (New Haven: Yale University Press, 2012)

Perkin, Harold, *The Rise of Professional Society: England since 1880* (London: Routledge, 1989)

Peters Corbett, David, *The Modernity of English Art, 1914–1930* (Manchester: Manchester University Press, 1997)

Pevsner, Nikolaus, *Pioneers of Modern Design from William Morris to Walter Gropius* (Harmondsworth: Penguin Books, 1960)

Pope-Hennessy, John, *Learning to Look* (London: Heinemann, 1991)

Powers, Alan, *Britain: Modern Architectures in History* (London: Reaktion, 2007)

Pugh, Martin, '*We Danced All Night*': A Social History of Britain between the Wars (London: Bodley Head, 2009)

Quinalt, Roland, 'London and the Land Question, c.1890–1914', in Cragoe, Matthew and Readman, Paul (eds.), *The Land Question in Britain* (Basingstoke: Palgrave Macmillan, 2010), pp.168–81

Readman, Paul, 'The Edwardian Land Question' in Cragoe, Matthew, and Readman, Paul (eds.), *The Land Question in Britain* (Basingstoke: Palgrave Macmillan, 2010), pp.181–200

422 BIBLIOGRAPHY

Richards, James M, 'Architectural Criticism in the Nineteen-Thirties' in Summerson, John (ed.), *Concerning Architecture: Essays Presented to Nikolaus Pevsner* (London: Allen Lane, 1968), pp.252–257

Richards, James M, *Memoirs of an Unjust Fella* (London: Weidenfeld and Nicolson, 1980)

Richardson, Margaret, *66 Portland Place: The London Headquarters of the Royal Institute of British Architects* (London, 1984)

Richardson, Margaret, *66 Portland Place: The Headquarters of the Royal Institute of British Architects* (London, 2004), rev. Hind, Margaret

Richmond, Peter, *Marketing Modernisms: The Architecture and Influence of Charles Reilly* (Liverpool: Liverpool University Press, 2001)

Ridley, Jane, *Edwin Lutyens: His Life, His Wife, His Work* (London: Pimlico, 2003)

Ritschel, Daniel, *The Politics of Planning: The Debate on Economic Planning in Britain in the 1930s* (Oxford: Oxford University Press, 1997)

Saint, Andrew (ed.), *Politics and the People of London: The London County Council, 1889–1965* (London: Hambledon, 1989)

Saint, Andrew, *Richard Norman Shaw* (New Haven: Yale University Press, 1976)

Saint, Andrew, *The Image of the Architect* (New Haven: Yale University Press, 1983)

Saint, Andrew, *Towards a Social Architecture: The Role of School-Building in Post-War England* (New Haven: Yale University Press, 1987)

Saler, Michael T, *The Avant-Garde in Interwar England: Medieval Modernism and the London Underground* (Oxford: Oxford University Press, 2001)

Samuel, Flora, *Why Architects Matters: Evidencing and Communicating the Value of Architects* (London: Routledge, 2018)

Saumarez Smith, Otto, *Boom Cities: Architect Planners and the Politics of Radical Urban Renewal in 1960s Britain* (Oxford: Oxford University Press, 2019)

Schuldenfrei, Robin, *Luxury Modernism: Architecture and the Object in Germany, 1900–1933* (Princeton: Princeton University Press 2018)

Sennett, Richard, *The Fall of Public Man* (London: Penguin, 2003)

Service, Alastair (ed.), *Edwardian Architecture and Its Origins* (London: Architectural Press, 1975)

Service, Alastair, *Edwardian Architecture: A Handbook to Building Design in Britain, 1890–1914* (London: Thames & Hudson, 1977)

Sonne, Wolfgang, *Representing the State: Capital City Planning in the Early Twentieth Century* (Munich: Prestel, 2003)

Sonne, Wolfgang, 'The Enduring Concept of Civic Art' in Pendelbury, John, Erten, Erdem, and Larkham, Peter J, (eds.), *Alternative Visions of Post-War Reconstruction: Creating the Modern Townscape* (London: Routledge, 2015), pp.14–31

Stamp, Gavin (ed.), *AD Profiles: Britain in the Thirties* 49.10–11 (1979)

Stamp, Gavin, *Telephone Boxes* (London: Chatto & Windus, 1989)

Stamp, Gavin, *Telephone Boxes* (London: Chatto & Windus, 1989)

Stephen, Daniel, *The Empire of Progress: West Africans, Indians and Britons at the British Empire Exhibition 1924–25* (New York: Palgrave Macmillan, 2013)

Stevenson, Jane, *Baroque between the Wars: Alternative Style in the Arts, 1918–1939* (Oxford: Oxford University Press, 2018)

BIBLIOGRAPHY   423

Stone, Dan, *Breeding Superman: Nietzsche, Race and Eugenics in Edwardian and Interwar Britain* (Liverpool: Liverpool University Press, 2002)

Strong, Roy, *Country Life 1897–1997: The English Arcadia* (London: Country Life, 1996)

Sugg Ryan, Deborah, *Ideal Homes, 1918–1939: Domestic Design and Suburban Modernism* (Manchester: Manchester University Press, 2018)

Summerson, John, *The Architectural Association, 1847–1947* (London: Pleiades Books, 1947)

Summerson, John, 'The Past in the Future' in *Heavenly Mansions* (London: Cresset Press, 1949), pp.219–41

Summerson, John, *Georgian London* (Harmondsworth: Penguin, 1962)

Summerson, John, 'Architecture' in Ford, Boris (ed.), *The Cambridge Guide to the Arts in Britain 8: The Edwardian Age and the Inter-War Years* (Cambridge: Cambridge University Press, 1989), pp.212–45

Sutcliffe, Anthony (ed.), *British Town Planning: The Formative Years* (Leicester: Leicester University Press, 1981)

Swenarton, Mark, *Homes Fit for Heroes: The Politics and Architecture of Early State Housing in Britain* (London: Heinemann Educational Books, 1981)

Swenarton, Mark, *Artisans and Architects: The Ruskinian Tradition in Architectural Thought* (Basingstoke: Macmillan, 1989)

Swenarton, Mark, *Building the New Jerusalem: Architecture, Housing and Politics 1900–1930* (Watford: HIS BRE Press, 2008)

Swenarton, Mark, *Cook's Camden: The Making of Modern London* (London: Lund Humphries, 2017)

Swenarton, Mark, Avermaete, Tom, and van den Heuvel, Dirk (eds.), *Architecture and the Welfare State* (London: Routledge, 2015)

Thirties, British Art and Design before the War: An Exhibition Organised by the Arts Council of Great Britain in collaboration with the Victoria and Albert Museum, held at the Hayward Gallery (London: Arts Council of Great Britain, 1979)

Thompson, James, *British Political Culture and the Idea of 'Public Opinion', 1867–1914* (Cambridge: Cambridge University Press, 2013)

The Transactions of the Royal Institute of British Architects Town Planning Conference (London: Royal Institute of British Architects, 1910, facsimile edn. London: Routledge, 2011) with introduction by Whyte, William, n.p.

Watkin, David, *The Rise of Architectural History* (London: Architectural Press, 1980)

Watkin, David, *Morality and Architecture Revisited* (London: John Murray, 2001)

Wellington, PS, and Silvey, Valeria, *Crop and Seed Improvement: A History of the National Institute of Agricultural Botany, 1919 to 1996* (Cambridge: National Institute of Agricultural Botany, 1997)

Wheeler, Katherine, *Victorian Perceptions of Renaissance Architecture* (Farnham: Ashgate, 2014)

Whittick, Arnold, *Eric Mendelsohn* (London: Faber & Faber, 1940)

Whittingham, Sarah, *Sir George Oatley: Architect of Bristol* (Bristol: Redcliffe Press, 2011)

Wildman, Charlotte, *Urban Development and Modernity in Liverpool and Manchester, 1918–1939* (London: Bloomsbury Academic, 2016)

424 BIBLIOGRAPHY

Williamson, Philip, *National Crisis and National Government: British Politics, the Economy and Empire 1926–32* (Cambridge: Cambridge University Press, 1992)

Wilson, William Henry, *The City Beautiful Movement* (Baltimore, 1989)

Wittman, Richard, *Architecture, Print Culture and the Public Sphere in Eighteenth-Century France* (London: Routledge, 2007)

Wright, Myles, *Lord Leverhulme's Unknown Venture: The Lever Chair and the Beginnings of Town and Regional Planning, 1908–1948: the 1st Lord Leverhulme, Sir Charles Reilly, Stanley Adshead, Sir George Pepler, Sir Patrick Abercrombie, Lord Holford* (London: Hutchinson Benham, 1982)

Yelling, James Alfred, *Slums and Redevelopment: Policy and Practice in England, 1918–1945, with particular reference to London* (London: UCL Press, 1992)

Youngson, AJ, *Urban Development and the Royal Fine Art Commissions* (Edinburgh: Edinburgh University Press, 1990)

Yusaf, Shundana, *Broadcasting Buildings: Architecture on the Wireless, 1927–1945* (Cambridge, Mass.: MIT Press, 2014)

Žantovská Murray, Irena, (ed.), *Le Corbusier and Britain: An Anthology* (Abingdon: Routledge, 2009)

Zweiniger-Bargielowska, Ina, *Managing the Body: Beauty, Health, and Fitness in Britain 1880–1939* (Oxford: Oxford University Press, 2010)

Index

For the benefit of digital users, indexed terms that span two pages (e.g., 52–53) may, on occasion, appear on only one of those pages.

Abbey Road Building Society 102–3
Abercrombie, Patrick 21–3, 112, 271–2, 279–80, 304–5, 396–7, 403
Acworth, Angus 250–1, 254–7
Adelaide House, London Bridge 3–5
Adshead, Stanley Davenport 21–3, 119–20, 219–22, 229, 246–7, 263, 272–3, 279–80, 284–5, 358–9, 385–6
Advertising Association 58–61, 68–9, 91–3, 119, 210–11
Advertising Exhibition, Olympia 90–3
Architects' Journal (*see* The Architectural Press)
Architects Registration Act
(1931) 20–1, 31–8, 121–3
(1938) 122–3, 261
Architects Registration Council of the United Kingdom (ARKUK) 33–4, 110, 121–2
Architectural Association, London 1–5, 32–3, 42–3, 183–5, 187, 195, 222
Materials Bureau 147, 155–6
Architectural Design and Construction 117–18, 263–4
Architectural Periodicals Index 197
The Architectural Press 224–5, 382, 394
Architects' Journal 223–5, 259, 261, 382
Architectural Review 12–13, 127–8, 140–1, 224–5, 242, 252, 382
Architectural Review (*see* The Architectural Press)
Architectural Union Company 23, 168–70
Architecture Club 1–2, 37, 81, 115
Arts and Crafts 51, 53, 68–70, 279
Art Workers' Guild 68–9
Asplund, Gunnar 149–50
Association of Architectural Surveyors and Technical Assistants (formerly Architects and Surveyors Assistants Professional Union) 32–3, 36–7, 42–3, 104

Atkinson, Robert 5, 86, 147, 149–50, 155–8, 171–2, 233–5
Ayrton, Maxwell 66, 68–9, 113–14, 351–2

Baker, Herbert 24–5, 50–1, 183–5, 361
Bankart, George P 189
Barnes, Harry 33–4, 104–5
Belcher, John 213–14
Beresford–Chancellor, Edwin 221, 263
Betjeman, John 252–3, 256, 260
Bird, Eric 119, 140–1, 197, 202–3
Blomfield, Reginald 7, 9–10, 28, 32–3, 40–1, 91–2, 168–9, 208–9, 223–6, 230–2, 271–2, 295, 358–60, 369, 376–9
Bone, James 115, 330–2
Bone, Muirhead 330–2, 343
Bossom, Alfred 104–5, 107, 122–3, 254, 292–3
Bovis 155–6
BBC (British Broadcasting Corporation) 7, 123–4
Broadcasting House 195–6
Bressey, Charles 391
Brett, Lionel 394, 403–4
British Commercial Gas Association 66–8, 83–6
British Empire Exhibition, Wembley 8–9, 49–52, 206, 210–11, 403–4
Cotton Industries Section 73–81
Electricity Section 81
Gas Section 81–3
Industrial Chemistry Section 72–3, 75–81
Empire Stadium, Wembley 52–3, 57–8
Palace of Arts 58–61, 65, 86–90
Palace of Engineering 57–8, 65, 86–7
Palace of Housing and Transport 65, 83–6
Palace of Industry 57–61, 65–90
Poster Street 87–90
Pottery Section 72–3, 75–81

426 INDEX

British Empire Exhibition, Wembley (*cont.*)
  Rubber Industries Section 73–5
  Ulster Industries Section 75–81
British Film Institute 123–4
British Government
  Barlow Report (Commission on the
    Redistribution of the Industrial
    Population) 296, 310–11, 314–15
  Board of Agriculture 54–5
  Board of Trade 56–7
  Commissioners of Woods, Forests and
    Land Revenues 213–14, 219, 223
  Later, Commissioners for the Crown
    Lands 224–5, 227–8, 370
  Department of Overseas Trade 56–7, 90–1
  Empire Marketing Board 56–7, 87–92,
    155, 163–5, 185–6
  Committee on Crown Lands and
    Government Lands 213
  Committee on National Expenditure
    (May Report) 100
  General Post Office 141
    Telephone Kiosk 64–5, 323–4, 345–6
  Ministry of Agriculture 54–5, 57, 68–9,
    113–15, 225–6
  Ministry of Health 108–9, 113–14,
    272, 281
    Moyne Report (Ministry of Health
      Departmental Committee on
      Housing, 1933) 240–1, 288–9
  Ministry of Transport 367–8, 390–1
    Highways Development Report
      (Bressey-Lutyens Report)
      391–2, 395
  Committee on Local Expenditure (Ray
    Report, 1932) 100–1, 105
  National Government 100–3
  Office of Works 8–9, 37, 155, 213–14, 225,
    249–50, 254, 369
  Royal Commission on Cross River
    Traffic 362–7
British Institute of Industrial Arts 56–7,
  64–5, 86–7
Bryant, HB 107, 124–5
Budden, Lionel 124–5, 183–5
Building Centre 123–4, 147, 153–67, 185–6,
  195, 197, 206
Building Industry Advisory Committee 107
Building Industry Council of
  Review 104–5, 107

Building Industries National Council
  19, 99–111, 124–5, 167, 172, 206
Building 5–7
Building Research Station 19, 163–5, 195, 197
Builder, The 23–4, 211–12
Burnet and Tait 3–5
Byron, Robert 224–7, 239–42, 249–52,
  256, 335

Cambridge University Library 12
Carlton House Terrace Defence
  Committee 224, 226, 248
Caröe, WD 211–12, 370–6
Carter, EJ 'Bobby' 43, 119, 125, 194–7
Central Electricity Board 293–6, 376–9
  National Grid 293–4, 376–9
Champneys, Walpole 149–50, 156–8
Church of England 315–18
  Malvern Conference 316–17
Civic design 384–5, 394–5
Coates, Wells 40–1, 119–20, 205, 292–3,
  304–5
Committees 38, 209
Communist Party 235–6, 241–2, 246
Congrès Internationaux d'Architecture
  Moderne (CIAM) 40–1, 43,
  205, 403–4
Connell, Lucas, and Ward 7
Conservative Party 254
  Municipal Reform Party (London County
    Council) 240–1, 332–3, 361–2,
    387–9
Construction industry 97–126
Copnall, Edward Bainbridge 129–30, 183–6,
  190, 193–4, 197
Coppock, Richard 105, 109–10, 189, 389–90
Council for the Preservation of Rural
  England (CPRE) 111–12, 119–21,
  250, 323–4, 369
Country Life 49–50, 53–4, 115, 367
Courtauld's, St Martin-Le-Grand 3–5
Crawford, William 91, 116–17
Creswell, HB 94
Cripps, Stafford 53, 402
Cullen, Gordon 382, 394
Curtis Green, William 66, 68–9, 392

Daily Telegraph 58–61, 219–21, 230–2
Dancehalls (see *Wornum, George Grey*)
Dawber, Guy 28, 111–12, 147, 250

INDEX 427

de Cronin Hastings, Hubert 222, 394
de Keyser, Polydore Weichand 213–15
De La Warr Pavilion, Bexhill-on-Sea 12
de Soissons, Louis 150–1, 155–6, 237–8,
    304–5, 392
Dell & Wainwright 128, 136–9
Denby, Elizabeth 86, 119–21, 123–4, 304–6
Derwent, Lord (see *Vanden-Bampde-
    Johnstone, George Harcourt*)
Design and Industries Association (DIA)
    50–1, 54, 64–5, 70, 83, 92, 140–1, 143,
    153, 190, 198, 206
Deutscher Werkbund 64, 140–1
Dircks, Rudolph 194–5
Documentary film movement 123–5,
    129–30, 136–41
Dorman Long 86–7, 279–80
Dower, John 119–20
Duncan, Ronald Avery 120–1, 202–4

Ecclesiastical Commissioners 370–6
Edwards, Arthur Trystan 5–7, 9–10, 25,
    113–14, 117–18, 209, 211–12,
    221, 229, 246–7, 250, 256,
    263–326, 382–4
    'Forbidden Houses', Housing Centre
        304–6, 314–15
    *Good and Bad Manners in
        Architecture* 250, 273–5
    Hundred New Towns Association 229,
        270, 275, 285–326
    Modern Terrace Houses 309
    The Things Which Are Seen 272–4,
        315, 318–19
    Three Rows of Tape 275
Electricity Development Association
    (EDA) 81
Electric Lamp Manufacturers' Association
    (ELMA) 161
    Lighting Service Bureau 161
Eltham Palace, Kent 151
Emberton, Joseph 3–5, 66, 68–9, 87–92
Empire Marketing Board (*see* British
    Government)
Empire Timber (*see* Empire Marketing
    Board, British Government)
Esdaile, Katherine Ada (Mrs Arundell
    Esdaile) 253
Eugenics 320–1
Everyday Things 197–205

Exhibition of British Industrial Design for
    the Home, Dorland Hall 197–8,
    201–2

Fabianism 28, 53, 272–3
Faculty of Architects and Surveyors
    (FAS) 36, 42–3, 116–17
Festival of Britain 357–8, 402–3
First Commissioner of Works (see *Office of
    Works*) 37–8
First World War 26
Fleetwood–Hesketh, Peter and Roger 224
Fletcher, Banister 116–17, 224–5
Forbes, Mansfield 287–8, 300–4
Fry, Edwin Maxwell (Max) 40–1, 86, 119–20,
    204, 224, 304–5, 370–6, 381–2

Gardiner, Clive 73–5
Gas Light and Coke Company (GLCC) 83
Gaumont–British 123–5
Gaye, Arthur S 224–6, 228
Georgian Group 209, 239, 246–62, 280
Gill, Eric 197
Goldring, Douglas 209, 211–12, 237–40,
    246–52
Glass 161–2
Gloag, John 140–2, 145–8, 162–3, 198,
    202–5, 402
    Artifex 141–2
    House of Factory 145–6
    Industrial Art Explained 143–4, 204
Gluckstein, Sidney and Vincent 155–6
Goodenough, Francis 81, 83–6, 155
Goodhart–Rendel, Henry Stuart 211–12,
    222, 258
Great Depression (*see* Great Slump)
Great Slump 97–8, 106–7, 388–9
Green, Arthur 213–14
Grierson, John 124–5, 140–1

Hall, Edwin Stanley 116–17
Hall, Herbert Austen 5, 81, 392
Harcourt Smith, Cecil 56–7, 64–5
Hare, HT 28, 169–70, 213–14
Harvey, JDM 130
Heal's Department Store 140–1
Hendry, HD 66–8
Hepworth, PD 156–8, 392
Herrick, FC 70–1
Hill, Oliver 68–9, 75–81, 152, 201–2

428 INDEX

Holden, Charles 52, 171–2, 210–11, 351–2, 381
Holford, William 127
Housing Centre 289, 304–7, 314–15
Hudson, Edward 145–6
Hundred New Towns Association (*see* Edwards, Arthur Trystan)
Hunter, Alec 193–4
Hussey, Christopher 151, 238–9, 252, 256, 391

Imperialism 49–51, 57–65, 179–80, 183–6, 218–19, 246–7, 342–3
Imrie and Angell 81
Incorporated Association of Architects and Surveyors (IAAS) 35–6, 42–3, 116–17, 367–8
Industrial Christian Fellowship 317–18
Institute of Chartered Accountants 175
Institute of Registered Architects 35–6, 367–8
Institution of Civil Engineers 175
International Advertising Convention 58–61, 83–6, 91–2, 116–17, 210–11

Jackson, Thomas Graham 144–5
James, Charles Holloway 12, 83–6, 119–20, 155, 392
James, Walter (4th Lord Northbourne) 310–11, 314–15
Joass, JJ 102
Johnson, Hewlett 300–3, 316
Joseph, Delissa 102
Juta, Jan 188–9

Keen, Arthur 169–70
Kensington Housing Trust 123–4
Keynesianism 101–2, 107–8, 110–11, 292–3

Labour Party 100–1, 239–41, 272–3, 298, 332–3
Lancaster, Osbert 13–14
Lanchester, HV 28, 171–2, 370
Land Settlement 54–5, 70, 386–7
Lee, Arthur (1st Viscount Lee of Fareham) 54–5, 362–7
Le Corbusier 151–3
Lethaby, WR 28, 144–5, 189, 198, 376–9
Lever, WH (1st Viscount Leverhulme) 58–61, 93–4, 384–5

Leverkus, Gertrude 179–80
Liberalism 15–16, 53, 241–2, 269–70, 360, 384–7
Liberal Anglicanism 270, 315–16
Liberal Party 33–4, 100, 292–3, 330
Liberty's, Regent Street 12
Lighting (of buildings) 161
Joint Committee of Architects and Electric Lighting Experts 161
Lighting Service Bureau (*see* Electric Lamp Manufacturers' Association)
Lindsay, David (27th Earl of Crawford and 10th Earl of Balcarres, Lord Crawford) 211–12, 246–7
Listing 208, 254–5
Liverpool School of Architecture 42–3, 93–4, 183–5, 263, 271–2, 384–6
Llewellyn Smith, Hubert 56–7, 64–5
Lloyd George, David 27, 101, 314–15, 320–1, 386–7
London
Bankside Power Station 398–9
Battersea Power Station 259–60, 323–4, 345–6
British Medical Association, Strand 210–11
Carlton Gardens 223
Carlton House Terrace 207–9, 223–9, 250
County Hall 330, 361–2, 379–80, 388–9, 398–9
Haig Memorial Homes, Morden 68–9
Hamilton Terrace, St John's Wood 68–9
Hungerford Railway Bridge, Charing Cross 130, 327–8, 358–81
Kensal House, Ladbroke Grove 72–3, 260
Kingsway 357, 385–6, 389–90
New Adelphi 227–8, 330
Palace of Westminster 130
Piccadilly Circus 212–15
Piccadilly Hotel 212–15, 218–19
Portland Town, St John's Wood 229–47
Regent Street 207–9, 213–23, 263–9, 280–1, 385–6
Liberty's 267
Swan and Edgar's Department Store 264
Vigo House 264
Rex House, Lower Regent Street 227–8
River Thames 130

INDEX   429

South Bank 327–8, 357–8, 367–8, 388–91, 398–9
St Paul's Cathedral 130, 242
Strand 263–4, 379–80
Stratton House, Piccadilly 250–1
Vauxhall Bridge 211–12
Waterloo Bridge 25, 130, 208–9, 250, 332–58
London County Council 33–6, 100–1, 211–12, 240–1, 297–8, 330, 338–41, 347–9, 367–9, 376–9, 385–6, 392, 395
Charing Cross Bridge Advisory Committee 369–81, 387–8, 390
Greater London Regional Planning Committee 335–8
Haig Memorial Homes, Morden 68–9
Highways Committee 335, 389–90
Housing Committee 237–8
Town Planning Committee 239–40
Londoners' League 232–3, 248
London Press Exchange 83, 91
London Society 29, 104, 211–12, 219–20, 329, 358–9, 361–2, 370–6
London Underground 52, 369
Lutyens, Edwin 28, 35–6, 49–50, 52–5, 66–9, 147, 168–9, 230–2, 358–9, 362–8, 384–6, 393–6
Deanery Gardens, Sonning 146

MacAlister, Ian 9–10, 34–5, 38, 43, 121–2, 196–7
MacDonald, Ramsay 100–3, 105, 314
Machine-craft 141–8, 187–8, 190, 194, 345–6
Maitland, Waldo 156–8, 161, 190–3
Manchester Guardian and Observer 8–9, 21–3, 115, 330–2, 384–5
Mass Observation 241–2
Maufe, Edward 66, 71–2, 75–81, 201–2, 392
Maule, HPG 68–9, 113–14, 145–6
Marfell, George 202–3
McGrath, Raymond 156–8, 197–8, 204, 292–3
Memorialists 144–5
Mendelsohn, Erich 1–2, 9–10, 152–3
Milne, Oswald 66, 68–9, 113–14
Modern Architectural Research Group (MARS) 40–1, 43–4, 119–20, 143, 195, 205, 224, 256, 392
Modernism 40–4, 119–20
Monck, Margaret 242

Morley Horder, Percy 54–5, 66–9, 73–5
Morrison, Herbert 332–5, 357–8, 367–8, 388–91, 398–9
Mortimer, Raymond 127
Municipal Reform Party (*see* Conservative Party)
Murray, John 28–31, 370
Myerscough-Walker, Raymond 128

Nash, John 208–9
National Federation of Building Trades Employers 105
National Federation of Building Trades Operatives 99–100, 105
National Grid (*see* Central Electrictiy Board)
National Institute of Agricultural Botany 54–5
Neo-Georgian architecture 5, 12–14, 46–7, 68–9, 151, 205, 255–8
Georgian architecture 208, 229–30
New Delhi 183–5, 361–2, 384–5, 387
New Olympia 3–5
Newton, WG 11–12
Niven, David Barclay 370–6
Northbourne, Lord (*see* James, Walter)
Norwich, City Hall 11–12

Office of Works (*see* British Government)
Official architecture 35–8, 108–9
Oliver, Basil 147

Pall Mall Gazette 219–21
Palumbo, Rudolph 230
Parsons, Michael (7th Earl of Rosse) 250–3, 260
Pick, Frank 5–6, 64, 119–20, 226, 260, 368–9
Political and Economic Planning group (PEP) 119–20
Portland stone 330–2
Preservationism 207
Prince Eugen 153
Prince Sevgard 153
Pritchard, Jack 152–3, 162–3, 292–3
Pritchard, Wood and Partners 162–3
Professionalism 38–40, 42–3
Propaganda 49–96, 105–6
Public opinion 219–21, 224–7
Public Relations 56–7, 95–6, 105

Quennell, CHB and Marjorie 198

430 INDEX

Rainbow Circle 53, 68–9
Ramsey, Stanley 120–1, 123–4, 275, 284–5
Reconstruction 26–31, 387–8
Registration (campaign for statutory
        registration) 31–8, 121–2, 175, 367–9
Reilly, Charles Herbert 21–3, 94–5, 183–5,
        263, 271–2, 279–80, 295–6, 384–6
Rhodes, Cecil 50–1
Richards, JM 198, 242, 249–50, 256–7
Richardson, Albert 87–90, 147, 230–2, 246–7,
        250, 256–7, 271–2, 279, 392
Rix, Reginald 116–18
Robert McAlpine and Sons 52–3
Robertson, Howard 1–2, 5, 41–2, 106–7,
        155, 190–3
Robertson, Manning 113–15
Rosse, Lord (see Parsons, Michael)
Rotha, Paul 124–5, 140–1
Rowe, Reginald 304–5, 314–15, 317–18
Rowland Pierce, Stephen 12, 204
Royal Academy 9–10, 215, 369
    Exhibition of Art in Industry 201–2
    Planning Committee 392–402
Royal College of Art 66–8
Royal Fine Art Commission 224, 259, 323–4,
        347–9, 361–2, 369, 393
Royal Navy 54–5
RIBA (Royal Institute of British
        Architects) 8, 17, 23, 27, 29, 81, 118,
        121–2, 127, 305–6, 338–9, 367–8
    Allied Societies 39–40
    Arts Standing Committee 202–3
    Centenary Committee 173
    Code of Professional Practice 112
    Council 39–40
    Defence League 33
    Executive Committee 39–40, 115
    Exhibition (Sub-)Committee 202–3
    Finance and House Committee 171
    International Town Planning
        Committee 168–9
    Joint Contracts Tribunal, Standard Form
        of Contract 19, 110
    Joint (Publicity) Committee 116–17
    Journal of the Royal Institute of British
        Architects 7, 197
    Membership 39
    New Premises Committee 166–7
    Official Architecture
        Committee 122–3, 369

Premises Committee 171
Public Relations Committee 34–5,
        118–23, 125, 173–4, 197, 202–3
Public Relations Officer 119, 202–3
Practice Standing Committee 112–13, 119
Provincial Conference (Liverpool) 94–5
Publicity Committee 117–18
Registration Committee 34–5
Salaried Members Committee 36–7
Silver Medal 328
Thames Bridges Conference 367–8
Unemployment Committee 104
Women Members Committee 179–80
9 Conduit Street 39, 168–71, 194–5
66 Portland Place 12, 127, 171–2,
        260, 335–8
    Aston Webb Committee Room
        130–5, 178–9
    Competition 166–7, 171–3
    Council Chamber 181–2, 185–6
    Henry Jarvis Memorial Hall 130–5,
        183–5, 187, 190–3
    Henry Florence Memorial Hall 130–5,
        173–4, 185–6, 188–94, 202–3
    'International Architecture, 1924–1934'
        Exhibition 202–3, 381–4
    'Everyday Things' Exhibition
        147–8, 202–6
    Library 181–2, 194–7
    Members' Room 179–80
    Opening Ceremony 173–5
    Women's Members' Room 179–80
Royal Society of Medicine 175
Ruskinain thought 108–10, 140–1,
        145, 215–18
Russian Constructivism 187–8

St Pancras House Improvement
        Society 123–4
Scott, Geoffrey 25, 276–8, 346–7, 384–5, 387
Scott, Giles Gilbert 9–10, 64–5, 128, 171–2,
        224–5, 227–8, 230–2, 323–4, 328–9,
        342, 345–58, 369, 376–9, 382–4,
        388–9, 392, 395–402
Scott, Leslie 369–70, 387–8, 390
Senate House, University of London 12
Shakespeare Memorial Theatre,
        Stratford 12, 127
Sharp, Thomas 288–9, 292–3, 382
Shaw, Richard Norman 144–5, 213–19

Simpson, John 32–3, 66
Sitwell, Osbert 210, 224–7
Social Credit Movement 290–3, 300–3, 312–14
Socialism (*see also* Communist Party) 242, 272–3
Society of Architects 29, 81, 155
Society for the Protection of Ancient Buildings (SPAB) 211–12, 248–53, 258
Society of Industrial Artists 193–4
South Eastern Railway Company (later Southern Railway) 360–1, 368–9
Southern Railway (*see* South Eastern Railway Company)
Squire, JC 1–2, 115, 224
Standardisation 158–9
Statham, H Heathcote 211–12
Summerson, John 6–7, 246–7, 250, 254–6, 328–9, 393–4
Sweden
Anglo–Swedish Society 86–7
Exhibition of Swedish Industrial Art 153
Skandia Cinema, Stockholm 149–50
Stockholm Concert Hall 189
Stockholm Library 189
Stockholm Town Hall 189
Svenska Slojdforeningen 140–1, 153
Svensk Form 153
Swedish Grace 68–9, 189
Swedish Society for the Improvement of Seeds 54–5
Swinton, George C 361–2
Sylvester Sullivan, Leo 3–5

Tallents, Stephen 56–7, 91, 140–1, 155
Tapper, Michael 86
Tapper, Walter 83
Tasker, Robert 35–6
Tatchell, Sydney 104–5, 107, 110
Taylor, John 213–14
Tecton 42–3, 195, 256, 260
Temple, William 315–16
Thomas, Percy 40, 125, 172–3
Timber 162–5, 342
Empire Timber 163–5, 185–6
Forest Products Research Laboratory 163–5
Timber Development Association 163–5

The Times 64, 224, 226, 342
Towndrow, Frederick 5–6, 8–10, 117–18, 166–7
Town Planning 226, 255, 316
Architectural Amenities Bill 254
Town and Country Planning Act (1944) 254–5, 387–8
Town and Country Planning Act (1947) 248, 255, 258, 387–8
Town Planning Act (1932) 387–8
Town Planning Conference (1910) 168–9
Town Planning Institute 29, 369
Town Planning Review 271–2
Townscape 382, 394, 403–4
Trotter, Dorothy Warren 230–3, 238–9, 246–7

Unemployment 97–8
Unwin, Raymond 99–100, 104–5, 107–9, 113–14, 122–3, 226, 272, 281, 313, 358–9, 369, 395–6

Vandepeer, Donald 225
Vanden–Bampde–Johnstone, George Harcourt (3rd Lord Derwent) 248–52, 259–61
Vane–Tempest–Stewart, Charles (7th Marquess of Londonderry) 37–8
Vigilance committees 210–11, 258–62
Central Vigilance Society 210–11
London Architectural Vigilance Committee 211–12
National Vigilance Association 210–11
National Vigilance Committee 210–11
Oxford Vigilance Committee 210–11
South African Vigilance Society 210–11

Warner Textiles, Braintree 175, 193–4
Ward, Basil 119–20, 123–4
Weaver, Lawrence 49–57, 61–3, 65–8, 81, 86–7, 91–2, 113–15, 140–1, 145–6, 386–7, 392
Webb, Aston 28, 211–14, 221, 358–60, 385
Webb, Maurice 107, 110–11, 128, 147, 155–6, 166–8
Webb, Sidney 28
Welfare state 19–21, 37–8, 402–3
Wellesley, Gerald 86–7, 252
Wembley, Middlesex 57–8
Williams–Ellis, Amabel 10–11, 242

432 INDEX

Williams–Ellis, Clough 9–11, 53, 66, 70–2, 75–81, 92, 114, 117–18, 210, 242, 329
Williams, Owen 362–7
Windsor–Clive, Robert (Lord Windsor, Earl of Plymouth) 211–12
Winser, JK 155, 158–9, 195
Wintour, Ulick 56–7
Woodford, James 129–30, 188–9
Workers' Educational Association 316
Wornum, George Grey 5, 9–10, 41–2, 68–9, 86, 119–20, 125, 127, 143, 145–56, 187–8, 197–8, 201–4
Bellometti's Restaurant, Soho 162–3

Building Centre 160–1
Derby Palais de Danse 149–50
King's Hall, Bournemouth 149–50
Royal Academy Exhibition of Art in Industry 201–2
Wornum (née Gerstle), Miriam 148–52, 162–3, 179–80, 188–9, 197–8, 204
Worthington, Hubert 66–9
Worthington, Percy 171–2, 384–5
Wren, Christopher 49–51, 54–5, 66–8, 130, 208–9, 279, 328, 361–2

Yerbury, FR 117–18, 123–4, 155–6